T0083508

Karolinum Press

Miroslav Petříček

Philosophy en noir

Rethinking Philosophy
after the Holocaust

VÁCLAV HAVEL SERIES

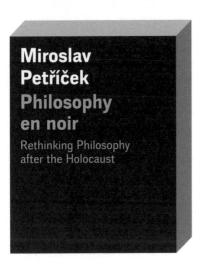

Miroslav
Petříček

Philosophy
en noir

Rethinking Philosophy
after the Holocaust

KAROLINUM PRESS

KAROLINUM PRESS is a publishing department of Charles University
Ovocný trh 560/5, 116 36 Prague 1, Czech Republic
www.karolinum.cz

Originally published in Czech under the title *Filosofie en noir*
by Karolinum Press in 2018.

EUROPEAN UNION
European Structural and Investment Funds
Operational Programme Research,
Development and Education

MINISTRY OF EDUCATION,
YOUTH AND SPORTS

This work was supported by the European Regional Development Fund project
"Creativity and Adaptability as Conditions of the Success of Europe
in an Interrelated World" (reg. no.: CZ.02.1.01/0.0/0.0/16_019/0000734).

Cover and graphic design by /3.dílna/
Frontispiece photo author's archive
Set and printed in the Czech Republic by Karolinum Press
First English edition

Cataloguing-in-Publication Data is available from the National Library
of the Czech Republic

ISBN 978-80-246-3853-9 (pb)
ISBN 978-80-246-3854-6 (pdf)
ISBN 978-80-246-3855-3 (epub)
ISBN 978-80-246-3856-0 (mobi)

To Aunt Hermanová
and Ms. Doris

CONTENTS

PART ONE
CRISIS

1

Between that which is departing and that which is only now arriving, sleepwalking spirits are materialising. Fantômas, Eduard Raban, von Passenov. Perhaps the key to these ciphers might be that which we call the *event horizon*.

2

Every reader remembers the sentence beneath the illustration of a particularly dastardly deed in an old penny dreadful: "He rang up the Yard about an hour ago and said his chambers had been invaded by Chinamen." Reading on we learn that the burglary had been reported using Bell's "electrical speech machine" by no less than the inventor of the aero-torpedo, plans to which had been seized by the Chinese. A century on and the aficionado of lowbrow literature will already have realised that the book in question is *The Insidious Doctor Fu Manchu* by the English author Sax Rohmer. The book was published in 1913 and was the first in a series spread over more than thirty years, with the last published in 1959 (leaving aside various posthumous continuations). The main character is the eponymous oriental villain who heads a secret organisation of Asians. Fu Manchu's nemesis, Nayland Smith, a colonial police commissioner with extraordinary powers of access and arrest, offers us a description of just how fiendish is Fu Manchu right at the start of the series, when he tells Dr. Petrie, his loyal companion:

"This man, whether a fanatic or a duly appointed agent, is, unquestionably, the most malign and formidable personality existing in the known world today. He is a linguist who speaks with almost equal facility in any of the civilized languages, and in most of the barbaric. He is an adept in all the arts and sciences which a great university could teach him. He also is an adept in certain obscure arts and sciences which no university of to-day can teach. He has the brains of any three men of genius. Petrie, he is a mental giant."

"But, Smith, this is almost incredible! What perverted genius controls this awful secret movement?"

"Imagine a person, tall, lean and feline, high-shouldered, with a brow like Shakespeare and a face like Satan, a close-shaven skull, and long, magnetic eyes of the cat-green. Invest him with all the cruel cunning of an entire

Eastern race, accumulated in one giant intellect, with all the resources of science past and present, with all the resources, if you will, of a wealthy government – which, however, already has denied all knowledge of his existence. Imagine that awful being, and you have a mental picture of Dr. Fu Manchu, the yellow peril incarnate in one man."[1]

So why do I feel the need to return to what is a pretty bizarre book? In fact I was reminded of the novel, which sketches out the radical threat faced by the whole of European (Western) civilisation, while reading the last published work by Edmund Husserl entitled *The Crisis of European Sciences and Transcendental Phenomenology*, based on the lectures he gave in Prague and Vienna entitled "Philosophy and the Crisis of European Humanity". In other words, I was put in mind of a classic of pulp fiction while reading a work that takes the state of emergency as its central theme. Though the crisis Husserl speaks of is manifest on the surface in the blind objectivism of science, on a deeper level it involves a forgetting of the original meaning that Western rationality was born both with and into. Interestingly, this period also saw the emergence of a new literary genre generally deemed lowbrow or trivial, and in this literature too we find what we might call a description of *crisis*, albeit a crisis refashioned into criminal and other such storylines. In the two years either side of Husserl's lecture, two more novels were published featuring Doctor Fu Manchu: *The Trail of Fu Manchu* and *President Fu Manchu*. The thriller by Eric Ambler *The Dark Frontier* (1936) also came out, the plot of which revolves around the discovery of atomic energy being misused in order to create a weapon. The hero, who loses his memory and is only subsequently informed of the events that have taken place, is Professor Barstow, an eminent physicist and expert in atomic energy, who, under the influence of the chance discovery of a volume of pulp fiction, is mentally reincarnated as the superhero

---

1   Sax Rohmer, *The Insidious Dr. Fu Manchu,* Methuen, London 1913, ch. 2.

Conway Carruthers and decides to feign collaboration with the armament manufacturers in order to thwart their dastardly plans. But do not be confused by the farfetchedness of the plot – Ambler's book is one of the first examples of the political thriller and masterfully evokes the atmosphere of living under the threat of atomic death, as well as its cultural and political backdrop. And just as Doctor Fu Manchu, though of oriental origin, is a master of Western science, so science and its soft underbelly form the theme of Ambler's book, as is clear from the conversation Professor Barstow has with a representative of the weapon manufacturers:

> "The ideals of science are constructive, not destructive," answered the Professor stiffly. "Science in the past has been shamefully exploited. But it has learnt to protect itself."
> Simon Groom shook his head.
> "No, Professor, you are wrong. While scientists are men, science cannot protect itself. The desire for supremacy which is in the hearts of all men prevents it. Even as I talk to you now, events are proving you wrong. The first atomic bomb has been made!"[2]

We might also note that the ominous collocation "atom bomb" first appears in literature intended for "the widest readership", namely the novel by H.G. Wells *The World Set Free* (1914). This book not only predicts the discovery of atomic energy almost twenty years before it happened (1933), but also the industrial applications that saw nuclear power definitively replace steam in 1953. However, in the book the discovery of cheap, easily available energy (nuclear plants are not only safe but smaller than traditional plants and can be situated everywhere) causes the complete collapse of civilisation, growing unemployment, unrest, and eventually a devastating war and

---

2   Eric Ambler, *The Dark Frontier*, Fontana Books, London 21967 (1936), ch. 1.

the dropping of an atom bomb on Berlin. The soldier in the plane carrying this new weapon,

> sat with his legs spread wide over the long, coffin-shaped box which contained in its compartments the three atomic bombs, the new bombs that would continue to explode indefinitely and which no one so far had ever seen in action.[3]

During the mid-1920s, H.G. Wells still imagined that a devastating world war would be the first stage in the establishment of a new system in a world liberated from work in which man is transformed into artist. However, after the end of what was the First (bona fide) World War and in the period immediately preceding the Second, such a dream was scarcely any longer feasible.

Eight years after Husserl's lectures on crisis, Graham Greene, whose early novel *A Gun For Sale* came out in 1936, published the next of what he termed his "entertainments", the thriller *The Ministry of Fear*. The book depicts the atmosphere of a kind of general but now unquestionably genuine crisis, firstly by setting the events in a London exposed night after night to German bombing, and secondly by virtue of the fact that what had hitherto been deemed fiction is now undeniably real. In the following passage, the hero of Greene's novel has a dream in which he speaks with his deceased mother and attempts to describe the world in which he is obliged to live:

> I'm hiding underground, and up above the Germans are methodically smashing London to bits all round me. (…) It sounds like a thriller, doesn't it, but the thrillers are like life — more like life than you are, this lawn, your sandwiches, that pine. You used to laugh at the books Miss Savage read — about spies, and murders, and wild motor-car chases, but, dear, that's real

---

3   H.G. Wells, *The World Set Free. A Story of Mankind*, MacMillan, London 1914, ch. 2, sec. 3.

life: it's what we've all made of the world since you died. I'm your little Arthur who wouldn't hurt a beetle and I'm a murderer too. The world has been
remade by William Le Queux. (…) Let me lend you the *History of Contemporary Society*. It's in hundreds of volumes, but most of them are sold in
cheap editions: *Death in Piccadilly, The Ambassador's Diamonds, The Theft
of the Naval Papers, Diplomacy, Seven Days' Leave, The Four Just Men…*[4]

The books he refers to are real and identifiable. William Le Queux
is the author of exciting (albeit interminable) novels in which he
gives vent to his concern for British politics with a fictional description of the invasion of Britain by the German army. His *Invasion of
1910* came out in 1906. However, in *Spies of the Kaiser* (1909), *Rev-
elations of the Secret Service* (1911), and many other semi-fictional,
pseudo-documentary books he exposed the danger to Britain of German spy rings and other forms of international conspiracy. *Death in
Piccadilly* is a whodunit from 1936 written by Elliot Bailey, *Seven
Day's Leave* is a film (a romantic comedy) made in 1942, and *The
Four Just Men* is Edgar Wallace's first novel, written in 1905. This
last is especially noteworthy for its ambivalence: the four just men of
the title, while murderers of noble origin and method, only liquidate
those who represent a menace to society and whom the police do not
have enough proof to prosecute. And finally there is Gregory Bellairs,
author of detective stories written in the 1930s and 40s, who is possibly present in Greene's novel in the guise of Mrs Bellairs, one of
the conspirators.

In order to ease out the links between these sensation novels and
Europe's crisis, let us remain a moment with the best known of the
authors referred to, Edgar Wallace, the harbinger of this style in
many respects. The blurb to the Czech translation of *The Four Just
Men*, though referring to detective fiction, captures very accurately
the emerging subgenre of pulp fiction, when it says of the author:

4   Graham Greene, *The Ministry of Fear*, Penguin, Vintage Classics, pp. 95–96.

Edgar Wallace is an author with the mind of a genius. This novel, which displays masterly ingenuity, is a good example of his detection skills. The reader's imagination is refined and exercised by the inexhaustible combinations that pervade the complex web of intrigue. One is unable to resist the excitement of being caught up in this detective story. To turn a page of this book is to close the doors of the present and to be swept away from everyday life, to forget everything and to live with Wallace. And a moment spent in Wallace's company is simply priceless.[5]

The "four just men" are actually three (the fourth is hired). The novel is the first of a series. Six books in total feature the same protagonists, the last being *Again the Three Just Men* published in 1929. In the first, the quartet of conspirators attempts to dissuade a British MP from submitting a draft bill on the extradition of foreigners who are in danger of being executed by their political opponents upon returning to their home country. They begin by sending warning letters that mysteriously find their way directly to the table of their addressee. However, the MP is determined and so the subsequent warnings (always announced in advance) are more spectacular: a bomb planted in parliament, a secret visit to a newspaper editor, etc. All of this foments panic in the population at large. The perpetrators are invisible and elude capture: there is no saying where or when they will turn up next. State officials keeping their own private vigil over justice are apoplectic and sense a threat to the very foundations of civilisation itself:

"It is monstrous," said the Colonial Secretary hotly; "it is inconceivable that such a state of affairs can last. Why, it strikes at the root of everything, it unbalances every adjustment of civilisation."[6]

5   Edgar Wallace, *Čtyři spravedliví* (The Four Just Men), transl. Běla Vrbová-Pavlousková, Julius Albert, Prague 1940.
6   Edgar Wallace, *The Four Just Men*, House of Stratus, Cornwall 2001, p. 72 (ch. VIII).

The inhabitants of London are horrified by the seeming ubiquity and omnipotence of these just men (not even the police can save the life of the MP, who is electrocuted by his telephone), and the atmosphere of the city on the day of reckoning is reminiscent of a state of war or emergency.

> And within an hour there was witnessed in London a scene that has no parallel in the history of the Metropolis. From every district there came a small army of policemen. They arrived by train, by tramway car, by motorbus, by every vehicle and method of traction that could be requisitioned or seized. They streamed from the stations, they poured through the thoroughfares, till London stood aghast at the realisation of the strength of her civic defences.[7]

Edgar Wallace undoubtedly created the prototype, though his was a very free model allowing for considerable variability within a genre it is difficult to put a name to. Perhaps this is why we speak of a "sensation" novel (even though the term was originally applied to Victorian authors), since the category of detective story would be too narrow. The sensation novel sometimes contains the seeds of a political thriller, and in this respect Eric Ambler's precursor was H.C. McNeile (Sapper) in books featuring Bulldog Drummond (the first of which, *Bulldog Drummond: The Adventures of a Demobilised Officer Who Found Peace Dull*, was published in 1920), in which a faint echo could be heard of J. Conrad's *The Secret Agent*, published in 1907. All of these books are about more than merely untangling a criminal plot. The sensationalism of their narratives was not driven simply by an attempt to attract the most readers, nor did it reflect the gradual commodification of literature, a phenomenon very visible in the serialised novels and booklets sold in railway station kiosks referred to by Walter Benjamin[8]. These books also act as

---

7   Ibid., p. 98 (ch. X).
8   Walter Benjamin, "Kriminalromane, auf Reisen", *Gesammelte Werke* 4.1, ed. Rolf Tiedemann – Hermann Schweppenhäuser, 7 vols, Suhrkamp, Frankfurt am Main 1972–1989.

a mirror, however distorted, held up to that which is already here in that it is in the process of arriving. In their own way, sensation novels model an uncertain and indefinable, yet still real fear – the heart of darkness at the very core of civilisation, something akin to *crisis*.

This disquiet, this testing of the boundaries of the classical whodunit (it was during this time that authors such as Agatha Christie, S.S. Van Dine, Freeman W. Crofts, Dorothy Sayers, et al. published their first books), is perhaps best illustrated in the books of H.C. McNeile, who wrote under the pseudonym Sapper, since as a serving officer in the British Army he was not permitted to publish under his own name. His hero, Hugh Drummond, is a man of action, though it is not only his superb physical condition that distinguishes him from his companions, but also his natural intelligence. His adversary in the first books is Carl Petersen, a criminal mastermind who operates under various different guises but whose modus operandi involves contract work for plutocrats with the aid of puppet conspirators. The sole aim of these plutocrats is to subvert the existing order and benefit from the ensuing chaos. In the very first novel we encounter a Bolshevik revolutionary who has moved to England, where he is bent upon applying his skills:

> I know not what this young man has done: I care less. In Russia such trifles matter not. He has the appearance of a bourgeois, therefore he must die. Did we not kill thousands – aye, tens of thousands of his kin, before we obtained the great freedom? Are we not going to do the same in this accursed country?[9]

In his bruising struggle with the conspirators and their puppet masters, Hugh Drummond is reluctantly reminded of his wartime experiences:

---

9   H.C. McNeile (Sapper), *Bulldog Drummond*, Hodder & Stoughton, London 1920, VII, ch. I.

He felt singularly wide-awake, and, after a while, he gave up attempting to go to sleep. The new development which had come to light that evening was uppermost in his thoughts; and, as he lay there, covered only with a sheet, for the night was hot, the whole vile scheme unfolded itself before his imagination. The American was right in his main idea – of that he had no doubt; and in his mind's eye he saw the great crowds of idle foolish men led by a few hot-headed visionaries and paid blackguards to their so-called Utopia. Starvation, misery, ruin, utter and complete, lurked in his mental picture; spectres disguised as great ideals, but griming sardonically under their masks. And once again he seemed to hear the toc-toc of machine guns, as he had heard them night after night during the years gone by. But this time they were mounted on the pavement of the towns of England and the swish of the bullets, which had swept like swarms of cockchafers over No Man's Land, now whistled down the streets between rows of squalid houses...[10]

Anarchists continue to undermine civilisation in Sapper's next novel, *The Black Gang* (1922), in which, with the aid of corrupt politicians, they try to hammer "another nail in the coffin of Capital. And, by heaven! A big one"[11] and infect England with Bolshevism. In the third in the series (*The Third Round*, 1923), Carl Petersen muses on the workings of the world and says to his partner in crime and mistress:

Take Drakshoff: that man controls three of the principal Governments of Europe. The general public don't know it; the Governments themselves won't admit it: but it's true for all that.[12]

10 Ibid., IX, ch. II.
11 Sapper (H.C. McNeile), *The Black Gang*, Hodder & Stoughton, London 1922, ch. 5.
12 Sapper (H.C. McNeile), *The Third Round*, Hodder & Stoughton, London 1923, ch. 1.

3

"Only from its extremes can reality be revealed," wrote Siegfried Kracauer in 1929 at the start of his study *The Salaried Masses*.[13] However, the same could be said of the relationship between the high and the low, the dominant and the marginalised, and, as the philosophical treatise *The Detective Novel*[14] by the same author shows, the relationship between the sensation novel and serious reflections upon the phenomenon of crisis. Philosophers have displayed but a sporadic interest in lowbrow literature. However, along with Walter Benjamin, who alludes to the novels of Gaston Leroux, Frank Heller and Sven Elvestad (highly popular in his day, though whose detective Asbjörn Krag is rather too similar to the master of disguise Nick Carter[15]) and others, Siegfried Kracauer is one of the exceptions. He wrote a study of the detective novel in 1922–25, though only the chapter "Hotel Hall" was published during his lifetime as part of the collection *The Mass Ornament* (1963).

In its own way Kracauer's treatise also aims to diagnose and describe the concept of crisis, and his reading of detective stories provided him with the appropriate language, since the detective traditionally embodies the modern form of rationality. However, Kracauer's diagnosis is also facilitated by his Kierkegaard-inspired ontological differentiation of a higher and lower realm that corresponds approximately to nature and transcendence. Man is the

---

13 Siegfried Kracauer, *Die Angestellten*, Suhrkamp, Frankfurt a.M., 1971 (first published in 1929 in *Frankfurter Zeitung*).

14 Siegfried Kracauer, *Der Detektiv-Roman. Ein philosophischer Traktat*. Suhrkamp, Frankfurt a. M. 1979. There is useful material to be found on Siegfried Kracauer in Gertrud Koch, *Kracauer. Zur Einführung*. Junius Verlag, Hamburg 1996; Frank Grunert, Dorothee Kimmlich (eds.), *Denken durch die Dinge. Siegfried Kracauer im Kontext*. Wilhelm Fink Verlag, Paderborn 2009; Nia Perivolaropoulou, Philippe Despoix (eds.), *Culture de masse et modernité. Siegfried Kracauer sociologue, critique, écrivain*. Ed. de la Maison des Sciences de l'homme, Paris 2001.

15 I am also acquainted with Elvestad's work from Czech translations, e.g. *Ples dobrodruhů*, Nakladatelství Vendelina Steinhausera in Pilsen 1921, or *Stíny dvou mužů*, Obelisk, Prague 1925. *Motrose* was translated into Czech by Milena Jesenská (Borový, Prague 1928).

interbeing (*Zwischenwesen*), because humanity is determined both naturally and by its relationship to annunciation and redemption. The locus of the detective novel is (human) reality, a reality that is in crisis because it has lost its relationship to the higher realm, even though it is only this relationship that grants the real any meaning: without this relationship, reality is de-realised. We are afforded a glimpse of this situation by lowbrow literature, which acts as a surface upon which phenomena are recorded (like a photographic negative) without being interpreted and without that which is recorded being deprived of its specificity. In this way, lowbrow literature makes phenomena accessible to diagnostic tools, which are capable, as Benjamin says, of returning the world of the dream to the world of wakefulness, transforming the detective story into *Denkbild* or thought image. This is a crucial concept for Kracauer, by which he defines himself in opposition to the *Neue Sachlichkeit* (New Objectivity) movement and the popularity of reportage that describes reality instead of searching for traces of its design flaws. An illustrative example of this is Kracauer's harsh criticism of the famous "film symphony" *Berlin* by Ruttmann. Kracauer observes that the film aims to encapsulate the metropolis by presenting a series of microscopic individual traits. However, instead of interrogating these traits

> in a way that would betray a true understanding of its social, economic and political structure (...) it leaves the thousands of details unconnected, one next to the other. There is nothing to see in this symphony, because it has not exposed a single meaningful relationship.[16]

The film fails to reveal the connections offered to our gaze by the *Denkbild*, the image of a thought (a thought in the form of an image, a thought-image).

16 Siegfried Kracauer,"Film 1928", in: *Ornament der Masse*, Suhrkamp, Frankfurt a.M. 1977. *The Mass Ornament,* transl. T. Y. Levin, Harvard University Press, Cambridge, Mass. 2005.

The *Denkbild* is illustrative reflection and reflected illustration in one. It combines (...) both methods of cognition. Shaping (*Gestaltung*) is permeated by theory, theory is absorbed by shaping. Cognition and experience, reflection and opinion, content and form, or however else this antinomy is referred to, permeate each other. And as they reach their limits, material reality is suddenly transformed into significant image.[17]

The origin of this new instrument of thinking is to be found in the "Erkenntniskritische Vorrede" (Epistemo-Critical Prologue) preceding Benjamin's essay on tragic drama and in his theory of ideas as constellations (ideas are to phenomena as constellations are to stars). The constellation is the tissue of an idea, which is objective in the sense that its parts are determined by concrete phenomena and its organisation expresses the internal logic implied in and distilled from reality. The concept was adopted in the 1930s by Theodor W. Adorno, who formulated more generally the meaning and objective of thinking, which now aims to grasp reality by means of the construction of thought-images instead of concepts. Adorno's interpretation is perhaps the more comprehensible, albeit at the expense of simplifying somewhat the original version propounded by Benjamin. For instance, in "The Actuality of Philosophy" he writes:

Philosophy distinguishes itself from science not by a higher level of generality, as the banal view still today assumes, nor through the abstraction of its categories nor through the nature of its materials. The central difference lies far more in that the separate sciences (*Einzelwissenschaften*) accept their findings (*Befunde*), at least their final and deepest findings, as indestructible and static, whereas philosophy perceives the first findings which it

---

17 Helmut Stalder, "Das anschmiegende Denken", in: Grunert – Kimmlich (eds.), Denken durch die Dinge, p. 70; trans. here by Phil Jones. Regarding the term "Denkbild" see Gerhard Richter, *Thought-Images: Frankfurt School Writers' Reflections from Damaged Life*, Stanford UP, Stanford 2007.

alights upon as a sign that needs unriddling. Plainly put: the idea of science is research; that of philosophy is interpretation (*Deutung*).

In this remains the great, perhaps the everlasting paradox: philosophy persistently and with the claim of truth, must proceed interpretively without ever possessing a sure key to interpretation; nothing more is given to it than fleeting, disappearing traces within the riddle figures of that which exists and their astonishing entwinings. The history of philosophy is nothing other than the history of such entwinings. Thus it reaches so few "results". It must always begin anew and therefore cannot do without the least thread which earlier times have spun, and through which the lineature is perhaps completed which could transform the ciphers into a text.

(...)

...the function of riddle-solving is to light up the riddle-*Gestalt* like lightning and to negate it, not to persist behind the riddle and imitate it. Authentic philosophic interpretation does not meet up with a fixed meaning which already lies behind the question, but lights it up suddenly and momentarily, and consumes it at the same time. Just as riddle-solving is constituted, in that the singular and dispersed elements of the question are brought into various groupings long enough for them to close together in a figure out of which the solution springs forth, while the question disappears – so philosophy has to bring its elements, which it receives from the sciences, into changing constellations, or, to say it with less astrological and scientifically more current expression, into changing trial combinations, until they fall into a figure which can be read as an answer, while at the same time the question disappears. The task of philosophy is not to search for concealed and manifest intentions of reality, but to interpret unintentional reality, in that, by the power of constructing figures, or images, out of the isolated elements of reality, it negates questions, the exact articulation of which is the task of science.[18]

---

18 Theodor W. Adorno, *Gesammelte Schriften*, ed. Rolf Tiedemann, Suhrkamp, Frankfurt a.M. 1986, here *GS* I, pp. 334–345. English translation from "The Actuality of Philosophy", *Telos*, vol. 31, 1977, pp. 126–127.

To simplify somewhat: what appears at first sight to be a continuous and straightforward social reality ("existing relations" in Adorno's words) must be deconstructed by means of the isolation of its elements (including those seemingly not worthy of attention) and the rearrangement thereof in order to discover in them something like an "image" rendering visible the contingency of a seemingly unshakeable reality – to expose its crisis. In adopting this cognitive tool, Adorno especially was motivated by Marx (the relationship between the forces and relations of production must be decoded in the form of goods), as explicitly evinced by aphorism 124 of *Minima Moralia*. The same aphorism also makes it clear that he was inspired by the "picture-puzzle" (*Vexierbild*), which was the privileged form of Benjamin's *One-Way Street* (1928). Analysing Antonín Dvořák's *Humoresque* in the essay *Quasi una fantasia*, Adorno writes:

> At one time there used to be a craze for a certain type of puzzle in the entertainment and theatre section of the daily newspapers. They were called picture-puzzles. A caption might read: Can you find the burglar? The picture showed an empty street without any people. A long ladder is leaning against a house, but it too has no one on it. Dark spots of rain are shown falling on the white houses. There is no sign of a burglar. The trick was to turn the page this way and that, sideways or upside down, until you discovered that the lines signifying rain, when taken with a bulky chimney, formed a grimacing gaze which could be arrested.[19]

However, Siegfried Kracauer had already carried out similar operations involving these thought images (*Denkbilder*) in *The Detective Novel*. The detective brings to light deracinated reason, the policeman the ineffectually functioning machine of legality, blindly obeying the law and detached from any relationship with justice. Nevertheless, the figure of the detective is remarkable. It is a cipher of

19 Adorno, *GS* 16, p. 28.

modern society inasmuch as it elucidates that liminal state that is human destiny and which now takes on a very special form. Like the priest before him, the detective is an intermediary. Like the priest, he too relates to the mysterious and secret, he mediates between the covert and the communal. However, while the priest invoked faith (i.e. mediated the relationship to that "higher" realm), the detective relies solely on the *ratio* appropriate to this world and in this way represents modern rationality, reason, which is no longer aware of its limitations and therefore also lacks a sense of morality. In the picture puzzle of the detective novel we can see that rationally fabricated reality, though at first sight cohesive and compact, is in actually fact incomplete and truncated.

Around the same time, Walter Benjamin in his early texts (e.g. "On the Programme of the Coming Philosophy" of 1918 et al.) ponders the possibility of expanding Kant's concept of experience and arrives at the concept of *speculative experience*. For Kant there is no room in experience for the idea of reason. Benjamin wants to show that in the final experience (subordinate to space-time, hence final) the absolute may also be manifest, but – since this is the experience of a finite being – only *indirectly, distortedly, in a kind of broken way.* Accordingly, this experience must be deciphered.

It is likely that Siegfried Kracauer had this in mind when he writes in *The Detective Novel*: "clouded sense becomes lost in the labyrinth of distorted events whose distortion it no longer perceives."[20] The labyrinth in which modern man loses himself is reality de-realised by rationality, which means that this is not only the realm of finality (because finality in itself is related to a higher realm, for instance to a transcendental idea of justice), but the realm of finality shattered by mechanical rationality. The policeman mechanically obeys the law without relating to the meaning to which it refers. The *ratio* is unmasked as a mere substitute: it is not capable of guaranteeing

20 Kracauer, *The Mass Ornament*, p. 173.

the meaning of that which it investigates, the events that it reveals, the reality that it explains.

It would be no exaggeration to claim that Kracauer, too, in his own way diagnoses crisis: a crisis of meaning, but also the meaning of crisis and meaning as crisis. However, this can only be corroborated more convincingly if we examine in more detail his *Denkbilder*. That "hotel lobby", for instance. And possibly it will become clearer why Kracauer focused on so-called "trivial" literature, something he hints at near the start of the chapter on the detective novel, when he writes:

> Just as the detective discovers the secret that people have concealed, the detective novel discloses in the aesthetic medium the secret of a society bereft of reality, as well as the secret of its insubstantial marionettes. The composition of the detective novel transforms an ungraspable life into a translatable analogue of actual reality.[21]

The hotel lobby, which is a venue that puts in frequent appearances in the classical detective novel, can be read as the "mirror image of God's house". Man visits here as a guest, but unlike the house of God, which is dedicated to the service of the one whom people wish to encounter, the "hotel lobby accommodates all who go there to meet no one". People are scattered around the lobby and receive their hosts incognito and without question; this is why the hotel lobby does not unite but simply emphasises their dispersal: the community in the hotel lobby is without meaning. Though it is not a quotidian space (man is not at home, he is a guest), in the hotel lobby man finds himself – albeit outside the everyday – *vis à vis rien*: the hotel lobby creates a gratuitous distance from the everyday.

---

21 Kracauer, *Der Detektiv-Roman*, p. 51.

In tasteful lounge chairs a civilisation intent on rationalisation comes to an end, whereas the decorations of the church pews are born from the tension that accords them a revelatory meaning.[22]

If, in the pure realm of Man as understood to include that which transcends it, equality is given by the relationship of the last things before the last (I am paraphrasing the title of Kracauer's last, unfinished book *Geschichte - Vor den letzten Dingen*, which was first published in English in 1969 as *History - The Last Things Before the Last* and in German translation as late as in 1971), in the hotel lobby equality is based on the "relation to nothingness", i.e. an equality that means emptying out within the framework of rational socialisation.

Here, the visitors suspend the undetermined special being, which, in the house of God, gives way to that invisible equality of beings standing before God (out of which it both renews and determines itself) by devolving into tuxedos.[23]

Tranquillity reigns in the hotel lobby, a solemn stillness holds court "that is the pride of all large hotels", as Thomas Mann wrote in his *Death in Venice*. However, the "contentless solemnity" of this quiet in the hotel lobby is a

silence that abstracts from the differentiating word and compels one downward into the equality of the encounter with the nothing, an equality that a voice resounding through space would disturb. (...) Remnants of individuals slip into the nirvana of relaxation, faces disappear behind newspapers, and the artificial continuous light illuminates nothing but mannequins.[24]

---

22 Kracauer, *The Mass Ornament*, p. 178.
23 Ibid., p. 181.
24 Ibid., p. 183.

The hotel lobby is a cipher, the key to which is the house of God, but a hotel lobby of the kind that appears in detective novels. The ciphers are not to be found in the depth of (high) art, but take shape on the surface, in trivial, i.e. superficial literature. Kracauer discovered *Oberfläche* (the surface) as text, and it is for this reason that his best known essay "The Mass Ornament" explains wherein resides the importance of the surface in a modern age permeated by rationalism. At the start of the essay there are dancers produced by the entertainment industry, then dance revues, and finally mass gymnastics in stadiums reported on by weekly film magazines: on the screen we can see "ornaments (...) composed of thousands of bodies, sexless bodies in bathing suits. The regularity of their patterns is cheered by the masses, themselves arranged by the stands in tier upon ordered tier."[25]

It is these patterns, these ornaments and monograms, that could be termed a "cipher" or *Denkbild*, carried by the very "mass" that participated in the creation of these ornaments as material, because people are merely the building blocks of ornament, fragments of some image. The ornament does not grow from within them or within the community, but "appears despite them". In this sense it *creates* something that can be made legible. "Creates" – in many senses of the word. The cipher can be read: the ornament is rational, it consists of the geometrical degrees and circles of Euclidian geometry, of the waves and spirals of physics, it is laid out in accordance with the rational principles of the organisation of labour, it is the aesthetic reflex of the rationality of production. But it is a cipher, which is why Kracauer writes:

No matter how low one gauges the value of the mass ornament, its degree of reality is still higher than that of artistic productions which cultivate out-

25   Ibid., p. 76.

dated noble sentiments in obsolete forms – even if it means nothing more than that.[26]

The ornament qua cipher is ambiguous: by virtue of its abstractness it makes reference to rationality (whose abstractness sets it apart from empiricism). However, that which is beyond the reach of the empirical, which is lost in abstraction, is nothing concrete in the vulgar sense of the word, for we can say that abstraction is simply a distorted form of universality that belongs to transcendence – without abstraction it would be impossible to relate not to the law, but to the idea of justice. However, just to be clear, I would add that Kracauer's topology in *The Detective Novel* is somewhat more complex:

If an existential tension is to be manifested, the law cannot be the last frontier. Instead, joint being within the sphere of sanctioned forms must retain its connection with the mystery over fixed forms. Since most people remain in a space surrounded by the law, from a sociological point of view attempting this connection is a matter for the individual. This connection takes place in a zone in which the power of the law does not apply without breakage, in the zone of that which contradicts the law and is above it, a zone that conceals mystery and danger within itself. Inasmuch as the law determines the true centre, it must turn away that which contradicts the law in the same way as it itself is impeded by what is above the law. Upper and lower powers outside the law are connected in such a way that the thread runs through the law. The human intermediate therefore demands that the whole life of existential community is played out in two spaces: in the space in which the law exerts control, and in the space in which the law is recognised as conditional.[27]

---

26 Ibid. p. 79.
27 Kracauer, *Der Detektiv-Roman*, p. 15 (trans. here by Phil Jones).

According to Kracauer, meaning resides precisely in the traces of the non-contingent present in the contingent. As soon as one is torn from the other, reality is meaningless.

Returning to the diagnostics of crisis, we observe certain similarities with Husserl. Here and there its source is rationality that has either forgotten its relationship with the founding idea (Husserl) or with the realm of the non-contingent (Kracauer). However, Kracauer, more expressively than Husserl, considers "objectivism" an important symptom of crisis, especially if it is manifest in a mechanisation pervading not only science but the level of the lived world. Several chapters are devoted to this idea of Kracauer's extensive study on the hitherto unexplored "tribe" of employees,[28] in which he examines the Taylorization of administration in large corporations.

More important (and this applies to both Kracauer and Husserl) is the relationship of "meaning" and history, even if in Kracauer's case this relationship is gradually developed, especially in his last, incomplete work on history from his exile in America.[29] While for Husserl the crisis is situated on the boundary between forgetting and recollecting (it is this irresolution that is the impulse for *Besinnung* in the sense of the clarification of meaning that is somehow here but obscured by scientific achievements), Kracauer, especially in his essay on photography devoted to the mechanism of memory and recollection, speaks of crisis as a *"go-for-broke game of history"*.[30] However, unlike Husserl he does not look for a clear therapy (which for Husserl is phenomenology), but rather for an approach appropriate to the situation that appears as crisis. He formulates this approach (present in the title itself) in the essay *Die Wartenden* of 1922.[31]

---

28 Kracauer, *Die Angestellten*.

29 Siegfried Kracauer, *Geschichte – Vor den letzten Dingen*. In: *Siegfried Kracauer Werke* 4, ed. Ingrid Belke, Suhrkamp, Frankfurt a.M. 2009. Original ed.: Siegfried Kracauer, *The Last Things Before the Last*. Completed after the death of the Author by Paul Oskar Kristeller. Marcus Wiener Publishers, Princeton 1995 (1. ed. Oxford University Press 1966).

30 Kracauer, *The Mass Ornament*, p. 61.

31 Kracauer, "Those Who Wait", in: *The Mass Ornament*.

Crisis is defined here as "metaphysical suffering from a lack of some higher meaning in the world" and as residing in an empty space, which is perceived as exile and isolation. This can then lead to extreme relativism (there exists no binding horizon of values or ideas), or even to *horror vacui*. However, this unfortunate state of affairs has a positive aspect: *waiting*. Waiting is "hesitant openness", *zögerndes Geöffnetsein*. This does not entail focusing on the last things, but a receptiveness to what cannot be predicted and what is unenforceable. In this respect the last sentences of the essay are crucial:

> Must it be added that getting oneself ready is only a preparation for that which cannot be obtained by force, a preparation for transformation and for giving oneself over to it? Exactly when this transformation will come to pass and whether or not it will happen at all is not at issue here, and at any rate should not worry those who are exerting themselves.[32]

Kracauer returns from the opposite pole, in a polemic with the spectre of universal history, to the restrained openness displayed by those who wait from the other side in his last book devoted to "the last things before the last". He rejects the idea of the chronological, homogenous, linear time accepted without question by historiography, and on the contrary seeks to understand it as a tissue of various shapes or forms in a synchronous cross-section, i.e. he foregrounds the discovery (inspired by Kubler, the theoretician of ancient art) that contemporary events are in fact mostly asynchronous if they belong to different time series or sequences whose character is always specific (a claim he again corroborates with the example of human memory). From this perspective space-time is the meeting place where unexpected encounters take place between different series of events – he uses the image of a railway station waiting room (not a million miles from a hotel lobby). But for this very reason

---

32 Ibid., p. 120. Cited in Gertrued Koch, *Siegried Kracauer: An Introduction*, Princeton University Press, Princeton, New Jersey 2000, p. 117.

historical reality is like that which has no end, something like *Vorraum*, a lobby or waiting room. And this calls for a different way of thinking (*Vorraum-Denken und -Verhalten*) – to remain on this earth and think through concrete things. If the subject of philosophy is to be the "ultimate truths" formulated in complete generality and with a claim to objectivity, and if it is so incontestable that, as such, philosophy has nothing to say of relevance about things pertaining to the lifeworld (Kracauer deliberately uses Husserl's term *Lebenswelt*), then the solution to this dispute can only be the "complementarity principle", i.e. not restricting ourselves to top down thinking, but thinking simultaneously in the opposite direction. Only this corresponds to that human "position in the middle" referred to in the book on the detective novel and which Kracauer now brings into convergence with the lifeworld of phenomenology in which, as he says, man does not deal with the last things but instead with the penultimate things as though they were the last (an idea captured more faithfully in the English rather than the German title of the book on history and historiography). If history is without end, it is deprived even of the aesthetic rescue of the past, the project attempted by Marcel Proust. And so history, like the present, must be viewed through the eyes of the exile, the extreme form of which in Kracauer's last book is Ahasver, the Wandering Jew. But then one thing is related to the other: he who waits is he who accepts his extra-territoriality as the basic human condition.

The immense importance of this shift in accent is not always obvious. In *The Detective Novel* the last reference point is atonement in the theological sense as mediated by the Judaic tradition of Messianism, something Kracauer studied in depth when in 1920–22 he, along with Leo Löwenthal and Erich Fromm, visited the Frankfurt *Freies Jüdisches Lehrhaus*[33], while in the essay on those who wait and in his last book the relationship to the last thing is character-

---

33 In this respect see Enzo Traverso, "Sous le signe de l'exteritorialité. Kracauer et la modernité juive". In: Perivolaropoulou – Despoix (eds.), *Culture de masse et modernité*.

ised as "hesitant openness". However, as Kracauer himself writes in a letter, we must turn our back on theology in the interests of theology itself. The emphasis is now on the insuperability of the boundary separating man from the absolute (which excludes any teleological speculation). Those who maintain permanent vigil awaiting the arrival of the Messiah or even want to expedite matters (such as Buber and Rosenzweig through the example of their Bible) are, according to Kracauer, *Kurzschluss-Menschen* or short-circuit people. In brief, history has no end, and yet it has (can have) meaning now as long as the unattainable, since absolute, "idea" is measured at every instant. This is a concept the final seal of which is surely the last sentence of the final aphorism of Adorno's *Minima Moralia* written immediately after the end of World War II:

> The more passionately thought denies its conditionality for the sake of the unconditional, the more unconsciously, and so calamitously, it is delivered up to the world. Even its own impossibility it must at last comprehend for the sake of the possible. But beside the demand thus placed on thought, the question of the reality or unreality of redemption itself hardly matters.[34]

Kracauer's exposure of monograms, that is to say significant patterns, and his reading of the ciphers on the surface of the quotidian in his book *Ornament der Masse* and elsewhere, clearly follows in the tradition of Simmelesque sociology. However, for this very reason it is easier to place his microanalyses within the wider context of "crisis", to a more precise understanding of which Georg Simmel contributed a range of important parameters aiding orientation. For example, it is impossible that Kracauer's theme and position of exile or extra-territoriality, which is closely connected with his *Vorraum-Denken*, was not influenced by Simmel's *Essay About the*

---

34 *Minima Moralia. Reflections from the Damaged Life,* trans. E.F.N. Jephcott, Verso, London and New York 2005, p. 247. I shall leave to one side the complex question of who inspired whom in the case of W. Benjamin, S. Kracauer and T. W. Adorno.

Stranger of 1908, and possibly by one of the first descriptions of the characteristic features of modernity contained in Simmel's essay *The Metropolis and Mental Life* of 1903.

Simmel's stranger is neither pilgrim nor traveller, neither outsider nor wanderer. He does not arrive today and leave tomorrow. On the contrary, the stranger is he who arrives today and remains tomorrow. He is still potentially a pilgrim or traveller (*der Wandernde*), since although he did not leave, he retains his freedom to come and go. He does not completely belong where he is, but lives within distance, with the consequence that for him that which is close is distant and that which is alien is close. However, this distance provides a specific objectivity to his perspective made possible both by his detachment and his participation, a perspective that "alienates" the given, tradition, and "habituality".[35]

Simmel, however, reveals the other side of this position in respect of the relationship the stranger has with the community in which he remains and of which he is a part, as is the indigent or, as Simmel states explicitly, the "enemy within".[36] If the community suffers internal division, unrest or revolt, whatever the cause, the party at threat will designate the stranger as an agitator or fifth columnist in order that it be possible to present the crisis as something originating from without.

His whole life Kracauer was fascinated by photography because it offered a picture of an epoch extracted from linear time. This is an eloquent example of that exterritoriality that he sought as a critical observer of his time. Like Benjamin's flâneur or Hannah Arendt's pariah,[37] he wanted to move "in the near-vacuum of exterritoriality", as he wrote in his book on history.

35 Georg Simmel, "Versuch über den Fremden", in: *Individualismus der modernen Zeit*. Suhrkamp, Frankfurt a.M. 2008, p. 269.
36 Ibid., p. 267.
37 During the 1930s, Hannah Arendt studied the tradition of the Jews as pariahs. She wrote a book on Rahel Levin-Varnhagen and came across the work of Bernard Lazar. See Enzo Traverso, *L'histoire déchirée,* Ed. du Cerf, Paris 1997.

However, exile was soon to become his very real fate. In 1933, the year the Weimar Republic came to an end, he was forced to leave Germany. While staying in Paris in 1934–37 he wrote a book on Jacques Offenbach, an Austrian emigrant in France and his kindred spirit. Eventually he left for the United States. His mother perished in Terezín.

4

This encounter between books that, on the face of it, have nothing in common – early examples of the thriller genre, Graham Greene's entertainments, and Husserl's *The Crisis of European Sciences* – raises some questions. Is the word "crisis" in the title of Husserl's work from the mid-1930s simply a somewhat exaggerated way of expressing certain misgivings harboured at that time regarding the exactness of the exact sciences? Or is it a reaction to the relatively profound transformation science was undergoing, a transformation that was driving a revaluation of traditional ideas of accuracy and scientism, and even of *rationality*, i.e. the deductive construction of an axiomatic system from irrefutably first and simplest principles? After all, this idea of rational knowledge is difficult to sustain in an era of relativity theory, quantum physics and intuitionism in mathematics.

All of these questions play a role in Husserl's book and Husserl himself refers tangentially to them. However, they are not the central issue, not the "crisis" he has in mind. In any case, Husserl was no doubt aware that revolutions in theoretical spheres rarely create panic in the population at large. Firstly, their scope is limited, and secondly, if they spread at all it is only after having been transformed and mediated by culture.

All the more remarkable, therefore, is the dramatic tone that Husserl adopts in the introductory paragraphs, in which he introduces us to the phenomenon of crisis. The very language of these preliminary considerations is striking. Husserl speaks of the crisis of the sciences as "an expression of the radical life crisis of European humanity" (the title of the first section of the book). What caused the crisis is the fact that the "genuine scientific character [of science] (...) has become questionable" and that this has given rise to a "general lament about the crisis of our culture" etc. In short, the "crisis of sciences" is a crisis of rationality. Though Husserl, unlike many of his contemporaries, does not speak of a crisis of culture or of "discontent" with culture as symptom of a loss of confidence in Enlightenment reason, his criticism of the instrumentalisation of science points in this direction, and it would perhaps not be going too far to claim that Husserl – albeit unwittingly, since he could not have suspected the extent of the future catastrophe (even though Benjamin's essay on mechanical reproduction was published in 1936, followed a year later by the opening in Munich of the exhibition *Entartete Kunst*) – anticipates the despairing question posed by Horkheimer and Adorno in *Dialectic of the Enlightenment*, namely "why mankind, instead of entering into a truly human condition, is sinking into a new kind of barbarism".[38]

It might appear as though Husserl is simply retracing a line of argument that has already been addressed either head-on or implicitly by earlier authors in texts ranging from what is often dubbed trivial literature (the precursor of the political thriller) to the distinguished essay by Max Weber entitled "Science as a Vocation" of 1919, in which Weber notes that "science has become a problem in calculation, fabricated in laboratories or statistical filing systems just as 'in a factory', a calculation involving only the cool intellect and not one's 'heart and soul'."[39] All this is hinted at, at least with hindsight, in *The Crisis of European Sciences*, where for instance the author observes "the appearance of puzzling, insoluble obscurities in modern, even mathematical sciences, and in connection with that (...) the emergence of a set of world enigmas which were unknown to earlier times."[40] It is clear that Husserl is by no means speaking

---

38 Theodor W. Adorno, Max Horkheimer, *Dialektik der Aufklärung*, in: *GS* 3, p. 11 ("die Erkenntnis, warum die Menschheit, anstatt in einen wahrhaft menschlichen Zustand einzutreten, in eine neue Art von Barbarei versinkt.").

39 Max Weber, "Science as a Vocation". Originally delivered as a speech at Munich University, 1918. Published in 1919 by Duncker & Humblodt, Munich, p. 5. English translation see http://www.wisdom.weizmann.ac.il/~oded/X/WeberScienceVocation.pdf Accessed January 2019.

40 Edmund Husserl, *The Crisis of European Sciences and Transcendental Phenomenology*, transl. with an Introduction by David Carr, Northwestern University Press, Evanston 1970, pp. 3 and 5.

of the special problems of the exact sciences, because that on which his "phenomenological philosophy" is now focused is the founding of science in subjectivity and therefore the relationship between reason and life. Hence the well known statement that summarises his perspective on the phenomenon of crisis: "In our vital need – so we are told – this science has nothing to say to us."[41] In fact all of Husserl's references to "crisis" have a particular, very ambiguous character. For instance:

> We make our beginning with a change which set in at the turn of the past century in the general evaluation of the sciences. It concerns not the scientific character of the sciences but rather what they, or what science in general, had meant and could mean for human existence.[42]

It is clear that the key phrase here is "scientific character", i.e. something along the lines of rationality (characteristic of European culture), from which, however, existing rationality in the form of the objectivism of the exact sciences has somehow split and whose meaning it has forgotten. Yet what is striking is the extent to which an uncharacteristically *personal* tone creeps into these considerations on rationality and science, even though both are in crisis. This tone tells us that something of genuine import is at stake.

> Scientific, objective truth is exclusively a matter of establishing what the world, the physical as well as the spiritual world, is in fact. But can the world, and human existence in it, truthfully have a meaning if the sciences recognise as true only what is objectively established in this fashion, and if history has nothing more to teach us than that all the shapes of the spiritual world, all the conditions of life, ideals, norms upon which man relies, form and dissolve themselves like fleeting waves, that it always was and ever will be so, that again and again reason must turn into nonsense, and well-being

41   Ibid.
42   Ibid.

into misery? Can we console ourselves with that? Can we live in this world, where historical occurrence is nothing but an unending concatenation of illusory progress and bitter disappointment?[43]

The world is in disarray. However, as Husserl tries to demonstrate and corroborate throughout the entire book, it is not the world itself, the world in which we live like foreign bodies in a foreign body – it is not the world's fault. The problem lies on the side of science, which is still science but has lost the *meaning* that is inseparable from science. In its self-forgetfulness it has become engrossed in its objectivism, and the result is that our world, the world founded by science, is in disarray. In *crisis*. "True science" is for Husserl something that relates to European Man, to Western culture, to Europe as a certain spiritual "achievement". Here too it is clear that he has in mind a *philosophical* meaning of crisis and that, in the final analysis, crisis in its capacity as a crisis of meaning is something that belongs to meaning.

Paradoxically, however, the path to this philosophical concept of crisis is, unwittingly, illuminated more by sensation novels than by scholarly essays.

---

43   Ibid., p. 28.

5

So how should we formulate the theme of crisis more accurately?

Husserl speaks of "crisis" in a dramatic tone, though this tone does not determine the very factual character of his reflections on the crisis of European sciences. The book is actually another of his introductions to phenomenology. At the same time it represents a new approach to the subject, since it includes the dimension of a certain *historicity* (Husserl speaks explicitly of "phenomenological history"), which it deems fundamental. Nevertheless, the dramatic tone of the introduction alerts us to the wider, let us say "cultural", context, namely the *awareness of crisis* in the 1920s and 30s that is evident in both "high culture", including philosophy, and in low-brow literature, specifically in thrillers. A portend of the decades that would follow the first world war is contained, for instance, in *The Decline of the West* by Oswald Spengler, published in 1918, of which Ernst Cassirer declared:

> At this time many, if not most of us, had realised that something was rotten in the state of our highly prized Western civilisation. Spengler's book expressed in a sharp and trenchant way this general uneasiness.

It is worth noting that Husserl himself did not share this feeling, and in a series of articles for the Japanese magazine *Kazio* in 1923, in an obvious allusion to Spengler, warned against believing in the decline of the West. Another work clearly reflecting the trauma of the First World War is Freud's *Civilisation and its Discontents*. But in fact the same is true of Husserl, when he introduces the series of articles referred to with the following words:

> Renewal (*Erneuerung*) is the general call in our miserable presence and within the entire sphere of European culture. The war of 1914 that laid waste to Europe and since 1918 has simply replaced military enforcement

techniques with "subtler" instruments of mental torture and morally de-
praved economic crises, has revealed this culture to be inwardly fake and
empty.[44]

In other words, the connection between differently formulated feelings of crisis and Husserl's book is not as loose as it might appear at
first glance. Husserl's crisis of European sciences is a reflection on
the crisis of *scientism*, the ideal of science, i.e. it is a reflection on the
crisis *inside* the history of European rationality itself. When reading
the book we must not forget his claim that Europe is a "spiritual
shape", that it is identical to this type of rationality, the Western
ideal of science. From this perspective, pulp fiction differs from
Husserl's concept of crisis inasmuch as it perceives the threat to
Europe as originating from *outside* (the "yellow peril"), but agrees
with Husserl that the external enemy has infiltrated Europe and
now poses a threat from within (London, the heart of civilisation,
a corrupt Member of Parliament). And when Graham Greene re-
suscitates the thrillers of the 1920s and 30s, he is saying clearly:
that which I used to read as fiction has in the meantime become
our reality. In other words, if we feel so inclined, we can situate
Husserl's work on crisis on a loose trajectory that includes on the one
hand *The Dialectic of Enlightenment* by Adorno and Horkheimer,
Benjamin's work and its predecessors, namely Georg Simmel, Max
Weber and Carl Schmitt, and on the other hand that which comes
later, e.g. Michel Foucault and Giorgio Agamben.

And so we have at least a rough coordinate for our deliberations:
we are justified in speaking of crisis when a threat moves from outside of that which is at threat and reappears inside. The exterior
enters the interior. This is a strange situation, since the "outside"
is now "inside". However, I think that intuitively this coordinate
can suffice for the purposes of orientation. At the same time, this

---

44 Edmund Husserl, *Vorträge und Aufsätze*, Husserliana XXVII, ed. T. Nenon and H.R. Sepp, Kluwer, Dordrecht 1989, p. 3; trans. here by Phil Jones.

"definition" is the shortest distance between two points, the points in question being Husserl's work on the crisis of European sciences and lowbrow (sensation) literature, since the theme is common to both: Europe is threatened with crisis; nay, possessed by crisis.

✕✕✕

As an example of this less serious literature I have cited what might be termed early "political thrillers": William Le Queux's *Invasion*, *Spies of the Kaiser* and Eric Ambler's *The Dark Frontier*, *Uncommon Danger* and others. However, we should not overlook John Buchan and his novel *The Thirty-Nine Steps* (1915), in which a group of German spies named *Der schwarze Stein* sabotages Britain from within and prepares the ground for invasion. And let us not omit the diabolical Doctor Fu Manchu from this company. Here the "exterior" has seeped everywhere in the form of a fifth column, the Orient in London, the exact sciences powerless against poisonous fungi, giant centipedes, thugs, etc. When Doctor Fu Manchu appears in the very heart of Old London Town, our protagonists feel as though they have been transported to "a dungeon in old Baghdad". In the centre of a metropolis they have the sensation of languishing "in the middle of a desert". The situation is similar when gangsters from Chicago relocate their activities to London.

However, no literary figure of the period is more characteristic of these themes than Fantômas. This is the exterior *par excellence*, as the very name suggests: a phantasmagoric existence within a European capital, in this case Paris. As such Fantômas embodies the most fundamental quality of the "exterior". He is *unidentifiable* in several respects. He is elusive to the point of invisible, because it is impossible to lay hands upon him – he resides outside the framework of "intelligibility", not least because he is *immeasurable by objective methods*. And his indecipherability is in direct relation to the terror that his very existence provokes. Fantômas could be anyone!

So let us remain briefly with this famous literary figure created by Pierre Souvestre and Marcel Allain (both journalists).[45]

In 1905, the Fayard publishing house began publishing a series entitled *Le Livre populaire* (with a colour dust jacket by Gino Starace). Since the print run of each book was a respectable 100,000 copies, price-wise *Le Livre populaire* could compete with a similar range recounting the adventures of Jean Laffitte. Between 1905 and 1914, Fayard published 112 novels, most of which first appeared as *feuilletons* in newspapers: Eugène Sue's *The Mysteries of Paris*, Paul Féval's *The Mysteries of London*, and others. The "mysteries" in particular continued in the vein of late Romanticism (Dumas, *Salvator, The Mohicans of Paris*), and so we find an aristocrat slumming it amongst ordinary folk, or the noble savage in the form of the native American. These books are a kind of social criticism tinged with sentimentality. The fact they were released in instalments impacted on their form, which included protracted dialogue (often in literary argot), convoluted subplots, etc. The genre was responding to the public's insatiable desire for crime (Arsène Lupin in newspapers starting 1905, Laffitte in book form starting 1907), something that was true of early cinema too. This demand was also met by a flood of American detective novels (e.g. Nick Carter – a bargain at 25 centimes for 32 pages a week).

In 1910, Fayard negotiated a contract with Souvestre and Allain, under the terms of which the writers would supply a complete novel of some 400 pages every month for 32 months. This was the genesis of the 32 works totalling some 12,000 pages featuring Fantômas (the authors dictated material onto a phonograph). In all around five million copies were published.

---

45 Regarding Fantômas see, for example, Thomas Brandlmeier, *Fantômas. Beiträge zur Panik des 20.Jahrhunderts,* Verbrecher Verlag, Berlin 2007; Robin Walz, *Pop Surrealism: Insolent Popular Culture in Early Twentieth-Century Paris.* University of California Press, Berkeley, Los Angeles 2000; special issue *Europe: Revue littéraire Mensuelle* (1978).

Fantômas is a ghostly figure who surfaces in the centre of Paris. He is a kind of cipher for the perpetrators of all mysteriously unresolved crimes, as indeed he is described by Bonnet in the first book:

> we have been distressed by a steady access of criminality, and among the assets we shall henceforth have to count a mysterious and most dangerous creature, to whom the baffled authorities and public rumour generally have for some time now given the name of Fantômas! It is impossible to say exactly or to know precisely who Fantômas is. He often assumes the form and personality of some definite and even well known individual; sometimes he assumes the forms of two human beings at once and the same time – Fantômas! His shadow hovers above the strangest mysteries, and his traces are found near the most inexplicable crimes, and yet...[46]

A burglar who cannot be apprehended, a homicidal maniac, but above all the bringer of destruction and chaos, who eludes even the indefatigable attempts of detective Juve and the journalist Fandor (Charles Rambert, the son of Etienne Rambert, whom Fantômas first disguises himself as, only later to murder by sinking the ferry on which Rambert is travelling by means of a fiendish machine). And there is no better description of the way the *exterior materialises within the interior* than that which begins the series:

> "Fantômas."
> "What did you say?"
> "I said: Fantômas."
> "And what does that mean?"
> "Nothing... And everything!"
> "But what is it?"
> "Nobody... And yet, it is somebody!"

46 Pierre Souvestre, Marcel Allain, *Fantômas*, transl. Cranstoun Metcalfe, Dover Publications, Inc. Mineola, New York, pp. 3–4.

"And what does that somebody do?"
"Spreads terror!"[47]

This terror is induced by the "elusiveness" of Fantômas: the outside that is now inside the inside escapes detection because within the "grid" of the interior it is unidentifiable. In the case of the Paris of Fantômas this grid comprises *science* in the form of anthropometry and the most highly advanced methods of police identification created by Alphonse Bertillon, one of the fathers of forensic science. And lest it escape our attention: this is another example of the "mathematisation" of the natural world, the numerical transcription of life (population statistics, taxes, birth and death rate curves, etc.): *bertillonage* is the numerical transcription of a person that is intended to allow for reliable *identification* but which in Fantômas' case fails repeatedly with catastrophic consequences. For

> (w)hile Bertillon's archive posited order for "the growing masses" of criminals, in which one criminal matched one series of numerical notations on one *fiche d'identité*, *Fantômas* disrupts the supposed numerical singularity of anthropometric identification by effecting multiple matches. Through the representation of a criminal whose identity corresponds to a constantly increasing number of *fiches d'identité*, the series systematically defies the singularity of numerical criminal identity, while simultaneously reproducing the generalised numbers of probably criminality that comprise the archive of *la police scientifique*.[48]

Fantômas is unidentifiable in all senses of the word. So, for instance, in the first book the actor Valgrand, who played Fantômas on stage, is executed in his place. Furthermore, Fantômas is capable of appearing as several persons simultaneously. He possesses a physical

---

47 Ibid, p. 1.
48 Nanette L. Fornabai, "Criminal Factors: Fantômas, Anthropometrics, and the Numerical Fictions of Modern Criminal Identity", *Yale French Studies*, No. 108 (Crime Fictions), 2005, pp. 60–73.

existence only at the moment he becomes someone else. Before this he is merely a *shadow* (in the later works dressed in black with a black cowl *en cagoule*, as he is portrayed in the films by Feuillade). In *Fantômas the Elusive* he is both man and woman in a single house. In *The Red Wasp* Juve expresses his doubts:

"Fandor, the unfathomable murder of Lady Beltham gives rise to a most disquieting thought. You hit the nail on the head when you were thinking out loud about the strange events that have taken place recently; there are possibly two Fantômases and we have only one of them under lock and key."[49]

In order to apprehend him, Commissioner Juve himself adopts a disguise in a move guaranteed to cause chaos. In *A Royal Prisoner*, Juve is arrested by his boss in the guise of Fantômas, while *The Corpse Who Kills* includes the following monologue by Juve:

"For, who is Fantômas – the real Fantômas, among so many probable Fantômas?
"Can you tell me that, Fandor?" continued Juve, who was getting excited at last. (...) "I grant you that we have seen, in the course of our chequered existence, an old gentleman, like Etienne Rambert, a thickset Englishman like Gurn, a robust fellow like Loupart, a weak and sickly individual like Chaleck. We have identified each one of them, in turn, as Fantômas – and that is all.
"As for seeing Fantômas himself, just as he is, without artificial aid, without paint and powder, without a false beard, without a wig, Fantômas as his face really is under his hooded mask of black – that we have not yet done. It is that fact which makes our hunt for the villain ceaselessly difficult, often dangerous! (...) Fantômas is always someone, sometimes two persons, never himself!"
Juve, once started on this subject, could go on for ever, and Fandor did not try to stop him: when the course of conversation led them to talk of Fantô-

---

49 Ibid., p. 450 (trans. here by Phil Jones).

mas the two men were as though hypnotised by this mysterious creature, so well named, for he was really "Fantômatic," a spectral entity: the two friends could not turn their minds to any other subject.[50]

By the end of the book the reader is inclined to ask: might not Juve actually be Fantômas? Not even Juve seems completely sure. And this is the horror of the outside inside: Fantômas can be anyone.

So have we learned something new about *crisis*?

Crisis is a state of *indistinguishability*. In the examples above the existing identification grid fails and there is no other to hand. This is a particular state of *transition* in which the world becomes increasingly unintelligible. Nothing makes clear sense, generally acceptable institutions prove less than dependable, routine modes of conduct are suspended, in short *ambivalence* reigns. In Husserlian terms, the meaning of science for life has been lost, and life has shown itself to be *immensurable*. Rationality appears to be at odds with itself. This is because, as Husserl himself says in his original lecture,[51] the scientist ceased being the subject of investigation. What he means is that the objectivism of modern science, i.e. its clear focus "outward" (on an "objective" reality that is supposedly completely independent of "subjectivity"), has stopped taking into consideration the fact that "no objective science can do justice to the very subjectivity which accomplishes sciences,"[52] which is why such a science has nothing to say regarding those questions that relate most closely to man. Rationality is at odds with itself inasmuch as the cause of the failure of rational culture, as Husserl states explicitly, "lies not in the essence of rationalism itself".[53] This is because reason has become embroiled in

50 Pierre Souvestre, Marcel Allain, *Fantomas se venge* [*Le Mort qui tue*], Livre de poche, Paris 1961, pp. 313–14.
51 Edmund Husserl, *The Crisis of European Sciences and Transcendental Phenomenology: An Introduction to Phenomenological philosophy,* trans. David Carr, Northwestern University Press, Evanston 1970.
52 Husserl, *The Crisis*, p. 295.
53 Husserl, *The Crisis*, p. 299.

"naturalism and objectivism". In other words, reason (in the guise of science) has forgotten its origin in the primordial element of subjectivity that is the life-world, *Lebenswelt*, or "natural world". It has become ensnared in its own exterior.

6

At the instant that the relationship between inside and outside ceases to involve clearly differentiated moments separated by a clear boundary, the situation becomes far more complex. This applies to the phenomenon of the crisis and the strange forms of mutual interpenetration of inside and outside consequent thereupon (the enemy/stranger within in the case of sensation novels, and a hesitant openness and unintelligibility in scientific theory in the case of serious reflection). This might involve, for instance, becoming entangled in the exterior as a consequence of the inexorable infiltration of the outside into the inside, which is indeed the situation being played out in the sensation novels referred to.

Here, however, we must broaden our field of investigation somewhat. Certain subgenres of the sensation novel (though not the classical whodunit) continue in a long, somewhat vague tradition of adventure literature. However, at the end of the nineteenth century and into the twentieth they begin to remould this tradition. The *event*, in the sense of that which arrives suddenly, that which is unforeseeable, now finds itself foregrounded. However, if the event thus defined is unexpectable, then upon its arrival it is *outside* the current horizon of expectations. This raises a question regarding identification of the event qua event and identification of its meaning, a meaning indecipherable from the current horizon of understanding. And all of this presupposes the event is even recognisable as an event. There are ambiguous clues or hints: something happened – but what actually happened? We might summarise our preliminary findings thus: the event is the *outside inside the inside* (*the outside-in*) (this would be crisis as event), though takes the form of something incomprehensible and foreign. This is why the event carries the horizon of its understanding within it (and is only distinguishable after it happens), and this horizon is incommensurate with the horizons of that world in which the event takes place.

This subgenre of the sensation novel dating back to the turn of the nineteenth and twentieth centuries, which stages this situation most effectively by appropriating certain features of adventure literature, is a depiction of the "war-to-come" that is closely associated with the spy novel.[54] It finds its predecessor in Chesney's *The Battle of Dorking* (1871), and then spreads rapidly, not only in England, but in Germany and France. The genre is prodigious and includes Wells' *War of the Worlds* (1898) and the technical science fiction by the same author (*The War in the Air*, 1908), as well as Le Queux referred to above (*The Great War in England in 1897*, 1888), and many others.[55]

The very term "adventure" would be hopelessly vague if not (again) for Simmel's essay "Philosophie des Abenteuers" from roughly the same time (1910), in which adventure is primarily defined as severance from the context of life. Its time (or "temporality"), if we may express it thus, stands outside the continuity of linear and (seemingly) homogenous time. However, this is an outside that "if only by a long and unfamiliar detour, is formally an aspect of the inside" and thus often takes the form of a dream). The fact that adventure exceeds the given horizon of expectation is shown by the fact of its being torn from the context of memory and of being centred on meaning "that exists as such". And this is a very accurate descrip-

54 Regarding the genesis of this type of novel, see I. F. Clarke, "Future-War Fiction: The First Main Phase, 1871–1900". *Science Fiction Studies*, Vol. 24. No. 3 (1997), pp. 387–412; I. F. CLARKE, "Forecast of Warfare in Fiction 1803–1914", in: *Comparative Studies in Society and History*, Vol. 10, No. 1 (1967), pp. 1–25; I. F. CLARKE, *Voices Prophecying War: Future Wars 1763–3749.* Oxford University Press, Oxford 21993; LeRoy L. Panek, *The Special Branch. The British Spy Novel, 1890–1980*, Bowling Green University Popular Press, Ohio 1981; David A.T. Stafford, "Spies and Gentlemen: The Birth of the British Spy Novel. 1893–1914." *Victorian Studies*, Vol. 24, No. 4 (1981), pp. 489–509; Robert Lance Snyder, *The Art of Indirection in British Espionage Fiction. A Critical Study of Six Novelists*, McFarland, Jefferson, NC 2011.

55 It suffices to cite but a few titles at random: *The Seizure of the Channel Tunnel* (the reaction to the plan to build a tunnel under the English Channel in 1882), *The Taking of Dover, The Siege of Portsmouth; La guerre franco-allemande de 1878* from 1877, the trilogy *La guerre de demain de capitaine danrit* (Emile Auguste Driant), *La fin de la Prusse et le démembrement de l'Allemagne* from 1913; *Die Abrechnung mit England* by Dr. Karel Eisenhart from 1900, and many others.

tion of the fact that the event (in respect of its meaning) carries the horizon of its understanding within itself.

> The adventure is freed of the entanglements and concatenations which are characteristic of (other forms of our existence) (it) is according to its intrinsic meaning (...) independent of the "before" and "after"; its boundaries are defined regardless of them. We speak of adventure precisely when continuity with life is thus disregarded in principle – or rather when there is not even any need to disregard it, because we know from the beginning that we have to do with something alien, untouchable, out of the ordinary.[56]

Temporality, which is actually the event in the strong sense of the word, could be called "adventurous time": this is the form of time staged by sensation novels. Its irruption into linear time – the irruption of the "exterior" – is a symptom of crisis in that form in which it becomes the theme of the sensation novel.

In this respect, novels about the war to come represent a curious paradox: they embody an expectation of the unexpectable. And this is precisely why spy thrillers develop in parallel, since the unexpectable can be expected only to the extent to which we are able to distinguish its traces in the current world. Spies must be unmasked as the ominous prelude to what is arriving. Spies are strangers set to become the "fifth column" and the "enemy within". This is how the unexpectable introduces itself on the threshold of an impending crisis: from within on the threshold of the outside.

The more complex time structure that characterises texts prophesying war is already powerfully present in the prototype of this literature, *The Battle of Dorking* by George T. Chesney from 1871, which reflects upon the transformation of power structures in Europe in

---

[56] Georg Simmel, "Philosophie des Abenteuers", in: Georg Simmel, *Gesamtausgabe,* 12, Suhrkamp, Frankfurt a.M. 2001.

the wake of the Franco-Prussian war.[57] An old man tells his grand-sons of the unhappy event that took place half a century before, when Britain, weakened by the need to protect its colonies, pacify Ireland and defend Canada, and by an unwarranted confidence in its own powers, succumbed within a matter of days to a better prepared enemy that routed its maritime fleet, penetrated the weak line of the army, and eventually reached London. The grandsons to whom all this is being recounted are preparing to emigrate from an England brought to its knees.

Here the war to come is projected into the past and the cause of the defeat is adjudged to be a failure to recognise the signs of what was to come.

> For us in England it came too late. And yet we had plenty of warnings, if we had only made use of them. The danger did not come on us unawares. It burst on us suddenly, 'tis true; but its coming was foreshadowed plainly enough to open our eyes, if we had not been wilfully blind.
>
> (...)
>
> After all the bitterest part of our reflection is, that all this misery and de-cay might have been so easily prevented, and that we brought it about ourselves by our own short-sighted recklessness. There, across the narrow Straits, was the writing on the wall, but we would not choose to read it. The warnings of the few were drowned in the voice of the multitude.[58]

Chesney's book is in reality characterised by a certain extratempo-rality. In 1914, it was republished and updated ("as though it were written yesterday" as it said in the new preface) and became one of many "admonitory essays in preparedness"[59] gravely warning of the

---

57 See for instance I. F. Clarke, "The Battle of Dorking, 1871–1914", *Victorian Studies*, Vol. 8, No. 4 (1965), pp. 309–328.

58 George Tomkyns Chesney, *The Battle of Dorking*, Grant Richards, London 1914, pp. 17 and 94.

59 I. F. Clarke, "Future-War Fiction: The First Main Phase, 1871–1900", p. 392.

short-sightedness of domestic policy and the decline of patriotism, and laying bare what the authors deemed a crisis of governance.

Though these projections of future war were based on thorough research, consultation with the military authorities, and a careful consideration of potential strategies, and, in the case of novels veering in the direction of science fiction (H.G. Wells and others), the invention of new weapons, they failed to break the barrier of the unexpectable. For instance, Le Queux in his *Invasion* (which combines fictive newspaper despatches from the battlefield with equally fictive official documents, posters, etc.) "quotes" the orders issued by the German General Kronhelm to the civilian populations in conquered territory. In fact, these are exact replicas of proclamations made in 1870. Not even forecasts of the damage wreaked are remotely hyperbolic – communiqués from occupied Essex announce the "destruction of one of our best golf courses" (chapter 5), and one searches in vain for any omen of Verdun or Ypres. When war finally broke out for real, the incommensurability of expectations with the unexpectable was shockingly apparent.

In their own way then, novels about an impending war offer a lesson in expectations of the unexpectable. They teach us that for our own sakes we have to learn how to read the signs, the writing on the wall, the auguries and portents, as they arrive. At the same time, however, it is clear that these pointers are unrecognisable through the identification matrix of the current world and hence ignored. The existing horizon of understanding is dis-interpreted. The "later" inscribed like a memento in these stories adumbrates the fundamental attribute of an event, the meaning of which is indecipherable within the context it threatens to infiltrate, is exterior to it, and as such only makes sense afterwards (after the event). The *war-to-come* genre unwittingly anticipates what Sigmund Freud, when speaking of wartime trauma, terms *Nachträglichkeit* or deferred action, which after the Second World War became subject to serious philosophical reflection intent on unearthing the paradoxes of temporality. The starting point of these reflections would often be Husserl's *Lectures on the Phenomenology of the Consciousness of Internal Time*, along with his concept of history as outlined in *The Crisis of European Sciences*.

The paradox resides in the fact that the "later" "then" appears avoidable by virtue of being visible. The sensation novel (drawing in part on the tradition of the detective story running in parallel) is also a lesson in the identification of clues, clues betraying the presence of the outside inside the inside, and is therefore inextricably linked to the espionage novel, since it is the spy, i.e. every foreigner getting through to "us", who is the visible materialisation of the warning signs of impending danger. This interpermeation of both genres is best documented by two classics: Childers' *The Riddle of the Sands* (1903) and *The Thirty Nine Steps* by John Buchan (1915).

In the first novel, Carruthers, a minor official in the Foreign Office, sets off with his friend Arthur Davies on a holiday in a yacht named *Dulcibella* in the Baltic Sea. However, Carruthers senses something fishy. Before he hooked up with Davies, a strange group of Germans had tried to kill his friend by luring him onto a sandbank during a previous trip. The two follow the Germans' tracks (three quarters of the novel, which is taken up with a detailed description of the difficulties of navigating narrow channels between shoals and negotiating the ebbs and flows of tides, might well test the patience of readers who are not as enthusiastic about sailing as Childers) and end up in an area in which the German navy is secretly preparing to invade England from its vulnerable north. They are being aided and abetted by a certain Dollmann, a former officer in the Royal Navy, who has stolen secret defence plans in England, travelled to Germany, and is involved in plotting war against his own country.

Even from this potted summary it is clear that the novel addresses (very effectively) one of the stumbling blocks of spy fiction: Carruthers and Davies are themselves forced into the position of spies. However, unlike the treacherous Dollmann, they are private individuals beholden to no-one, both amateurs, and both sportsmen, driven solely by patriotism. This distinction is crucial and explains the statement made by a character in William Le Queux's *Secrets of the Foreign Office*: "I am an Englishman, despite the fact that I am a spy." The employees of the British Secret Service are not spies, but secret agents, diplomats delegated with particularly delicate tasks and very often amateurs who reluctantly adopt this role for the sake of the common weal. This completely negates the equivalence spy = foreigner/outside(r). In *The Man from Downing Street*, Le Queux conveys this distinction faultlessly:

> "There is, I know, something repugnant to the British mind where the secret agent is concerned, but it must be remembered that England's enemies nowadays keep up a whole army of unscrupulous spies. She is compelled, therefore, both in her own interests and in those of European peace, to supplement her attachés at the various Embassies by a corps of secret agents."[60]

The second novel, *The Thirty-Nine Steps* by John Buchan from 1915, is quite explicit in this and other respects. The hero is Richard Hannay, who is returning from Rhodesia to England. One night he is buttonholed by a stranger, the American Franklin Scudder, who grimly sets out the situation in Europe and the balance of forces in the world in a way guaranteed to cause alarm. He makes special reference to plots against the Greek prime minister Karolides, who is the "only barrier between Europe and Armageddon" and is therefore to be assassinated (an event which duly takes place). Scudder is found murdered, but manages to leave behind a message in code. Richard Hannay, now being pursued by both the police and the conspirators, unravels the mystery, deciphers the code, and

---

[60] William Le Queux, *Secrets of the Foreign office*, ch. 1.

uncovers a vast network of German spies called *Der Schwarze Stein*, The Black Stone, fifth columnists preparing for a German invasion.

These examples too, in their own way, bear clear testimony to the crisis, to the cracks in the matrix allowing the meaning of events to be discerned, because they are unable to grasp and understand the signs of that which is arriving to such an extent that it seems that the present has lost its connection with the past. Something has happened. But what? In spy fiction these clues are largely material and visible, and it is therefore no surprise that back then this literature provoked an almost hysterical fear of a vague threat posed by revolutionaries, anarchists, Fenians, or German waiters and cooks in English hotels who might be soldiers in disguise. The world is a minefield: "A single stroke of the pen, a hasty or ill-advised action, and a war might result which would cost our Empire millions in money and millions of valuable lives."[61]

---

61 William Le Queux, *Of Royal Blood*, 1900. Cf. David A.T. Stafford, "Spies and Gentlemen: The Birth of the British Spy Novel. 1893–1914." *Victorian Studies*, Vol. 24, No. 4 (1981), pp. 489–509.

7

Luc Boltanski is a contemporary French sociologist who has examined detective novels and political thrillers. His *Enigmes et complots*,[62] published almost one century after Kracauer's *Der Detektiv-Roman*, has a similar starting point. Boltanski too is interested in the mysteriousness of mystery and introduces an important distinction between the world and reality that serves as a framework for an examination of that which we call a fact. This then permits us to define precisely the enigmatic character of "mystery". According to Boltanski (and according to detective stories), every event that conspicuously stands out against the background of the commonplace or leaves a kind of scratch on the otherwise seamless fabric of reality, no matter how negligible (e.g. sugar in a salt cellar, or the label "apples" on a basket containing nuts[63]), is mysterious. In brief, the mystery is an anomalous singularity in sharp contrast with how a thing is normally presented or how it behaves. If reality is that which is socially constructed and stabilised (by means of all kinds of institutions and various modes of schematisation), i.e. that to which we refer back as soon as we understand what the things we encounter every day are and what they are for, then according to Boltanski everything that happens unpredictably should be deemed the "world". The event is nothing more than the "emergence of the world in the middle of reality"[64] – an enigma within the regime of the exception. Reality is always "official" reality and the "world" makes itself known across reality. Faith in reality presupposes an implicit conviction that it is identical with the world.[65] However, the intervention of a detective is elicited by events whose occurrence

---

62 Luc Boltanski, *Enigmes et complots. Une enquête à propos d'enquêtes*, Gallimard, Paris 2012.
63 The example given by Boltanski is one of Chesterton's Father Brown stories.
64 Ibid, p. 22.
65 Ideology is the attempt to dissolve the non-identity of world and reality. Cf. Boltanski, *Enigmes*, p. 86.

disrupts the fixed tissue of reality, which up till now has appeared unblemished.[66] The detective's investigation seeks the origin of this flaw and culminates (directly or indirectly) in the discovery that something is concealed beneath reality, namely the immensurability of the world. Or to put it another way: the adventurous temporality of the world arises like a mysterious event from linear time.

The detective novel (and this applies to all types of sensational-ist literature) is the manifestation of a situation in which the en-deavours made by official (state) institutions to assign recognisable contours to reality and thus to stabilise it have come to naught. The official interpretation of reality as enforced by the police apparat or (in spy novels) the secret services is put to the test that mystery rep-resents. The investigation resolves a particular problem, but with-out eliminating the implicit enigmaticity of reality itself, since the policeman "has a tendency to see evil only where the conduct of the accused transgresses an explicitly legal rule. This is why he so often makes errors in judgement that are apt to turn into legal errors. The detective, for his part, *sees evil everywhere.*"[67]

Boltanski's book, which "conducts an investigation into investiga-tions", aims to show how the work of a sociologist and her position vis-à-vis the social is close to the investigation of a detective. The same rationale lies behind the choice of basic terminology: reality (the stabilised order) versus the world (the dimension of events). "Everything that happens emanates from the world, but in a spo-radic and ontologically uncontrollable fashion, while reality, which is based on a selection and an organisation of certain possibilities offered by the world at a given moment in time, can constitute an arrangement apt to be grasped synthetically by sociologists, histo-rians and local actors."[68] However, if we come to Boltanski from Husserl's phenomenology and do not wish to forfeit the connections

---

66 See Ibid, p. 158.
67 Ibid, p. 84.
68 Ibid, p. 18.

and contiguities, we must transform what are primarily sociological categories into philosophical concepts. This means inverting their positions, since (this is something we shall shortly deal with in more detail) for Husserl the world is "the horizon of all horizons",[69] i.e. the horizon is that which serves as a basic reference point allowing for the identification of the meaning of everything we might possibly encounter. It is a (passively self-constituting) product of the sedimentation and habituation of experience. In its own way (and as Boltanski would have it) it is a *stabilising* element.[70] However, apart from the substitution of one word for another, everything that Boltanski says applies unchanged and perfectly describes what I have in mind when I speak of the matrix of intelligibility or the horizon of understanding into which *reality* irrupts (as I have used the word up till now) in the form of an event.

At the same time (though again not explicitly), the sensation novel, which recounts the emergence of the outside (of reality) within the inside (the world), also thematises their non-identity inasmuch as it records a deferral and the consequent incommensurability of the horizon of expectations (and understanding) in respect of what is arriving. To put it another way: not only the protagonists of a detective novel, but the various heroes of sensationalist plots (agents, private detectives, investigators and inventors), are in a unique position vis-à-vis the world that is symmetrical to the position of criminals: both parties are aware that the tissue of the world is not inviolable. Hence the tradition of the criminal mind of the detective initiated by Sherlock Holmes and followed immediately (with a certain swaggering nonchalance) by J. G. Reeder, the creation of Edgar Wallace:

---

69 Cf. for example *Die Krisis,* p. 282 (Husserliana VI). In Husserl's terminology every "something" is always "from the world".

70 Similarly, in Lacan's differentiation between the imaginary, symbolic and real something unidentifiable would suddenly emerge more on the side of the "real", while the world would be more on the side of the symbolic.

"A brilliant criminal — it is a terrible thing to confess, but I have a reluctant admiration for him. You see, as I have so often explained to you, I am cursed with a criminal mind. But he was mad."[71]

Mr Reeder shook his head. "A romantic surmise." He sighed heavily. "You have to realize, my dear Gaylor, that I have a criminal mind. I see the worst in people and the worst in every human action. It is very tragic."[72]

Taking this eccentric position as our starting point we may also note the rigidity characteristic of schematisations of current horizons of expectation when confronting an event that is irreducible to the present state of the world, in the form either of unreadiness (for the war to come) or an inability to keep step with the unforeseen interventions of events. When in Wells's *The World Set Free* a legal battle breaks out over the patent to the atomic bomb, the inventor, impassively observing what takes place in court, looks with amusement at the archaically robed judge with his mad wig, and while taking in this absurd theatre in the gloomy building, observes to himself:

The law is the most dangerous thing in this country. It is hundreds of years old. It hasn't an idea. The oldest of old bottles and this new wine, the most explosive wine. Something will overtake them. (...) While almost all the material and methods of life had been changing rapidly and were now changing still more rapidly, the law-courts and the legislatures of the world were struggling desperately to meet modern demands with devices and procedures, conceptions of rights and property and authority and obligation that dated from the rude compromises of relatively barbaric times.[73]

Leaving aside certain differences, the robes of this panoptical judge are not that different from the uniforms donned by Joachim von Pasenow in Broch's *The Sleepwalkers*, a novel written at approxi-

---

71 Edgar Wallace, "The Treasure Hunt"
72 Edgar Wallace, "Red Aces".
73 Herbert George Wells, *The World Set Free*, ch. I/3.

mately the same time as Husserl's *The Crisis of European Sciences.* The job of the uniform is to

> manifest and obtain order in the world, to arrest the confusion and flux of life, just as it conceals whatever in the human body is soft and flowing, covering up the soldier's underclothes and skin, and decreeing that sentries on guard should wear white gloves. So when in the morning a man has fastened up his uniform to the last button, he acquires a second and thicker hide and feels that he has returned to his more essential and steadfast being. Closed up in his hard casing, braced in with straps and belts, he begins to forget his own undergarments, and the uncertainty of life, yes, life itself, recedes to a distance.[74]

Literature deemed trivial, no matter how closely bound by conventions, is in a certain sense free because it is situated in the interstices between worlds: between the world passing by and the world that is yet to arrive. At this point conventions become spectres, since the past, sedimented convention becomes entangled with that which is arriving and so is suspended. Convention still binds, but becomes a game. The sensation novel does not wish to decipher a mysterious code, but transforms it into the protagonists of its stories. Literature deemed highbrow, on the other hand, attempts to construct a horizon of understanding in this interspace intrinsic to that event that is only beginning to announce its arrival using the method of abduction. This interstice and this interspace is *crisis.*

---

74 Hermann Broch, *The Sleepwalkers*, trans. Willa and Edwin Muir, New York 1947, pp. 20–21.

8

By taking the non-serious seriously, by introducing into the high the low that is excluded from it by deep-seated cultural antithesis, we arrive at a way of demonstrating the outside inside the inside (the outside-in). In this respect Fantômas is the perfect example: one only has to reference French surrealism and the circle of authors associated with it. The Fantômas series became part of the iconology of high modernist art by virtue of its implicit anarchy and a treatment of time and space verging on the deranged. Moments of fantasy are released from the Victorian corset of the classic detective novel (and Fantômas stands completely outside the domain of deductive rationality and identification), and as for finding some kind of moral instruction... au contraire. The surrealists were fascinated by the wild, phantasmagorical poetics of this literature, and as Roger Caillois says, the energy concealed in the anarchy of these novels is so strong that it is capable not only of confronting but undermining the power of the system.

So far, so indisputable. However, if necessary these findings can be bolstered by various cross-sectional comparisons. The traditional detective story has a clear structure: the mystery emerges against the backdrop of a clearly organised world that the crime has destabilised. According to Luc Boltanski, the detective and spy novels represent an innovation in the sphere of 20th century literary fiction. The crime is a kind of anomalous singularity in stark contrast with the way that things normally present themselves: it is the "emergence of reality in the middle of the world". The crime (the enigma) sows confusion in the world in its capacity as that which does not belong to the horizon of expectable events and therefore causes something we might term a *crisis of the world*. The traditional whodunit (Poe, Doyle, Agatha Christie et al.) chronicles the derailment of the system and its return (a return realised by purely rational means). It depicts the *restoration of order*, the restitution of the world conceived as *de iure* stable order. Inasmuch as the crime operates as a kind of temporary aberration there is an analogy with Husserl: with the resolution of the crisis things return to normal. However, the restoration of order obliges Husserl to introduce another factor, namely *responsibility*. As in the thriller, in the traditional detective novel the restoration of order would not be possible without a *private* investigator (no matter what his motivation is), who then in the American hardboiled school of detective novels shoulders this "responsibility" explicitly. Philip Marlowe does not relate to the world but *corresponds to the reality* that has emerged in the middle of the world. This emergence of reality is dealt with in even more detail in the "Flitcraft parable", unobtrusively inserted into *The Maltese Falcon* by Dashiell Hammett (published in 1930) and recounted by Sam Spade.

9

During the 1930s, Husserl explored the phenomenon of crisis in detail in what is commonly termed his late work. In 1936, he published in the Belgrade journal *Philosophia* the first of a planned series of essays that were to examine the intellectual crisis of that time, especially the crisis afflicting the sciences. The aim was to advance his transcendental phenomenology as the only means of overcoming this crisis. This essay is all that was published of his last work; the text published in the collected works includes Husserl's continuation, unfortunately incomplete.[75] His late period also includes *Formale und transzendentale Logik* of 1929 and *Erfahrung und Urteil*, published after Husserl's death by Ludwig Landgrebe in 1939 in the Academia Verlagsbuchhandlung publishing house in Prague. However, the firm was closed down that year following the German occupation and dissolution of Czechoslovakia, and though the book had already been printed it did not enter the distribution network. The entire print run was pulped, apart from 200 copies that the publishing house had managed to send to their London partners. In 1948, a photomechanical reprint of the first edition was published using one of these copies. At this point in the proceedings Prague enters the scene, since the *Cercle philosophique de Prague*, whose members had attempted to rescue Husserl's manuscripts from his estate prior to the German occupation, were keen that the book be published. However, when it became clear that Prague was unsafe, Pater van Breda created the Husserl Archives in Leuven.

The starting point of both the Vienna lecture and the book is the concept of crisis. Inasmuch as it appears that the Western world is

---

75 Edmund Husserl, *Die Krisis der europäischen Wissenschaften und die transzendentale Phän-omenologie*, ed. Walter Biemel, (Husserliana VI), Martinus Nijhoff, Haag 1976. Edmund Husserl, *Die Krisis der europäischen Wissenschaften und die transzendentale Phänomenologie. Ergänzungs-band.Texte aus dem Nachlass 1934–1837*, ed. Reinhold N. Smid (Husserliana XXIX), Kluwer Academic Publishers, Dodrecht 1993.

caught up in crisis, then according to Husserl this is because it has betrayed the very idea that defines it, i.e. the idea of philosophy, the idea of universal knowledge (including the special sciences), and the idea ensuing therefrom of an existence striving toward the ideal and norms of autonomous reason. European man has lost his relationship with this idea mainly due to the influence of a positivist conception of science and the concomitant process of specialisation (fragmentation) and technologisation (mechanical application). Science has eliminated questions relating to values and meaning (both of science itself and of human existence) from its sphere of interest and has capitulated to "naturalisation" (i.e. the investigation of man as object and the dominant status of the "fact"). However, in so doing the sciences have become incomprehensible (if not in respect of their content, then most decidedly in respect of their cultural or "existential" function). Science is the product of a certain intellectual, spiritual activity, and yet spirit has gradually been excluded from science as a legitimate field of enquiry. As a consequence, science has lost its relevance to man because it has nothing to say about what matters to him most. And yet if Western man loses his faith in reason, he loses his faith in himself. The solution to this crisis could only reside in a return to the original ideal, i.e. the primal establishment of scientificity (rationality as the cultural value of the West par excellence). This is the task of this new "introduction to phenomenology" and at the same time an explanation of why phenomenology must engage with history. (For that matter the concept of "crisis" implies "history".) Phenomenology now attempts to unravel the complex history of the very idea of philosophy, this idea being something like the *verborgene Einheit intentionaler Innerlichkeit* (concealed unity of intentional interiority), which makes it possible to speak of Europe as of a certain "formation". For if words such as "Europe", "science" and "philosophy", notwithstanding all empirical transformations (scientific discoveries, different philosophical theories, historically empirical events, etc.), delineate something identifiable as a unity (an object), this is thanks to this primal establishment, from which everything is endowed with a certain (completely specific) meaning and which is both constitutive of and constituted by Europe.

As we have seen, Husserl believes that Europe is a spiritual shape, something that originated, and so he turns his attention to history as a philosophical problem. Origin is the same as establishment: Europe is a project identical to the establishment of philosophy in ancient Greece, and this philosophy is established with the creation of the ideal of universal knowledge, i.e. a knowledge aimed at an idea that transcends man and that therefore man can only set for himself as ideal, as *telos*, a mission by which he will henceforth gauge his knowledge (and, of course, his entire life). *Telos* – ultimate object, i.e. *entelecheia* – the endless pursuit of an objective set at the outset. An orientation on this *internal* teleology is at the same time a norm in the sense of constant self-normalisation. A focus on the idea or ideal implies responsibility: by his every action man takes upon himself responsibility for abiding by this norm. A completely specific type of rationality or reason operates and appears within history, "the epoch of mankind that now seeks to live, and only can live, in the free shaping of its existence, its historical life, through ideas of reason, through infinite tasks."[76] This rationality characterises Europe as a certain whole, forever unified by its internal, immanent teleology. And so, for instance, Husserl can write:

> In the spiritual sense the English Dominions, the United States, etc., clearly belong to Europe, whereas the Eskimos or Indians presented as curiosities at fairs, or the Gypsies, who constantly wander about Europe, do not.[77]

The latter represent Europe's *exterior*.

76 Husserl, *The Crisis*, p. 274.
77 Ibid, p. 273.

Husserl explains this concept of a specific European rationality in detail in *The Crisis of European Sciences*, and it is enlarged upon both by the original lectures and the annexes to the treatise (manuscripts from his estate), especially *The Origin of Geometry*[78]. These additional texts contain, for instance, references to the "critical attitude" associated with this teleology, with Western rationality. The theoretical attitude (a synonym for European reason) is characterised by the universality

> of his (the "philosophical man's") critical stance, his resolve not to accept unquestioning any pregiven opinion or tradition, so that he can inquire (…) after what is true in itself, an ideality (…) The ideal truth becomes an absolute value.[79]

However, Husserl does not only diagnose the crisis, but devotes his essay to a detailed description of a cure. And given that the text also serves as an introduction to phenomenology, it is clear that it is in fact phenomenology that represents the sought-after therapy. This is a phenomenology enriched by what the phenomenon of the crisis has brought to it, namely the dimension of history, a phenomenological interpretation of historicity. However, in many respects this is very specific and it is therefore not surprising that a thinker who from the outset was concerned with the method of describing essences and essential structures should finally turn his attention to history. For such a thinker, history is like the essence of Europe itself. It is a specifically European phenomenon in the same way as science qua philosophy and philosophy qua science. Both one and the other are established at the outset, from which point onward they have *meaning*, and this meaning not only evolves but emerges from history. For history (not necessarily in the traditional sense of the word) is *teleological*. If meaning is put in jeopardy by cri-

78 *The Crisis*, pp. 353–378 and Supplementary Texts, Appendix VI.
79 Husserl, *The Crisis*, pp. 286–287.

sis because science has abandoned it, then this meaning must be rediscovered. The quest for the primal meaning is what Husserl terms *Rückfrage*: "regressive enquiry" or "backwards reflection" as a recollection of the original ideal, which (as this recollection reveals) is also a "task", which means that this origin or original establishment of science (identical with Western rationality) somehow contains within it the dimension of directionality. There is a close connection here between the ideal of "knowledge from the original insight" (the imperative of "evidence"), rationality (science, philosophy), and Europe. Husserl's book is an attempt to *reanimate* this origin and this connection. Fascinating though this connection is, I will leave to one side the relationship between Husserl's "regressive enquiry" and Heidegger's "destruction of the history of ontology", the purpose of which is to release Being from its forgetfulness.

To conceive of *Rückfrage* as the simple retracing of its own tracks would be to simplify matters. The purpose of "regressive enquiry", i.e. the "return to origin", is to reveal the innermost *cause* of the crisis (which cause, as becomes clear, is the "forgetting" of the origin). It is therefore within tradition (*tradere*: to deliver, betray – tradition passes down and hands over the origin, the primal establishment) that the origin of "crisis" must also be revealed; tradition must evince some kind of discontinuity. In simple terms: this regressive procedure should be hampered somewhere along the way. This of course is not completely accurate. Husserl does not allow for anything like this. However, using this observation I would like for the moment simply to hint at a certain internal difficulty associated with the project of "the way back". If I wanted to explore the problem in greater depth by means of a comparison, then for Bergson, for instance, every way back would of necessity be a way forward, and in this respect Bergson is at odds with Husserl, despite the fact that both proceed on the basis of an "internal sense of time".

Husserl is convinced that it is necessary somehow to correct tradition, which is clearly somehow unreliable in and of itself. It is for this reason that a pure relationship to the origin as established by this very origin is a relationship of *responsibility* to the original establishment. It is a task. Tradition guarantees nothing; it is only tradition if man accepts responsibility for "traditionalising". However, in general terms this means that *traditionalising* is inherently a risky relationship to that which is to be traditionalised.

A discomfiting question arises: is this "instability", this "discontinuity" of tradition, i.e. the disconnectedness that threatens it (this is what Husserl diagnoses as the "forgetting" that, as it were, periodically jeopardises tradition) – is this something contingent or necessary? If it is necessary, then it threatens the very possibility of regressive enquiry, and in a certain sense the traditional concept of tradition would thus be annulled. If it is contingent, then it would threaten the "transcendental" dimension of the whole of Husserl's meditation on crisis, because "forgetting" would not have a philosophical but simply a historical resolution. Forgetting and remembering: is this a symmetrical or asymmetrical relationship?

This is basically the first circle of problems that need to be looked at.

However, there is a second circle too.

In principle it is clear that this *Rückfrage* has been necessitated by the present era, i.e. the "crisis" itself, the present era as "critical" – the era finds itself in crisis. However, this means that the place from which to pose the question of origin is not contingent. For instance: previously it was impossible to sense, observe and diagnose this deviation on the part of tradition from tradition itself. It is only at the *peak* of a crisis that a crisis is apparent as such, and therefore necessitates critical reflection or *Besinnung*.

However, if the present is (historically) privileged in this way, if it is a questioning of the "situated", and if its situatedness is the essential perspective of our view of the past, does this mean that we can genuinely look back to the "origin" as it was? Is not every presence the relationship between forgetting and remembering? And if we cannot look back in this fashion on the "origin", then how does it appear now? And this would entail a large difference; this would mean that the recommencement born of remembrance is less a return or a new acceptance than it is a *new establishment*, and not merely the repetition of what has already been established at some point, a continuation of the way the whole of this constellation (European rationalism, Europe) was established. The new acceptance of tradition would then be something like a new, equally primal establishment, and would by no means have to be at odds with this tradition's concept of *telos*, with its teleologicality. We could, for instance, be inspired by Wittgenstein's conception of the rule, which *only emerges through its use*, and is "re-established" anew at every step. This would be a strange situation: it would be possible to speak of a base, and yet there would at the same time be a moment of a certain fundamental *baselessness* or *Grundlosigkeit*.

I will try to demonstrate that Husserl must always stand on one side in respect of these various alternatives, and yet is immediately obliged to take the other side into consideration; that he operates within a strange force field that is determined simultaneously by both sides. The side on which he stands has a boundary and Husserl ends by operating on this boundary as though to extend beyond it and into the other side.

These first two points give rise to several themes and a generalising problem.

Firstly, there is historicity and the concept of the "origin" or the "original (primal) establishment", i.e. the relationship between the empirical and the ideal, between that which is *de facto* and that which should be *de jure*. However, if it is impossible to separate and distinguish between the two – if the empirical is within the ideal, the historical within the ahistorical or essential – then we are faced with an exemplary case of crisis, i.e. of the outside-in.

It is for this reason that one of the "appendices" to the *Crisis*, "The Origin of Geometry", is so important (and the subject of so many interpretations). This is a text that *on the one hand* concretises the primary establishment, not as a single act but rather as a certain process that necessarily includes several successive stages, and *on the other* demonstrates the "internal teleology" that, just as internal teleology allows us to speak of Europe, allows us to speak of one geometry, a single geometry, which

> continued to be valid with this very same meaning (...) continued and at the same time was developed further, remaining simply "geometry" in all its new forms.[80]

At the same time, this text clearly suggests that we are not operating here on the level of historical investigation but on the "transcendental" level, i.e. on the level of the conditions of possibility: we do not enquire how geometry genuinely arose, but we enquire

> into the submerged original beginnings of geometry as they necessarily must have been in their "primally establishing" function (...) we inquire into that sense in which it appeared in history for the first time – in which it had to appear, even though we know nothing of the first creators and are not even asking after them.[81]

It *had* to be thus in order that we have the geometry that we know. Our geometry involves a certain (historically manifest) *apriorism*.

And this *must necessarily* have been linked to itself: the discovery of geometry in the mind of the first geometrist, the intersubjective fixation of this discovery by means of communication, and later on its exchange through speech and writing, which is the *necessary* source of each *ideal objectivity* shared by a certain community. Said

---

80 *The Crisis*, p. 353.
81 Ibid., p. 354.

community is constituted by this sharing and thus lives permanently on the horizon of what is thus shared (the idea of geometry, the idea of Europe), and because it is the horizon, i.e. potentiality, openness, the origin within this horizon is further (historically) developed without losing its timeless existence. It is therefore the establishment of a certain *teleology*, or to express it in basic phenomenological terms: it is *the fulfilment of a certain primary intention.*

But why, for instance, must we also speak of "responsibility" and a "task"?

This question is answered by the phenomenological principle of all principles, which Husserl again cites in *The Origin of Geometry*:

> evidence means nothing more than grasping an entity with the consciousness of its original being-itself-there.[82]

Applied to the origin of geometry this means that every act of the geometrist must be subject to this principle: though she works with traditionalised ideally objective objectivities (the word *Gegenständlichkeit* is used very broadly by Husserl), if she is to operate on a horizon established by the original observation, she must always revive this objectivity anew, i.e. have it in front of her as evidence. This is a task and in this sense the geometrist is also *responsible* for the traditionalising and continued development of the origin. She is summoned to a re-awakening, which is the only guarantee that the continued development of the primarily established coincides (and in this sense is somehow identifiable) with the initial intention, that it is the fulfilment of the initial intention. Husserl formulates this completely generally (because it refers to any linguistic expression of ideal objectivities), and though his formulation is somewhat complicated, overall it is fairly clear:

---

82   Ibid., p. 356.

In the contact of reciprocal linguistic understanding, the original production and the product of one subject can be *actively* understood by the others. In this full understanding of what is produced by the other, as in the case of recollection, a present coaccomplishment on one's own part of the presentified activity necessarily takes place; but at the same time there is also the self-evident consciousness of the identity of the mental structure in the productions of both the receiver of the communication and the communicator; and this occurs reciprocally.[83]

For the sake of later considerations I would briefly refer to the requirement of "coverage", i.e. identification, the primacy of *identity* (which does not conflict with creativity precisely because it is played out within a specific horizon established once and for all). However, it is in this "condition of the possibility" of the traditionalisation (submission, sharing, communication) of ideal objectivities that there is also the *possibility of crisis*, loss, petrification.

It is easy to see that even in (ordinary) human life, and first of all in every individual life from childhood up to maturity, the originally intuitive life which creates its originally self-evident structures through activities on the basis of sense-experience very quickly and in increasing measure falls victim to the *seduction of language*. Greater and greater segments of this life lapse into a kind of talking and reading that is dominated purely by association; and often enough, in respect to the validities arrived at in this way, it is disappointed by subsequent experience.[84]

This bare acceptance without verification by means of a return to evidence is something that deforms even such a strict science like geometry, inasmuch as each science proceeds *deductively* (from the undeniable to that ensuing directly therefrom):

83   Ibid., p. 360.
84   Ibid., p. 362.

The process of deduction follows formal-logical self-evidence; but without the actually developed capacity for reactivating the original activities contained within its fundamental concepts, i.e., without the "what" and the "how" of its prescientific materials, geometry would be a tradition empty of meaning; and if we ourselves did not have this capacity, we could never even know whether geometry had or ever did have a genuine meaning, one that could really be "cashed in".
This is our situation, and that of the whole modern age.[85]

Among other things it is clear here that what Husserl says about geometry applies both to science (i.e. rationality), and, given the way that Western culture is bound up with science, to Europe and its tradition. Europe is in *crisis* because it forgot the meaning traditionalised by this tradition.

In his *Against Epistemology: A Metacritique*,[86] Adorno characterises phenomenology as the attempt at a pure realisation of the principle of identity by means of a continuous reduction to subjective immanence (all acts constituting ideality, objectivity, are acts of consciousness, i.e. of subjectivity), and says that in Husserl knowledge takes the form of the absolute form of identitarian/identifying thinking. In light of the above this is indisputable. However, both Adorno and later Derrida especially elaborate on this theme in a way that is fundamental with regard to our own theme, saying that Husserl's texts are an example of how thinking, by virtue of its intentions, transcends itself under the pressure of its own contradictions, and so surpasses its own boundaries by applying its own strategies. In his essay "Genesis and Structure" Derrida says the same thing, albeit from the opposite end:

---

85 Ibid., p. 366.
86 Theodor W. Adorno, *Zur Metakritik der Erkenntnistheorie*. In: T.W. Adorno, *Gesammelte Schriften* 5, pp. 31, 34 and 37.

Husserl has always indicated his aversion for debate, dilemma and aporia, that is for reflection in the alternative mode whereby the philosopher, at the end of his deliberations, seeks to reach a conclusion, that is to close the question, to enclose his expectations or his concern in an option, a decision, a solution (...) by his rejection of system and speculative closure and by virtue of the style of his thought, Husserl is attuned to the historicity of meaning and to the possibility of its becoming, (...) and is also respectful of that which remains open within structure.[87]

I mention all of this now because I am trying gradually to reveal the "structure" of the phenomenon of crisis. As well as the most general relationship of outside-in, now would be a suitable moment to articulate the ambiguity already referred to several times, which is this: exceeding a thing's own boundaries from within. This is something that also characterises the strange "temporality" of the crisis in the present: past frameworks of comprehension (this was Husserl's original phenomenological project) cannot be applied, and yet those frameworks of comprehension that would allow for the decipherment of suddenly unreadable meaning are only just arriving. However, it is in their direction that Husserl's later philosophy appears to point under the pressure of internal contradictions and "mysteries".

What contradictions and mysteries? We come across some of them in *The Origin of Geometry*: genesis versus observation, or the proceduralism of the constitution of ideality that is somehow established "in time" notwithstanding that fact that, in its capacity as "essence", ideality is timeless. Secondly: forgetting as a possibility linked with traditionalisation. However, if traditionalisation is tied to the medium of speech, it is something like a "necessary" possibility, and this is why forgetting can only be confronted by "responsibility", a responsibility that we can but do not have to subscribe to. This

87 Jacques Derrida, *Writing and Difference*, trans. Alan Bass, Routledge, London and New York, pp. 154–155.

means that such subscription is contingent, a completely empirical act, in which case it is difficult to understand traditionalisation otherwise than purely empirical history – the concept of teleological history comes under significant threat.

10

The most detailed analysis of this movement within Husserl's phenomenology was conducted by Jacques Derrida in his introduction to "The Origin of Geometry".[88] A return to acts establishing subjectivity presupposes a *phenomenological history*. Husserl will never investigate empirical history. He is interested in ideal history, i.e. the movement from the establishment of meaning via its ongoing development in recurrent reactivation until the moment of crisis, when evidence was lost from science. He is interested, then, in "intentional history" as a tradition that nevertheless reproduces the very structure of intentionality, the basis of which is the temporality of consciousness (intention gravitating towards its fulfilment). A present that, in the movement of protention, holds onto and surpasses itself as past present, makes possible a retention of the past in the mode of sedimentation, and therefore allows for a "return" to the past, since the past remains held by the order of retention: it is a "deposit". However, this deposition is possible only through the abandonment of the immanence of consciousness, the *externalisation* of the deposited in language, which is simply this deposit established as an intersubjectively shared objectivism. It thus becomes a "document" separated from purely intentional history (which makes possible various "lapses"), a poor reading of the deposited, an associative interpretation instead of evidence, etc. This is the first point.

The second point is that ideal objectivity is always constituted within the lifeworld, within natural experience, for instance in the case of geometry through the gradual idealisation of natural, and not ideal, forms wholly similar to each other, i.e. through the process of "infinitisation", through advancement to a limit. This is science, rationality: *the transcending of all sensory or factual limits.*

88 Jacques Derrida, "Introduction", in: E. Husserl, *L'Origine de la géométrie.* P. U. F., Paris 1962). Jacques Derrida, *Edmund Husserl's Origin of Geometry: An Introduction,* trans. John P. Leavey Jr., Nebraska UP, Lincoln and London 1989.

Thus the institution of geometry could only be a *philosophical* act (...) The philosopher is a man who inaugurates the theoretical attitude: the latter is only the spirit's radical freedom, which authorises a move beyond finitude and opens the horizon of knowledge as that of a prehaving, i.e. of an infinite project or task (*Vorhaben*).[89]

In "The Origin of Geometry" Husserl wants to grasp at its source the origin of apriority itself, i.e. that which establishes infinitisation.

But if each infinitisation is a new birth of geometry in its authentic primordial intention (which we notice still remained hidden to a certain extent by the closure of the previous system), we may wonder if it is still legitimate to speak of *an* origin of geometry. Does not geometry have an infinite number of births (or birth certificates) in which, each time, another birth is announced, while still being concealed? Must we not say that geometry is on the way toward its origin, instead of proceeding from it?[90]

In his essay on the origin of geometry, Derrida, already prepared for a reading of phenomenological texts by his doctoral thesis entitled *The Problem of Genesis in Husserl's Phenomenology*,[91] written in the first half of the 1950s, tracks step by step how the highly paradoxical idea of non-linear teleology is outlined. "A primordial consciousness of delay can only have the pure form of anticipation",[92] we read in conclusion. In other words, the objective that history has (teleologically) in its sights, as described by Husserl and established by its commencement, only ever becomes clear later (*nachträglich*), always in aspects determined by situation. The objective is *inside* history (teleology), though not in the sense of some *arché* (*principium*)

89 Ibid., p. 125.
90 Ibid., p. 129.
91 Jacques Derrida, *Le problème de la genèse dans la philosophie de Husserl*. P.U.F., Paris 1990. Jacques Derrida, *The Problem of Genesis in Husserl's Philosophy*, trans. Marian Hobson, The University of Chicago Press, Chicago and London 2003.
92 Derrida, *Origin of Geometry. An Introduction*, p. 153.

that right from the start controls the movement flowing from it. It is for this reason that the continuity of this movement (tradition) is clear only in retrospect. *Rückfrage* or the retrospective questioning of the beginning is therefore productive. *Rückfrage* is a moment of this teleology, it reconstitutes this beginning, it repeats anew the establishment and discovers or revives meaning anew. However, "anew" means both "again" and "for the first time".

This summary, however, does not do justice to all the implications and consequences contained in the *Crisis*. Especially unclear is the analogy between the establishment of European science, i.e. specifically European rationality, the personification of which is the task of philosophy, and the establishment of geometry as a concrete science with which Husserl works as with an example intended to illuminate his teleological conception of the history of meaning. Above all, this summary does not make clear how Husserl works with his concepts, by means of which his conception of crisis takes shape.

If, when interpreting these concepts, we proceed "chronologically", we quickly discover in *The Crisis of European Sciences* that there is a curvature of the time of factual history: we find ourselves in "phenomenological" history. The starting point must be the *Urstiftung* or primal establishment. In the case of science (rationality, philosophy, Europe) this is the discovery of the idea of knowledge as a resolution by which man, adopting a theoretical approach to the world, transcends the finitude of his existing awareness. The closed horizons of understanding in which practical actions take place are thus traversed by an infinitely open horizon, by the horizon of the ultimate purposeful idea of knowledge from evident observation.

(W)hat is most essential to the theoretical attitude of philosophical man is the peculiar universality of his critical stance, his resolve not to accept unquestioningly any pregiven opinion or tradition so that he can enquire, in respect of the whole traditionally pregiven universe, after what is true in itself, an ideality (...) Thus ideal truth becomes an absolute value.[93]

This overcoming of the finitude of knowledge is described in detail in *The Origin of Geometry* as it reconstructs the path to ideal objectivities as timeless and intersubjectively communicable, extricated from the situational conditionality of cognition. This new, completely unique horizon of human life is the horizon of infinite orientation upon the objective that man opts for, and because it is targeted upon infinity its fulfilment cannot be viewed as anything but a task. Science is primarily a project that becomes a new purpose to life, and this affords it a specific (European, rational) *meaning*.

It is this meaning that is in the state of crisis that Husserl diagnoses when he discovers a significant deviation from this project, the cause of which is forgetting, specifically forgetting the meaning within which the project was originally founded. However, if such a deviation is *de facto* possible, this would mean that teleology is not some application of the norm, but the acceptance and continued renewed acceptance of responsibility for said norm. Perhaps this is a very fine distinction. However, it is of crucial significance and must therefore be somehow concretised.

Husserl often refers disparagingly to the "objectivism" of modern science. And yet a significant aspect of true science is its orientation on ideal objectivities. This is not a contradiction. Objectivism entails forgetting the subsoil of the lifeworld from which it emerged (this is analysed by Husserl in §§ 34–36 of *The Crisis*). Furthermore, the construction of ideal objectivities is not an end in itself. It has a meaning, namely to overcome finiteness by virtue of the infinite alignment of the original resolution (cognition as finite can only take possession of the infinite in the form of a task). The problem therefore resides in the "traditionalisation" of the original

---

93 Husserl, *The Crisis*, p. 286.

plan. Husserl addresses this problem not only in the published text of *The Crisis*, but also in manuscripts dating back to the period after the publication of its first version, e.g. in an essay entitled "Teleology in the History of Philosophy", where we read:

> The only people who have objectives and tasks are those that set themselves tasks. To an extent this is so even when we accept a task on the basis of tradition. It is not simply subsequent comprehension or empathy (*Nachverstehen*). The same applies to every communication. Understanding it does not mean that it is accepted, but that by our own action we co-enact the validity in which the party communicating intends them (*selbsttätig mitvollziehen*). The judgement accepted will become our own, the assumed wishes and will our own.[94]

This is a subtle distinction that in the later work is a clear echo of the early *Logical Investigations* and its phenomenological semiology, the study of the sign and signification – *Bedeutung*.[95] The sign is presented as something binary: on the one hand it is *expression* (*Ausdruck*), on the other *indication* (*Anzeichen*). Expression is determined as the immediate *presence* of the intended significance in a sign and is thus primary, while indication is a derived mode of the sign because it only secondarily refers to the immediately seen. Husserl, as Derrida will formulate it,[96] privileges full, unmediated presence, whose very possibility is the condition for the possibility of phenomenology, since its necessity is already implied by the "principle of all principles" articulated in the first volume of Husserl's *Ideas*:

94 Husserl, *Die Krisis der europäischen Wissenschaften und die transzendentale Phänomenologie. Ergänzungsband. Texte aus dem Nachlass 1934–1937,* p. 373 (trans. here by Phil Jones).
95 Edmund Husserl, *Logical Investigations,* Vol. 1 (International Library of Philosophy), trans. J. N. Findlay, Routledge 2001, pp. 183–233.
96 Once in the "Introduction" to "The Origin of Geometry", and once in *Voice and phenomenon,* Jacques Derrida, *La voix et le phénomène.* P.U.F., Paris 1967.

No conceivable theory can make us err with respect to the *principle of all principles: that every originary presentive intuition is a legitimizing source of cognition, that everything originary* (so to speak, in its "personal" actuality) *offered to us in "intuition" is to be accepted simply as what it is presented as being*, but also *only within the limits in which it is presented there.*[97]

The originary or original cannot be contaminated by anything unoriginal and must be present to the opinion that grasps it. This is the basis of phenomenological "evidence". This is why both here and in the *Crisis* the primacy of "idealities" (ideal objectivities and thus pure meanings), which as idealities are *repeatable* within different contexts on the basis of the identity of their *presence*, were of fundamental significance for Husserl.

However, is the implicit primacy of "presence" sustainable within the context of this differentiation (i.e. the possibility of a clear differentiation between expression and indication)?

Let's sum up what we have so far. Inasmuch as Husserl takes crisis to entail a forgetting of the original meaning, this can mean several things in respect of the distinction between expression and indication, or, as the case may be, subsequent understanding and co-execution: a factual omission during the fulfilment of the founding resolution, the cause of which (completely external) is factual or empirical history randomly diverting the direction of teleological historicity. This situation creates a need for critical thinking (*Besinnung*) about the relationship to tradition, i.e. it makes it necessary to conduct retrospective questioning (*Rückfrage*) of the primary establishment (*Urstiftung*), its ideal meaning, and should therefore take

---

97 Edmund Husserl, *Ideas Pertaining to a Pure Phenomenology and to a Phenomenological Philosophy*, transl. F. Kersten, Martinus Nijhoff, Haag 1982, § 24, p. 44. For Husserl, *Anwesenheit* is: "die volle und vollständige Anschauung, die Unmittelbarkeit des Augenblicks, die Selbstgegenwart in der reinen Innerlichkeit", cf. Rudolf Bernet, "Differenz und Anwesenheit. Derridas und Husserls Phänomenologie der Sprache, der Zeit, der Geschichte, der wissenschaftlichen Rationalität", in: Ernst Wolfgang Orth (ed.), *Studien zur neueren französischen Phänomenologie*, Karl Alber, Freiburg and München 1986, p. 57.

the form of an explicit awareness. It is only necessary to penetrate the sedimented, passively stored and hitherto unconscious layers of historical acceptance of the project and thus rediscover its true meaning – for instance, an infinite movement in the direction of ideal objectivities can always be seen behind objectivities. However, if Husserl is speaking of a revival motivated by crisis, if crisis is exclusively the work of empirical history, and if reactivation is the *answer* to a concrete situation in the light of an idea, i.e. a decision taken on its meaning in the present and from the present, then every such reactivation of meaning is also *productive* insofar as it reveals aspects that could not have been evident at the outset. The *Rückfrage* conducted is *Nachstiftung*, i.e. something like a second foundation or re-establishing. This is a term that appears in *The Crisis of European Sciences*, for instance when Husserl writes:

> This we seek to discern not from the outside, from facts, as if the temporal becoming in which we ourselves have evolved were merely an external causal series. Rather, we seek to discern it from the inside. (…) For it (our history) has spiritual unity through the unity and driving force of the task which stands before us not merely as factually required but as a task assigned to us, the present-day philosophers. For we are what we are as functionaries of modern philosophical humanity; we are heirs and cobearers of the direction of the will which pervades this humanity; we have become this through a primal establishment which is at once a reestablishment (Nachstiftung) and a modification of the Greek primal establishment. In the latter lies the teleological beginning, the true birth of the European spirit as such.[98]

James Dodd explains this point very adeptly while at the same time respecting Derrida's reading:[99] to have a tradition means dealing

98 Husserl, *The Crisis*, pp. 70–71.
99 James Dodd, *Crisis and Reflection. An Essay on Husserl's Crisis of the European Sciences*, Kluwer Academic Publishers. Phaenomenologica 174, 2004, pp. 72 et seq.

with problems that relate to that which tradition means *for us*; the beginning, though already begun, must nevertheless continue to be clarified and stipulated, or the full extent of the assigned task will remain concealed in the apparent manifestness of traditionalised knowledge. The term *Nachstiftung* is therefore saying the same, again and *anew*, because it is saying it in a (historically) different world. The second time is the first time. (When Husserl speaks of *Endstiftung*,[100] it is this movement he has in mind.)

While "The Origin of Geometry" can still operate within a teleological horizon (something that must have happened for geometry to come into being, i.e. those deeds and actions that established it), then the "crisis" that motivates the retrospective questioning of the origin thus focused arrives from within, since the wider context of the entire volume on the crisis of the European sciences indicates, however Husserl wished to avoid this, that at least potentially the outside (indication, *Nachverstehen*) is always already inside, because without an active return to the passively accepted, teleology is impossible. However, this implies an essential moment of *responsibility*: meaning appears only through responsibility because it appears *in a response to crisis*. Teleological movement is the movement of *Nachträglichkeit* ("afterness" or deferred action), which only now, for the first time, reveals the meaning of the original establishment. The crisis is therefore itself already *Urstiftung*.[101] The crisis is the irreducible dimension of phenomenological history. It is therefore *inside*. It does not arrive from outside, though the exterior (empirical history) is essential in order that this fact shows itself. Husserl's texts from the period of the *Crisis* are always characterised by a certain ambiguity, inasmuch as they allow for the conclusion that "the very meaning of science, its function not only as the project of discovering the world but of opening the world to and for a 'genuine' life in truth, is itself perpetually in a state of crisis. From the

100 Husserl, *The Crisis*, p. 72.
101 For more on this point see Dodd, *Crisis and Reflection*, pp. 44 et seq.

latter perspective, the opening of the world to understanding in the form of the true is never simply positive, but is always at the same time the opening of an experience of the questionableness of the world."[102]

102 Dodd, *Crisis and Reflection*, p. 52.

11

It appears, therefore, that the meaning of the word "crisis" is weightier than we might have thought. It does not involve simply a recognition of the productivity of crisis in the Popperian concept of falsification or Kuhn's conception of the structure of scientific revolutions. Not only does Husserl not regard these examples as crises, he explicitly states that the radical transformation of concepts in theoretical disciplines has nothing in common with his concept of crisis. The key to what he diagnoses as crisis is the "crisis of scientificity", i.e. a threat to the very *framework* within which paradigm shifts and the falsification of theories take place.

For this reason, the problem with Husserl's phenomenology as philosophical thinking resides in the question of whether this *framework*, i.e. "scientificity" as a specific type of rationality that characterises Europe as a cultural formation, is as unproblematic as Husserl appears to think it is. This impression is given by the fact that the concept is the precondition of all his other reflections, which are framed by the feeling of the uninhabitability of the world inasmuch as man feels exiled in his own world.[103] This is an issue that needs to be addressed if we are to reflect on the phenomenon of crisis on a more general level, albeit inspired by phenomenology.

At first glance it is clear where doubts might arise in connection with Husserl's conception of crisis and history. It suffices to mention the name of Michel Foucault, an author whose conception of discontinuity makes him in this respect the antithesis of Husserl. However, the concept of such a framework (idea, telos, founding ground) is difficult to sustain even from within and is problematic in Husserl's work itself (the founding ground inasmuch as it presupposes the possibility of reactivation, identifying its repetition with its beginning).

For in opposition to this imperative of a return to the founding or originary ground, on the obverse of considerations justifying

---

103 This is how the feeling of crisis in Husserl is formulated by James Dodd, ibid., p. 39.

this imperative, stands the possibility that a return is impossible, that repetition is somehow productive other than in the interstices or boundaries of the original "intention", that there is no first beginning, and that therefore the very concept of the first "founding ground" is highly problematic. This, as we have seen, is an indication that non-linear teleology implies another "adventurous" temporality of an event, occasionally breaking through the linear, chronological or continual flow of time, the coherence of which is given by the mutual interpenetration of the retention, impression and protention of Husserl's *Lectures on the Consciousness of Internal Time*. And it is this other temporality that is indirectly thematised in Husserl's question as to how the existence of ideal objectivities is even possible. We can only answer this question after conducting the *Rückfrage*, the regressive enquiry. Since ideal objects unquestionably exist (numbers, geometric forms, general meanings, etc.), we have to ask about the *conditions of their possibility* (transcendental phenomenology: what must have come before?). However, here our deliberations up till now are somewhat complicated by the fact that this search for the conditions of possibility comes up against not "structure", but genesis, and we therefore have to perform a *reconstruction of this genesis*. Phenomenology thus turns our attention towards the history of meaning. Every ideality arises in the realm of the natural world, and, as we have said, this is by means of a process of idealisation and "infinitisation", i.e. advancement toward a limit. However, this also means that every ideality is established by the transition from the sensibly perceivable (something round, circular or non-angular) to the non-sensibly perceivable (a circle, ring or spiral). Ideality is established on the "bedrock" of the world accessible to the senses. However, this bedrock cannot be regarded as a "founding ground", because it is surpassed by idealisation. And because this involves advancement toward a limit, at the same time a horizon opens up of *endless continuation*, openness, i.e. something like the idea in the Kantian sense of the word, hence "infinitisation". Here, as we know, we find ourselves at the source of the equivalence of science/rationality and Europe, since aiming for an endless limit is *eo ipso* a task.

However, this is ideal history and not empirical history, because what Husserl is attempting to reveal is the very "eidos" of historicity, the *meaning* of history, i.e. something like the condition of the possibility of empirical history. He is attempting to reveal that which he designates as phenomenological history, which he has no intention of abandoning during his analyses of idealities.

Nevertheless, infinitisation in itself is not the *entire* establishment of ideality, because there is no ideality without its universal communicability, and this assumes the possibility of its preservation by means of the fixation of idealities. The establishment of ideality, meaning, only *culminates* with this essential fixation, which mediates ideality for *tele-communication*. As soon as ideality is established as tele-communicable between contemporaries and in time by means of tradition, it is communicated not by means of pure expression (this is only in the mind of the first founder), but via the sign as *indication*: it is not *bedeutet*, it is not meant, but rather "implied" by means of its material manifestation in the signs by means of which it is exteriorised. This is at the core of Derrida's argument in his *Introduction to The Origin of Geometry*. However, indicativity necessarily implies the interpretability of the idealities thus mediated (meanings, sense), i.e. the possibility that the original intention will be distorted or deformed. Husserl confronts this with a *demand*: *there must be responsibility, i.e. the task of re-animating the original meaning, reactivating it* (the re-execution of the original act of observation, the acquisition of primary evidence). It is therefore necessary to accept that, beyond responsibility to the infinite task, there exists no ideal communication that would guarantee the continuity of the traditionalisation of the original establishment (the meaning thus established). However, if this ideal communication is supposed to belong to "duration" within the framework of an intentionally teleological horizon, an ideal historicity and orientation on the ideal limit (from the order of in-finity), it is extremely difficult, if not impossible, to separate it from the sphere of empirical historicity to which it is necessarily related by virtue of its dependence on the *indicativity* of traditionalisation, to the sphere of indexes and interpretations, which for Husserl is a field in which "omission", "forgetting" and "defeat" take place, i.e. a field in which *meaning is lost*, in which rationality misses itself, without its being possible to push this field beyond the boundary of phenomenological history: it is the outside that is inside history. Or to put it another way: responsibility is not a necessary but a free act (or after Schelling: freedom resides in the capability of responsibility and irresponsibility), and this means it is impossible to eliminate the possibility of a complete forgetting of the original evidence. What for Husserl is the *ground* changes during the course of his deliberations into the *postulate*.

Derrida again:

> But since, in order to escape worldliness, sense *must* first *be able* to be set down in the world and be deposited in sensible spatiotemporality, it must put its pure international ideality, i.e., its truth-sense, in danger. Thus a possibility, which even here accords only with empiricism and nonphilosophy, appears in a philosophy which is (at least because of certain motifs) the contrary of empiricism: the possibility of truth's *disappearance*.

And when in this respect he mentions Husserl's distinction between expression and indication, he writes in a note:

> Using this distinction we could interpret the phenomenon of crisis (which for Husserl always refers to a disorder or illness of language) as a degradation of the sign expression into a sign indication, of a "clear" intention into an empty signal.[104]

---

[104] Derrida, *Edmund Husserl's Origin of Geometry*, footnote 96, p. 92.

The irruption of another temporality. The movement of searching and finding should be under the control of a teleological horizon guaranteeing the continuity of tradition as tele-communication – this would be pure "transcendental historicity". However, a condition of the possibility of finding (in the sense of reactivation) is forgetting. This is a figure that is already present in Husserl's *Lectures on Internal Time-Consciousness*: the *Ur-impression* is conscious only as grasped retention. Here though in concrete form: the first is secondary in relation to the second, loss is the condition of the possibility of further development, the original meaning is traditionalised only if empirical history and finiteness are in play contaminating each ideality as tele-communicated. In other words, risk is linked with contamination, with irreducible entanglement. Meaning is always in crisis.

But then we can say: the phenomenological method will grow into a reflection upon what phenomenology does not possess, what it lacks, how it *deviates* from its original establishment. This means, however, that legible traces of this absence are present in it.

However, this is the same as the question: how will phenomenology fulfil its telos (the *idea* of phenomenology)?

If it identifies a "crisis" as a) a severance of the relationship to the origin, and b) the exterior (forgetting, succumbing to the temptations of language), then phenomenology itself is in a special relationship with this crisis inasmuch as it itself is the *crisis* (albeit unreflectedly). This special position of phenomenology itself as *deviating from its origin, its constant iteration that is always a new foundation*, is the crisis (factoid: all of Husserl's published texts are conceived of as an "introduction to phenomenology" intended to demonstrate the teleological necessity of phenomenology against the backdrop of "recent philosophy" after Descartes).

In order to complete our sketch of all contiguities perhaps we simply have to answer a single question. Husserl wants to understand crisis as something extraordinary or exceptional in light of the intentional teleology of the phenomenological history of meaning. But what does the exceptionalism of the exception mean? For history under the administration of teleology it should – *de jure* – be a factual deviation *within, albeit also without* the horizon of the original foundation of rationality. Restitution should therefore always be possible, even though the restoration of the teleological movement has up till now revealed (necessarily) concealed aspects of the original idea albeit somehow already implied at the start. The exception would then be something against which history can always be immunised by critical reflection and acceptance of the appropriate responsibility. On the other hand, we might say: the exception is – *de jure* – the necessary medium of the manifestation of meaning, which is why *Urstiftung* needs *Nachstiftung* (from the perspective of *Endstiftung*); it is the medium of an act in which a decision is always reached anew (i.e. always for the first time) regarding in what sense we are *now, at this very moment*, to understand the original idea. Exception as a moment of crisis would then be a far riskier *caesura*. This is also intimated by Husserl when he says that the condition of *Besinnung* or critical thinking is *epoché* in respect of the entire preceding tradition:

> We can (...) subsequently (*nachträglich*) adopt a position of critical reflection and enquire of the original motives of the traditionalised that conferred meaning upon it..., in order to legitimise the task as a task for us, or to eliminate it as illegitimate. For in this resides the cornerstone of our freedom, namely that *epoché* is also always possible in respect of the past (*nachträglich*).[105]

Crisis is a moment in which tradition is suspended as a whole. We become aware (Husserl's example) of the failure of our attempt to accomplish what we promised ourselves.

---

[105] Husserl, *Die Krisis der europäischen Wissenschaften und die transzendentale Phänomenologie. Ergänzungsband.Texte aus dem Nachlass 1934–1937*, p. 374 (trans. here by Phil Jones).

This is why – if failures proliferate – one says: "This is no way to live", and, on the contrary, a successful person asked "How are you?", replies with a simple "Fine thanks".[106]

It is for this reason that the exception could qualify as a state of emergency. In the case of Husserl this would lead to a new confirmation of the norm if by means of the *epoché* it were to be possible to reinstate the *status quo ante*, inasmuch as this involves the meaning of heading for the original objective. However, it also seems, if we read his texts from the 1930s with greater detachment, that rules are possible only thanks to the exceptions in which they are first established as rules. To express this in the language of political and legal philosophy: this would be more a case of the exceptionalism of an exceptional state as the condition of the reactivation of meaning. However, there is then no return to what is departing and a general *epoché* in respect of tradition would be the condition of an openness to what is arriving.

None of this is without risk. Husserl wrote his text on the crisis facing Europe in the period immediately following the collapse of the Weimar Republic. Its dissolution and takeover by the National Socialists was made possible, inter alia, by Article 48 of its Constitution, which authorised the president to suspend completely or partially certain fundamental rights temporarily, i.e. to declare de facto an exceptional state (a state of emergency)[107]. Only a few years later, Walter Benjamin had the following to say in his *Theses on the Philosophy of History*:

The tradition of the oppressed teaches us that the state of emergency in which we live is not the exception but the rule.[108]

106 Ibid., p. 384.
107 Regarding this point see Dan Diner, *Beyond the Conceivable. Studies on Germany, Nazism, and the Holocaust*. University of California Press, Berkeley, Los Angeles, London 2000, pp. 11–25.
108 Walter Benjamin, *Über den Begriff der Geschichte. Kritische Gesamtausgabe* 9. Ed. Gérard Raulet, Suhrkamp, Frankfurt a.M. 2010, pp. 74, 87 and 97.

All of this had already been predicted by sensationalist literature in which, in its way, this exceptional structure of meaning is also revealed: the meaning of meaning itself, meaning as crisis, meaning as the event of a crisis: the outside is inside, the crisis is a state and an event, action that is manifest as a state because it paralyses and suspends the existing order (*suspense novel*). But this paralysis has its own strange dynamic, an almost hectic movement: the city is teeming with police, the chaotic excitement of crowds, an atmosphere of general uncertainty and a tense expectation of what is to follow. Think of the literature already quoted: Paris terrorised by Fantômas, London in the power of the Chinese, or London being fought over by gangsters. This last novel cited, by Edgar Wallace (*When the Gangs Came to London*), at one point even describes the "suspensive" aspect of the phenomenon of the "crisis" with almost clinical precision in a conversation between the American detective Jiggs Allerman and cabinet members at a meeting of what these days would be called a "crisis management team":

The prime minister asks:

"What are we going to do, Captain Allerman? You know these people, you're acquainted with the methods employed to deal with them – what's your suggestion?"
Jiggs did not speak for a moment. He sat by the table, drumming his fingers on the polished surface. Presently he lifted his head.
"Any suggestion I make, gentlemen, will sound immodest. The first is that I be given absolute control of the Metropolitan police force for a month. The second is that you suspend all your laws which protect criminals – these fair play methods of yours are going to get you in worse than you're in already. I suggest you scrap every rule you've laid down for Scotland Yard; that you suspend the Habeas Corpus Act, and give us an indemnity in advance for any illegal act – that is to say, for any act which is against your law – that may be committed in the course of that month. If you'll do this, I'll put these two gangs just where they belong."

"In prison?"

Jiggs shook his head.

"In hell," he said.

It was perhaps unfortunate that he used this extravagant illustration. The Home Secretary was a very earnest Nonconformist, who took his religion seriously.

"That, of course, is..." He paused.

"Fantastical," suggested Jiggs. "I'm getting quite used to the word. It's the one you pull when any hard-sense suggestion is made to you."

"In the first place," said the Home Secretary stiffly, "we could not give you complete control of the police. That, as I say, is--um--impossible. I'm not so sure that it isn't against the Constitution."

Jiggs nodded. "She's a new one to me."[109]

---

109 Edgar Wallace, *When the Gangs Came to London*, House of Stratus, 2001, ch. 7.

12

In the same year that an American policeman was searching for a way of stemming the flood of gangsters into London, Carl Schmitt, whose ideas were probably inspired by Article 48 of the Weimar Constitution, was preparing the second edition of his *Political Theology* (1st edition 1922, 2nd edition 1933). Schmitt also published an expanded version of *The Concept of the Political*, as well as the no less well known essay *Legality and Legitimacy* (1932), and in all of these works we find what approximates to a juridico-political commentary on what Captain Jiggs Allerman proposes in crude terms in Wallace's *When the Gangs Came to London*, namely a theory of sovereignty and the "state of exception". "Sovereign is he who decides on the exception" reads the first sentence of *Political Theology*[110]. And because the *Ausnahmezustand* or state of exception is simply another name for a crisis, it would be possible to draw on Schmitt's considerations as the backdrop against which to examine Husserl's concept of crisis, nonlinear teleology, and above all the emphasis laid on responsibility.

Leaving terminology to one side, Schmitt's state of exception is a particular manifestation of the general phenomenon of crisis (though this formulation could be inverted) in the sense that it displays the same underlying structure. The link between crisis and a state of exception is clear to the legal scholar Clinton L. Rossiter, as we see in the title of his *Constitutional Dictatorship: Crisis Government in the Modern Democracies* (New York 1948), in which he writes: "... in time of crisis a democratic, constitutional government must be temporarily altered to whatever degree is necessary to overcome the peril and restore normal conditions (...) the government will have more power and the people fewer

---

110 Carl Schmitt, *Political Theology: Four Chapters on the Concept of* Sovereignty, trans. George Schwab, MIT Press, Cambridge, Massachusetts 1985, p. 5.

rights...".[111] The "necessary degree" (clearly formulated in the demands set by Jiggs Allerman) is vague: are we still talking of a legal state or, on the contrary, a complete suspension of the rule of law as handed down by precedent? Or is this a state in which political (state) and executive power has merged with legislative power and can no longer be distinguished? For this reason too, since the time of Roman law the state of exception has been associated with civil war, rebellion, an extreme threat to the state, states of emergency, etc. In brief, the problem is as follows: if the declaration of a state of exception were a purely political decision, it would be illegal and there would be a risk of chaos, because a state of exception must somehow be "legitimised" even though it suspends legality. This is where Carl Schmitt comes in, who understands the state of exception as a *borderline concept*, as the *threshold of the law* (the border or threshold implies ambiguity: neither-nor, both-and)

> Because the exception is different from anarchy and chaos, order in the juristic sense still prevails even if it is not the legal order. The existence of the state is undoubted proof of its superiority over the validity of the legal norm. The decision frees itself from all normative ties and becomes in the true sense absolute. The state suspends the law in the exception on the basis of its right of self-preservation, as one would say. The two elements of the concept legal order are then dissolved into independent notions and thereby testify to their conceptual independence. Unlike the normal situation, when the autonomous moment of the decision recedes to a minimum, the norm is destroyed in the exception. The exception remains, nevertheless, accessible to jurisprudence because both elements, the norm as well as the decision, remain within the framework of the juristic.[112]

---

111 Cited in Giorgio Agamben, *State of Exception (Homo Sacer II)*. The University of Chicago Press, Chicago and London 2005, p. 8.
112 Schmitt, *Political Theology*, p. 12.

This is not simply to say that the crisis is something that can be encountered or experienced in reality (up to the very boundary of banality or familiarity: I will leave to one side life or economic crises and even worse examples), though this is not without interest, because in such cases the crisis is something like a borderline situation, a state of limitation that, like *state and event, being and becoming*, is such that one cannot be separated from the other. This is why the "crisis" is also a situation of irreducible ambiguity.

However, this complicates matters considerably, because the simple topological antithesis outside/inside implied in various theories of the state of exception is insufficient to explain the phenomenon it sets out to explain. Giorgio Agamben puts it thus in his monograph on the state of exception:

> If the state of exception's characteristic property is a (total or partial) suspension of the juridical order, how can such a suspension still be contained within it? How can an anomie be inscribed within the juridical order? And if the state of exception is instead only a de facto situation, and is as such unrelated or contrary to law, how is it possible for the order to contain a lacuna precisely where the decisive situation is concerned? And what is the meaning of this lacuna? In truth, the state of exception is neither external nor internal to the juridical order, and the problem of defining it concerns precisely a threshold, or a zone of indifference, where inside and outside do not exclude each other but rather blur with each other.[113]

But let us return for a moment to Schmitt and the quote from his *Political Theology*: "... the state of exception is something other than mere anarchy and chaos". A state of emergency is *declared* and is therefore the subject of a decision, a sovereign decision, because it is a decision on an exception, which is always outside the norm, since the general norm can never cover an exception – neither indeed can

---

113 Agamben, *The State of Exception (Homo Sacer II)*, p. 23.

the general norm justify the decision that the situation in question is a genuinely exceptional case. It is a decision that cannot be extrapolated from any legal norm. Nor is it possible to claim that the state of exception arises necessarily from an emergency situation, since a state of emergency is not an objective fact: a state of emergency is simply that which is *declared* to be a state of emergency.[114] This is why Schmitt says that the sovereign decides whether there exists a state of emergency.[115] However, he also says: "The sovereign stands outside of the normally valid juridical order and yet belongs to it."[116] If this is true, then it is also true that the state of exception remains something other than anarchy and chaos. But how can this possibly be true? Easy – the state of exception is a borderline or liminal state, the *threshold* of the (juridical) order.

Schmitt concretises and elaborates on the problem. A decision that *annuls* the juridical order in this way manifests a *specific legal moment*: the norm requires a normal form of life circumstances or it cannot be applied, which is why a decision on a state of exception first creates a situation in which legal provisions can apply and therefore in which norms may be applied. Order must first be established so that the rule of law be meaningful, and this in turn makes possible the declaration of a state of exception. Schmitt generalises this question as follows:

> Precisely a philosophy of concrete life must not withdraw from the exception and the extreme case, but must be interested in it to the highest degree. The exception can be more important to it than the rule, not because of a romantic irony for the paradox, but because the seriousness of an insight goes deeper than the clear generalizations inferred from what ordinarily repeats itself. The exception is more interesting than the rule. The rule proves nothing; the exception proves everything: It confirms not only

114 Ibid., p. 30.
115 Schmitt, *Political Theology,* p. 7.
116 Ibid.

the rule but also its existence, which derives only from the exception. In the exception the power of real life breaks through the crust of a mechanism that has become torpid by repetition.[117]

The norm is possible on the basis only of the exception: for Schmitt the *fundamentum inconcussum* of his legal theory, for Husserl the unintended yet possible consequence of his concept of crisis and teleology, which, on the contrary, is supposed to avert the threat of complete discontinuity in relation to tradition. In the case of Schmitt the *Urstiftung* or original foundation would be the sovereign decision that first creates the possibility of normativity and in its capacity as sovereign is itself without foundation, because there are no rules available pertaining to the decision to call a state of exception, and such a decision is not subject to any (juridical) control: however, as the boundary of juridical order it is both outside and inside. The state of exception is the moment when the order (law) detaches itself from its own power, suspending its power. In the case of Husserl this is in the name of a decision preceded by the suspension (in the sense of the problematisation) of the entire tradition heretofore as normalising, i.e. *responsibility*. However, in this case too we could say that this is an act that is both inside and outside. Husserl wants to retain the performance of responsibility within the framework or horizon of teleology, which is why he views it as a conscious endorsement of the original idea – this is why each new establishment in the sense of *Nachstiftung* is inside. However, if this *Nachstiftung* is somehow productive – if it is a response to crisis, i.e. if it corresponds to a historically arising situation – then it is not entirely clear whether it is possible to speak of a "ground" of responsibility inasmuch as no response can be passively inferred from the founding idea. The non-groundlessness recognised by Schmitt is a threat to Husserl that he fails to avert convincingly. He might indeed para-

---

117 Ibid., p. 16.

phrase Schmitt: in a crisis "the power of real life breaks through the crust of a mechanism that has become torpid by repetition."

This comparison could be transferred to a level of greater abstraction. In a highly original monograph, Michael Marder[118] interprets Schmitt's "political ontology" on the basis of the relationship between line and point, i.e. a kind of proto-geometry of the original act of *Landnahme*, which Schmitt in his book *Der Nomos der Erde*[119] describes as his form of *Urstiftung*. The earth as the antithesis of the sea, in which no structuration can leave any permanent trace, is a realm allowing for the establishment of a fixed locus and border, a stable order of localisation. This establishment of a visible *nomos* is "a constitutive historical event – an act of *legitimacy*, whereby the legality of a mere law first is made meaningful."[120] *Rechtsetzung* is manifest in the fixed lines thus charted that are born of the "punctuating" moment of establishment without this point being broken or surmounted by a line, since a line itself is nothing other than an infinite number of points. In Schmitt's concept of the political this basic scheme (line-point) is mirrored in the sovereign decision on a state of exception, in the exception or the irrepressible potentiality of the point. The exception is part of the line and yet transcends it. Schmitt extrapolates from this a radical political idea in which the decision on a state of exception is a permanent reminder that continuity lives in intermittency or discontinuity.[121]

To compensate for the normative groundlessness of its origination, the line appeals, in the last instance, to definite divisions (*bestimmte Einteilungen*) and demarcations engraved in the literal ground, the soil: the firm line and

118 Michael Marder, *Groundless Existence: The Political Ontology of Carl Schmitt*, Continuum, New York 2010.
119 Carl Schmitt, *Der Nomos der Erde im Völkerrecht des Jus Publicum Europaeum.* Dunckler & Humblot, Berlin 21974 (1950). Carl Schmitt, *The* Nomos *of the Earth*, trans. and annotated by G.L. Ulmen, Telos Press, New York 2003.
120 Schmitt, *The* Nomos *of the Earth*, p. 73.
121 Cf. Marder, *Groundless Existence*, p. 15.

nomos that flourishes from it can always fall back on the earth for their onto-phenomeno-political support. Rooted in such solidity (...) are the acts of appropriation consonant with the most elemental sense of *nomos* as well as the "standards and rules", *die Masse und Regeln*, for human conduct that, much later, will generate the abstractions of normativitiy forgetful of their grounding in the earth. The repression of the concrete similarly isolated by Husserl as the cause of the crisis plaguing European sciences and collective consciousness, is further exacerbated by the extension of linearity to the whole planet. (...) The budding cold and uninhabitable abstraction of globality, which is but a geographic representation disengaged from the life-world of human beings, overrides the earth and the soil that bore the first lines of nomic demarcation.

Yet, the extension of linearity is, in an equal measure, a rupture, a "headlong leap into the nothingness" that, strangely, mimics the accomplishments of decision-making. It punctuates that which it extends, unhinging and ungrounding the line removed from its material support in the soil. Comparable qualitative leaps and punctuations will, henceforth, accompany every attempt at redrawing the global lines and remaking the international order (...) Akin to the decision that signals the end of indeterminacy and asserts its independence from infinite deliberations and rationalisations, the point is absolved from all relationality even as it negatively mediates the self-relatedness of space. This exceptional determination, this extra-normative eruption, this performative declaration that is not buoyed up by anything but itself, aptly illustrates the sovereign decision on the exception in *Political Theology*.[122]

A comparison with Husserl's idea of teleological history and its beginnings in the establishment of the original idea will serve to demonstrate this strange borderline position, a position that is not easy to understand. Unlike Walter Benjamin, who views the (juridical) order as permeated by the violence by means of which it was founded

[122] Marder, *Groundless Existence*, p. 16.

and thus constantly in the power of fateful forces, capable of being annulled only by "divine" violence completely exterior to the history to which it will one day put an end[123], Carl Schmitt inclines to the idea of discontinuous continuity as an inexhaustible potentiality of history, and so acknowledges both the continuity of the line and the radical discontinuity of the sovereign decision, without postulating any external factor. Husserl's teleology also rejects and at the same time accepts both one and the other, but only inasmuch as both ensue from the potentiality of a single origin and the idea founded within it; though it takes the moment of crisis seriously, the decision is only a decision if it is a *response*, if it responds to the original idea. Even here he applies to history (albeit in modified form) his concept of temporality, the flow of which guarantees the intentional interconnectedness of retention, impression and protention. However, impression here is something akin to a crisis that is a response bound anew to a past story (tradition), while the response opens a future in which meaning will once again have the chance to limber up, as it were, a meaning that is to explain authentic traditionalisation. Hence recollection of the origin of event as responsibility for the history of meaning and as response.

In simple, approximate, terms, the ambiguity of Husserl's nonlinear teleology is concentrated in the semantic proximity of the words "responsibility" and "response", which can become an irreducible difference. Responsibility relates to a certain horizon – it is responsibility for traditionalisation in respect of its original establishment. However, the response is close to the performative utterance: if I do not respond, I do not know how I respond and by what means in the singular moment of crisis I seize the original idea in order to reincorporate it into the history in which it has been forgotten. Only then can we say that the basis of history is present in

---

123 Cf. Walter Benjamin, "Zur Kritik der Gewalt", in: *Gesammelte Schriften* II.1, ed. R. Tiedemann – H. Schweppenhäuser, Suhrkamp, Frankfurt a.M. 1999, pp. 179–204; Walter Benjamin, *Über den Begriff der Geschichte*.

history as long as it is made present again and again. However, this making present is always only ever possible in situationally relative and thus new responses. Each second time is somehow the first time. However, it is then difficult to understand this method of connection using the retention/protention model (primarily "passive"), inasmuch as the response simultaneously bears witness to what is yet to arrive and what is very possibly incommensurate with the existing horizons of expectations. Then, of course, the response would be far more a search for the traces of projects that until now could not be realised in this history even though they were in fact possible.

13

The present, if we take it seriously as present, is crisis. This is borne out by Husserl's phenomenology, which constantly operates on the border of itself, because in relation to its own tradition as created by *The Philosophy of Arithmetic* and *Logical Investigations* it adopts a critical approach, fearing that it has forgotten its founding idea and has forfeited its meaning. It comes face to face with a crisis: it finds himself repeatedly beyond the boundary of its original project and repeatedly attempts to avert this threat. Husserl wishes to protect the idea of reason and Europe, seemingly in vain.

And yet Husserl's descriptions and concepts allow for a suitable response. Not to crisis, but to the catastrophe that, like a shadow of that which is on the point of arriving, somehow indirectly announces itself in his texts from the 1930s, even though Husserl only circles around this shadow. The hitherto absent is now inside, but Husserl is forever attempting to force it out beyond the boundary of European teleology.

PART TWO
CATASTROPHE

14

Black milk of dawn.

15

Thinking after the end of the Second World War finds its original establishment, its *Urstiftung*, in the categorical claim made by Theodore W. Adorno in 1949 that first appears in the essay *Cultural Criticism and Society*:

> Cultural criticism finds itself faced with the final stage of the dialectic of culture and barbarism. To write poetry after Auschwitz is barbaric. And this corrodes even the knowledge of why it has become impossible to write poetry today.[124]

The emphasis here is on both parts of the sentence, which is clear when Adorno cites himself and in the essay *Art and the Arts* writes:

> While the present situation no longer has room for art – that was the meaning of the statement about the impossibility of poems after Auschwitz – it nevertheless has need of it.[125]

Adorno never rescinded his original statement, though over time he clarified it:

> Perennial suffering has as much right to expression as a tortured man has to scream; hence it may have been wrong to say that after Auschwitz you could no longer write poems.[126]

This correction was in order if only because Adorno himself was a great admirer of the poetry of Paul Celan, as we see in his *Aesthetic Theory*, where we read that Celan's poetry

---

124 Theodor W. Adorno, "Kulturkritik und Gesellschaft", in: *GS* 10.1, p. 30. Regarding the context of and changes to Adorno's statement on poetry after Auschwitz, see Klaus Hofmann, "Poetry After Auschwitz – Adorno's Dictum", *German Life and Letters*, 58, 2, 2005, pp. 182–194.
125 Theodor W. Adorno, "Die Kunst und die Künste", *GS* 10.1, pp. 452–453.
126 Theodor W. Adorno, *Negative dialektik*, *GS* 6, p. 355.

is permeated by the shame of art in the face of suffering that escapes both experience and sublimation. Celan's poems want to speak of the most extreme horror through silence. Their truth content itself becomes negative.[127]

This then gives rise to a question that it would be possible to answer in a similar way, i.e. on the basis of Adorno's own work: is philosophy possible after Auschwitz? And if so, then how?

127 Theodor W. Adorno, *Aesthetic Theory,* trans. Robert Hullot-Kentor, Continuum, London & New York 1977, p. 322.

16

At the same time as Husserl was attempting to salvage Europe's identity on the basis of its original idea and find a way of reducing that which is exterior in respect of European rationality, a plan was being hatched for a final solution to this exterior, a plan for its physical elimination. Husserl grappled with ideality and phenomenological historicity. What was about to arrive, however, was real history.

No matter when it may be written, every story will henceforth be before Auschwitz,

as Maurice Blanchot was to write much later.[128] He is referring to a kind of paralysis brought on by the facticity of an event that cannot be incorporated within the existing horizon of rationality, cannot be explained and thus accorded a meaning, a meaning that, notwithstanding, it must not be allowed to possess. This is not a logical contradiction, but a trauma. The ability to think is not only occluded, as Adorno says, but is removed from the game by the time of an event by which we are marked, an event we are obliged to maintain an awareness of and are unable to rid ourselves of because we are unable to retrieve it within the imagination. It is irreparable, somehow lost for us, but for this very reason we are still implicated in it.[129] It is the original oblivion, the antecedent of the memory in which, nonetheless, it persists. However, if it is something irredeemable, this event can never be absent: that which we cannot encounter, we cannot escape from. Thinking can only *testify*. The outside is inside

128 Maurice Blanchot, *Après coup*, Les Ed. de Minuit, Paris 1983, p. 99. "A quelque date qu'il puisse être écrit, tout récit désormais sera d'avant Auschwitz."
129 See, for example, Steven Shaviro, "Complicity and Forgetting", *MLN*, Vol. 105, No. 4 (1990), pp. 819–832, here p. 820: "But the deepening tendency of thought, its political situatedness, is precisely this: that it cannot escape the unexpected demands of the present moment, or the return, the uncanny insistence, of a longburied past. "

and remains before us. Not teleology, but the irruption of traumatic temporality into linear chronology.

Adorno and Horkheimer's *Dialectic of the Enlightenment* is also a form of "retrospective questioning", i.e. *Rückfrage*, in that it seeks a response to the question of "why humanity, instead of entering a truly human state, is sinking into a new kind of barbarism".[130] This, too, is critical thinking in the Husserlian sense of the word *Besinnung*, in that it involves a "reflection on the regressive moment"[131] by which reason consumes itself. This, too, reveals the loss of meaning in the instrumentalisation of science and the mathematisation of qualities (with explicit reference to Husserl's *Crisis*). However, its starting point is not crisis, but the catastrophe of the Holocaust. And in its response to the Holocaust it can no longer strive for a return, but for an openness in thinking for the future that cannot, however, be anything other than an openness to the radically *other*. This is not about preserving tradition, but rescuing hope. The place that for Husserl was home to remembrance is now occupied by the response to factual history. However, in both cases reflection on the meaning of rationality is a matter of responsibility. This can be corroborated very briefly with two quotes. The first is from Adorno's *Lectures on Negative Dialectics*:

> But that after Auschwitz one cannot seriously speak of a world in which that was possible, and in which the threat of a repetition in some other way looms daily, and in some comparable guise – I am reminded of Vietnam – is probably happening this very second, as being meaningful; i.e. to maintain that this world in which we live is supposed to meaningful, that seems to me to express a cynicism and a frivolity which is, simply, in terms of pre-philosophical experience, no longer justifiable. And a philosophy which, imbued with a foolish arrogance of the spirit refusing to take cognisance of

---

130 Theodor W. Adorno, Max Horkheimer, *Dialectics of Enlightment*, trans. E. Jephcott, Stanford University Press, Stanford 2000, p. xiv.
131 Ibid.

this reality – turns a blind eye to this and which insists, come what may, that there is meaning, that seems to me to be an exaction which cannot be imposed on anyone not entirely stupefied by philosophy; for philosophy can, without question, amongst the many other functions it fulfils, stupefy with success.[132]

The second is from *Minima Moralia*, in this case Adorno's reflections at the very end of the war (autumn 1944):

> The thought that after this war life could continue on "normally", or indeed that culture could be "reconstructed" – as if the reconstruction of culture alone were not already the negation of such – is idiotic. Millions of Jews have been murdered, and this is supposed to be only the intermission and not the catastrophe itself?[133]

The outside is irreducibly inside: a factual historical event has transformed post-war philosophy by compelling it to *respond* to factual history. Thinking lost the self-assuredness provided by its foundation in the idea of reason. As a consequence, philosophy during the second half of the twentieth century is often difficult to understand. It invents new terms and searches for other traditions and other forms of argumentation. It will perhaps become more understandable if we read it as a response to the event that was Auschwitz, the very character of which excludes any rational assimilation. It would even be possible to show that the texts of many of philosophy's most renowned practitioners, from Adorno via Levinas, Blanchot and Derrida to Agamben and Didi-Huberman and so on, also have a kind of personal dimension inasmuch as they search for an appropriate philosophical language in which to express (personal) experience.

132 Theodor W. Adorno, *Lectures on Negative Dialectics*, trans. Rodney Livingstone, Polity Press, Cambridge 2008, p. 19.
133 Theodor W. Adorno, *Minima Moralia. Reflections from Damaged Life*, trans. E.F.N. Jephcott, Verso, London and New York 2005, p. 55.

The Holocaust is an event that has necessitated the radical transformation of philosophical discourse, and unless we understand this transformation, their books will seem too complicated, paradoxical, or even capricious. However, the idea that they were merely involved in proposing academic solutions to academic problems could not be further from the truth. These writers are interested in the very meaning of thinking, and all of them share the conviction that philosophical thinking is only present where philosophy transcends itself. Now it is about something else, it is about bearing witness. And yet this bearing witness represents a completely different type of *showing*. This is the lesson of the Holocaust. Auschwitz is a radical event inasmuch as we have to ask ourselves whether our conceptual understanding, interpretation and analysis are appropriate responses to it. Thinking reconstructs nothing in such a way as to lend the event a narrative arc. It is touched by the event and responds to it, reflects upon it, while at the same time being a reflection upon the concept of the event and its own relationship to the event. All of this is part of the process of bearing witness.

All of this is stated clearly and harshly in Adorno's *Negative Dialectic*:

> After Auschwitz, our feelings resist any claim of the positivity of existence as sanctimonious, as wronging the victims; they balk at squeezing any kind of sense, however bleached, out of the victims' fate. And these feelings do have an objective side after events that make a mockery of the construction of immanence as endowed with a meaning radiated by an affirmatively posited transcendence. Such a construction would affirm absolute negativity and would assist its ideological survival – as in reality that negativity survives anyway, in the principle of society as it exists until its self-destruction. The earthquake of Lisbon sufficed to cure Voltaire of the theodicy of Leibniz, and the visible disaster of the first nature was insignificant in comparison with the second, social one, which defies human imagination as it distils a real hell from human evil. Our metaphysical faculty is paralysed because

actual events have shattered the basis on which speculative metaphysical thought could be reconciled with experience.[134]

134 Theodor W. Adorno, *Negative Dialectics,* trans. E. B. Ashton, Routledge, London 1973, pp. 361–362.

17

Between the response and the event, the event and experience, experience of the event and testimony thereof, there is clearly a very close relationship, all the more so if it is necessary to respond to the experience from the order of *de facto*. The event is something that happens out of the blue. At the same time it touches us and awakens us to life, inasmuch as that which we call life, as Jean-François Lyotard says, emerges from the violence that impacts upon our lethargy from without.[135] Because we are not furnished with a special organ for perceiving the event, we have no choice but to describe our relationship to it in different ways. We are "struck by" the event, "caught unawares", the event "relates to us". These descriptions always contain an important lesson for thinking that ventures to deal with the event: philosophy must emerge from within itself and transcend itself. The fact of experience in relation to an event problematises the relationship between philosophical reflection and its subject matter. Experience of the event tests the boundary of thinking, and for this reason it seems that it bursts in upon the realm of philosophy like an unwelcome intruder from without. However, if the close relationship between event and experience is to be accepted, two conclusions may be drawn. Firstly, experience is present only where there is an event. Secondly, experience is the place from which an event is perceived.

But if the experience of Auschwitz transformed thinking in the second half of the twentieth century, a basic question arises: *is experience of the Holocaust even possible? And if so, can it still be called experience?* These are questions in which the transformation of thinking is both enacted and reflected. If we know that in modern philosophy the term experience is subordinate to the function of recognition, then only that which is cognitively relevant is deemed

---

135 Jean-François Lyotard, *Moralités postmodernes*, Ed. Galilée, Paris 1993; idem, *Postmodern Fables*, University of Minnesota Press, Minneapolis, pp. 235–250.

to be the content of experience. Otherwise, to borrow from Adorno: concretely experienced reality is subordinate to instrumentalised rationality (or the "positivism" of the modern world). The concepts that experience organises separate it from that which Husserl named the life-world or *Lebenswelt*.

These questions are therefore basically self-evident, and on the eve of the Holocaust and still under the sway of the First World War, philosophy anticipated them in the texts by Walter Benjamin that relate to the specific experience of twentieth-century Man.

Right at the start of his long essay *The Storyteller* (1936), Benjamin observes a certain decline in the traditional art of storytelling (the essay examines the work of Nikolaj Leskov) and writes:

> experience has fallen in value. And it looks as if it is continuing to fall into bottomlessness (...) With the (First) World War a process began to become apparent which has not halted since then. Was it not noticeable at the end of the war that men returned from the battlefield grown silent – not richer, but poorer in communicable experience? What ten years later was poured out in the flood of war books was anything but experience that goes from month to mouth (...) the communicability of experience is decreasing.[136]

The experience of the First World War was already such that it paralysed experience and its link to the chronicling of that experience, for which it was no longer possible to find adequate (communicable) expression. Closely related to this is the inability to *relate* in the manner of erstwhile storytellers. In Benjamin this is a theme that is subject to many variations, for instance in his earlier essay *Experience and Poverty* (1933), where we read:

136 Walter Benjamin, *Selected Writings* 3, Belknap Press, Cambridge 2006, pp. 143–144.

this much is clear: experience has fallen in value, amid a generation which from 1914 to 1918 had to experience some of the most monstrous events in the history of the world...[137]

(Benjamin uses the same formulation almost word for word in *The Storyteller*, but now expresses his idea on the very boundary of self-contradiction.) However, we then read something that seems almost to anticipate Adorno and Horkheimer's *Dialectic of the Enlightment*, albeit from a different perspective:

Indeed (let's admit it), our poverty of experience is not merely poverty on the personal level, but poverty of human experience in general. Hence, a new kind of barbarism.[138]

Benjamin, however, has something different in mind. He is alluding to the "positive concept of barbarism". The barbarian, starved of experience, must begin anew, he is faced by a tabula rasa (Klee and Loos, among others, turn to "the naked man of the contemporary world who lies screaming like a newborn babe in the dirty diapers of the present"). Poverty would therefore entail people attempting to rid themselves of experience in order that they might apply their internal and external poverty so purely that something decent emerges from it.

This perhaps explains the "contra-dictoriness" referred to above: wartime "experience" is incommunicable because it has deprived man of everything in which he believed. He begins anew, and yet it is doubtful whether this will lead to his being able to return to experience in some original sense of the word. Rather, it involves the complete annihilation of tradition in the sense of the inherited traditionalised horizons of understanding (see Benjamin's *The Work of Art in the Age of Mechanical Reproduction*, the loss of aura, etc.)

---

137 Walter Benjamin, *Selected Writings* 2, p. 731.
138 Ibid., p. 732.

Whatever. The fact is that Benjamin discerns a clear connection between war and the erosion of experience, even if he still regards the etiolation of experience as embodying the possibility of reversal (stepping outside of tradition, i.e. in the final analysis outside of history) and ultimately the abolition of history.

Freud is preoccupied by a similar crisis of experience, and this leads him to a reformulation of psychoanalysis. In *Beyond the Pleasure Principle* (1920), in which he introduces the concepts of the pleasure principle and the reality principle, he works with the phenomenon of "trauma" as illustrated by war-induced neuroses.[139] Freud discovers that the war caused a significantly high number of traumatic neuroses and that these cannot any longer be explained simply as organic damage to the nervous system.[140] The striking symptom that accompanies this type of neurosis he terms *Wiederholungszwang* or repetition compulsion:

> the compulsion to repeat also recalls from the past experiences which include no possibility of pleasure, and which can never, even long ago, have brought satisfaction.[141]

Repetition compulsion – and herein resides its paradox – trumps the pleasure principle (its source being older). It appears when an excessively powerful experience breaks the natural barrier protecting the sensory organs against a "shock".[142] According to Freud, in this way that which is older than the pleasure principle, namely the death drive (the urge inherent in organic life to restore an earlier state of things), makes its presence felt:

---

139 Freud dealt with such neuroses separately, cf. "Zur Psychoanalyse der Kriegsneurosen", 1919.
140 Sigmund Freud, *Beyond the Pleasure Principle*, W.W. Norton and Company (Standard Edition), New York, London, 1990, p. 6.
141 Ibid., p. 14.
142 "We may (…) regard the common traumatic neurosis as a consequence of an extensive breach being made in the protective shield against stimuli." Ibid., p. 25.

it must be an old state of things, an initial state from which the living entity has at one time or other departed and to which it is striving to return by the circuitous paths along which its development leads. If we are to take it as a truth that knows no exception that everything living dies for internal reasons becomes inorganic once again then we shall be compelled to say that *"the aim of all life is death"* and, looking backwards, that *"inanimate things existed before living ones"*.[143]

Freud goes on to develop this idea in *The Ego and the Id*.

However, so as to ensure the context is complete, we should recall that Freud had of course already examined "traumatic neurosis" in his *Introductory Lectures on Psychoanalysis*, especially in the eighteenth lecture "Traumatic Fixation, the Unconscious", in which he discusses the fixation on a certain segment of the past, which, though a significant symptom of every neurosis, is demonstrated especially powerfully by the war:

The closest analogies to these conditions of our neurotics are furnished by the types of sickness which the war has just now made so frequent – the so-called traumatic neuroses.

It is as if these patients had not yet gotten through with the traumatic situation, as if it were actually before them as a task which was not yet mastered...[144]

After the war, what Freud terms "Nachträglichkeit" – "afterness" or deferred action – becomes one of the key intersections of the different lines forming the (new) philosophical discourse. At the same time, it is clear that this is not speculation but an attempt to capture

---

143 Ibid., p. 34.
144 Sigmund Freud, *Introductory Lectures on Psychoanalysis*, trans. James Strachey, W.W. Norton, New York 1977, p. 241.

the *experience* and the strange temporality contained therein that disrupts linearity.

This was confirmed in the aftermath of the horrors of the Second World War and the Nazi genocide.

Otto Dov Kulka, who recollects life in Auschwitz in his book *Landscapes of the Metropolis of Death*, says:

> I am after all a child, who was bound with those chains as a child and remained bound by them throughout every stage of growing up: I say that I was bound and remained bound, or fettered by chains, but that is because I was never there, because my foot never stepped into those courtyards, inside those buildings. I circled them as a moth circles a flame, knowing that falling into it was inevitable, yet I kept on circling outside, willingly or unwillingly – it was not up to me – all my friends, the butterflies, not all of them, but almost all of them were there and did not come out of there.[145]

His whole life bound to an experience he did not have and could not have had. "Bound", i.e. he continues to live with it (it is still present), it returns again and again. However, we're still not quite there... It's more radical than that. What we are talking about is *non-experience*, an *absence* of experience. If this is experience, it is constantly being experienced *outside the place within which the experience would have been possible* (the crematorium at Auschwitz). However, it is for this reason (the absence of experience, the impossibility of experience) that he who recounts this experience/non-experience is someone who bears witness (to the experience of the absence of that experience to which he is "bound"). That which returns is the *impossibility of having any experience of that to which I bear witness and which, paradoxically, legitimises me as witness.*

Kulka's text thematises the return, the repetition. It is not driven by an endeavour to understand or explain, but on the contrary

---

145 Otto Dov Kulka, *Landscapes of the Metropolis of Death*, trans. Ralph Mandel, Belknap Press, Cambridge 2013, p. 10.

reflects upon the inexplicability of experience. For this reason his book features an ongoing internal conflict between the reflexive language of memory and the method by which the historian apprehends events.[146] The reflexive language here, though not "enlightening" experience, is nevertheless still inclined towards experience, forever re-returning experience.

Traumatic narrative on a more general level is examined, for instance, by Michael Rothberg, author of *Traumatic Realism*, who reveals the specific traumatic temporality in which that repetitiveness and "afterness" of experience asserts itself strongly. Within this framework he then investigates the possibility of the representation of the Holocaust as event. The endeavour of re-presentation is to document (so that the event is not forgotten), but also somehow to reflect. Whence a return of the "old" genre of *realism*, which would appear to be the genre best suited to both tasks. However, the event of the Holocaust drives classical realism to its furthest limit, because that which is to be re-presented can only be submitted "traumatically", i.e. by means of the registration of the repetitive structure of time (*Nachträglichkeit* and *Wiederholungszwang*). Hence the "discourse of extremity", hence *traumatic realism*.

> Traumatic realism develops out of and in response to the demand for documentation that an extreme historical event poses to those who would seek to understand it (...) (it) is an attempt to product the traumatic event as an object of knowledge and (...) to transform its readers so that they are forced to acknowledge their relationship to posttraumatic culture.[147]

The narrative (storytelling, the narrative text) points to the event, but does so by means of a very special form of indexical relationship. The traumatic index does not point to the present, but to the

---

146 Ibid., "Introduction", p. xii.
147 Michael Rothberg, *Traumatic Realism: The Demands of Holocaust Representation.* University of Minnesota Press. Minneapolis, London 2000, pp. 100–101.

irrevocable absence of its referent (from Kafka to Beckett and other authors in whom philosophy took a keen interest during the latter half of the twentieth century).

So what we have is something like a collapse, the implosion of linear (historical) time. We have an event that is not within this time, as thought it were itself "temporalising" from a different temporality that the event itself establishes, an event that conjugates itself differently. It is present as past, endlessly deferred in relation to itself, and yet only "present" in this deferral.

Is experience of the Holocaust really experience? Or more precisely: how "is" the event of the Holocaust in experience? Not simply in the sense of being present, initially as fact and then endlessly deferring its own presence in its capacity as fact, but somehow transcending itself by virtue of the fact of its having happened (it is possible only at the point it has happened). In fact, as Claude Romano says, in the case of traumatic time the antithesis of memory is not forgetting but *repetition*. The event insists, persists, it is "stuck" within repetition. It is intolerable, and the impossibility of remembering (the configuration of the event as retrievable) is manifest in the repetition of the unappropriated and inappropriable event (the trauma). We are not in a position to remember *freely* what happened as having already taken place (completed, literally past). Or we are *incapable of experience*, i.e. that distance that memory provides. The past has not passed but continues to haunt the present (scaring it, stalking it, following in its footsteps, as Derrida will later write). The forgotten survives as a *vector* of repetition that does not retain the fact of the event but attempts (in vain) to break free from this fact, to escape it.

Otto Dov Kulka again captures this perfectly when he describes a dream that recurs with slight variations. After many years he returns to Auschwitz and goes downstairs. He has the feeling he has

as in those recurrent dreams in which I descend these stairs together with all my friends and all those who are close to me. It's the dream that always takes me back there, when I know that there is no way to avoid that place, that everyone is bound to arrive at that place because it is an inalterable law of the place, one from which there is no escape, and there is no chance for the fantasy we conjure up about liberation and an end, like playful childish fantasies, for an iron law leads everyone there and no one will escape from there. I also knew... that at the last moment I would be saved. (...) That night dream always brings me back to the same immutable law by which I end up back inside the crematorium and, by some roundabout way, through canals of dark water, through trenches and hidden openings, I dig beneath the barbed wire and reach freedom and board a train, and at one desolate station at night a loudspeaker calls my name, and I am returned to the place I am bound to reach: the crematorium. And however much I know that I must be caught, I always know, too, that I must be spared. It's a kind of circle, a cycle of Tantalus or Sisyphus, or of whatever myth we choose to invoke that is germane here, which returns in an endless vicious circle to the same place.[148]

Escape ... is possible. But every escape is simply the first step on the path back to that from which he is escaping. And so that from which there is no escape is constantly present, albeit forevermore in absence.

However, this dream is a *form of experience* because it "repeats" the real experience. Experience is "given" as a dream. When the so-called family camp at Auschwitz is liquidated, the children are taken elsewhere. Their journey leads to the crematorium.

We gazed at the smokestacks of one of the crematoria there. Step by step we drew closer. That primal experience of looming horror and of being sucked into it, swallowed within it — that is what persisted; that, and not

148 Kulka, *Landscapes of the Metropolis of Death*, pp. 13–14.

the relief, the overwhelming feeling of relief as we walked past the gate and continued toward the 'sauna camp' and entered it and through the windows could even see into the crematorium compound – all this I somehow remember, but this experience did not persist in the memory. The primal experience, the one that persisted, is the trauma, recurring numberless times and encapsulating, like a highly concentrated essence, the immutable law of the Great Death. A law that prevailed and applied to each and every one of us. Grappling with it – hopelessly – yet aspiring compulsively to escape its clutches, was a formative experience.[149]

Though Benjamin's pre-war theme of experience and its paralysis returns after the war in the writings of Adorno, the words remain but the meaning is completely transformed. In *Minima Moralia* Adorno writes:

The sheer incommensurability of the body to the war of attrition the previous time around already made authentic experience impossible. No one could have talked about it the way the battles of the artillery-general Napoleon Bonaparte were recounted. The long interval between war memoirs and the armistice is not an accident: it testifies to the laborious reconstruction of memory, which remains conjoined to something powerless and even inauthentic in all those books, regardless of whatever horrors the writer witnessed. (...) World War II however is as completely devoid of experience as a machine is to the movements of a body, (the less can it leave behind) a continuous and unconsciously preserved picture of memory. Everywhere, with each explosion, it has broken through the protective shield in which personal experience formed, the duration between the healing forgetting and the healing memory. Life has transformed itself into a timeless succession of shocks, between which gape holes, paralysed intermediary spaces (...) No one will be able to think of this, that every trauma, every unprocessed shock of that which recurs, is a ferment of coming destruction.[150]

149 Ibid., p. 33.
150 Adorno, *Minima Moralia*, pp. 54–55.

18

The experience of the Holocaust is perceived as a traumatic experience. This means that its very re-presentation (leaving to one side the problematic nature of this term) by a philosophical discourse that draws on the language of tradition is impossible if it does not want to falsify the event that this experience – in shock – encountered. Although this involves grasping something past historically, any attempt to reflect upon this experience makes it clear that the very structure of linearly conceived time is incommensurate with this experience. In brief: we are faced with the experience of the *impossibility of experience*. The past is not securely deposited in memory. The event is still with us, but not in the manner of something – literally – past, but as something that coming to terms with is a task we are forever faced with.

It is for this reason that philosophical discourse seeks a foothold in the Freudian concepts of repetition compulsion (*Wiederholungszwang*) and afterness, or deferred action (*Nachträglichkeit*), since it is clear that with their help a more acceptable description of "traumatised" experience is possible. However, philosophy then comes up against temporality, which *excludes the possibility of identification*, since understanding comes up against the *evasiveness* of that which it is attempting to re-cognise, its irreducible *absence in presence*. This temporality is manifest in different ways and very often in paradoxes (which, given the traditional language of philosophy, is to be expected). For instance, the first sentence of Adorno's *Negative Dialectics* reads as follows:

> Philosophy, which once seemed obsolete, lives on because the moment to realise it was missed.[151]

---

151 Adorno, *Negative Dialectics*, p. 3.

The Holocaust is thus a kind of consequence of the radical *crisis* of European rationality. If we wish to find *causes*, we must return and search in the tradition of European reason for that which remained overlooked until the outbreak of this radical crisis. We must reflect on the European tradition of rationalism. Inasmuch as the starting point of Husserl's critical reflection (*Besinnung*) is crisis, and crisis itself calls for retrospective questioning (*Rückfrage*) aimed at the original establishment and the remembrance thereof, then for Adorno the starting point of a no less critical thinking (*Nachdenken*) is catastrophe. Though Adorno's retrospective questioning is also directed at the "original establishment", which is what he terms the Enlightenment and is basically identical to European rationality (even though its origin resides elsewhere, with Bacon, at the crossover point to myth or in myth itself), this is not in order to resuscitate some original idea but to find in it the "regressive moment" that caused the idea of the Enlightenment to repudiate itself. This does not entail – and in this respect there is an analogy with Husserl, though Adorno is far more radical – rejecting this idea, because freedom is inseparable from enlightened thinking. No, the therapy is more complicated than that. If the Enlightenment does not want definitively to seal its own fate, it must also include in itself a critical reflection upon this "regressive moment".[152] Clearly this does not imply teleology. However, like Husserl, Adorno identifies a crisis leading to catastrophe in the fact that science, as a consequence of its instrumentalisation, has lost its meaning. In this respect Adorno and Horkheimer's *Dialectic of Enlightenment* is the continuation of Husserl's *The Crisis of the European Sciences* through the prism of the event that was the Holocaust, and thus marks the beginning of a radical transformation of philosophical discourse.

The title *Dialectic of Enlightenment* tells us clearly what direction, *pace* Husserl, this *Rückfrage* conducted by Adorno and Horkheimer

---

152 Theodore W. Adorno, Max Horkheimer, *Dialectic of Enlightenment*, trans. E.F.N. Jephcott, Stanford UP, Stanford 2002, p. xvi ("rückläufiges Moment").

will take (the preface is dated May 1944, and the entire volume was published in 1947, which means it came out in the same year as Primo Levi's *If This is a Man*). The Enlightenment of its title is much broader in scope. The word is usually associated with the idea of "progress". However, if this is how we choose to understand it, we are soon brought up short by the following sentence: "The curse of irresistible progress is irresistible regression."[153] From this we glean that, whereas for Husserl crisis is something that appears at a certain moment in history, for Adorno and Horkheimer the *crisis* is the very idea of the Enlightenment in that form in which it has developed up until the present day. The aim of the Enlightenment in the most general sense of the term was to release people from fear and grant them mastery. "Yet the wholly enlightened earth is radiant with triumphant calamity."[154] Or in other (better) words: the cause of the crisis is contained in the very establishment of the idea of enlightenment, i.e. in the very basis from which that rationality evolves in which the "regressive moment" is contained from the start.

Adorno and Horkheimer are at their most provocative and radical when they overthrow the whole idea of a chasm separating myth and (rational) science. An example of this is when they claim that the Enlightenment is mythical fear radicalised,[155] which now emerges in the manifest form of an always latent crisis, right now as we pose the question of "why humanity, instead of entering a truly human state, is sinking into a new kind of barbarism".[156] Another example would be when they say that "the myths which fell victim to the Enlightenment were themselves its own products".[157] This is a paradox only if we cleave to the idea of a discontinuity between myth and reason. If, however, we take reason to mean *explanation*, then myth already

---

[153] Ibid., p. 28 ("unaufhaltsame Regression").
[154] Ibid., p. 1.
[155] Ibid., p. 11.
[156] Ibid., p. iv.
[157] Ibid., p. 5.

fulfils this function, myth is already science (and on the contrary science succumbs to myth, e.g. the "myth of progress"). What is to be achieved through explanation? The answer to this question involves a critical reflection on the "regressive moment" when it shows that the ultimate goal of explaining is to achieve *mastery over nature*.

Just as for Husserl the history of Europe is identical with a certain idea of reason, so the same is true of the *Dialectic of Enlightenment*. However, at the same time the two ideas are virtually incommensurate. For Husserl, science is identical with responsibility for the evidence of cognition, with insight, with an "intrusion" into the essence of the thing itself. However, according to Adorno and Horkheimer, science establishes itself as the attempt to gain dominion over reality by explaining it. The aim of science is to overcome a mythicised world characterised by a fear of nature in its capacity as unfathomable *exterior*, which is why power and knowledge are synonymous (though this is the basis of the tradition of enlightened rationality). Reason is instrumentalised, and this then means that it is not superior to purposes (sovereignty over nature), but is subordinate to them.

Leaving aside the different frameworks, in many respects this analysis of the instrumentalisation of reason builds on Husserl, at times explicitly (Adorno's dissertation was concerned with the transcendence of the noematic object, i.e. it was intended to reveal the implicit "materialism" of phenomenology through the irreducibility of the empirical moment in an intentional relationship). Adorno and Horkheimer cite Husserl and his account of how mathematics gained independence:

> An infinite world, here a world of idealities, is conceived, not as one whose objects become accessible to our knowledge singly, imperfectly, and as it were accidentally, but as one which is attained by a rational, systematically coherent method. In the infinite progression of this method, every object is ultimately attained according to its full being-in-itself (...) Through Galileo's mathematisation of nature, nature itself is idealised under the

guidance of the new mathematics; nature itself becomes – to express it in a modern way – a mathematical manifold (Manningfaltigkeit).[158]

In its way the *Dialectic of Enlightenment* is saying something similar: the Enlightenment establishes only formal rationality because instrumental reason prioritises mathematical formalism and formal logic without reflecting on the goals to be achieved. Thinking becomes an automatic process (it competes with the machine, which it would like to replace[159]). The idea of science is positivistically diminished and becomes indifferent to questions of meaning. The problem is that only questions of meaning mean anything to Man. The world is a gigantic analytical judgement.

However, as I mentioned, the framework is different and this modifies the perspective. According to the *Dialectic of Enlightenment*, the driver of enlightenment is reason, rationality, science as power over nature (the outside), i.e. *Herrschaft* or sovereignty, dominion. However, both the nature without and the nature within, i.e. "human nature", must be mastered in this way. At the same time, reason controlled by reality is rationalisation (the level of the general), to which the individual (or everything particular or specific) must be subordinate: a new collapse into myth, because a universe controlled by general necessity then necessarily appears as *fatum*. Society, too, is "rationalised":

The generality of the ideas developed by discursive logic, power in the sphere of the concept, is built on the foundation of power in reality... Power confronts the individual as the universal, as the reason which informs reality."[160]
The generalisation of instrumental rationality rules here and there.

158 Husserl, *The Crisis*, p. 22.
159 At the very start of his career, Husserl had already subjected the first attempts at the formalisation of logic to the same critique and called for a logic of content.
160 Adorno, Horkheimer, *Dialectics of Enlightenment*, p. 10, 16 ("rückläufiges Momen").

This already anticipates the thesis of *Negative Dialectics* that "the whole is untrue", since the philosophical concepts by which the world is interpreted and that are instruments of power raise the social conditions that justify them to the level of true reality by demanding general recognition (just as only the world as it is re-presented by science is raised to the status of "true world" by means of mathematisation). The idea of the Enlightenment contains the seeds of its own destruction in the form of instrumentalised rationality. This is the "regressive moment", reflections upon which must be embraced by reason if it does not want to seal definitively the fate of the founding idea. In other words, reason must reflect upon its outside-in and not eliminate it by passing it off as something that is "outside" it. (This is Husserl's gesture, a gesture that, one might say, wants to force the "regressive moment" out into the outside). Reason must somehow be true to that which so-called progress destroys. This is because

enlightenment must reflect on itself if humanity is not to be totally betrayed. (...) What is at stake is not conservation of the past but the fulfilment of past hopes.[161]

It is impossible to quit the Enlightenment or to remain within it without reflection. This paradox can only be resolved if historical development understands itself differently, if it follows the path to this other understanding illuminated by the catastrophic culmination of the history of European rationality. One might say that the history of European reason has from the very beginning been controlled by a strange *dialectic* – strange, because it is neither the Hegelian dialectic (the gradual sublation of contradictions on increasingly higher levels of consciousness, or "spiritualisation"), nor it is the Husserlian "dialectic", which in the final analysis is not a dialectics at all

---

161 Ibid, p. xvii.

since empirical history only derives meaning from the perspective of ideal teleology. A strange dialectic indeed... it is difficult so much as to consider it as "movement". Every progress goes hand in hand with regression. The revelation of the beginning reveals the end, overcoming myth is a myth, catastrophe illuminated the *Urstiftung* of rationality as *crisis*. Auschwitz does not mean a return to a point prior to the modern era, but is somehow the moment of just this era. After Auschwitz the mutual "constellation" of culture and barbarism swap places, and this helps us understand the claim that "to write poetry after Auschwitz is barbaric". Without reflection upon the "regressive moment", every example of progress is the progress of barbarism. The assiduous cultivation of culture can only mask the fact that we are once again falling back into barbarism. All this is complicated by the fact that the Holocaust is incomprehensible and unnameable and therefore in the realm of the incommensurable while at the same time being within rationality.

Henceforth Adorno's dialectic will work within a different, "traumatic" temporality. Adorno is uncompromising in this respect and his texts are often accompanied by a complicated network of prolepsis and analepsis (in film language: flashback and flash forward). Take, for example, this aphoristic observation from *Minima Moralia*:

What the Germans have committed is beyond comprehension, even the psychological kind, given that the horror seems to have been perpetrated more as blindly planned and alienated measures (*Schreckmassnahmen*) of terror than as spontaneous gratification. According to the reports of eye-witnesses, the torture and murder were carried out without enthusiasm, and perhaps for that reason went so far beyond all bounds. Nevertheless, the consciousness which would like to withstand the unspeakable sees itself thrown back again and again to the attempt to understand, so that it does not subjectively fall prey to the madness which objectively rules. The thought irresistibly obtrudes that the German horror was something like a revenge taken in advance. The credit system in which everything, even world conquest, can be advanced, determines also the actions which prepared its end and the end of the entire market society, all the way to the suicide of the dictatorship. In the concentration camps and gas chambers the downfall of Germany is, as it were, being discounted (...) At the beginning of German imperialism stands Wagner's *Twilight of the Gods*, the rapturous prophecy of their own doom, whose composition was undertaken simultaneously with the victorious war of 1879. In the same spirit, two years before WW II, the German public saw a film of the downfall of their zeppelin in Lakehurst. Calm, posed, the ship went on its way, only to suddenly plummet straight down. If there remains no way out, then the destructive drive becomes completely indifferent as to what it never firmly established: as to whether it is directed against others or against its own subject.[162]

162 Adorno, *Minima Moralia,* pp. 103–104.

19

Traumatic temporality is that in which the impossibility of experience is experienced, an experience that endures in consciousness as an unassimilable exterior. And so reason, as founded in the enlightenment project, can only be saved if a method is found of reminding us of this experience. For this experience is paralysed, it must be brought to speech within philosophical reflection. Because this reflection moves within the element of concepts, it is necessary that a concept become its *expression* without ceasing to be a concept, i.e. it is essential that it also become an index of its exterior.

Traumatic experience is (the experience of) suffering – *Leiden*. This word, which has many different meanings, is also used by Adorno as the keystone of different registers of reflection. Generally speaking, *Leiden* is the consequence of violence perpetrated against everything individual or other insofar as it is identified as such, i.e. apprehended in re-cognition by intellectual categories and concepts. However, *Leiden* is also experienced by the subject as an identifiable part of rationalised society. *Leiden* ultimately refers to the final solution, to the physical elimination of the unidentifiable exterior. European history is the history of suffering that surpasses identifying thought while at the same time being the last condition for the possibility of the transformation thereof.

Within critical reflection upon itself, conceptual thinking must become an expression of suffering. The crisis of conceptual thinking consists of a misconception (in the case of Hegel) of contradiction as an index of the falsehood of identity, which is why it always left to one side that which escaped it. This explains the necessity for the *negative* dialectic: at the very instant the concept fails, it illuminates that which experience prevented it from expressing, and everything that had been suppressed and rejected by concepts comes to light. In respect of the concept this sedimented exterior is sedimented *Leiden*, and the truth is only articulated by the decaying remains of conceptual thinking.

The basic terms of Adorno's philosophy – experience, nonlinearity, expression and concept – are constellated, as it were, in this way. However, every idea contained within and owing its existence to this constellation has a specific meaning. Each idea refers to a range of others, without the significance of any of these terms being dominant or central. The constellation has no centre or, as Adorno says, in a philosophical text everything should be in the same proximity from the centre. Each moment contains traces of all other moments within itself. From a different perspective, the method by which thought proceeds has no reason for proceeding thus but is legitimised by its outcome.

It is undeniable that *constellation* is a word with a Benjaminian pedigree. An "idea" that is neither illustrative nor immediately communicable since it belongs to a temporality other than historical temporality only makes an appearance if it is possible to organise the concrete fragments, i.e. the elementary elements of phenomena that remain when their false unity is shattered. This is because for Benjamin, "... the value of fragments of thoughts is all the greater the less direct their relationship to the underlying idea."[163] Benjamin thus locates a point of departure from the following paradox: we have to respect the uniqueness of the fragment without projecting it into some kind of whole as a part thereof, because then the unique significance it has as a fragment would be invalidated.[164] (Adorno's "The whole is untrue" points in the same direction.) In Adorno the constellation is intended to offer a glimpse of that which disappears in the concept. It is in its way a complex indexical symbol.[165] The constellation

163 Walter Benjamin, *The Origin of German Tragic Drama. Epistemo-Critical Prologue*, trans. John Osborne, Verso, London and New York 1978, p. 29.
164 Regarding Benjamin's concept of the constellation see especially Takao Tsunekava, "Konfiguratives Denken und Allegorie", in: Klaus Graber, Ludger Rehm (eds.), *Global Benjamin* 1 (Internationaler Walter-Benjamin-Kongress 1992), Fink Verlag, München 1999, p. 192 et seq.
165 Siegfried Kracauer works analogously with the idea of the "ornament". However, it is his *Passagen-Werk* that most approximates to Benjamin's work with fragment. A more remote response can also be found in G. Didi-Huberman, e.g. in *Devant l'image*, Ed. de Minuit, Paris 1990.

illuminates the specific side of the object, the side which to a classifying procedure is either a matter of indifference or a burden. (...) By themselves, constellations represent from without what the concept has cut away within: the 'more' which the concept is equally desirous and incapable of being. By gathering around the object of cognition, the concepts potentially determine the object's interior. They attain, in thinking, what was necessarily excised from thinking. (...) Instead, what is indissoluble in any previous thought context transcends its seclusion in its own, as nonidentical. It communicates with that from which it was separated by the concept. It is opaque only for identity's claim to be total; it resists the pressure of that claim. But as such it seeks to be audible. Whatever part of nonidentity defies definition in its concept goes beyond its individual existence; it is only in polarity with the concept, in staring at the concept, that it will contract into that existence. The inside of nonidentity is its relation to that which it is not, and which its managed, frozen self-identity withholds from it. (...) The object opens itself to a monadological insistence, to a sense of the constellation in which it stands; the possibility of internal immersion requires that externality. (...) Becoming aware of the constellation in which a thing stands is tantamount to deciphering the constellation which, having come to be, it bears within it. The chorismos of without and within is historically qualified in turn. (...) As a constellation, theoretical thought circles the concept it would like to unseal, hoping that it may fly open like the lock of a well guarded safe-deposit box: in response, not to a single key or a single number, but to a combination of numbers."[166]

However, Adorno's *Nachstiftung*, the new establishment of conceptual thinking as thinking in constellations, has radical implications. Philosophy does not resign itself to systematic interpretation. Instead, interpretation now has a strange and unique architecture that is described very effectively by Hermann Broch at the beginning of *The Sleepwalkers* (in the episode dated 1888, though the novel was

---

166 Adorno, *Negative Dialectics*, p. 3.

written between 1928 and 1932, almost in parallel with Husserl's *The Crisis of European Sciences*), when Joachim von Pasenow is assailed by the feeling that "some pillar or other of life had become shaky, and though everything still remained in its old place, because the parts reciprocally supported each other, yet along with a vague wish that the vaulted arch of this equilibrium might cave in and entomb beneath it all that was tottering and uncertain..."[167]

---

[167] Hermann Broch, *The Sleepwalkers*, trans. Willa and Edwin Muir, Vintage, New York 1966, p. 11. This image probably finds its origin in Heinrich von Kleist's letter of 16 November 1800 to Wilhelmine von Zenge: "Engrossed in my thoughts I returned via the arched gate to the city. Why, I wondered does the arch not collapse given that it is not supported by anything? It remains standing, I answered, because *all the blocks want to come tumbling down upon each other.*" Kleist also used the image in the tragic drama *Penthesilea*, v. 1348–9.

20

That which is only hinted at in Husserl is made explicit in Adorno, beginning with the *Dialectic of Enlightenment*, namely that critical theory tracks rationality from the start of its journey to the catastrophe that is its shocking, traumatising outcome. This outcome is shocking and traumatising because it is irrational. The only possible philosophical response is relentless self-reflexive thinking.

> Having broken its pledge to be as one with reality or at the point of realisation, philosophy is obliged ruthlessly to criticise itself.[168]

If philosophy is not in agreement with reality because that which is real (the traumatising reality of the Holocaust) is not rational, and that which would appear to be reasonable is clearly not real, then the prerequisite of the identity of thinking (rational "science" in the sense in which Hegel uses this word) and being is unsustainable because it is refuted by reality. Reflection upon the genuine history of rationality opens the way to criticism of the basic condition of classical ontology. If *Dialectic of Enlightenment* responds to this reflection (analogously to Husserl's *Besinnung*) with a request for self-criticism on the part of reason, then one of the central themes of *Dialectic of Enlightenment* is self-criticism on the part of the concept[169], which discovers in Hegel's positive dialectic the possibility of negative dialectic. The aim will not be to hypostasise the concept of the non-conceptual, but rather to show that the non-conceptual moment is the guarantor of the *material* congruity of the concept (its *Sachhaltigkeit*, or substantiality), and that it must therefore also be a measure of such thinking that, precisely for material reasons, relinquishes the classical claim to "totality".

---

168 Adorno, *Negative Dialectics*, p. 3.
169 Ibid, p. 136.

The thoughts of transcendental apperception or of Being could satisfy philosophers as long as they found those concepts identical with their own thoughts. Once we dismiss such identity in principle, the peace of the concept as an Ultimate will be engulfed in the fall of the identity. Since the basic character of every general concept dissolves in the face of distinct entity, a total philosophy is no longer to be hoped for.[170]

At this juncture it is worth nothing that Adorno often calls as witness Samuel Beckett and his *Endgame*:

Hence interpretation of Endgame cannot pursue the chimerical aim of expressing the play's meaning in a form mediated by philosophy. Understanding it can mean only understanding its unintelligibility, concretely reconstructing the meaning of the fact that it has no meaning.
After the Second World War, everything, including a resurrected culture, has been destroyed without realizing it; humankind continues to vegetate, creeping along after events that even the survivors cannot really survive, on a rubbish heap that has made even reflection on one's own damaged state useless.[171]

It is from this seed that Adorno's *Negative Dialectic* gradually grows. It is notoriously "difficult", not least because it features a particular "composition" (the musical term is entirely appropriate in this case):

Ideas should be driven to testify not by the logical necessity of systematically organised arguments, but by the configuration of moments within their context... Philosophy is not essentially "referencable"... Adorno's language is dramatically escalated, as though catastrophe or salvation depended on

---

170 Ibid., p. 136; cf. Theodor W. Adorno, *Ontologie und Dialektik (1960/61)*, ed. Rolf Tiedemann, Suhrkamp, Frankfurt/M. 2008, pp. 325–326.
171 Theodor W. Adorno, *Noten zur Literatur*, Suhrkamp, Frankfurt a.M. 1981, pp. 283 and 286.

the completely minute movement of thought. His guiding principle is exaggeration.[172]

If we return to the quote from the beginning of *Negative Dialectic*, it becomes clear that the "negativity" of the dialectic refers to nothing more than the necessity of integrating the outside inside, without this meaning that the resulting whole is ever an enclosed whole.

The promise that philosophy (thinking, reason) is/will be at one with reality is contradicted by the fact that the concepts by which reality was/is to be understood *diverge in an irreducible way* from reality. The idea that thinking would one day be able (conceptually) to grasp reality in its entirety (with no remainder) is not only unsustainable, but dangerous, because it postulates that cognitive reason is (in the final analysis) identical with the order that it reveals in reality, i.e. that reality is rational along the lines of rational thinking inasmuch as it postulates the identity of thinking and being. However, this means that the assumption that establishes the Enlightenment version of reason must be subject to criticism, and the irreconcilability of concept and thing must be borne in mind. The promise that enlightenment reason made (in the sense of the *Dialectic of Enlightenment*, i.e. Western philosophy) is broken in the most shattering way in the complete and utter irrationality of the Holocaust, an event that is incomprehensible by reason that was played out *within* a history that was thought to be leading towards the definitive permeation of reality by reason.

The contours now become clearer of that revealed by the analysis of the genesis of enlightenment and instrumental reason undertaken in *Dialectic of Enlightenment*. The concept that "identifies" a thing also violates it (the thing "suffers" identification) and reveals that the driving force of conceptual thinking is *power*, namely the

172 *Interpretationen. Hauptwerke der Philosophie. 20. Jahrhundert*, Reclam, Stuttgart 1992; Dieter Birnbacher, "Negative Dialektik" pp. 336–337.

attempt to control and eliminate the uncontrollable. Not even Marx escapes censure. In his *Lectures on Negative Dialectics* Adorno says that, for Marx too, the unlimited control of man over nature is beyond question, which is why his dream of a classless society is akin to a giant joint-stock company for the exploitation of nature.[173] The remedy to this situation must be just as remorseless, but at the expense of the concept, the system, and the act of identification (i.e. the belittlement of a unique entity by means of a general concept), at the expense of systematic, controlling, totalising thinking that forbids anything to remain outside. The task is to protect this outside.

Adorno's philosophy, i.e. his *negative* dialectic, is thus on the boundary of the modern and postmodern. It is about rescuing the "modern" (the idea of the Enlightenment) through a reinterpretation of it that takes the form of a certain overthrow: "...consummate negativity, once squarely faced, delineates the mirror-image of its opposite"[174] This would be the elementary form of the *search for traces of the possibility of another modernist project within modernism itself.* The authors who emerged in the 1960s differed from Adorno in that they were operating *on the other side* of this boundary (Lyotard, Levinas, Derrida, Blanchot, Agamben et al.)[175]

But why should this involve *another modernist project*? Because it involves the search for a different rationality to that which was not only unable to prevent the Holocaust, but actually made it possible, while acknowledging that reason cannot be surrendered. It is

---

173 Theodor W. Adorno, *Vorlesung über Negative Dialektik. Fragmente zur Vorlesung 1965/66*, ed. Rolf Tiedemann, Suhrkamp, Frankfurt a.M. 2008, p. 89. *Lectures on Negative Dialectics: Fragments of a Lecture Course 1965/1966*, Polity Press, Cambridge 2008, p. 89.
174 Adorno, *Minima Moralia*, p. 247.
175 Perhaps as (from the perspective of "postmodernism") *post-metaphysical thinking*. In the case of Adorno is it relatively clear: it is the consequence of the maximum tightening of modern concepts to their limit (which is how he treats Hegel); pushing modern and classical philosophical concepts to their limit. Openness also means going beyond these limits. In philosophy it is therefore necessary to protect something from the system, namely that phenomena create coherence objectively, and not only on the basis of the classification to which the cognising subject subordinates them.

therefore essential to find the traces of another reason *within* rationality itself. This is clearly the sense of the passage from *Minima Moralia* quoted above ("mirror-writing of its opposite"). Reflections upon history should reveal the *traces* of another modernism, or, as Husserl might put it, should be a recollection of its original primary establishment. This is a good way of interpreting Adorno's *negative dialectic*. Philosophy is thinking in concepts. It emerges from the act of identification (the recognition of the individual by means of the concept). However, the underbelly of the act of identification is that something inevitably leaves its *trace* in it, something that resists identification, something unidentifiable, i.e. the outside in relation to the identifying concept. Adorno calls this *das Nicht-identische* or non-identical. (And for that reason the "other" modernism referred to above would be unidentifiable within the context of the historical since its traces would only be visible later.) This reflection allows us to perceive in the act of identification the *exercise of power* (the acquisition of knowledge for the purpose of control, *Herrschaftswissen*), and thus the fundamental ambivalence of modern rationality. Furthermore, insofar as only one aspect of rationality prevails, namely that of power, we also perceive in that rationality the basis of the catastrophe of reason: the dominion of that claim to power that leads to rationality in the form of instrumental reason. Or to put it another way: rigorous reflection will lead us to recognise the disregard paid to ambivalence, the disregard paid to the *dialectic* of the Enlightenment. According to Adorno, this neglect can only be confronted or remedied by dialectical reason, regarding which he states very "dialectically" in *Minima Moralia*:

Dialectical reason is, when set against the dominant mode of reason, unreason: only in encompassing and cancelling this mode does it become reasonable.[176]

176 Adorno, *Minima Moralia*, pp. 72–73.

We therefore need to examine in detail what Adorno means by "dialectical". In the lectures *Einführung in die Dialektik* of 1958 Adorno offers the following explanation: the concept must be appropriate to the thing, it should be the *expression* of the thing, since concepts are formed through their confrontation with that which they "conceive". This means that

> The dialectic is indeed a method which refers to the proces of thinking, but it also differs from other methods insofar as it constantly strives not to stand still, constantly corrects itself in the presence of the things themselves. We could define dialectic as a kind of thinking which does not content itself merely with the order of concepts but, rather, undertakes to correct the conceptual order by reference to the being of the objects themselves (...). Dialectic is the method of thinking which is not merely a method, but the attempt to overcome the merely arbitrary character of method and to admit into the concept that which is not itself concept.[177]

The word "dialectic" implicitly presupposes that thought equals conceptual thinking. However, the concept must be appropriate to the thing. The concept should be an explanation of the thing and therefore the thing must (constantly) correct itself, because concepts are formed through their conflict with that which they "apprehend". The concept should not overcome the resistance of the thing (which is the struggle of instrumental reason serving "control"), but should unfold by means of this resistance. Though Adorno's concept of dialectic is clearly inspired by Hegel, it represents a muscular reinterpretation, since Hegel's dialectic assumes, in the last instance, the absolute identity of all designations thus obtained about the thing. This is why in the end Hegel's dialectic assumes a whole in which all of the thing's resistance has been annulled and the concept and the thing become as one (truth is the whole, the outcome; this is the

---

177 Theodor W. Adorno, *Einführung in die Dialektik (1958)*, ed. Ch. Ziermann, *Nachgelassene Schriften*, IV: Vorlesungen, 2, Suhrkamp, Frankfurt a.M. 2010, pp. 10–11.

significance of the term "totality" used by Adorno). For Adorno, on the other hand, the meaning of the dialectic derives from the fact that the "dialectic of the concept" is placed in opposition to the traditional ontology of the highest categories (the defining attribute of which is timelessness, immutability, a constant structure[178]), in other words that the concept must follow its thing, it must forever compare itself with what it intends (the "intention" of the concept), and it must do this in such a way that a difficulty (*Schwierigkeiten*) emerges between the concept and the thing that obliges us to change this concept during the process of thinking (without its being necessary to relinquish earlier designations): the divergence of concept and thing, *Begriff und Sache auseinandertreten*. Adorno's dialectic is characterised by the *priority granted the object*.

> Perhaps I may add here that what motivated me personally to turn to dialectics in a decisive sense is precisely this micrological motif, namely the idea that if we only abandon ourselves unreservedly to the compulsion exercised by a particular object, by a particular matter, and pursue this single and specific matter unreservedly, then the ensuing movement is itself so determined out of the matter that it possesses the character of truth even if the Absolute, as an all-embracing totality, can never be given to us.[179]

It should now be clear why Adorno refers specifically to "negative" dialectics. Firstly, something is revealed in this movement, something substantive (*Sachhaltiges*), something that *is not identical* with thinking. Secondly, this movement is inexorable, it can never be

---

178 Adorno, *Lectures on Negative Dialectics*, p. 40: "Thinking would be a form of thinking that is not itself a system, but one in which system and the systematic impulse are consumed; a form of thinking that in its analysis of individual phenomena demonstrates the power that formerly aspired to build systems. By this I mean the power that is liberated by blasting open individual phenomena through the insistent power of thought. This power is the same power that once animated the system, since it is the force which enabled individual phenomena, non-identical with their own concepts as they are, to become more than themselves."
179 Theodor W. Adorno, *Einführung in die Dialektik (1958)*; idem, *An Introduction to Dialectics*, trans. Nicholas Walker, Polity Press, Cambridge 2017, p. 21.

terminated. From which we may conclude (*pace* Hegel's phenomenology of spirit): *the whole is untrue*. The form in which we think of the thing is not the form of the thought thing itself. Dialectical thinking is the consequence. It is a sustained critique of those very concepts with which thinking works conceptually. It must forever act with the concept in the name of the concept.[180]

Perhaps, therefore, we are justified in claiming that Adorno is on a quest to find the traces of a different modernist project, the traces of a different rationality. The first trace: *Begriff und Sache auseinandertreten*, or the divergence of concept and thing. This is virtually the "fundament" of the different thinking that will appear in a variety of forms, especially in *thinking of and from difference*. And here we find a second important trace: reason (rationality) is intrinsically linked with the *idea of justice*, since it is about constantly being true to the thing as apprehended by the concept, while justice is the knowledge of the irreducibility of the non-identical moment, i.e. it is the unrealisable extent of the reality of our thinking.[181]

Thinking that is not measured against the idea of justice cannot prevent something like the Holocaust: nay, it bears responsibility for Auschwitz. It is thinking that eliminates, annihilates the outside, to oversimplify matters somewhat. In negative dialectics the outside is in a certain sense both outside and inside, inasmuch as truth is both a process and the outcome of this process that, however, is *open*, open for and to the outside.[182]

And here is where we find the third trace, namely the priority granted the object in negative dialectics. Everything (recognition,

---

180 According to Adorno a version of this traditional ontology is Heidegger's use of "existentiells", i.e. categories by which the "structure of the being of Dasein" can be described.

181 Jacques Derrida: deconstruction is justice, because justice cannot be converted to law, "there is always a remainder", c.f. *Force of Law* et al.

182 In his essay on Eichendorff, a poet in the tradition of German idealism, Adorno cites a passage in which Eichendorff reproaches the whole of post-Kantian philosophy for omitting everything dark, dissonant, i.e. that which cannot emerge in the glow of rationalism, the moment of the "irrational" (*An Introduction to Dialectics*, p. 37) as the ground of *another* thinking that implies a different *rationality*.

the articulation of experience) takes place in the element of thinking, but always with reference to the real (contemporary) world. Negative dialectics is the path to the articulation (expression) of the experience of the fundamental *historicity of the world*. In reality it is nothing more than *Bewegtes und Werdendes*, or movement and becoming; history (real history), i.e.the events of a world in which the same is constantly becoming its own other, its own antithesis, takes priority over being. The price paid for failing to understand and act upon this is what the critical theorists of the Frankfurt School (inspired by Lukacs) termed reification (*Verdinglichung*).

These three "traces" are artfully woven together so as to bring out their mutual implications by Roger Foster in his book *Adorno: The Recovery of Experience*, when he writes:

> This failure opens a breach within immanence, in which the transcendent appears within it as what cannot be said (and therefore as external to concepts). What Adorno calls the 'unfreedom' of philosophy is its dependence on historical experience, which, in turn, is not the idealist story of a self-realising subject, but rather the subordination to 'nature', by which Adorno means that it is driven by blind, nonrational forces. But because interpretation retains the striving of thought to say the unsayable, even though it is impossible within current experience, it maintains the possibility of redemption in the form of hope. It is therefore the constant exertion of thought to say what it cannot say that preserves the transcendent within thinking.[183]

The divergence of thing and concept monitored and elaborated on by negative dialectics can in simple terms be expressed thus: there is never any *equivalence* between the concept and the thing. However, this very fact reveals – *ex negativo* – equivalence as a basic tool of a controlling knowledge, of instrumental rationality: equivalence is the original principle of conceptual thinking that, through

183 Roger Foster, *Adorno: The Recovery of Experience*. State University of New York Press, New York 2007, p. 84.

the identification of the particular by means of the concept, *levels off* the diverse as non-identical: identificatory thought is thought in equivalents (of things themselves) – the word *Gleichschaltung* is not far off. And so like goods, something like a construct emerges by means of abstraction from qualities and use value (reduction to an exchange value that allows for the comparability of the incomparable), and so the most diverse realities are comparable whensoever they are mediated by a concept. Total convertibility permits nature to become controllable (the result on the level of society is "the abstract monotony of the administered world", according to *Negative Dialectics*).[184] Adorno of course adopts the concept of general equivalence from Marx's analysis of the function of money,[185] but generalises it and in particular elicits further consequences from it: philosophical expression seeks to communicate something that is *outside* the plane of convertibility (it is not tied to "existing relations") and must therefore reflect the method by which it is expressed. The philosophical text must be capable of communicating a philosophically articulated experience of reality – of being its "equivalent", albeit incommutable: it will help that which has no equal to itself to find expression. So again the problem of justice arises and with it a question: *how not to speak of the Holocaust*, to paraphrase Derrida.

Perhaps this would suffice to legitimise the assumption that thinking after Auschwitz cannot be understood as a break with

---

184 Adorno, *Negative Dialectics*, p. 6.
185 Nevertheless, mention is made of the principle of equivalence even by Georg Simmel: "money, with its colourlessness and its indifferent quality, can become a common denominator of all values, it becomes the frightful leveller – it hollows out the core of things, their peculiarities, their specific values and their uniqueness and incomparability in a way which is beyond repair. They all float with the same specific gravity in the constantly moving stream of money. They all rest on the same level and are distinguished only by their amounts. In individual cases this colouring, or rather this de-colouring of things, through their equation with money, may be imperceptibly small. In the relationship, however, which the wealthy person has to objects which can be bought for money, perhaps indeed in the total character which, for this reason, public opinion now recognises in these objects, it takes on very considerable proportions." Georg Simmel, *The Metropolis and Mental Life*, Blackwell, Oxford 2002, p. 16.

modernism but as a search for the traces of a different project of modernity. The discovery of these traces leads to the transformation of philosophical discourse. *Identificatory thinking* in its capacity as eliminatory thinking, the deconstruction of which leads to a situation in which an *other rationality* is revealed in it, is the basic characteristic of modernist thinking, i.e. that against which philosophy of the latter half of the 20th century turns.

Adorno's *negative dialectics* slot perfectly into this context because his texts, by virtue of their style and their relationship to conceptual thinking and systematicity, exemplify the transformation of philosophical discourse. In order to demonstrate this I would like to take a typical passage from *Negative Dialectics*.

A new categorical imperative has been imposed by Hitler upon unfree mankind: to arrange their thoughts and actions so that Auschwitz will not repeat itself, so that nothing similar will happen. When we want to find reasons for it, this imperative is as refractory as the given one of Kant was once upon a time. Dealing discursively with it would be an outrage, for the new imperative gives us a bodily sensation of the moral addendum – bodily, because it is now the practical abhorrence of the unbearable physical agony to which individuals are exposed even with individuality about to vanish as a form of mental reflection. It is in the unvarnished materialistic motive only that morality survives.

The course of history forces materialism upon metaphysics, traditionally the direct antithesis of materialism. What the mind once boasted of defining or construing as its like moves in the direction of what is unlike the mind, in the direction of that which eludes the rule of the mind and yet manifests that rule as absolute evil. The somatic, unmeaningful stratum of life is the stage of suffering, of the suffering which in the camps, without any consolation, burned every soothing feature out of the mind, and out of culture, the mind's objectification.[186]

186 Adorno, *Negative Dialectics*, p. 365–366.

The formulation of this idea is characteristically complicated. Our understanding of it depends on our finding in it a figure outlined by the relations between individual moments. It is to be found in Part 3, "Models", of which it is the third, entitled "Meditations on metaphysics", which begins with the "section" (though Adorno does not sectionalise but uses brief indications in the form of headers) "After Auschwitz". We can therefore read this as "metaphysics after Auschwitz", though if metaphysics is traditionally *prima philosophia* or "ontology", then we can also read it as *philosophy after Auschwitz*. However, Adorno's "meditation" is upon the impossibility of ontology after Auschwitz (in the sense that philosophy after Auschwitz must be different and must rest on foundations other than traditional or modern philosophy consisting of metaphysics and ontology). The word "meditation" is deliberately ambiguous inasmuch as the best known "meditation", i.e. Descartes', (re)laid the foundations of modern systematic ontology or metaphysics.

Adorno advocates thinking in models rather than thinking in a system ("thinking after Auschwitz" is a kind of *model analysis*). How should we understanding "model"? In the introduction to *Negative Dialectics* under the heading "Argument and Experience" Adorno offers a general critique of *Systemphilosophie*, which is based on a given intellectual order (categories and first principles, i.e. the tradition of Aristotelian *prima philosophia*), into which intellectual content is inserted. However, this method eliminates its "own content": the thought as bearer of (real) experience is subjected to regimentation. For this reason the opposite applies: the unregimented idea is by elective affinities connected with the dialectic that as criticism of the system reminds us of that which is outside the system. The force that in the act of cognition releases the dialectical movement is the force that revolts against the system.[187] Models (in the plural) replace system (always in the singular). What

187 Cf. ibid., p. 31.

is fundamental in models is the "force field" that arises through the configuration of moments that, like iron filings in a magnetic field, create a certain "figure" on their surface, an "image" that is its own "content" and that refers to the experience that the model is to apprehend. For this reason, too, the *essay* is the privileged form of philosophical discourse for Adorno:

> It is not so much that the essay neglects indubitable certainty as that it abrogates it as an ideal. The essay becomes true in its progress, which drives it beyond itself, not in a treasure-hunting obsession with foundations. Its concepts receive their light from a *terminus ad quem* hidden from the essay itself, not from any obvious *terminus a quo*, and in this the method itself expresses its utopian intention. All its concepts are to be presented in such a way that they support one another, that each becomes articulated through its configuration with the others. In the essay discrete elements set off against one another come together to form a readable context; the essay erects no scaffolding and no structure. But the elements crystallize as a configuration through their motion. The constellation is a force field, just as every intellectual structure is necessarily transformed into a force field under the essay's gaze.[188]

The basis of the *discourse* of traditional philosophy must be the "system", since the idea cannot be contingent, but necessary, i.e. *binding* in some way – this guarantees its place in the system. However, if the (negative) dialectic represents thinking that reflects traces of the resisting exterior of the system, then its presentational form (*Darstellungsform*) cannot be a systematic interpretation, though this does not make it "unbinding". And again we find ourselves at the "model":

---

[188] Adorno, *Noten zur Literatur*, p. 21.

The call for binding statements without a system is a call for thought models (...) A model covers the specific, and more than the specific, without letting it evaporate in its more general super-concept. Philosophical thinking is the same as thinking in models; negative dialectics is an ensemble of analyses of models.

Regarding this binding quality Adorno adds:

(T)he stringency (*Stringenz*) of a philosophical thought requires its mode of proceeding (Adorno is careful to avoid the word "method") to be measured by the forms of inference. Philosophical proof is the effort to give statements a binding quality by making them commensurable with the means of discursive thinking.[189]

Expression, i.e. the attempt to express experience, is the deictic field, i.e. the field open towards the outside. On the one hand, it is the "rhetorical moment" (concretising, individualising, specifying), and on the other the "mimetic moment" (the concept is shaped by that which it wants to apprehend). Philosophical *Darstellung* or *presentation* is the objectivisation of this entirety.

After this localisation it also is possible to define the introductory quote under the heading "Metaphysics and Culture" in the third part of *Negative Dialectics* in light of its context. The immediately preceding considerations headed "After Auschwitz" clearly show that, for Adorno, Auschwitz is a fundamental event to which he must devote his thinking if he is not to part company with his own presence, i.e. "reality". His criticism of "metaphysics" or "ontology" now becomes implicitly understandable: it is essential we revise our relationship to god, freedom, immortality, etc. as *eternal* ideas guaranteeing the intelligibility of that which we encounter. Above all, we must review the claim that truth equals "permanence" and

---

189 Adorno, *Negative Dialectics*, p. 64.

transience (history) equals appearance. This is something that leads to the "binding character" as the criterion of another rationality that differs from the "necessity" of the system – the rationally *non-legitimisable* is clearly that which is emotionally intolerable by virtue of being unbearable. This means that Auschwitz did not only destroy, but, on the contrary, revealed the emotional basis of rationality – the attempt to lend genocide some kind of meaning by means of interpreting it already *feels* completely irrational. To do so is to perpetrate violence against its victims (whence the feeling of guilt of its survivors). The feeling is something that points to the non-conceptual in that which we are attempting to apprehend.

And in this respect Auschwitz is the "model", an event that cannot be subsumed or classified without remainder under some rational principle. Not even a simple causal principle suffices. The task is *to research the entire web of conditioning factors through which (by means of reflection) the contours of a different thinking will hopefully shine through.*

Adorno's description of the situation is as follows:

> The administrative murder of millions made of death a thing one had never yet to fear in just this fashion. There is no chance anymore for death to come into the individuals' empirical life as somehow conformable with the course of that life. The last, the poorest possession left to the individual is expropriated. That in the concentration camps it was no longer an individual who died, but a specimen – this is a fact bound to affect the dying of those who escaped the administrative measure.
>
> Genocide is the absolute integration. It is on its way wherever men are levelled off – "polished off", as the German military called it – until one exterminates them literally, as deviations from the concept of their total nullity.[190]

190 Adorno, *Negative Dialectics*, p. 362.

Adorno describes the event that was Auschwitz in such a way that it becomes clear in his description (which quite deliberately omits concrete "facts") how in this event the basic tendency of instrumental rationality (administration, *Verwaltung*), as well as the *systematic* thinking associated with it, becomes reality, and by doing so points to something that could roughly be called "the conditions of the possibility of Auschwitz in modern rationality". His description is also interesting in that it takes us to the very boundary of abstraction (the philosophical concept of identity, the paradigm genus-species, the basic themes of his negative dialectics), and it is precisely in this way that his thinking touches upon something concrete, namely that the outcome of the system is the extermination of the individual. And so the "concept" (e.g. the concept of the "theory of knowledge", the concept of "identity") disintegrates completely. It becomes unsustainable, its origin in "power" (administration, *Verwaltung*) exposed. And this in turn takes us back to the introductory quote:

A new categorical imperative has been imposed by Hitler upon unfree mankind: to arrange their thoughts and actions so that Auschwitz will not repeat itself, so that nothing similar will happen. When we want to find reasons for it, this imperative is as refractory as the given one of Kant was once upon a time. Dealing discursively with it would be an outrage, for the new imperative gives us a bodily sensation of the moral addendum – bodily, because it is now the practical abhorrence of the unbearable physical agony to which individuals are exposed even with individuality about to vanish as a form of mental reflection. It is in the unvarnished materialistic motive only that morality survives.

The course of history forces materialism upon metaphysics, traditionally the direct antithesis of materialism. What the mind once boasted of defining or construing as its like moves in the direction of what is unlike the mind, in the direction of that which eludes the rule of the mind and yet manifests that rule as absolute evil. The somatic, unmeaningful stratum of life is the stage of suffering, of the suffering which in the camps, without any consolation, burned every soothing feature out of the mind, and out of culture, the mind's objectification.

What we observe here (at least on the level of "discourse") is a striking use of rhetoric as a form of argument (Hitler imposed a new imperative upon people by virtue of the fact that what he caused became unacceptable): something positive emerges from a rejection of the existing. Adorno takes interpretation to be something like the practice of resistance (in language itself) to communicative tendencies. This is another reason why Adorno's text is always more process than thesis.

1. The reason why it is necessary "to arrange [our] thoughts and actions so that Auschwitz will not repeat itself, so that nothing similar will happen", is not a reason in the sense of a principle from which something (a certain kind of conduct) necessarily ensues, but a physical resistance to something factual, which is why it cannot be established "discursively". What is essential is *das Hinzutretende* or the addendum (the moment that must accede). However, this is also *das Austretende* or escape, because it deflects us from the order of principles on the basis of which we are to act. A large theme in Derrida's deconstruction of justice: to act in accordance with a prescription cannot be "good".

2. That which "accedes" in this way and allows for the boundaries of the system (clearly distinguishing between exterior and interior) to be breached is the "body" (the rejected outside inside). If instrumental reason eliminates individuality, which it reduces to that which is convertible from the individual subjected to *Gleichschaltung*, or unification, then only the physical feeling remains (irreducible precisely because it is physical, i.e. beyond the reach of the "spirit") of suffering as the site of resistance to "power" (whether this be the power of the concept or the power of the administrative world, etc.). "It is in the unvarnished materialistic motive only that morality survives." (We also encounter this motif in Lyotard.)

3. Another formulation of the "priority of the object" over the subject thinking it: the response to Auschwitz must be "other thinking", because the traditional (modern) is *somatically* intolerable.

4. This is how identity thinking itself is problematised ("what the spirit produces as being equal to it" is that from which we always escape *physically*). It is disjointed into its exterior, to that which is dissimilar to it, which is the body. Though the body is outside inside, it is also something that is in real history, so that it is impossible to conceptualise history as something external to bodily anchored thought. But this "outside" is that in which the dominion of the spirit still *exclusively* appears in its true form, i.e. as controlling *power*, as "evil".

This was how the whole of modern culture was destroyed in the concentration camps (the site of unbearable physical suffering), a culture that had until that moment been able to conceal the fact that its paradigm of cognition (science, philosophy) resided in violence perpetrated against that which it re-cognised.

The imperative thus formulated is already an "other rationality". It cannot be justified, firstly because it is beyond the order of justification, and secondly because its origin resides in concrete history, i.e. concrete, real historical events and our reflection thereon, reflection that is at the same time the self-reflection of reason. Not, therefore, the necessity of system, but historical necessity: *there is nothing left but to...*, *I can do nothing else but...*. On the very boundary of the concept *we have no choice but to* transcend the *boundary of the concept*.

In other words, this quote reveals Adorno's relationship to the philosophical concept in general, and in this particular case to the concept of "metaphysics" and to the associated concept of the "theory of knowledge" within the framework of a certain concept of the "system" and the postulate/concept of "identity" (the identity of thinking and being, or of thinking identifying the thought thing). The concept is confronted with historical reality in the latter's instrumentally irredeemable experience in the body. It thus comes face to face with its own boundary, from which that which is "enshrined" in it is suddenly illuminated, and this then allows for the entire system in which these concepts are arranged to be transcended. Adorno himself describes this very precisely in the essay *Zur Metakritik der Erkenntnistheorie* (which begins as a critique of Husserl's phenomenology)

> Even the decaying concepts of epistemology point beyond themselves. Right up to their highest formalisms and, before that, in their miscarriages, they are to be rescued as a bit of unconscious transcription of history. For they must be helped to procure self-consciousness against what they explicitly mean. This salvation, mindfulness of the suffering that sedimented itself in concepts, waits for the moment of their ruin. It is the idea of philosophical critique. It has no other measure than the ruin of illusion. ... It is time not for first philosophy but last philosophy.[191]

Here we also see the influence of Walter Benjamin and his essay *The Origin of German Tragic Drama*. The world of the baroque poet is located in the chasm between a fallen world and salvation.[192] *Ratio* is unable to create the concept of reality as a whole. What is left are the ruins of the philosophical system, and philosophy's task is to interpret and arrange these fragments. As soon as the ruination is clear, the truth content of systematic philosophy is revealed, as Adorno wrote in his lectures of 1964/65, in which Benjamin's concept of allegorical interpretation appears in the form of a "deep allegorical insight" (*allegorischer Tiefblick*).[193] But he has already arrived at this point in his interpretation of Husserl:

---

191 Theodor W. Adorno, *Against Epistemology. A Metacritique*, trans. Willis Domingo, Polity Press, pp. 39–40.
192 Foster, *Adorno: The Recovery of Experience*, p. 78.
193 Adorno, *Vorlesung über die negative Dialektik*, p. 188. See the commentary by Foster, *Adorno: The Recovery of Experience*, p. 79.

The concept of natural history does not appear in this passage gratuitously. Husserl believes he is giving a phenomenology of spirit by presenting and cataloguing its cabinet of natural history specimens. Just as in natural history museums, relics of vanished life are assembled into a collection and put on show, though 'nature' in these specimens just allegorically means past history, and their history is nothing other than a simple natural pastness (Vergängnis) – so there is also a phenomenological exhibit of its 'excursions', which has to do with fossils and fossilized syntheses whose 'intentional life' faintly reflects the past-real.[194]

By plucking its items from existence and historical change, phenomenology deadens them (the ideals of the bourgeois era as relics), but at the moment of the fall – the crisis – theoretical creations allow for a glimpse of their utopian impulse, whence is born the endeavour to protect such a form of knowledge that would be an expression of the world of things.[195]

Philosophical thought that can be reduced to its bare bones or net profit is useless. The superficiality of many philosophical works that take no account of this is more than just aesthetic insufficiency: it is an index of their own falsehood. Wherever a philosophical idea, in the most important texts, lags behind the ideal of unremitting renewal, it is defeated. To think philosophically means to think the intermittent, to be disturbed by that which is not thought itself. In vigorous thinking the analytical judgement that must inevitably be used becomes untrue. The power of thinking so as to swim against one's own current is the power of resistance to that which has already been thought. Proper thinking requires civil courage.[196]

194 Adorno, *Against Epistemology*, p. 217.
195 Cf. Foster, *Adorno: The Recovery of Experience*, p. 110.
196 Theodor W. Adorno, "Anmerkungen zum philosophichen Denken", *GS* 10.2 (Kulturkritik und Gesellschaft), pp. 603–604 (trans. here by Phil Jones).

It is necessary to push the antagonism of concepts to the very boundary of that which they are still capable of saying and to subordinate concepts of the theory of knowledge to the "logic of disintegration". In this way, concepts operate as an expression of the experience that permits this theory of knowledge (the separation of subject and object). The concepts come to a halt and become images. They begin to attest to the experience enshrined within them. They are as intelligible as the surface upon which the whole is legible in the figure as it is created by the interpretation of its elements.

This is also a procedure not without a certain proximity to Bergson,[197] and this is important, for instance, in relation to Deleuze. According to Bergson, perception is the selection of the instrumentally useful features of a thing that allows for the commensurability of the non-identical. Perception is structured *habit* (habitual responses to stimuli), and habit is the plane from which general ideas emerge, including concepts (the concept is a habit rising up from the sphere of action into the realm of thought). Perception, which consists of "habitual memory", is placed in opposition to pure memory: though habitual memory dominates in each current experience, the experience is always tinged by the *entire* memory. In light of Adorno's deconstruction of the concept, we can say, à la Bergson, that beneath the concepts that it is possible to "dilate", i.e. expand into ever larger circles that contextualise the concept in question by means of its "memory" in such a way that the concept begins to be dissolved and that which is otherwise retraced beneath the instrumental organisation of perception (the encounter with reality) shines through it. In this way the boundary between habitual response (a sensomo-

---

197 Foster, *Adorno: The Recovery of Experience*. Cf. Adorno's reformulation of Bergson's "intuition": "Only lightning bolts of knowledge are saturated with memory and prescience. Official and 'obligatory' knowledge (...) fall as such directly out of time and memory. The cogniser is overwhelmed at the moment of intuition and delivered out of subsumption alone and from the current present of past judgements, conclusions and especially rleations whose unimfication brings to light what in the object is more than a placeholder in the systematic." See also the chapter devoted to this in: Foster, *Adorno: The Recovery of Experience*. ("5. Failed Outbreak II: Bergson").

toric mechanism) and pure memory disintegrates; homogenous multiplicity is permeated by heterogeneous multiplicity (pure memory, duration), which is a different concept of the "whole" or "totality". The whole is transformed *in its entirety* by the addition/subtraction of a certain element. Perhaps this is what Adorno's "constellation" and his *Darstellung* or presentation might look like.

21

Adorno's *Minima Moralia* came out in 1951, though individual sections had been written between 1944 and 1947, i.e. at the same time as Adorno was working with Horkheimer on the *Dialectic of Enlightenment*. It closes with an aphorism (or *Denkbild*) entitled "Zu Ende", "At the end", which is at once a brief summary and broad outline of Adorno's thinking. Moreover, as Alexander Garcia Düttmann wrote, in this work philosophy "converges with art, since understanding it does not involve grasping its arguments but comprehending its gestures."[198] He is referring to *Aesthetic Theory* and its concept of the unattainable promise of happiness. However, since Adorno's thinking must be understood as an attempt to analyse non-discursive rationality, it is clear that aesthetic experience as a dimension other than discursive truth will play a pivotal role (as Adorno himself says in his early essay on "The Actuality of Philosophy").

Aphorism 153 reads as follows:

Finale. – The only philosophy which can be responsibly practised in face of despair is the attempt to contemplate all things as they would present themselves from the standpoint of redemption. Knowledge has no light but that shed on the world by redemption: all else is reconstruction, mere technique. Perspectives must be fashioned that displace and estrange the world, reveal it to be, with its rifts and crevices, as indigent and distorted as it will appear one day in the messianic light. To gain such perspectives without velleity or violence, entirely from felt contact with its objects – this alone is the task of thought. It is the simplest of all things, because the situation calls imperatively for such knowledge, indeed because consummate negativity, once squarely faced, delineates the mirror image of its

198 Alexander Garcia Düttmann, *So ist es. Ein philosophischer Kommentar zu Adornos >Minima Moralia<*, Suhrkamp, Frankfurt a.M. 2004, p. 12.

opposite. But it is also the utterly impossible thing, because it presupposes a standpoint removed, even though by a hair's breadth, from the scope of existence, whereas we well know that any possible knowledge must not only be first wrested from what is, if it shall hold good, but is also marked, for this very reason, by the same distortion and indigence which it seeks to escape. The more passionately thought denies its conditionality for the sake of the unconditional, the more unconsciously, and so calamitously, it is delivered up to the world. Even its own impossibility it must at last comprehend for the sake of the possible. But beside the demand thus placed on thought, the question of the reality or unreality of redemption itself hardly matters.[199]

This demonstrates the basic gesture of thinking after the Holocaust: the ultimate acceptance of the radical exterior into the interior, without a self-enclosed whole resulting from this operation, i.e. without the Other being reduced to the Same, to borrow terms from Levinas's *Totality and Infinity*. The noticeably theological framework of Adorno's reflections, which links him to Walter Benjamin and which philosophically thematises the "damaged" life at the end of the war, is suspended – or perhaps erased – by the last sentence. "Erasure" is a semantic operation that appears in Heidegger (indeed it could be said to be Husserl's form of "bracketing"). Later on it will feature large in the work of Jacques Derrida: something is so, but *sous rature* (deconstruction is justice, justice is something impossible). This too is negative dialectics – the sentence as the index of the unidentifiable non-identical. The last words act as a kind of punctuation after which there is nothing more to say. However, in this way an internal dynamic is opened of this brusquely concluded whole, and paradoxically confirms the thesis that the whole is untruth. In this constellation of beginning and end we can observe a sublation (*Aufhebung*) that does not retain anything from that which is overcome,

199 Adorno, *Minima Moralia*, p. 247.

but liquidates it in order that something radically different is able to rise up against it.[200]

Likewise, one could say that Husserl's teleology of history is present here as erased. Philosophical thinking is not situated outside real history, even though the concept of history that here provides the background and against which the meaning of events is understood from the radical end of history is radically other in respect of the history of progress. Adorno carries Benjamin's inspiration forward over the boundary of the Holocaust. The shock that Stalin's pact with Hitler represented to Benjamin and which led him to formulate his *Theses on the Philosophy of History* is compounded at the end of the war. We have no choice but to understand history differently. Similarly, it is essential we subject even philosophical language itself to criticism.

> The power of the facts has become so appalling that all theory, even true theory, seems ridiculous by the side of it. This has been burnt into the organ of theory, namely language, and has left its mark on it.[201]

A different relationship to history is called for. We no longer need to explain history but to find a philosophical response to it that is at the same time a change of attitude. We must look at things as they would appear from the perspective of the end of history, from the standpoint of redemption. Parting company with their current manifestation means seeing them as they are not. In this, as Gerhard Richter so perceptively observes, there is something of Benjamin's understanding of allegory as being radically different to that which it allegorises. However, Adorno's text actually highlights its own al-

---

200 For an interpretation of this text, cf. especially Gerhard Richter, "Aesthetic Theory and Nonpropositional Truth Content in Adorno", in: Gerhard Richter (ed.), *Language Without Soil: Adorno and Late Philosophical Modernity*, Forham University Press, New York 2010, pp. 131–146.
201 Theodor W. Adorno, "Bar Harbor Notebook", *Frankfurter Adorno Blätter* 4 (1995), p. 7; cited from Richter (ed.), *Language Without Soil*, pp. 2–3.

legoricality by explicitly "thematising" the standpoint of redemption as unattainable. The paradoxical figure with which Adorno works in this aphorism thus doubles the *Nachträglichkeit (afterness)* by means of its anticipation of the unavailable. However, that which is outside history has always left its traces in the existing world and appears in it through "cracks and fissures". This is also why thinking whose true home is elsewhere can operate here: it transposes negative traces of that which it cannot incorporate into itself into philosophical discourse by means of the mirror writing of its opposite, even though it is able to express this legacy through its concepts. If this thinking does not want simply to reproduce or prolong reality, it must have its measure elsewhere. In fact, the aphorism "Finale" serves simply to radicalise the *Dialectic of Enlightenment*: if enlightened thinking fails to take into account its own residual connection with that which it wishes to overcome (to sublate), then it is unaware of its own position within regressive tendencies and will, on the contrary, not be a sublation or turn, but a re-turn to the darkness that it wished to illuminate.

The final aphorism in *Minima Moralia*is is characterised by a kind of internal surge of energy: we must seek recourse in that which in knowledge necessarily eludes this knowledge as unpresentable. However, what is important is not some kind of "content" that evades knowledge, but the process of escape itself, as though philosophical thinking were characterised by a permanent state of emergency. This is also why the aphorism is one of the privileged forms of philosophy. Adorno explains this in brief in a note in the margins of Heinz Krüger's *On the Aphorism as Philosophical Form*:

> While Krüger is indebted to German philology for the thematic and methodological bases of his work, his intention was to reveal the aphorism to be a specific, independent philosophical form. In other words, he wanted to develop the aphorism and its unique qualities from the content of the very philosophy that discloses itself by means of this form... He laid an emphasis

on the antithesis of open and closed thinking, on "ignorance" reflecting itself, on the intensification of the exception to the rule and on the paradox as a medium of truth and enemy of convention, so as to uncover the inner unity of that which appears to banal preconceptions to dissolve in a completely undisciplined way into plurality.[202]

If, as Krüger claims, the aphorism evades formal logical understanding because it chops in two the question of how it justifies its own existence in the position of judgement before even raising it, then it is clear what is at stake, both in the literary form of the aphorism and in the unattainability of that last measure of thinking. This is thinking that does not stand within any fixed realm, though this does not mean that it is random; it is necessary in some other way since it does not have the guarantee of the "foundation". This is one of the characteristics of post-war thinking, i.e. thinking without foundation that is nevertheless "established" on the absent foundation in its capacity as the erased foundation. In Derrida this takes the form of "ellipticity", in Lyotard the "dispute" between two legitimate claims, and in Michel Foucault the "impossible" position of his archaeological knowledge. It is also manifest in a philosophical interest in writers such as Maurice Blanchot, Georges Bataille, Samuel Beckett and others, since a similar shift is visible in their work. "The essence of literature is that it has no essence," says Maurice Blanchot. If, as Adorno is convinced, the possibility of thinking forces thinking to understand its impossibility, then it must remain open to that which is on the point of arrival so as to be open from within to the outside – an essay, a fragment, a configuration. Where language is disrupted, the form of communication is itself the expression. The reference to the theological concept of redemption is the index of the need for something other than an Enlightenment-based or modern concept of history, the need to

202 Theodor W. Adorno, "Heinz Krüger zum Gedächtnis", GS 20.2, p. 473.

rescue the openness of thinking which, however, in Adorno's case (and in this he is close to the "cracks and fissures" in Husserl's texts, though this was not his intention) does not surrender the idea of the absolute, notwithstanding the fact that the relationship with it is reversed: it is a mistake to close oneself off to one's own contingency because of the non-contingent, since thinking beyond the borders is only possible from within.

At the same time, Adorno's version of unfounded thinking, the measure of which is beyond its reach, displays a striking kinship with Kracauer and his waiting for the last things before the last. There is also a link with the radicalisation of that relationship to that which is coming in Blanchot's *L'Attente L'Oubli*. The concept of redemption here designates the position of radical criticism that prevents any premature appropriation of the truth, i.e. of all concepts of universal history that would like us to have the basic mosaic of history in front of our eyes right now if we know upon what goal history is supposed to focus. But more importantly, a criticism that reveals the falsity of everything existing and that sees that any framework of universal history with its teleology necessitates the suffering of those whose life was not about this life because it was subordinate in advance to the goal, i.e. those who suffered because their life could not attain its expression, is at the same time a criticism saving the past. It wants to be true to that which history (according to this interpretation) eliminated. However, this salvation requires a fundamental transformation of the philosophical discourse, something that is abundantly clear in the conclusion to *Negative Dialectic:*

Nothing on earth and nothing in the empty heavens is to be saved by defending it. The 'yes, but' answer to the critical argument, the refusal to have anything wrested away – these are already forms of obstinate insistence of existence, forms of a clutching that cannot be reconciled with the idea of rescue in which the spasm of such prolonged self-presentation would be eased. Nothing can be saved unchanged, nothing that has not passed through the portal of its death. If rescue is the inmost impulse of any man's spirit, there is no hope but unreserved surrender of that which is to be rescued as well as of the hopeful spirit.[203]

203 Adorno, *Negative Dialectics*, pp. 391–392.

22

The transformation of philosophical discourse that is the response to the event of the Holocaust includes as retrospective questioning (*Rückfrage*) *sui generis* both reflection upon conceptual thinking and reflection upon the language of philosophy itself, and in addition the rehabilitation of expression or the "rhetorical moment": the concept must at the same time become an expression of historical experience, an expression of suffering. The concept is open to expression, which attempts to become concept. All of this in light of the necessity of the relationship to that which, on the boundaries of the phenomenological definition of phenomenality, surpasses these boundaries. This involves showing what misses the phenomenon and escapes from it within this escape itself, by means of which it eludes identification. Since it involves experience resisting its own reification, objectifiability and convertibility, it is the act of testimony that finds itself at the forefront rather than cognition. In the conflict between real experience and philosophical discourse their incommensurability must be attested to. Husserl's semiology continues to be unsustainable inasmuch as, beginning with *Logical Investigations*, it excludes indexicality as the original modus of the relationship and subjugates it to intentionality focused upon fulfilment. Now, on the contrary, the significant relationship is the index: the trace or testimony, often in a radical escalation, as is so in the case of Emmanuel Levinas, when he speaks of the trace of a past that has never been present. However, we find something similar in other writers, for instance Maurice Blanchot and Jacques Derrida, who take up Adorno's negatively dialectical critique of the concept (either consciously or not) with an emphasis on the radical diversity of the Same and the Other. It might therefore seem that the exterior finds itself once more irreducibly outside the inside. This is not so. Both resistance and escape are meant as distinctive methods of relating. In other words, this is a unique relationship, a relationship that, as a relationship across difference, is both relationship and separation simultaneously.

23

The calm, the burn of the Holocaust, the annihilation of noon – the calm of the disaster.[204]

Though Maurice Blanchot may have summed it up in one word, disaster, *désastre*, this most extreme form of the outside, is an idea whose entire significance acquires its contours only gradually and within a variety of contexts. In 1940, it was the word most frequently used to describe the military defeat of France. After the war, especially in Blanchot's book *L'ecriture du désastre*, it refers directly to the horrors of the final solution. More generally it refers to something unthinkable by thinking: to the trace of the encounter with the radical exterior, which is non-actualisable because it is outside memory (and inasmuch as it exhibits signs of trauma).

If we want to understand this use of the word *désastre* (from the Italian *disastro*, dis + astro "star", from Latin *astrum*), which originally referred to the deviation of a star from its orbit or to a star that had ceased to exert a positive effect, we must return to the structures of thought within which it is inscribed. However, we must then turn once more to Edmund Husserl and to the early articles by Emmanuel Levinas, in which he was one of the first to introduce phenomenology to France and in which his own conception of ethics as the "first philosophy" began to take shape.

In Husserl's work, whose "truly new accents will never reverberate to any but the sensitive or the practiced ear, but – obligatorily – alert",[205] Levinas, as he later said, was attracted above all by the discovery of the intentionality of consciousness and its broader scope:

---

204 Maurice Blanchot, *The Writing of the Disaster*, trans. Ann Smock, University of Nebraska Press, Lincoln and London 1986, p. 1.
205 Emmanuel Levinas, *Discovering Existence with Husserl*, trans. Richard A. Cohen and Michael B. Smith, Northwestern UP, Evanston, Illinois 2000, p. 111.

Without the idea of intentionality understood in a more originative sense than in objectification, without intentionality removed from the logic of objectification because it traces out truly transitive relations, all the contemporary philosophy of art would have been impossible or incomprehensible.[206]

Intentionality, the intentional relationship, is the movement of stepping out of itself, and as such (insofar as this movement implies that consciousness is somehow forced to submit to the objects to which it relates) would liquidate the concept of the representing consciousness establishing the exteriority of the exterior (a concept in which interiority controls exteriority[207]). However, Husserl himself operates on the periphery of this discovery. He somehow retains the model of representation at the moment it allows itself to be seduced by the endeavour to establish a new objectivism (and to return European science to its original idea). However, this has the effect of pushing into the background the fact that, in its analyses of intentionality, phenomenology reveals a deeper movement behind objectivations, a concrete life focused on exteriority that is not objective – the equivalent in fact to Wahl's movement to the concrete world, *vers le concret*.[208]

On the one hand, therefore, Levinas regards the discovery of the intentionality of consciousness to be liberating, since consciousness is forever beyond its own boundaries, its primary act being to step outside of itself, which underpins all its other acts[209] – consciousness equals presence in the world. A second important moment then arises: the correlation of intentional thought and its subject, which is unregulated by any a priori schema. However, there is a certain price to be paid: the intentional object is in this way constituted as

206 Ibid., p. 199 note.
207 Cf. ibid., p. 53–54.
208 Cf. Jean Wahl, *Vers le concret*, Vrin, Paris 1932.
209 Cf. Levinas, *Discovering Existence*, p. 135.

ideal and intentionality is characterised as idealising (this on a pre-predicative level).

> For Husserl, the object, even in cases where it is sensible and individual, will always be what is identified through a multiplicity of intentions. To say that all consciousness is consciousness of something is to affirm that across these correlative terms of a multiplicity of subjective thoughts, and thus transcending them, an identity is maintained and affirmed. The intentional object has an ideal existence in relation to the temporal event and spatial position of consciousness.[210]

It is clear that *time* is implied in this relationship, the *temporality* essential for the *ideal* object to reveal itself to consciousness (perception runs through various aspects of the intended thing, i.e. it performs acts of synthesis and identification of this thing as this thing): something identical (hence ideal) can only reveal itself in time. On the other hand, according to Levinas this represents a certain problem as far as the status is concerned of that which from *Ideen* I onwards Husserl calls "hyletic givens" ("primary contents" in *Logical Investigations*). Husserl uses the term "hyle" to refer to sense data that operates as a "substance of intentional shaping or *Sinngebungen* on different levels" (III/1, 193). The material of intentional functions (colourful, olfactory, tactile, etc.) is not the same as the objective moments (the colourfulness of a thing, the roughness of a thing), which can only become evident through this material. In Husserl's concept, therefore, intentional form is, as it were, above the sensory substance as a "revitalising" or sense-giving layer, and so the concrete sensory experience emerges from sensory material that in itself *has nothing of intentionality*. Late Husserl then clarifies and complicates this interpretation, especially in connection with

---

210 Ibid., p. 203.

his analysis of "affection" within the framework of analyses of passive syntheses.[211]

Levinas examines the problem of "hyletic givens" in great detail, firstly devoting his attention to the "character" of this hyle (and noting that the significance of this *reel* moment increases in Husserl over time), and then in connection with temporality. The connection of the first and second is clear from his description of intentional consciousness.

Intentions that mean and identify a transcendent object are not like simple windows onto the outside, but contents filling a certain duration: intention is "temporal reality". Furthermore, consciousness that renders objects present to us is also present to itself. It is lived (experienced), which is what enables us to speak of "experiences" (*Erlebnisse*): consciousness, which is consciousness of an object, is at the same time non-objectifying consciousness of itself. "The intention is *Erlebnis*". However, this term "is also applied to contents that are not acts, to non-intentional contents.... there exist states of consciousness that are not conscious of anything!"[212] and herein lies the problem of sensory or hyletic contents.

In short, Levinas reveals in the fissures of Husserl's intentionality something like a *trace of alterity* (the *exterior*), and this allows him (though he is still operating within Husserl's texts and often answers questions Husserl has posed himself) to discern a kind of double modality in intentionality.

1) Intentionality in the mode of idealising identification, which makes it possible for the "impression" (or *sensation*) to be experienced as a certain identifiable unity (as the same) appearing within a multiplicity of moments, because this impression is retained in "outline" (and in abbreviated form, as it were) as a whole in each (different) moment thanks to specific, immanent intentionality (re-

211 Edmund Husserl, *Analysen zur passiven Synthesis*, ed. Margot Fleischer (Husserliana XI), Martinus Nijhoff, Haag 1966, p. 148 et seq.
212 Levinas, *Discovering Existence*, p. 139.

tention). The impression is a "shadowing" or *Abschattung*, which, however, gives itself through *Abschattungen* in the immanence (of intentional consciousness that is forever being "temporalised") in which it is alive. This is the origin of Husserl's concept of the inner consciousness of time, which is consciousness itself. Time as a continuous flow or passage is the condition of the possibility of consciousness being able to reveal (by means of gradual self-profiling) something identical to itself, i.e. that as this.

2) However, in the case of "hyletic" data, something is shown that is somehow to the side of this idealising and identifying intentionality. The object showing itself is possible only in that intention intends, i.e. it "revives" a "sensation", an impression, which, however, must already have elapsed to a minimal extent in order for intention to have been able to revive it. The act of its "apprehension" (*Auffassung*) arrives only after the material of the constituted object (see the roughness and colour as hyletic data). This means that consciousness is delayed, it lags behind the past, that is, it lags behind that which must be presumed to be the *Urimpression*, the "primary" or "original" impression. As *escaping* or preceding it is free of any ideality, it is non-ideality par excellence.[213] It is non-identifiable and as such is the perpetually escaping basis of identification.

The unpredictable novelty of content that emerges in this source of all consciousness and being is the original spontaneous generation (*Urzeugung*), the transition from nothingness to being (to being that is transformed into being-for-consciousness, but is never lost), the spontaneous generation that deserves to be called absolute activity, *genesis spontanea*; however, it is also completed outside of any anticipation, expectation, outside any embryonic origin, any continuity, and as a consequence it is complete and utter passivity, the receptivity of the "other", which penetrates the "identical", it is life and not "thought". As "inner consciousness" it becomes conscious-

213 Ibid., pp. 215–216.

ness by means of the temporal modification of retention, which perhaps characterises the essence of all thinking as the retention of a certain fleeting fullness. Consciousness is the process of growing old and the search for lost time.[214]

The secrecy of intentionality resides in the "deviation from..." or in the modification of the time flow.

In this respect Levinas would agree with what Derrida writes in "Violence and Metaphysics":

> The absolute alterity of each instant, without which there would be no time, cannot be produced – constituted – within the identity of the subject or the existent.[215]

The outside is somehow inside, which it permeates through the interstices of the intentional relationship to the world without being explicitly present as a pre-reflexive level of consciousness for this consciousness itself, since the activity of the identifying (re)cognition aimed at objectivisation and thematisation incessantly pushes this otherness into the background. Phenomenology reveals the world and at the same time tacitly eliminates all non-intentional moments. To put things in the more expressive language of Levinas, in which one of the important themes of Derrida's deconstruction is also expressed, phenomenology's reflection upon the phenomenon violates and does not acknowledge the secret. However, the intentional relationship always, albeit only implicitly, includes something that sees by means of consciousness without catching sight of. In showing, the disappearance is present of that which shows itself as unseen.

However, as far as thinking after Husserl is concerned, the close connection between this involuntary discovery of radical alterity (of

214 Ibid., p. 216.
215 Jacques Derrida, "Violence et métaphysique" in: Derrida, *Writing and Difference,* p. 113.

the outside-in) and the perforation of the continuity of time is important, and is addressed by both Levinas and Derrida. This is also why Levinas speaks of consciousness lagging behind itself and whence the highly complex network of references and other links begins to unfold as though from a spring. And so, for example, it is evident we can interpret this escape as unassimilated experience linked with shock and trauma (Freud and Benjamin). However, it is equally possible – and this will be Levinas's strategy – to focus on a description of this level prior to *Sinngebung*, prior to the apprehending identification, i.e. to focus on a description of the absolutely other before it is lost by being absorbed by the interior or totality.

It is this that forms the "hard core" of Levinas's essay *Existence and Existents* of 1947, in which that which the level of the identifiable and nameable covers is designated using the French idiom *il y a* or "there is". The essay is therefore also an escalation of the polemic against Heidegger's ontology as expounded in *Being and Time*, since *il y a*, this "barren, haunting and horrible nature of being"[216], is both beneath the threshold of the ontological difference between being and existence and beneath the threshold of the world as the (Husserlian) horizon of all horizons.

However, a description of this being before being requires an extreme escalation of conceptual thinking (the concept is form), i.e. it is no surprise that Levinas here appeals to the "exoticism" of art, since the hyletic data already referred to appears in it. This is because in artistic creation, materiality or sensory qualities are not subject to representation and do not refer to the world, but return perception to the impersonal element in which the outside and inside cannot be differentiated and which involves "not only the disappearance of every object, but the extinction of the subject."[217]

---

216 Preface to the 2nd ed. Emmanuel Levinas, *De l'existence à l'existant.*
217 Emmanuel Levinas, *Existence and Existents*, trans. Alphonso Lingis, Martinus Nijhoff, Haag 1978, p. 67.

Something analogous must apply to Levinas's language, which wants to approach this radical *otherness* without depriving it of its otherness. This language, too, must be "obscure", because it relates to a sphere that is outside the light that is the prerequisite of identification (it is only in light that shape or form can emerge, that something may reveal itself to be something and thus become apprehendable), outside the light that is the phenomenological condition of the phenomenon and that is therefore simply another word for the world or totality, objectivising intentionalities, and the horizons thereof. The night, which is complementary to this light, means simply obscurity, illegibility, confusion. For this reason, the night of the element, the night of the *il y a*, must be a *different night*, night as the content of the space without horizons, essential anonymity, in which anything applies to anything, the night that bears down upon us in the form of fatigue and insomnia and in which (outside the antitheses of day and night) we experience how our "I" is flooded with anonymity.

> The exterior – if one insists on the term – remains uncorrelated with an interior. It is no longer given. It is no longer a world. What we call the I is itself submerged by the night, invaded, depersonalised, stifled by it. The disappearance of all things and of the I leaves what cannot disappear, the sheer fact of being in which one *participates* whether one wants to or not, without having taken the initiative, anonymously.[218]

However, we must view this *il y a* as simply a "rustling" or "murmuring" (*murmure*) of silence, a word and an "experience" that we will henceforth frequently encounter in the work of Michal Foucault and many others.

It was around this time that Levinas's lifelong friend Maurice Blanchot appeared on the scene, not only in the novels (the first

218 Ibid., p. 58.

version of *Thomas l'Obscure* was written in 1941, and *Aminadab* came out a year later), but also in the essays on literature collected and published as *L'Espace littéraire* (1955). Both genres involve an encounter between writing, *écriture*, and language. The writer who writes is at the same moment dragged down into the depths of speech, into his own being, i.e. into language that is not tied to a representation of the world and which is free of references and designations, but in and out of which an incalculable game between words is constantly flitting that does not depend on any speaker. The "whisper" in the background confusion of the written text does not refer to a human being, but is the operation of language itself outside of that speech that refers by means of its precisely convertible signs to our world (thus articulated in the instrumental utilisation of language): it is the operation of the endless deferral of meaning that cannot be stabilised in any interpretation. It is therefore the movement of constant deferral or *différance* of meaning, as Jacques Derrida puts it. It is for this very reason, claims Blanchot, that the writer is unable to read his own work, which for him too is a mystery from which he is separated (later variations on the theme of the "death of the author" clearly find their antecedents here). This mystery, though it hints that it exists without allowing itself to be deciphered, only makes itself known by means of rustling or murmuring beneath denotative speech.

> To write is to make oneself the echo of what cannot cease speaking – and since it cannot, in order to become its echo I have, in a way, to silence it. I bring to this incessant speech the decisiveness, the authority of my own silence. I make perceptible, by my silent mediation, the uninterrupted affirmation, the giant murmuring upon which language opens and thus becomes image, becomes imaginary, becomes a speaking depth, an indistinct plenitude which is empty.[219]

219 Maurice Blanchot, *The Space of Literature*, trans. Ann Smock, University of Nebraska Press, Lincoln, London 1982, p. 27.

As Blanchot sees it, literature seeks to be the expression of the experience of that which precedes life. To put it even more precisely, literature *is* this very experience, since, as he says in *L'Entretien infini*: "How can I, in my speech, recapture this prior presence that I must exclude in order to speak, in order to speak it?"[220] This is experience "structured" by revealing the disappearing in its disappearance, i.e. in its resistance to being revealed, experience as testimony to the absolute exterior, to which it relates as separated from it.

However, this is still insufficient for an understanding of the term *désastre*.

This is how things stand at present. Firstly, we have *il y a* as experience, as something that penetrates experience without being able to become experience. Secondly, we have the thought of the relationship that is also an absolute separation, a relationship across irreducible difference, by means of which even the phenomenological concept of showing is fundamentally modified: in the foreground is the revelation of that which evades revelation, or the revelation of that which disappears in its disappearance. This is roughly the line along which Blanchot's thinking, and that of others, moves.

However, to begin with Blanchot approaches this non-phenomenon through literature and its relationship to language. This is about experience exposed to the inexpressible *murmure* (rustling, whispering or droning) behind words that refer to things by means of general meanings. That which allows literature to be literature and which Blanchot designates using the word *écriture* fundamentally modifies our understanding of language in philosophy, which gradually becomes almost the norm as soon as Roland Barthes, Michel Foucault, Jacques Derrida, Jean-François Lyotard, Gilles Deleuze and others begin to move away from structuralist linguistics as a model. Blanchot arrives at this other concept during the course of a polemic with Hegel, and his argument runs something like this: in

---

220 Maurice Blanchot, *The Infinite Conversation*, trans. Susan Hanson, University of Minnesota Press, Minneapolis and London 1993, p. 36.

speech aimed at communication the concreteness of the thing communicated is negated and replaced by a general meaning or idea. The language of communication is "essential" language. However, if language is freed from this function and if words do not refer to things, speech becomes an autonomous element, a neutral dimension (neither a thing nor an idea) without subject. A speech without subject that has no speaker and that the speaking subject drags into his murmur (*murmure*). This is the outside, which is the bedrock of the language of communication that refers to things by identifying them. The work, the *œuvre*, as the manifestation of *écriture*, is at the same time *désœuvrement* or worklessness, the corrosion of isolation, within whose interstices appears that which cannot be named and apprehended (mystery, absolute otherness). This dimension of speech – the rustling, whispering, droning or *murmure* – is clearly that apparition of the linguistic expression that Husserl's semiology wants to eliminate.

Il y a is experience in which we confront that which *always already* threatens to absorb this experience as the radical outside. Novels may evoke it, bear witness to it, insofar as the reader is exposed to speech that says something and simultaneously denies its communicative function. Many passages in Blanchot's novel *Thomas l'Obscur* can be read in this way, and it is impossible not to recall Levinas's *il y a* and its combination with the "second night" referred to in Levinas's essay *Existence and Existents*:

> Whereas just a moment ago I felt nothing, simply experiencing each feeling as a great absence, now in the complete absence of feelings I experience the strongest feeling (…) am at grips with a feeling which reveals to me that I cannot experience it, and it is at that moment that I experience it with a force which makes it an inexpressible torment. And that is nothing, for I could experience it as something other than what it is, fright experienced as enjoyment. (…) I discover my being in the vertiginous abyss where it is not, an absence, an absence. (…) The darkness hides nothing. My first

perception is that this night is not a provisional absence of light. Far from being a possible locus of images, it is composed of all that which is not seen and is not heard, and, listening to it, even a man would know that, if he were not a man, he would hear nothing. (…) Along with the feeling that everything has vanished, this night brings me the feeling that everything is near me.[221]

In the words of Michel Foucault from his essay entitled *The Thought from Outside*, Blanchot's *écriture* refers to the being of speech itself at the moment that "language appears as a leave-taking from that which it names": Upon reaching the brink of itself,

what it finds is not a positivity that contradicts it, but the void that will efface it. Into that void it must go, consenting to come undone in the rumbling (*murmure*), in the immediate negation of what it says, in a silence that is not the intimacy of a secret but a pure outside where words endlessly unravel.[222]

Why, however, in the case of Blanchot should the word *désastre* – something inauspicious but also immemorial – be another name for Levinas's *il y a*? This is a question to which there does not have to be a clear answer. It must be clear that that which Blanchot named in this way, observed from various angles, necessarily shows itself in different ways and embodies different aspects of that which cannot be subordinated to a single meaning. But this is exactly why this word is appropriate, since, like *il y a*, it is outside the antithesis of positive and negative. It refers to *otherwise than being*, to quote the title of Levinas's second large book. And Blanchot himself speaks of

221 Maurice Blanchot, *Thomas the Obscure*, trans. Robert Lamberton, Station Hill Press 1998, Barrytown, New York, pp. 102–105.
222 Michel Foucault, "The Thought from Outside", trans. Brian Massumi, in: *Foucault Blanchot*, Zone Books, New York 1987, p. 22.

the loosening of the meaning of words that in his texts seem to occupy the position of concepts:

> These names, areas of dislocation, the four winds of spirit's absence, breath from nowhere – the names of thought, when it lets itself come undone and, by writing, fragment. Outside. Neutral. Disaster. Return. Surely these names form no system. In their abruptness, like proper names designating no one, they slide outside all possible meaning without this slide's meaning anything – it leaves only a sliding half-gleam that clarifies nothing, not even the outside, whose frontier is nowhere indicated. These names, in a devastated field, ravaged by the absence which has preceded them – and which they would bear within themselves if it weren't that, empty of all inferiority, they rise up exterior to themselves (stones petrified by the endlessness of their fall and forming the walls of an abyss) – seem remainders, each one, of another language, both disappeared and never yet pronounced, a language we cannot even attempt to restore without reintroducing these names back into the world, or exalting them to some higher world of which, in their external, clandestine solitude, they could only the irregular interruption, the invisible retreat.[223]

Il y a is thus radical exteriority, just as Levinas's "face" is radical exteriority. In both cases the encounter with the outside is played out in a past that was never present, because the encounter with the other is inscribed in me, as Levinas would say, before I encounter it in reality. The other is somehow always already in my place and this original co-implication explains the consciousness of vulnerability. This always involves the event of separation that is present only in forgetting: "The disaster is related to forgetfulness – forgetfulness without memory, the motionless retreat of what has not been treated – the immemorial, perhaps. To remember forgetfully: again, the outside."[224] *Désastre*, therefore, as absolute loss (but also as original

---

223 Blanchot, *Writing of Desaster,* pp. 57–58.
224 Ibid., p. 3

passivity and the unattainability of immediacy). These are also signs of trauma (*désastre* in the sense of disaster), as well as a deviation to a radical, since non-totalisable, asymmetry (*dés-astre*, disconnection from the stars, dis-orientation). However, it is only a traumatic experience inasmuch as it makes its presence felt in a world (the horizon of all horizons) that has a centre and in which that which *is* is that which "is thought about, seen, acted on, willed, felt – an object",[225] in a world already formed by the intentional (i.e. symmetrical, noetic-noematic) relationship of the interior to the exterior that Levinas calls the *totality*, the basis of which is the possibility of owning, i.e. suspending otherness.[226]

A preliminary summary: *désastre* refers simultaneously to two fundamental transformations of philosophical discourse. Above all, the relationship must be thought of as a *relationship across irreducible difference*. The basic form of showing is the *showing of that which is escaping from the phenomenon in the very act of its escape*. But now we have a problem. The outside is somehow inside.

225 Levinas, *Existence and Existents*, ch. 2.
226 Emmanuel Levinas, *Totalité et Infini. Essai sur l exteriorité*. Martinus Nijhoff, Haag 1961, p. 8.

24

However, in the word *désastre* there is also an echo of the Holocaust: *The calm of the holocaust, the burn of the holocaust, the annihilation of noon – the calm of the disaster* (désastre).

The second novel by Maurice Blanchot is called *Aminadab*. It bears the name of Levinas's brother, who, along with his father, stepmother, another brother Boris and other relatives, was murdered by the Nazis in Lithuania. Levinas's mother and daughter in France were saved from transportation by Maurice Blanchot, Levinas's classmate from the University of Strasbourg and a lifelong friend, who hid them with friends in the Normandy countryside. Levinas himself, serving from 1939 in the French army, was captured and interned, first in Rennes and then in Germany in Stalag 11 B.

> The Bergen-Belsen concentration camp was very close: we met prisoners from it. We knew that people were disappearing in a strange way in Poland. We knew that they were rounding up Jews and deporting them. But we simply couldn't believe it...[227]

Levinas's teacher, the sociology professor Maurice Halbwachs, also died in Bergen-Belsen. Levinas called the dog that greeted the prisoners with pleasure every day the last Kantian in Nazi Germany. "We were stripped of our human skin... [and only] a small inner murmur (...) reminded us of our essence as thinking creatures."[228]

From the perspective of traditional philosophy Levinas is often associated with an almost scandalous thesis: ethics takes precedence over ontology, because the fundamental situation is the relationship

---

[227] *La conscience juive face à l'histoire: le Pardon*, ed. Eliane Amado Levy-Valensi, PUF, Paris 1965, p. 75.

[228] Emmanuel Levinas, *Difficult Freedom*, trans. Seán Hand, Johns Hopkins University Press, Baltimore 1997, pp. 152–153.

of man with his fellow man as the radical other, his relationship to exteriority. If this *alteritas* or otherness is to be sustainable, we must conceive of this relationship as asymmetrical: I am here only if addressed by another, though I am always already in the position, vulnerable and naked, of he who answers. Unlike the founding acts of consciousness or subjectivity, which both phenomenology and the modernist tradition both privilege, in Levinas the primary "relationship" is one of passivity, because it accentuates the moment of response or patience.

However, the idea as reduced in this way leaves unanswered the question of what philosophical concepts are actually supposed to communicate. What testimony do they offer? To what do they refer? Philosophical thinking is exhausted neither by reflections upon its own history nor the creation of systems, because then it would be difficult to show how it relates to real experience. However, for this very reason each transformation of philosophical discourse is a specific philosophical response to a certain historical experience. If this were not so, then concepts would not emerge and evanesce, and it is only in this way that they are legitimised.

Penetrating the thicket of Levinas's thinking is not easy. It is rooted in the Judaic tradition, though Levinas is careful always to distinguish his philosophical books from Judaic exegesis. Nevertheless, it is impossible to make such a separation and, on the contrary, a certain overlap offers a kind of key to his "ethics" in his texts dealing explicitly with the Holocaust, because this is an event that represents a challenge to both theology and philosophy. Levinas rises to the challenge not only in *Totalité et Infini* and *Autrement qu'être*, but in other texts too.

Born in Lithuania to a rabbinical family, in 1946 Zvi Kolitz wrote a short story entitled *Yosl Rakover Talks to God*. The original version, published in Argentina, was in Yiddish. In the story, a work of fiction, Yosl Rakover recounts how he is spending the last hours of the Warsaw Ghetto Uprising. In a dramatically realist style that does not shy away from depicting the inordinate cruelty of the Germans and sometimes the Poles, he describes the fate of his family (including his six children, all of whom die), and that of his other relatives and friends. And then at the end of the story he says something strange: "I believe in the God of Israel, even when He has done everything to make me cease to believe in Him." The text was translated into English (and later into Hebrew) and from English into other languages. However, the English translation did not feature the name of the real author (a fact repeated in many translations), and for a long time the text was thought to be an authentic document. Only much later was it "returned" to its true author. Levinas read it and called it "both beautiful and true, true as only fiction can be" (indicating that he had his doubts regarding its authenticity as a document but, as is clear, felt that the question of authorship was not of crucial importance). His essay "Loving the Torah More Than God" makes reference to the story. Three points are crucial here. Firstly: what is the suffering of innocents actually supposed to mean? Is it not proof of a world without God? In which case would not atheism be the proper response?

Secondly: according to Levinas the answer presupposes that we are aware of the specific nature of the Jewish concept of God. To resort to atheism is the response of those who live in a childish fantasy of a God who punishes evil, distributes rewards and forgives sins, a God who treats people as thought they were children. If Yosl Rakover does not lose his faith in God, it is because his faith has its origin in the religion of adults. The heavens are empty, the God of adults is revealed in the emptiness of the heavens of children. Yosl is alone, God has concealed his face, the just are without succour. However, Yosl has been left alone precisely in order to shoulder the burden of God's own responsibility for others. The path to God must pass across a section without God (which is why true atheism must find a response to the *legitimate* requirement of atheism). And thirdly: the specifically Jewish meaning of suffering as an invitation to man to become adult. This represents a rejection of theodicy as a remnant of a mythical understanding of God.

> Theodicy, in other words, was never a fact of life. But if we ever thought it was and needed a demonstration of its insufficiency, the Holocaust was such a demonstration with a vengeance. The Holocaust as an event for Levinas aligns itself with the deepest order of human catastrophe. It is the return of the moment of the exile, the beginning of the first diaspora. All responsibility is in our hands, not because there is no God, or because God has concealed or veiled His Face, but because, he tells us, there never was such a God to begin with, because the dream of such a God is the dream of children who would deflect human responsibility onto the divine. To become adult for Levinas is to assume a full responsibility for human behaviour that is not the product of my freedom but ironically its condition, that is given in the created fabric of the world. And to become such an adult – infinitely responsible for the other individual (and here is really the second part of it) – is clearly in fact to engage God in relationship, a God who is otherwise than being, a God who demands of us nothing less than shouldering God's own responsibility for others, for their lives, for the responsibility, even for their deaths.[229]

The experience of suffering is fundamental. For instance, Levinas says that the just may only live separated in this way from God through his *consciousness that necessarily includes suffering*. If we want to understand Levinas's philosophy it is important to know that for him "conscience" is not part of consciousness (consciousness that in the distance explores the world as it shows itself to him, for instance during reflections upon himself): on the contrary, consciousness is made whole by virtue of "conscience" (the French word *conscience* means both consciousness and conscience). In philosophi-

---

229 Sandor Goodhart, "Conscience, Conscience, Consciousness. Emmanuel Levinas, the Holocaust and the logic of witness." In: J. Roth, E. Maxwell et al., *Remembering for the Future: The Holocaust in an Age of Genocide*, Palgrave, New York, 2001, pp. 98–113.

cal language: without *moral* consciousness there is no consciousness. However, this means that consciousness is somehow established through suffering, exposure, not by intentionality but by means of a readiness and openness to encounter the Other.

This provides us with an entrée into another of Levinas's texts dealing with the Holocaust, *A Religion for Adults*[230], closely related to the first text by title. Again, at first sight Levinas would appear to be grappling with a theological problem, namely, the different conception of God in Judaism and in connection with the question of human freedom. The voice of Israel is usually heard as the voice of an *ancestor*, and this has its own tradition, because the particularity of Jewish monotheism resides in its oral tradition, which is crystallised in the Talmud and the commentaries thereto. It eschews the path taken by Christianity and does not view man as being party to a drama that arises independently of his will (from divine power), because according to Judaism this is an offence to human freedom and has another source, namely the numinous idea of the sacred that empowers man and carries him (actually a form of violence). The god of the Jews is not he who is most powerful, and therefore the survivors emerged from the contest of these numinous, mythical deities. Judaism *rejects* these deities, which is why it is always open to the threat of atheism. However, atheism (absolute separation from god) is essential if the relationship to the transcendent is to be understood as a *relationship*. Several important points need to be made here. Firstly: the theological problem is simultaneously a philosophical problem. What is crucial is the interpretation of suffering, i.e. that which gave rise in Christianity to the idea of theodicy. The invitation to the religion of adults marks the end of theodicy. According to Levinas the Holocaust represents

---

230 Both in Levinas, *Difficult Freedom*, p. 17.

the destruction of all balance between the explicit and implicit theodicy of Western thought and the forms which suffering and its evil take in the very unfolding of this century. (...) The disproportion between suffering and every theodicy was shown at Auschwitz with a glaring, obvious clarity.[231]

Theodicy is a response to the search for the meaning of the "scandal" of evil in the overall plan of creation. Suffering is therefore subordinate to a certain "metaphysical expediency". When Adorno rejects any attempt to "understand" the Holocaust as an insult to the victims, then, indirectly, like Levinas he rejects theodicy. And in the case of both writers the theological idea of theodicy is somehow inscribed into the Enlightenment idea of progress as its own type of "overall plan" of history. Secondly: the relationship to God is an ethical one, because the presence of God can only be experienced through my relationship to the other, to another person and within this relationship. Thirdly: the meaning of separation. Man is primarily "egoism". However, he must not persist in this. Unlike the Western, Christian tradition following on from ancient times (Plotinus and later Augustus and the contemplation of the soul within), Judaism emphases real transcendence, without which the soul cannot be for itself. The separated I senses a chink in itself. It discovers itself as (always already) affected by the other both arbitrarily and violently. Egoism: everything the "ego" has within range is transformed into "its own". However, in order to own it, it must accept – take – it, which is in itself problematic, because the discovery of its own "abilities" is simultaneously the discovery of their illegitimacy in respect of the Other. "Self-consciousness inevitably surprises itself at the heart of a moral consciousness" without the other being a new edition of myself. Through the other I am in touch with God (in a relationship of *transcendence*). The ethical relationship is pri-

---

231 Emmanuel Levinas, "La souffrance inutile", in: *Entre nous.* Grasset, Paris 1991, pp. 114–115.

mary. Justice towards the other drives me towards an unsurpassable proximity to God.

There is only a hint of "suffering" here. Though I suffer if an injustice is done to another, I am also primarily "sufferance" (*passio* and *patientia*) inasmuch as I can only be self-conscious if I am already "subverted" in my egoism as always already "affected" by the Other.

If we still take phenomenology as our referential framework, we could, along with Levinas, formulate the same thing once again in the following way: I meet someone; they issue a command with their face; their vulnerability prevents me from murder; along with this instruction there is astonishment that I cannot understand the other: I cannot kill, I cannot assimilate, I am bound to the other by an endless obligation. The intentionality of consciousness is overturned: the other "intends" me, I myself am "accused" by the other. The isolated I is breached by the other, the intentionality of someone else, the I is extra-verted:[232]

Suffering is surely a given in consciousness, a certain "psychological content", like the lived experience of colour, of sound, of contact, or like any sensation. But in this "content" itself, it is in-spite-of-consciousness, unassumable. It is unassumable and "unassumability". "Unassumability" does not result from the excessive intensity of a sensation, from some sort of quantitative "too much", surpassing the measure of our sensibility and our means of grasping and holding. It results from an excess, a "too much" which is inscribed in a sensorial content, penetrating as suffering the dimensions of meaning which seem to be opened and grafted on to it. For the Kantian "I think" – which is capable of reuniting and embracing the most heterogeneous and separate givens into order and meaning under its *a priori* forms – it is as if suffering were not only a *given* refractory to synthesis, but the *way* in which the refusal opposed to the assembling of givens into a meaningful whole is opposed to it: suffering is at once

232 Robert Gibbs, *Correlations in Rosenzweig und Levinas*, Princeton University Press, Princeton 1992, p. 26.

what disturbs order and this disturbance itself: a backwards consciousness, "operating" not as "grasp" but as revulsion. It is a modality, or the
categorical ambiguity of quality and modality. Taken as an "experienced"
content, the denial and refusal of meaning which is imposed as a sensible
quality is the way in which the unbearable is precisely not borne by consciousness, the way this not-being-borne is, paradoxically, itself a sensation of a given. This is a quasi-contradictory structure, but a contradiction
which is not formal like that of the dialectical tension between the affirma-
tive and the negative which arises for the intellect; it is a contradiction by
way of sensation: the plaintiveness of pain, hurt.[233]

Suffering as a given in consciousness is a feeling, a "sensation",
which means that it too is something akin to a "hyletic datum",
inasmuch as it defies synthesis, i.e. the act of identification. However, its resistance is stronger because it rejects "intentionality". It
is "inside-out consciousness", the consciousness of something that
refuses to be consciousness (it is unacquirable or unassumable). It is
also therefore the experience of this unacquirability (unassumability), unbearability. But what does inside-out consciousness mean? It
means openness to the outside, into the outside – in relation to the
Other (albeit on the level of "feeling"). The outside is thus always
already inside.

And the text continues as follows:

Suffering, in its hurt and its in-spite-of-consciousness, is passivity. Here,
"taking cognisance" is no longer, properly speaking, a taking; it is no longer
the performance of an act of consciousness, but, in its adversity, a submission; and even a submission to the submitting, since the 'content' of which
the aching consciousness is conscious is precisely this very adversity of
suffering, its hurt. But, here again, this *passivity* – in the sense of a modality – signifies as a *quiddity*, and perhaps as the place where passivity

233 Levinas, "La souffrance inutile". In: *Entre nous,* p. 107.

signifies originally, independent of its conceptual opposition to activity. (...) The passivity of suffering is more profoundly passive than the receptivity of our senses, which is already the activity of welcome, and straight away becomes perception. In suffering sensibility is a vulnerability, more passive than receptivity; it is an ordeal more passive than experience. It is precisely an evil. It is not, to tell the truth, through passivity that evil is described, but through evil that suffering is understood. Suffering is a pure undergoing.

The ethical relationship is established on a pre-reflexive level, on the level of sensibility, i.e. on a deeper level than intentional consciousness.

Let's return for a moment to the story of Yosl Rakover. For me it is intolerable to share in (the co-experience of) his suffering: I am aware of his *vulnerability*. But where does my understanding of vulnerability come from? From the openness of the human being that is not openness of the consciousness of characterised intentionality (an openness to everything that is shown to me), but openness as "the denuding of the skin exposed to wounds and outrage. This openness is the vulnerability of a skin exposed, in wounds and outrage, beyond all that can show itself...".[234] This is the core of Levinas's concept of subjectivity, of the subject, which in classical (and modern) philosophy is defined by consciousness and its reflexive relationship – by a closing off – within itself. Levinas is searching for the origin of subjectivity *prior* to this consciousness: its source is the experience (sensation) of *radical passivity*, of that which is implicated in vulnerability.

The subjectivity of the subject is a radical passivity of man, who also posits himself, declares himself to be, and considers his sensibility as an attribute.

---

[234] Emmanuel Levinas, *Collected Philosophical Papers,* trans. Alphonso Lingis, Nijhoff, Haag 1987, p. 146.

This passivity is more passive than every passivity; it is repressed in the pronominal particle self (se) which has no nominative form.[235]

Clearly an extraordinarily complex "experience". Vulnerability is the "capability" to receive a strike. Openness. However, this is openness *as the relationship to another Other*. I am injured by the other, injured by his suffering, which I understand from my own vulnerability. This is why for me Yosl's fate is intolerable, unacceptable. Subjectivity is primarily this sensitivity, sensibility.

> Vulnerability is obsession by the other or an approaching of the other. ... To suffer from another is to have charge of him, to support him, to be in his place, to be consumed by him. ... Nothing is more passive than this being implicated prior to my freedom, this pre-original involvement.[236]

235 Ibid.
236 Ibid., p. 147.

25

However, in the word *désastre* there is an echo of the Holocaust:

The unknown name, alien to naming:
The holocaust, the absolute event of history – which is a date in history –
that utter-burn where all history took fire, where the movement of Meaning
was swallowed up, where the gift, which knows nothing of forgiving or of
consent, shattered without giving place to anything that can be affirmed,
that can be denied – gift of very passivity, gift of what cannot be given. How
can it be preserved, even by thought? How can thought be made the keeper
of the holocaust where all was lost, including guardian thought?
In the mortal intensity, the fleeing silence of the countless cry.[237]

This echo is to be heard most clearly in an understanding of "human-ism" that is different to Sartre's existential version or Heidegger's ontological version by virtue of being highly impacted by the experience that the concentration camps survivors recorded and that can be summed up as follows: Man is the indestructible that can be destroyed, *l'indestructible, qui peut être détruit.* This was how Blanchot responded upon encountering Robert Antelme, who in 1947, after his return from Buchenwald, published *L'espèce humaine*, his testimony of experiences that he describes as "surpass-ing all imagination".[238] For Blanchot, who soon became acquainted with the author, this book became a kind of bridge to thinking the outside through the relationship to the other as a "relationship with-out relationship", a relationship via irreducible difference, as well as another opportunity to offer a dialogic commentary on Levinas's concept of ethics.

---

237 Blanchot, *The Writing of the Disaster*, p. 80.
238 Robert Antelme, *The Human Race*, trans. Jeffrey Haight and Annie Mahler, The Marlboro Press, Evanston, 1992, p. 2.

In this text, part of the collection *L'Entretien infini*, Blanchot first examines Antelme's book from the broader perspective of the "final solution of the Jewish Question" in order to base his reading on a consideration of what it means "to be a Jew". Crucial to this is the idea of exodus and exile as an essentially nomadic idea,[239] an existence unfettered by appropriation and ownership (identification), i.e. the idea of a positive relationship to exteriority in which another dimension opens up to Man, namely a relationship to that which is beyond his reach. The true meaning of this relationship is suggested by the prefixes to the words that describe it: exile, exodus, exteriority, ex-istence (or separation, *dés-astre*).

> The Jew is the man of origins, who relates to the origin, not by dwelling, but by distancing himself, in this saying that the truth of beginning is in separation.[240]

(Derrida's commentary on *The Origin of Geometry*, more Husserlian in style than Husserl himself, infers something very similar.)

Antelme's book contains an extreme form of the relationship to another, namely the relationship to the Other in myself, i.e. a relationship by means of which, without its being possible for me to be aware of the fact, I always already am. In a state of extreme crisis, Man (a concentration camp prisoner) found himself on a boundary on which he was deprived of the power to say "I". He was deprived of the world and there is now nothing but this Other, by which he "is not". Existence in the first person singular is outside him, i.e. it is affirmed only in this (his) anonymous presence without speech. He lives an egoism without ego, his adherence to life is an adherence to

---

239 Baudrillard and especially Deleuze later revived the idea of "nomadicism", linking it more closely to Nietzsche than Blanchot.
240 Maurice Blanchot, *The Infinite Conversation*, trans. Susan Hanson, University of Minnesota Press, Minneapolis and London 1993, p. 125.

an *impersonal* life – and yet it is this that is experience of ex-istence, experience of the *il y a*.

> As though the inexorable affirmation in man that always keeps him standing were more terrible than universal disaster (*désastre*). (…) Having fallen not only below the individual, but also below every class and every real collective relation, the person no longer exists in his or her personal identity. In this sense the one afflicted is already outside the world, a being without horizon. And he is not a thing; even useless, a thing is precious. The deported person is not a thing belonging to the SS: when still working as a labourer, his work gives him, however little, the value of a man exploited; but for the essentially deported person, the one who no longer has either a face or speech, the work he is forced to do is designed only to exhaust his power to live and to deliver him over to the boundless insecurity of the elements. Nowhere any recourse: outside the cold, inside hunger; everywhere an indeterminate violence.[241]

The destruction of existence in an actualising world in which the relationship of the appropriated and identified holds sway, i.e. the relationship of power eliminating everything inappropriable, reveals the indestructibility of ex-istence, inasmuch as it returns it to the element from which it was torn as "hypostasis" (the term is Levinas's), inasmuch as it returns it to the impersonal and neutral *il y a* (neither subject nor object, neither inside nor outside, neither night nor day but another night, neither speech nor silence but a *murmur*). It finds itself outside the relationship of control, it is the experience of the relationship to the Other as Other. Separated from itself it relates to the strangeness of otherness, it is this relationship to that which is indestructible in it by virtue of being non-actualisable.

This can also be read as a commentary on Levinas's equation of ontology and war or totality. *Désastre*: the negative lesson of the Ho-

---

241 Blanchot, *The Infinite Conversation*, p. 130.

locaust, but also *désastre* as the separation that is the prerequisite or condition of the relationship to the Other and otherness.

A more careful reading of the texts by Blanchot reveals an important shift in comparison with Levinas's ethics as first philosophy. In the case of Blanchot the relationship to another is not meant solely as the relationship to the Other, but is generalised. It is a relationship to the unknown as unknown, in which the unknown is affirmed in that which makes it unknown. Unveiling it leaves it in its veiledness. That which is thus "unveiled" must remain intact. The unknown is neutral. Not only does it not belong to our horizon, but it does not belong to any representable horizon (in the Husserlian sense of the word).[242] As so often in Blanchot, here too the experience returns of literature, the work, writing as *écriture*: every interpretation inter alia points to what is apprehensible only at the moment of ineluctable loss – the rustle or drone of speech, the murmur that captures the work, is the presence of things prior to the existence of the world (as the horizon of all horizons).[243] To formulate this conservatively: the meaning of the work is inexhaustible, not as a consequence of the deep thinking of its author, but thanks to the historical depth and autonomous life of speech.[244] Derrida will go on to say that no interpretation is capable of holding back the deferral of meaning in its articulations. And prior to this, Charles Sanders Peirce had already intuited at the end of the semiotic process the constantly escaping final interpreter. The uniqueness that interpretation wishes to highlight is always already lost in said uniqueness as mediated by interpretation. *Désastre*: immediacy is unattainable, it is outside.

242 See "Connaissance de l'inconnu", in *The Infinite Conversation,* p. 51.
243 Also in the essay "La littérature et le droit de la mort", in: Maurice Blanchot, *La part du feu,* Gallimard, Paris 1949.
244 For more on this see Ulrich Haase, William Large, *Maurice Blanchot,* Routledge, London and New York 2001, p. 55.

Immediacy not only rules out all mediation; it is the infiniteness of a presence such that it can no longer be spoken of, for the relation itself, be it ethical or ontological, has burned up all at once in a night bereft of darkness. In this night there are no longer any terms, there is no longer a relation, no longer a beyond – in this night God himself has annulled himself. Or, one must manage somehow to understand the immediate in the past tense. This renders the paradox practically unbearable. Only in accordance with such a paradox can we speak of disaster. We can no more think of the immediate than we can think of an absolutely passive past, but patience in us vis-à-vis a forgotten affliction is the mark of this past, its oblivious prolongation. When we are patient, it is always with respect to an infinite affliction which does not reach us in the present, but befalls by linking us to a past without memory. Other's affliction, and the other as affliction.[245]

The philosopher is not marked by astonishment but by fear, fear as a "disposition" in which, flung out of himself, he experiences the Outside, the Unknown. However, in this respect Blanchot refers to the question posed by René Char: How can we live without the unknown before us?[246] If the unknown is outside the horizon of all horizons, that is, outside our understanding, apprehension and authorisation, outside the field of the visible (including both the visible and its symmetrical counterpart the invisible), and if it cannot ever be part of any whole, then it can only be that which is forever on the point of arriving without in any way being possible to anticipate and without ever being able to become presence – the relationship to the unknown is *une relation de non-présence*, a relationship to which identity, unity and presence is foreign. *Désastre* is another name for difference (and in Derrida *différance*). Both implicate the relationship in radical separation. And so humanism may be destroyed, but a trace of it lingers as resistance outside the relationship of control.

245 Maurice Blanchot, *Writing of Disaster*, trans. Ann Smock, University of Nebraska Press, Lincoln and London, 1986, pp. 24–25.
246 "René Char et la pensée du neutre", in Blanchot, *The Infinite Conversation*, p. 298 et seq.

Désastre: Man is inseparable from his otherness, but only inasmuch as he is inassimilable by history. *Désastre*: the trace shows that to which it refers, in its escape and as escaping. However, for this very reason the outside is somehow inside and we are forever in the proximity of that which is on the point of arriving.

Kracauer and Adorno still in a certain sense hold fast to an idea of redemption, though as paleonymy or under erasure (*sous rature*). However, Kracauer's wait in the hotel lobby for the "last things before the last" displays a striking resemblance to Blanchot's thought from the outside, however different their starting points. Both Levinas and Blanchot speak of original passivity that is the sign of an asymmetric relationship. The appropriate response is waiting, *l'attente*, not in anticipation but as a display of the absence of the last foundation (the past that was never the present) or the non-actualisability of that which is on the point of arriving. This involves waiting for the sake of waiting, i.e. waiting as patience.

> the impatience at the heart of error is the essential fault, because it misconstrues the very trueness of error which, like a law, requires that one never believe the goal is close or that one is coming nearer to it. One must never have done with the indefinite; one must never grasp – as if it were the immediate, the already present – the profundity of inexhaustible absence (…) it is impatience which makes the goal inaccessible by substituting for it the proximity of an intermediary figure. It is impatience that destroys the way toward the goal by preventing us from recognising in the intermediary the figure of the immediate.[247]

247 Maurice Blanchot, *Literární prostor*, pp. 98 and 99–100. *The Space of Literature*, trans. Ann Smock, University of Nebraska Press, Lincoln, London 1982, p. 79.

26

The transformation of philosophical discourse is a process that is played out on many levels simultaneously. It is not linear and includes the interaction of a large number of elements, the effects of which only become apparent from a distance. A description of this transformation should therefore examine the dynamic of the comprehensive system rather than the structure. One starting point is a method that could be summarised in the form of a single principle: the same again but differently. Only by means of the re-layering of different perspectives in which the first description is repeated differently is it possible to see broader contexts shining through while at the same time noticing details, charting shifts in emphasis, monitoring other trajectories of lines, and being permanently aware of the openness of the field undergoing this transformation. Borrowing from mathematical topology, we might also call this method the baker's transformation. The distant finds itself in immediate proximity through a process of folding, while the proximate recedes from itself and different connections become apparent.

27

If we pursue our exploration of the unknown to its limit, we encounter what not only Blanchot but Derrida too called the *secret*. If, inspired by phenomenology, we ask ourselves how the secret is manifest (if we know of the secret then it has been manifested in some way while remaining a secret in this manifestation), the answer would be: the secret discloses itself by resisting its own disclosure. This is a surprising modality of the relationship of inside and outside: we know the inside of a secret that outwardly remains unknown. In a sense, the secret as the unknown is a crisis of disclosure, an example of a relationship through difference.

This relationship can be demonstrated in various ways. Let us return to Walter Benjamin and his examination of the middle class interior in nineteenth-century Paris.[248] The interior is a place in which a living space is established. An apartment is a person's universe, his salon a private theatre box, its owner's enclosure. It is the interior, insulated from the exterior, fenced off from the exterior, the exterior that is present in it but deprived of its exteriority in the manner of collectible items. Its occupant controls the without from within by means of sophisticated optical equipment, for instance using a spy mirror, very popular at the time, on a window. The owner thus usurps the outside, which is domesticated by means of the mirror.[249]

However, the spy mirror finds us not only in a middle-class drawing room functioning as a means of situating the exterior inside as the interior, but back at Husserl's phenomenology. The mirror is a highly accurate *diagram* of phenomenological reduction as the founding act and precondition for an investigation of the constitu-

---

248 Walter Benjamin, *DasPassagen-Werk*, Suhrkamp, Frankfurt a.M. 1983, pp. 281–300.
249 Negatively in the case of the *Straßenfilm*: the shadows of the strange, desolate world of a city street are projected into the ceiling of a room. This is how the famous film *Die Straße* by Karl Grune of 1923 begins.

tion of the world. One might hang the inscription "transcendence in immanence" or "reduction to pure phenomenon" beneath this window mirror, which projects the outside world into the room. If we are to understand wherein resides the mysteriousness of mysteries and eventually of the secret, we must clearly pass through classical phenomenology. However, let us bear in mind that this mirror could also be seen as a warning regarding philosophy itself. I will leave it to others to find examples of how this might be so.

Couched in the language of phenomenology and its concepts: I cannot doubt that I perceive, for when reflecting upon this experience I have in front of me (before the eyes of a reflecting or observing consciousness) the unmediated givenness of the *reel parts* of this experience (be that the experience of perception, fantasy, remembrance, etc.). Whether or not there is something outside the experience that really exists is a question I shall not ask. I did not lose the world after this reduction, because as well as *reel* immanence (the moments that are a *reel* part of the experience, that are in it), there appears ideal or *intentional immanence* (this is summarised by Husserl's definition of intentionality: every experience is an experience of something, means something). Both, i.e. the immediate givenness of the experience and that which is meant as intended, are an undisputed part of that which Husserl calls the *phenomenon* and which will be (the sole and exclusive) theme of phenomenological description and analysis.

To have an appearance before one's eye, which refers to something that is not itself given in the phenomenon, and to doubt whether it exists or how its existence is to be understood that makes sense. But to see and to intend nothing other than what is grasped in the seeing, and yet still question and doubt – that makes no sense at all.[250]

250 Edmund Husserl, *The Idea of Phenomenology*, trans. Lee Hardy, Kluwer Academic Publishers, Dodrecht 1990, p. 38.

Husserl is now in a position to claim that we must distinguish between a *reel* analysis of phenomena and an intentional (or ideal) analysis, between *reel* immanence and ideal or intentional immanence.

Perception includes perceiving the flowering tree, i.e. the tree so designated: this can be extracted from it by means of intentional analysis: the description of a tree qua tree by this perception of the perceived extracts something from the perception, something that belongs to it, something that "lies within it", but does not lie *reely* and does not have to have any "genuine being". The transcendent in some way, therefore, obviously belongs to the phenomenon, as perceived, conjured up, imaged in fantasy or otherwise cogitated.[251]

In other words, the outside is inside, but not as the outside, not as something that could be transcendent in respect of consciousness. Neither real nor *reel* transcendence, nothing of that kind can intrude into the phenomenological approach. Thanks to this immanence the problem of knowledge is "free from all mystery", as Husserl claims in *The Idea of Phenomenology*, i.e. the mystery is resolved by virtue of the outside being inside as the interior, transcendence transformed wholly into immanence.

However, this will not suffice. We must follow Husserl a lot further and in much greater detail.

Feelings, experiences, *Erlebnisse*, along with everything contained within them – these are phenomena, a kind of safe space that can be investigated and analysed using the phenomenological approach (excluding all external assumptions). A very important term in this investigation is "apperception", since this concept unites the delineation of the intentional relationship, i.e. the fact that every experience is always an experience of something. For instance, "I perceive

---

251 Edmund Husserl, *Einführung in die Phänomenologie der Erkenntnis* (1909), ed. Elisabeth Schuhmann, Husserliana VII, Springer 2005, p. 56 (trans. here Phil Jones).

something". To be even more precise, this means: "I perceive something as something". Apperception is this "as". I perceive a building if I perceive it *as* a building, if, as Husserl also says, in the perception of building I *intend* a building. In Husserl's lexicon a synonym for apperception is *Auffassung* or concept, or *Deutung* or something like (in a weaker sense of the word) interpretation: the intentional object, intentionally immanent objectiveness, is "constituted" (another key term in classical phenomenology) through apperception (which, however, usually takes place without our knowing: it is not a conscious act) from the material of sensory perception; that which is thus experienced content acquires its *meaning*, it is endowed with meaning (*Sinngebung*). This is then the topic of the investigation of the noetic-noematic correlation, which is the level of *static* phenomenology because it involves the investigation of essential structures within the framework of an intentional relationship.

However, this is still too brief. Two questions still need to be answered. Firstly: experience must be able to go back to "something, anything", and therefore we must investigate this "givenness of something". And secondly: apperception (interpretation) cannot be without some kind of guidance; if apperception (*Auffassung, Deutung*) is conceived of as the identification of something *as* something, there has to be something here with which it is identifiable (within certain limits), i.e. something like an advance prefigurement, on which the apperception of something can be based.

One, of course, leads to the other. And we are still operating on the level of "passivity" ("I mean a tree": quite simply I perceive a tree), and so everything takes place without explicit consciousness or explicit participation. Or on the level of "pre-predicative" experience.[252] Husserl resolves all of these problems (I am simplifying, but not much) within the framework of *genetic* phenomenology, usually

---

252 Cf. Edmund Husserl, *Experience and Judgment*, trans. James S. Churchill and Karl Ameriks, Routledge & Kegan Paul, London 1973. Part I . Prepredicative (Receptive) Experience.

associated with his later writings even though the very possibility of static phenomenology presupposes genetic phenomenology.

Perception is always the exemplary experience for Husserl. Perception is the perception of something, i.e. something must be given. This means that something must detach itself from a uniform background, it must be *abgehoben* or lifted, profile itself, stand out against the background as an approximately identical unit. If it is "to arise" (let us note in passing, so as not to push things beyond the bounds of the tolerably complex), it is clear that "time" is a condition. This means that consciousness is most deeply the "temporalisation of time", consciousness is the "stream of consciousness", the consciousness of time is the original site (*Urstätte*) of the constitution of something as something. And this "something" must somehow be identity, because if it were not, it would merge into something else. The fixing or retention of something is process, movement, and therefore (already) presupposes temporality, time, a duration within which it can take place. Only in this way does analysis arrive at something that stimulates perception by virtue of detaching itself from the field from which it "affects" us, as Husserl says.

Originally, then, there is the homogenous, uniform field from which "something" can emerge. However, even within this homogeneity something may be in contrast to something else: red stripes on a white background, for instance. In general, then, something detaches itself from the background and in contrast to the background. However, it is not static, because if this involves "standing out" from the background, it means that originally affinity and merger function as limits in every contrast (something almost merges with the background, but now it is also "something"). These are elementary visual givens. The limit here is sameness or *Gleichheit*, against which "something" emerges in "gradual cover" thanks to repetition and summarisation, but always in the familiarity-strangeness dynamic. If the "similar" is here, which detaches itself from the non-similar, it is the product of the "cover" or *Deckung* (which is why it is necessary that the last foundation be time). Husserl summarises the whole of this complex act in *Erfahrung und Urteil* thus: *associative* genesis controls the genesis of passive prefigured givennesses.[253] For the sake of basic orientation I would merely add, with caveats: that which is described in this way is something like the creative interplay of subjectivity and the world. However, I add this only in order to make clear what Husserl had in mind when he says that phenomenology is the uncovering of "hidden subjectivity", the *leistende Subjektivität* in whose acts the world as always already given to us becomes our world by virtue of what it is for us, etc.[254] I use the word "interplay" so that it is clear that this does not mean that the subject produces its own world. It "constitutes" its world, "reveals" it – this would perhaps be the most accurate description (and it would be possible to return to the *Crisis*, to the theme of responsibility for the inspection, fulfilment of the idea, etc.). However, at the same time it is clear that all of this still stands on the fundamental principle of transcendence in immanence in the form of *intentional immanence*, because it is impossible to abandon this dimension without abandoning phenomenology itself.

The whole of this initial phenomenological theme can be brought to a close with a much discussed quote regarding "association". In *Erfahrung und Urteil*, which deals extensively with the importance of associations, Husserl says the following:

Affinity or similarity can have different degrees within the limits of the most perfect affinity, of likeness without difference. Wherever there is no perfect likeness, *contrast* goes hand in hand with similarity (affinity): the coming into prominence of the unlike from a basis of the common. If we pass from likeness to likeness, the new like presents itself as *repetition*. Its content

---

253 Regarding Husserl's concept of association see Elmar Hollenstein, *Phänomenologie der Assoziation. Zur Struktur und Funktion eines Grundprinzips der passiven Genesis bei E. Husserl*, Martinus Nijhoff, Haag 1972.
254 Husserl, *Erfahrung und Urteil*, pp. 46–47.

comes into completely perfect coincidence with that of the first. This is what we refer to as *blending*. (…) What in a purely static description appears to be likeness or similarity must therefore be considered in itself as being already the product of the one or the other kind of synthesis of coincidence, which we denote by the traditional term *association*, but with a change of sense. It is the phenomenon of associative genesis which dominates this sphere of passive pregivenness, established on the basis of syntheses of internal time-consciousness. The term "association" denotes in this context a form belonging essentially to consciousness in general, a *form of the regularity of immanent genesis*. That association can become a general theme of phenomenological description and not merely one of objective psychology is due to the fact that the phenomenon of *indication* (*Anzeige*) is something which can be exhibited from the point of view of phenomenology. (…) Association comes into question in this context exclusively as the *purely immanent connection of "this recalls that"*, "one calls attention to the other."**255**

So what exactly is phenomenology capable of telling us?

Every experience has its own horizon; every experience has its core of actual and determinate cognition, its own content of immediate determinations which give themselves; but beyond this core of determinate quiddity, of the truly given as "itself-there", it has its own horizon. This implies that every experience refers to the possibility – and it is a question here of the capacity (*Ver-möglichkeit*) of the ego – not only of explicating, step by step, the thing which has been given in a first view, in conformity with what is really self-given thereby, but also of obtaining, little by little as experience continues, new determinations of the same thing. Every experience can be extended in a continuous chain of explicative individual experiences, united synthetically as a single experience, open without limit, of the same.**256**

255 Edmund Husserl, *Experience and Judgment*, pp. 74–75
256 Ibid, p. 32.

Husserl very appositely calls this "and so on" "induction" in the sense of *Vordeutung* – in the sense of anticipatory intentionality (the internal and external horizon).

So why the need for this digression? This is the connection point of both: *apperception*, thanks to which I perceive something as something, is "guided" by this (habituated) structure of reference, remembrance and suggestion. It is a strange "circle". "Something is reminiscent of something" is the demonstrable moment of experience (as Husserl wants). It becomes our guide to the analysis that ascertains the "conditions of possibility". At the end of this analysis we understand how *apperception* is possible. In other words, it is impossible to escape from the structure of "something refers to something different", which, however, is the same as sealing the outside inside. This different is different because something similar refers to it (both are the "same" within limits). The question is whether it would not be possible to find traces of *another limit* in this structure, which, it does not need to be emphasised, is guided by the model of *identifying knowledge.*

If it were not possible to discover any trace of something like this, if it were not possible to discover the hidden origin of some serious "crisis", this would mean that something like an intentional relationship to secrecy would be an absurdity for Husserl's phenomenology in the same ways as, for instance, Freud's unconscious. However, this does not mean that we have not obtained something. On the contrary, we now have a lexicon at our disposal using which we can very precisely formulate questions such as: how can we imagine an intentional relationship to mystery, and what should this act "mean"?

28

The mystery that emerges in phenomenology is the mystery of how something mysterious can disclose itself. And mindful of limits: how can the secret or, borrowing from Blanchot, the unknown, show itself? The problem resides in the very concept of the limit, that we might characterise very simply: if something is defined by its limit, then upon attaining this limit that which is thus defined is annulled and disappears. And this is how it is with secrecy as the limit-form of mystery.

Husserl's analysis of experience in the end reveals the particular ground of the pre-predicative experience that is structured by "horizons" that allow for anticipation and guide our understanding of that which is showing itself as showing itself in apperception. However, this texture is something that is constituted procedurally, by means of the sedimentation of the already experienced and the association of that which emerges in this process and differs by virtue of being in contrast to it. It is the level of passive functioning that is nevertheless the basis or footing for all other acts following on therefrom: perception, cognition, and finally science itself, which deals in general concepts.

Before I continue, I would like to take the liberty of a certain interpretative intervention and sketch out what in my opinion is a fundamental problem that has accompanied phenomenology from its very beginnings to recent texts. Phenomenological analyses are possible only given a certain approach. This does not simply concern impartiality (*epoché*, reduction); this approach must be free of all expediency and special interests. The phenomenologist is not interested in discovering something pertaining to the being of the so-called real world. In the final analysis his approach is detached even from that which is associated with the empirical I of the analysing philosopher, etc. For instance, in the *Introduction to Husserlian Phenomenology* by Bernet, Kern and Marbach the authors state very clearly that the last realm to which phenomenology descends, i.e. the world of our life, is given prior to the stipulation of all practical purposes and, according to Husserl, may be concretely and universally seen only in an attitude that is disengaged from all purposes.[257] From 1891 to 93, Husserl worked intensively on an investigation into the character of formal logic. Especially instructive in this respect is his critique of Schröder's *Vorlesungen über die Algebra der Logik,* 1 (1890), which Husserl reviewed in 1891.[258] One of Husserl's objections runs as follows: purely formal deduction does not refer to the specific content of terms in a judgement. Formalised logic includes only that which can be deduced on the basis of pure form. However, logic consists of mental operations that are beyond the realm of pure deduction. In contrast, Husserl demands, inter alia, a logic of pure content, all the more so since, in his opinion, every extensional logic is necessarily supported by intentional logic. It is clear how the study of arithmetic gives rise to the *Logische Untersuchungen,* in which (partly under the influence of Frege's critique) Husserl wishes to recognise logical and mathematical concepts as objective, namely ideal objects that have their own individual being independent of the psyche. An analysis of their originary givenness in consciousness becomes that which will be termed (static, descriptive) phenomenology, in which Husserl tries to prove the legitimacy of the "opinion of generality" and hint at a path leading to the constitution of generalities, i.e. pure logical content, and thus to correct logic as the basis of our relationship to the world. In other words, Husserl's interest, which is never suspended though is often only implicit, is in the establishment of "content" logic – *Weltlogik* in the final analysis – which presupposes a precursory, albeit completely peculiar "logic" of the natural world, the idealisation of which allows for logic and science. This is the birth certificate of his phenomenology. However,

257 Rudolf Bernet, Iso Kern, Eduard Marbach, *Introduction to Husserlian Phenomenology.* Northwestern University Press, Evanston 1993.
258 Edmund Husserl, *Aufsätze und Rezensionen,* ed. Bernard Rang, Husserliana XXII, pp. 3–43.

alongside this is the fact that for Husserl the last vanishing point of *Erkenntnis*, knowledge as the most fundamental relationship to the world, and, to put things as generally as possible, the last "horizon", is the modern world in the sense of the Enlightenment project (content logic as *Weltlogik* is the last version of the French revolutionary *Encyclopédie*). However, this means that, though his phenomenological approach is reduced, this intention inexplicably remains present in it, i.e. the unreflected assumption of the priority of cognition as re-cognition (identification), which phenomenology legitimises by virtue of the fact that its *Wesenschau* is a method of obtaining the *pure content* of our thinking (while at the same time revealing its intersubjective validity). The French would say that the basic position, the *Grundhaltung*, of classical phenomenology, is logocentrism. Husserl says the same thing, albeit in a more complicated fashion:

> (It is necessary) to traverse the path which leads from mute, conceptless experience and its universal interweavings; first to typical, vague, primary universality, which is sufficient in everyday life; and thence to the genuine and true concepts, such as genuine science must presuppose them to be.[259]

However, what this interest opens up in phenomenology is the irreducible dimension of crisis. In order to clarify matters, we must return to the quote above. In fact, I left out one sentence that in this context is highly significant. Husserl looks in detail at the horizontal structure of the pre-predicative, passively self-establishing realm of every experience in which every explicit, to wit, conscious relationship must be founded and thanks to which the "apperception" of something as something is possible. This must be borne in mind if we want, using this lexicon, to formulate the question of what and

---

[259] Ms. F 1 32, p. 39b/40a, quoted from Bernet et al, *Introduction to Husserlian Phenomenology*, Northwestern University Press, Evanston 1993, p. 221.

how the intentional relationship to secrecy as the limit-designation of something radically unknown should be "intended". In the passage, now cited in full, Husserl says:

Affinity or similarity can have different degrees within the limits of the most perfect affinity, of likeness without difference. Wherever there is no perfect likeness, *contrast* goes hand in hand with similarity (affinity): the coming into prominence of the unlike from a basis of the common. If we pass from likeness to likeness, the new like presents itself as *repetition*. Its content comes into completely perfect coincidence with that of the first. This is what we refer to as *blending*. *If we pass from the similar to the similar, a kind of coincidence also takes place, but it is only partial, being subject to the simultaneous opposition of the unlike.* In this overlapping in conformity with similarity there is also something on the order of a blending, but relative only to the element which is like; there is no pure and perfect blending, as with complete likeness. What in a purely static description appears to be likeness or similarity must therefore be considered in itself as being already the product of the one or the other kind of synthesis of coincidence, which we denote by the traditional term association, but with a change of sense. It is the phenomenon of associative genesis which dominates this sphere of passive pre-givenness, established on the basis of syntheses of internal time-consciousness.

The term "association" denotes in this context a form belonging essentially to consciousness in general, a *form of the regularity of immanent genesis*. That association can become a general theme of phenomenological description and not merely one of objective psychology is due to the fact that the phenomenon of *indication* (*Anzeige*) is something which can be exhibited from the point of view of phenomenology (…) Association comes into question in this context exclusively as the purely immanent connection of "this recalls that", "one calls attention to the other".[260]

---

260 Husserl, *Experience and Judgement*, pp. 74–75.

What follows is the sentence I omitted: "If we pass from the similar to the similar, a kind of coincidence also takes place, but it is only partial, being subject to the simultaneous opposition of the unlike (*Widerstreit des nicht Gleichen*)".

Husserl here describes in detail the passively proceeding (i.e. without the participation of the consciousness) performance of identification: the similar emerged that, in the flow of consciousness (in the temporality of the flow of consciousness), coincides with the similar (if the similar emerged, than this was because another similar emerged in this flow) – and the identifiable is identified. I do not see different red stains or shades of red, but the red colour of the object (homogenous). The unidentifiable is (without the participation of consciousness) *eliminated*. This is a condition of our being able (in conscious perception) to perceive the objectivity of any kind, and this is Husserl's interest linked with this analysis, this is the condition of the possibility of further objectivisation and idealisation. However, in these passively ongoing acts horizons are also formed, on the basis of passive associations, gradually, through the settling or sedimentation of identifications (or to put it another way: habituality or "custom"), which are like (limitlessly infinite and therefore insurmountable) extensions of similarities through their association. And in these horizons (the world according to Husserl is the "horizon of all horizons") they move (not completely consciously) within the framework of the intentional relationship of apperception, i.e. understanding, *Deutung*, "interpretation", because we are always moving in the texture of "something is reminiscent of something else". And it is also for this reason that in 1921, in one of the appendices to his early lecture *An Introduction to Phenomenology* from 1905, in which he analyses the example of "perceiving something as a tree" that I see for the first time, Husserl writes:

The unknown is experienced more in an apperception that is furnished with a horizon and within this horizon with an intentional structural form that in the lines of intentional genesis extends to earlier individual universal apperceptions of "well known trees", etc. The earlier, genuine knowledge originally established its own habitual experience and this experience is in the new cases awakened "through analogy" and tacitly implies the apperceptive horizon – in analogy. It is not re-cognition individually of the same tree, oven, etc., but of the same or similar tree and then with awareness of the distance from similarity, covered in difference.

Apperception (the perception of something as something) is possible only on the basis of *Weckung* or awakening, i.e. by virtue of the fact that the given "impression" awakens certain close "horizons" with which it is associated.

Awakening of the known (with phenomenological differences: the awakening of a certain individual knowledge, then of an uncertain concatenation of such knowledge) can then take place in such a way that something new, something unknown simultaneously awakes different series that are not connected by coverage to any type. The object resembles a fir tree, also a spruce, different conifers, etc. Under the title "fir tree" typical designations were formed, others under the title "pine tree", etc. However, the new does not correspond to any of these types, and yet it resembles all of them and has something in common with all of them. How is this possible? The pine tree I see for the first time reminds me of a "fir tree" – a certain order of typical coverage with a certain type, which, however, is not in genuine agreement with that tree which is seen and does not match it even upon further acquaintance.

We therefore have to say: everything we familiarise ourselves with can enter into series in which a type takes shape, either in its own, fully demonstrative comparison, or a "re-awakening" of an old apperception and through coverage by virtue of the transposition of empty ideas of the old perception onto empty ideas of the new experience. Every perception (like every originary appearing experience) leaves behind an "unconscious" remnant as permanent experience. This remnant is awoken as "empty idea", which is covered with a new opinion, one that is both in accordance with that which is actually perceived and in accordance with its horizons that through coverage become designated. The same takes place during its own comparison if during the transition the experience activated is already gone as a live act and the still vivid retention is already empty but accompanied by a relative larger empty designation that is translated via the sense of the new experience. This is how open series are created in passivity, as soon as in the necessary process of atrophy they lose their certainty of the awoken old experience and their subjects lose their individuality, the relationship to a firmly given temporal surrounding, i.e. their temporal position. This uncertainty lends the awoken the character of "some A", where A is a complex of moments that are awoken by a new perception in a certain way.[261]

Whence Husserl's oft repeated sentence from Section 80 of *Erfahrung und Urteil*: the unknown is a mode of the known, *Unbekanntheit als Modus der Bekanntheit*.

It is perhaps now clear what the purpose has been of this close reading of Husserl's texts and what point we have arrived at. We have made it possible to formulate the following question: In what sense is this level of passive, pre-predicative experience, this last realm, genuinely the final level beneath which there is nothing more? Husserl's text seems to encourage a strange hypothesis: the eliminated has not disappeared but is somehow (still) beneath the horizon of all horizons. It is something that, paradoxically, finds itself on the other side of the horizon, beyond the horizon, which is unsurpassable and which, in its capacity as the endless, cannot logically have any "beyond". This is how the "exterior" might "appear" (though we should by rights, following Heidegger, place the word "appear" under erasure) if it is true that the unknown is possible only as a mode of the known. But perhaps it would be more accurate to say that the non-identified in the act of overlapping

---

261 Husserl, *Einführung in die Phänomenologie der Erkenntnis*, pp. 84–86, note 1 (trans. here Phil Jones).

of the similar is somehow mixed in said act, blends (*verschmelzt*) with the identical. And so the last field would be heterogeneous in a dual, very different, sense. 1) It would be heterogeneous if contrasts emerged in it or it stood out against the background and something detached itself from something similar, etc. However, in terms of limits this heterogeneity is the homogeneity of associatively entwined textures, since everything similar has its origin in the same, emerges from the same. And 2) it would be heterogeneous to the extent that in its folds it is – being pushed away – the radical exterior, radical heterogeneity in respect of the homogeneity thus constituted. This of course is something completely different to transcendence in the immanence of phenomenological reduction. It would be the intentionally *reel* moment of consciousness as escaping this consciousness: *that which within the phenomenon can never become a phenomenon, radical resistance to the (identifying) identification.*

Modern science resides in this dual heterogeneity. The first guarantees its possibility, while the second implies its ongoing crisis. Modern science, as Ladislav Hejdánek wrote in the 1960s, is *objective thinking* and in order for it be possible to exist, it must push resistance back "beyond" the horizon.

The originality is clear from this confrontation – albeit only in hindsight – of what Ladislav Hejdánek in various articles written in the mid-sixties called "non-objective thinking". (The first of these articles was published in 1964, which is quite remarkable if we compare what Hejdánek was saying with French philosophy of that time.) At least a brief mention is necessary because, I believe, Hejdánek's intention is very similar to that which we are following here, while the only difference (which make these texts so fascinating) is that his ideas are neither for nor against phenomenology. Basically, Hejdánek is saying the following. Yes, every thought is necessarily a thought of something. A thought that does not relate to some object is impossible. However, a pitfall of objective thinking is that it confuses that which, as phenomenology would say, is constituted by identifications, i.e. intentional objectivity, with "ontological" objectivities (Hejdánek). In other words, objective thinking ignores the non-objective components that all thinking includes, whether this be by ignoring them, not reflecting upon them, or not even seeing them. One of the examples Hejdánek offers that illustrates his concept of non-objectivity is an event, or the event-character of an event – not an event as outcome, but a "live" event. A live event would be, for example, the emergence of something new *that renders the past by means of its past*. However, this means that neither that necessary component that is the past as it is transformed by an event representing the arrival of the new, nor the future, is "objectively" given, because that is non-objective: the event opens itself to something that is not here. And so we can say:

Nowhere is it guaranteed (on the contrary, the opposite is quite easily demonstrated) that everything to which we relate essentially in our ideas and without which we could not meaningfully think and speak is objectively comprehensible, i.e. is conceivable as a subject, an intentional subject.[262]

And one further quote (from 1982, though for our purposes the chronology is unimportant):

Genuinely objective thinking fully and exclusively focuses on these subjective intentions and connotations and eradicates from its awareness any interest and any deliberate or merely conscious relationship to its non-objective intentions and connotations. This of course does not mean that it lacks such non-objective intentions and connotations, but more that it does not consciously heed them and does not forget them, that it does not

262 Ladislav Hejdánek, *Nepředmětnost v myšlení a ve skutečnosti*, OIKOYMENH, Praha 1997, p. 52.

deem them important and therefore leaves them in the shadows, in the dark corners that "nobody attends to".[263]

I would now like to attempt to tie these strands together so as to obtain the material for further considerations and above all for the more precise formulation of questions.

The displacement of life "beyond" the horizon or, as Ladislav Hejdánek would say, into the shadow and dark corners (something akin to "folds") results in the exterior becoming something beyond reach. It is something that *de jure* may not appear inside if the order of objective reality is not to collapse. Whence the various, intuited ciphers of this exterior, its (only possible) form inside, a phantom arriving "from behind" the horizon of all horizons. But also the critical threat of science in its "folds", whence the fear aroused by the unidentifiable or non-identical. It is everywhere and nowhere, it might be anything. Fear as an index of the world, which wants to have the unknown simply as a mode of the known. This is the effect that Feuillade's film of Fantômas has on us:

> Reality is no longer that which it is. By its transformation it is earlier than figures are hidden and objects change (...) It is a world in which the home is radically negated: man cannot settle anywhere. That which is supposed to operate as home produces something strangely unwelcoming (*das Unheimliche*). Flowers are not flowers but convenient places for secretly installed microphones, an ambulance is not an ambulance but a car that participates in raids, gloves are not gloves but a spine filled with narcotic (...) Doors are simply ornamental accessories. Entry to buildings is by windows, chimneys and cellars. Anyone who carelessly enters via the doors immediately collapses in a heap (...) Every *déjà vu* evokes something unpredictable. Feuillade brings public anxiety into the salons and testifies to what Walter Benjamin has already implied:

[263] Ibid., p. 55.

"The bourgeois interior of the 1860s to the 1890s – with its gigantic side-boards distended with carvings, the sunless corners where potted plants sit, – fittingly houses only the corpse. "On this sofa the aunt cannot but be murdered." The soulless luxuriance of the furnishings becomes true comfort only in the presence of a dead body.[264]

On the other hand, the enthusiasm of avant-garde artists for pulp fiction (the sensation novel) bears witness to the potential of the "non-objective" in folds, an openess to the future, the event.

The reduction of the exterior to intentional immanence also implies the elimination of empirical history. In this respect it is instructive to recall how Hejdánek speaks of the event and its unattainability by means of objective thinking. Phantoms appear on the reverse side of every *Weltlogik*, which presupposes a secondary position of everything empirical (contingent) in light of the "essential".

The relationship to mystery and secrecy. What type of intentionality is this? We would know nothing of secrecy, the unknown, the other, if we had not come across its traces. However, the intentional relationship to the trace is necessary non-objective intention because the trace, in the strict sense of the word, is a *trace of the unidentified, a trace of the unidentifiable.*

264 Thomas Brandlmeier, *Fantômas. Beiträge zur Panik des 20. Jahrhunderts*, Verbrecher Verlag, Berlin 2007, pp. 25–26. Walter Benjamin, *One-Way Street and Other Writings*, trans. Edmund Jephcott and Kingsley Shorter, NLB, 1979, p. 48.

29

Beneath the world as the horizon of all horizons, but actually already in its interstices, which are only seemingly covered by the continuity of associative references or inductions, is the outside. The unidentifiable is not the background of the identifiable in the manner of Gestalt psychology. Though the unrecognisable disappears beneath the known and though the outside is always already eliminated, it is genuinely the past that was never the present, trauma, or, more importantly, the *désastre*. However, it cannot be otherwise if the postulate is to apply of the identity of thinking and being respectively (as Husserl would have it), the "universal covering or match-up (*Deckung*) between language and thinking",[265] and if it is to be possible to recall the original meaning in the form of its continual returnable clarification (*Besinnung* and *Rückfrage*).

Nevertheless, these traces of the outside are somehow visible inside, now registered under different names, such as Levinas's *il y a* in fatigue and insomnia, or Blanchot's other night and whispering behind the words, *murmuring*. It is for this reason that testifying, witnessing and testimony characterising the thinking of the outside becomes an important means of showing.

However, in this case we can say that thinking of the outside is a response to the founding elimination of the base, to the trace as an irreducible reference to that "remainder" for which Derrida coins the neologism *restance non-présente*,[266] i.e. that which remains when the thing is recognised without being actualised because it resists its own showing. Consciousness qua consciousness, in other words, consists of the consciousness of loss. Thinking the outside evades mourning, in which the lost is gradually replaced by something else, but cultivates a melancholy that refuses to lose the loss.

---

265 Edmund Husserl, *Formale und transzendentale Logik. GS 7*, ed. Elisabeth Ströker, Felix Meiner Verlag, Hamburg 1992, p. 28.
266 E.g. Jacques Derrida, *Limited Inc.*, Galilée, Paris 1990, p. 33.

In this respect, Foucault's texts on literature, written between 1962 and 1966 and seemingly isolated in his work as a whole, acquire added significance. Their central theme, the ontology of speech, follows on in many ways from Maurice Blanchot, while hinting at the "discourse analysis" using which Foucault will demonstrate how every order of discourse is supported by the outside, which both establishes said order while being covered by it.[267] When Foucault argues that the statement "I speak" subjects the whole of modern literature (as well as philosophical discourse, we might add) to a test, he is paraphrasing or indirectly citing Blanchot, whose book *L'attente L'oubli* begins as follows:

Here, and on this sentence that was perhaps also meant for him, he was obliged to stop. It was practically while listening to her speak that he had written these notes. He still heard her voice as he wrote. He showed them to her. She did not want to read. She read only a few passages, which she did because he gently asked her to. "Who is speaking?" she said. "Who, then, is speaking?" She sensed an error that she could not put her finger on. "Erase whatever doesn't seem right to you." But she could not erase anything, either. She sadly threw down all the pages. She had the impression that although he had assured her that he would believe her implicitly, he did not believe her enough, with the force that would have rendered the truth present. "And now you have taken something away from me that I no longer have and that you do not even have." Weren't there any words that she accepted more willingly? Any that diverged less from what she was thinking? But everything before her eyes was spinning: she had lost the center from which the events had radiated and that she had held onto so firmly until now. She said, perhaps in order to save something, perhaps because the first words say everything, that the first paragraph seemed to

267 See Arne Klawitter, "Von der Ontologie der Sprache zur Diskursanalyse moderner Literatur", in: *Foucault und die Künste*, ed. Peter Gente, Suhrkamp, Frankfurt a.M. 2004, pp. 122–140.

her to be the most faithful and so did the second somewhat, especially at the end.[268]

This is a strange dialogue. Strange, because it takes the form of an asymmetrical relationship and a relationship across an unsurpassable difference. The speech seeks to hear what it itself is saying and what is escaping from her words. The murmur, the whisper of speech, is like a guide,[269] whose words are audible only in the (distorting) answers of the one who speaks or writes.

The words not only (and less and less) refer to meanings, but reflect themselves, and as Foucault says, in this folding there suddenly arises "a kind of stubborn, amorphous anonymity", which deprives the subject of his simple identity (i.e. the position of the originator of the spoken, or the author), "divests it of its unmediated right to say *I*, and pits against its discourse a speech that is idissociably echo and denial".[270] From the murmur of speech there is heard the constant demand that he who speaks cannot meet, and that is a burden he would like to rid himself of. *Murmur*: "'language' is only a formless rumbling, a streaming; its power resides in dissimulation"[271] behind words. A space opens up between the clear and distinct, generally recognisable meanings of words and the unidentifiable murmur of speech, a space of waiting, patience, *Warten*.

The impatience at the heart of error is the essential fault, because it misconstrues the very trueness of error which, like a law, requires that one never believe the goal is close or that one is coming nearer to it. One must

---

268 Maurice Blanchot, *L'attente L'oubli*, Gallimard, Paris 1962, p. 7.
269 There is more than a hint of this in the very title of Blanchot's book *Celui qui ne m'accompagnait pas*, Gallimard, Paris 1953.
270 Michel Foucault, "The Thought of the Outside", in Michel Foucault, *Aesthetics, Method, and Epistemology*, ed. by James D. Faubion, trans. Robert Hurley and others (Essential Works of M. Foucault, Vol. 2), The New Press, New York 1998, pp. 163 and 167.
271 Ibid., p. 67.

never have done with the indefinite, one must never grasp – as if it were the immediate, the already present – the profundity of inexhaustible absence. (...) it is impatience which makes the goal inaccessible by substituting for it the proximity of an intermediary figure. It is impatience that destroys the way toward the goal by preventing us from recognising in the intermediary the figure of the immediate.[272]

272 Maurice Blanchot, *The Space of Literature*, trans. Ann Smock, University of Nebraska Press, Lincoln, London 1982, pp. 78–79.

30

Philosophy does not explain the event, it responds. Its response is itself a transformation of the philosophical discourse. If the event is that which does not coincide with existing horizons of understanding that allow for recognition, and if the event is the irruption of reality into the world and if it is that which carries its horizon of understanding in itself, then the event is the recognition of the incomprehensibility of the event, its discursive absence. But one could also say that the transformation of philosophical discourse is a response to the experience of loss that necessarily, albeit unreflectedly, accompanies every act of identification inasmuch as this act eliminates that which does not correspond to the known in the habitualised form of inductive reference within the structure "something as something". But is it experience? It is more the trace of a lack in experience, or a deficit that can only be removed by its erasure. For this very reason thinking of the event is thinking of the outside.

Within this thinking it is possible to discern various, albeit parallel lines.

Philosophy must first shine a light into the shadows and dark corners that the modernist project left behind it insofar as it drew on the Enlightenment ideal of rationalism, subscribed to the classical concept of a language purged of indications, and pledged allegiance to the idea of *mathesis universalis* (exact science). Whence the search for traces of other, unrealised projects of modernity in modernity itself. Indeed, we might interpret postmodernism in this way. Secondly, other forms of showing must be found in the name of saving not phenomena, but that which necessarily escapes from phenomena. The importance of indexicality, testimony as forms of showing. And thirdly: philosophy must search for a relationship to the other in its otherness – the transformation of philosophical discourse is essential if this otherness is to be respected.

What is the backdrop to all of these lines? The event of the Holocaust as the radical elimination of the event. And along with this, the elimination of any possible relationship to that which is on the point of arrival.

31

A prerequisite of the relationship to that which is on the point of arriving is patience, i.e. non-anticipation; patience inasmuch as this designates a state beyond the passive/active opposition; patience, i.e. waiting in the ultimate antechamber focused on the last things before the last, the restrained openness of the waiting, as Siegfried Kracauer would say, in a place that is both outside and inside. This patience does not attempt to recognise, it does not "intend". It suspends intentionality, and for this reason both Levinas and Blanchot speak of radical passivity, exposure to the experience of the neutral – neither inside nor outside. And this is another aspect of the experience of literature, *écriture*, if transposed to the question "Who is speaking?", which can then be concretised in various different ways.

For instance: who is speaking in the books of Samuel Beckett?

This is all the more exemplary an example when we consider that Blanchot's texts, and not only by virtue of their diction, often bring to mind Beckett. This is especially so in the case of the original form of asymmetrical dialogue that stages the Beckettian narrative, pursuing that which cannot be apprehended through narration. If the radical non-representability of that around which the dialogue circles is somehow to appear, non-representability itself must be represented.[273] "For what is it that remains representable if the essence of the object is to hide from representation? It remains to represent the conditions of this hiddenness (*dérobade*)."[274] This is exactly what happens in Blanchot's dialogue, which thus acquires a performative character. We do not know whether he who speaks is simply repeating that being said by another voice, a voice that,

---

273 Cf. Simon Critchley, "Who Speaks in the Work of Samuel Beckett?" *Yale French Studies*, No. 93, The Place of Maurice Blanchot (1998), p. 114.

274 Samuel Beckett, "Peintres de l'Empechement" (1948), in: Samuel Beckett, *Disjecta: Miscellaneous Writings and a Dramatic Fragment*, ed. Ruby Cohn, John Calder, London 1983, p. 136.

moreover, constantly claims that it has not been heard correctly. The result is that the speaker is haunted by the feeling that the meaning of that he is hearing is constantly eluding him. At the same time, however, he is

> led on by a wandering speech, one that is not deprived of meaning, but deprived of centre, that does not begin, does not end, yet is greedy, demanding, will never stop, one couldn't stand it if it stopped, for that is when one would have to make the terrible discovery that, when it does not speak, it is still speaking, when it ceases, it perseveres, not silently, for in it silence speaks eternally.[275]

The links between the two are obvious. However, Blanchot's text literally effectuates the situation of the speaker, dramatises it, establishes it performatively. It is a dialogue and at the same time a monologue. Or to be more precise, neither one nor the other. And this is why the question "Who is speaking?" is aporetic, like the question:

> Why do you listen to me as you do? Why, even when you speak, do you keep listening? Why do you attract in me these words that I must then say? And never do you answer; never do you make something of yourself heard. But I will say nothing; be aware of this. What I say is nothing.
> Undoubtedly she wanted him to repeat what she had said, merely repeat it. But never did she recognise her words in mine. Did I unwittingly change something in them? Did something change on their way from her to me?

---

275 Maurice Blanchot, *The Book to Come*, trans. Charlotte Mandell, Stanford University Press, Stanford 2002, p. 210. For an example of the similarities between the diction of Blanchot and Beckett, cf. "The ex-pression that there is nothing to express, nothing with which to express, nothing from which to express, no power to express, no desire to express, together with the obligation to express." (Samuel Beckett, in: *Disjecta*, p. 139) and Blanchot: "The writer finds himself in the increasingly ludicrous condition of having nothing to write, of having no means with which to write it, and of being constrained by the utter necessity of always writing it." (Maurice Blanchot, *Faux pas*, trans. Charlotte Mandell, Stanford University Press, Stanford 2001, p. 3). More on this see Curt G. Willits, "The Blanchot/Beckett Correspondence: Situating the Writer/Writing at the Limen of Naught", *Colloquy: text theory critique* 10 (2005), pp. 257–68.

In a low voice for himself, in a lower voice for him. An utterance that must be repeated before it has been heard, a traceless murmur that he follows, wandering nowhere, residing everywhere, the necessity of letting it go.

It is always the ancient word that wants to be here again without speaking.[276]

Who is speaking? Who is speaking if speaking and hearing almost overlap and the "speaker" – situated within an irreducible difference between both – is thrown into what Blanchot calls "*my* consciousness *without me*", and so experiences the failure of speech in relation to that which echoes behind his words as their guide, who, though he does not accompany his speech, does not so much as for a moment abandon it?[277]

That which the speaker (of Blanchot's dialogues) says is a reply striving to capture the voice whose speech is a *murmur*, thus penetrating the inside from outside like a phantom that does not permit the work ever to be completed, since the difference of this voice in light of the speech is irrevocable and every speech is in an asymmetric relation to it. "Murmuring in the mud", to quote Beckett, since the origin of this word (not only in Blanchot's texts) is clearly his *Comment c'est*. Yet *murmur* is another name for *il y a*, which brings us back to Blanchot and the experience of literature or *expérience littéraire*. It is clear that the locus of his dialogues (no less than his novels or fragments) is the literary space, *l'espace littéraire*, which in the act of writing opens itself up into another night: "To write is to make oneself the echo of what cannot stop talking". "Night is the book."[278] Literature (and the thinking based on this fundamental experience) consists of the unattainability of its base: "This discourse, as speech of the outside whose words welcome the outside

276 Maurice Blanchot, *Awaiting Oblivion*, trans. John Gregg, University of Nebraska Press, Lincoln and London 1997, p. 4.
277 Cf. Blanchot's book the title of which is *Celui qui ne m'accompagnait pas* (Gallimard, Paris 1953).
278 Blanchot, *The Space of Literature*, pp. 20 and 27.

it addresses, has the openness of a commentary: the repetition of what continually murmurs outside. (...) discourse, as a speech that is always outside what it says",[279] as Foucault describes it.

Though Blanchot is close to Levinas and adopts many of the latter's ideas while adding his own commentary, we should not overlook the important shifts and transfers of emphasis. These are clear both in the privileged status of writing or literature (*écriture*), and in the original phenomenology of the voice implied in his understanding of Levinas's *il y a*.

Levinas sees a crucial distinction between the Saying (*le dire*) and the Said (*le dit*).[280] This is based on the primacy of the encounter with another as the Other as a relationship involving separation, while the relationship of reciprocity in which the other is the addressee of a communication by means of language as a semiological system (*Dit*) is secondary. The encounter with another person (face-to-face in a situation of one for/on behalf of the other) is the event of exposure to the proximity of another and the fracturing of the closed "I", an uncovering of vulnerability: the experience of passivity, a passivity that precedes the passive/active distinction.

In Levinas's work proximity is another name for the relationship across irreducible difference, but also the field establishing the very meaningfulness of the meaning of the preceding semiotics. Proximity is the original dimension or primordial saying as *Dire*, which is beyond all acts of thematisation or identification and which precedes consciousness inasmuch as it (as in phenomenology) is defined by intentionality, i.e. by the noetic-noematic *correlation*. This is because the relationship to the other in proximity cannot be described by categories of consciousness, which mean something *qua* something and which are always already embedded within participation in gen-

---

279 Michel Foucault, *Essential Writings, Aesthetics, Methodology, and Epistemology*, p. 153.
280 At this point we might wish to consider analogous constructions (all of which find their source in the differentiation *natura naturans* versus *natura naturata*): Maurice Merleau-Ponty: "parole parlante" and "parole parlée", and Georges Didi-Huberman: *figure figurante* and *figure figurée*.

eral and generally transparent universality (the level of *le Dit*). In contrast, the relationship to the other is a relationship to singularity that is always (already) situated beyond the theme of discourse and as such is non-representable.

> This relationship of proximity, this contact unconvertible into a noetico-noematic structure, in which every transmission of messages (...) is already established, is the original language, a language without words or propositions, pure communication.[281]

Speech in the sense of *Dire* affects the interlocutor, without showing him in the sense of phenomenological showing, a showing that, Levinas is convinced, always has the structure of discourse to the extent that that which appears is necessarily mediated by meaning and cannot appear outside it. The other makes sense immediately, i.e. prior to our conferring meaning upon it in an intentional and thematicising relationship. And if consciousness is wholly intentionality, then in respect of the encounter with another as the other it is in an always (already) delayed proximity. The level of symbolic communication is the level of the said, *le Dit*.

In contrast, in the case of Blanchot the event problematising the relationship is not the correlation of an encounter with the other, but a literary experience that exposes both the reader and the writer to otherness in its capacity as "uncognisable" and is thus a privileged place for the experience of separation or difference. This is why his texts are dominated by *écriture*, the word, which denotes not only the letter and writing, but literature as an experience open to the murmur of *il y a*, which it listens to in such a way as to become its echo or response, similar to Levinas's responding and responsibility. Both cases involve the experience of that which manifests itself only by virtue of the fact that it flees its own manifestation or showing

---

281 Emmanuel Levinas, "Language and Proximity", in: *Collected Philosophical Papers*, trans. Alphonso Lingis, Nijhoff, Dordrecht, Boston, Lancaster 1987, p. 119.

(its thematicisation and identification). In the case of Blanchot the critical importance of *écriture* ensues from the fact that it filters Levinas's thinking through literary experience, the experience of the incompleteable work, which as performative text refers neither to fiction nor to representable (articulated because already endowed with meanings) reality. The work is at one with its incompleteability and, like the author, the reader experiences in it the very existence of speech, bears witness to a consciousness without subject in which things are liberated from that instance that shrouds them in meaning. The encounter with the *murmure*, with the *il y a* through *écriture*, thus becomes thinking of the outside, whose "discourse" can only be that which Beckett termed the *literature of the un-word*, since the existence of speech is experienced in it as a thing. *Ecriture* is that literature that wants "to draw into the light of day the elemental deep which the world, in order to affirm itself, negates and resists."[282] Its element is *fascination*.

Fascination as the experience of exteriority, though something like touch, is a vision of that which fascinates us, foists itself upon our gaze as though this gaze were understood by it. "What fascinates us robs us of our power to give sense. It abandons its 'sensory' nature, abandons the world, draws back from the world and draws us along. It no longer reveals itself to us, yet it affirms itself in a presence foreign to the temporal present and to presence in space." Another way, in other words, of describing the literary experience, the encounter with absolute otherness. Writing means enduring this experience in which "fascination threatens".[283]

If, to the question "Who is speaking?", Blanchot seeks an answer in writing, this does not mean that the voice has disappeared completely. However, it is essential the question be reformulated: "Who is speaking if the voice is speaking?" The speaker is not a subjective interior. The voice (in its materiality or sonance) is that which lib-

282 Blanchot, *The Space of Literature.*
283 Ibid., pp. 28 and 30.

erates the discursive utterance universalised by meaning, the voice of nobody. That which speaks is the element *il y a* itself, whispering, murmuring, droning and vibrating thus in the impersonality of the voice that has no duration within which it could be completed, which vanishes as soon as the words are uttered and escapes into the depth in which it neither began nor will it end. However, again and again it permeates everything said and echoes in literature inasmuch as it is turned to the outside, it resonates in speech inasmuch as it is waiting.

So we must still wait. And in waiting what is there to be done? What do we do?
Well, waiting, we chat.
Yes, listening to the voice. But what is this voice?
Not something to hear, perhaps the last written cry, what is inscribed in the future outside books, outside language.
But what is this voice?[284]

A scream. That most human utterance by which man defies identification. Graffiti on walls.

So the Jews shut up and the guard moved off. Then the Jews started talking again, in their language, as he says, ra-ra-ra, and so on
What's he mean, ra-ra-ra, what's he trying to imitate?
Their language.
No, ask him: was the Jews' noise something special?
They spoke Jew.
Does Mr Borowi understand "Jew"?
No.[285]

284 Blanchot, *The Infinite Conversation*, p. 331.
285 *Shoah. An Oral History of the Holocaust.* The Complete Text of the Film by Claude Lanzmann. Pantheon Books, New York 1985, pp. 30–31.

32

Thinking after the Holocaust definitively abandons the postulate of the identity of thinking and existence and with it the violence of identification. In doing so it reopens the question of the inside and the outside. The outside is inside as a trace of that which is escaping. If thinking relates to the outside, then this is an asymmetric relationship and one that also includes separation, radical difference and resistance to showing itself as these are understood by phenomenology. Philosophy responds to this event by transforming its discourse. By doing so it testifies to the experience that the existing discourse eliminates. If the philosophical response seems to be a paradox, this is only because it must investigate the very boundaries of understanding and teach itself to listen before it begins to speak. The experience of the Holocaust is above all the experience of a *radical discontinuity*, *rupture* or *cut*, radical because the linearity of time collapses in this experience and the before-after relationship implodes. This means that this experience itself makes the linear experience of time impossible.

People arrive. They look through the crowd of those who are waiting, those who await them. They kiss them and say the trip exhausted them.
People leave. They say goodbye to those who are not leaving and hug the children.
There is a street for people who arrive and a street for people who leave.
There is a cafe called "Arrivals" and a cafe called "Departures". There are people who arrive and people who leave.
But there is a station where those who arrive are those who are leaving, a station where those who arrive have never arrived, where those who have left never came back.[286]

---

[286] Charlotte Delbo, *Auschwitz and After,* trans. Rosette C. Lamont, Yale University Press (2nd ed.) 2014, p. 3.

This is the first paragraph of the first volume entitled *None of Us Will Return* of the trilogy *Auschwitz and After* by Charlotte Delbo. Delbo and her husband were arrested on 2 March 1942 in Paris, because both belonged to the French resistance. Her husband was executed in France and Delbo was moved to Romainville and then deported to Auschwitz on 24 January 1943. She spent time in the Birkenau women's camp before being transferred to Ravensbrück, where she remained until the camp was liberated on 23 April 1945. Her trilogy is remarkable not only as "testimony", but by virtue of its original literary form, namely an attempt at "literature after Auschwitz".

The first half at least of the passage above describes a mundane, quotidian situation. A station that exists simply so that people arrive and depart, a station that is not the destination of any journey that is not a place to stay. The station clock shows only the time of departure or arrival, but does not measure duration. This is an ordinary experience. All stations look like this. This is what they are like. A station is a junction between lines coming from somewhere and continuing somewhere else, between farewells and welcomes. The station has no intrinsic meaning beyond simply being a place *to be passed through*. But suddenly there are the "two streets" and those arriving who are departing: the quotidian is suddenly breached by the extreme experience of *non-returnability*. Arrival is the same as departure. According to Michael Rothberg, it is precisely this co-existence of the everyday and the extreme that is a trait of literature after the Holocaust, of *traumatic realism*.[287] In his introduction Rothberg describes very realistically the entrance to the concentration camp, the entry into death. "Arrival" is suddenly something that does not have its own name. There exists no before if there is no after, no after if there is no before. And not even the largest station in the world has a name – because it is called Auschwitz. Delbo

---

287 Michael Rothberg, *Traumatic Realism: The Demands of Holocaust Representation*. University of Minnesota Press, Minneapolis, London 2000.

avoids looking for names for what must remain nameless and thus unthinkable. The name would grant acceptance, the intertwining of the mundane and mass extermination. It is for this reason that Primo Levi wrote:

> At a distance of years, one can today definitely affirm that the history of the Lagers has been written almost exclusively by those who, like myself, never fathomed them to the bottom.[288]

However, the unobtrusive word "we" has also collapsed. Who writes of this experience if none of "us" who have it return, as the title of the first part of Delbo's trilogy implies? Arrival/departure: the rupture is the moment that separates them but in such a way that what follows, cannot follow. If there is anything after this separation, it is something that is *after the end*. Like the designation "survivor" that quickly surfaces in the preposition "after" – *Nachleben, survivre, living forth*.

I would add merely a short observation regarding the "end" that is the station.

Husserl's *The Crisis of European Sciences*, which is concerned with crisis, is actually a reaction to the *threat of the end*, an end that Husserl seeks to avert by means of his phenomenology. And yet it is unable to resolve the problem by returning to the beginning, by reviving it and continuing in the direction that was established at the start. In other words, it would like, without much success, to save the teleology of history. However, something paradoxical emerges athwart Husserl's attempt: the end is something that is constantly being deferred because "ending" is more like a moment of history, a "crisis" that is a part thereof. However, Husserl is unwilling to accept this.

---

288 Primo Levi, *The Drowned and the Saved*, trans. Raymond Rosenthal, Abacus, London 2013, p. 9.

Adorno speaks explicitly of philosophy after the end of philosophy. However, all of this is actually simply a giant prelude to a very complicated investigation of temporality in the philosophy of the second half of the twentieth century. One possibility is suggested in the trilogy by Charlotte Delbo, who seeks the language of the *testimony* of survivors. She alternates forms, e.g. autobiographical sections with micro-stories. Repetition does not indicate any movement. If philosophy qua discourse is bound to language, then it has no option but to constantly *transcend* language if it is to deal with that which cannot be named.

However, all of this is closely related to the act of *responding* and *bearing witness*, since it is possible to show that this rupture, this implosion of the before-and-after relationship, relates to the theme of the Holocaust and, by extension, to the theme of the "end". The theme of what follows after the end is not an abstract philosophical construction but a response to the responses to the trauma of Auschwitz. Perhaps the witnesses themselves demonstrate this most convincingly – or, to be more precise, the *absenting testimony*. The psychologist Dori Laub, co-founder of the *Video Archive for Holocaust Testimonies* at Yale University and himself a child survivor, says that, in the final analysis the event of the Holocaust was a singularity in that it "did not create its own witnesses". The unfathomable psychological structure of this event prevented its victims, and indeed any of its participants, from being able to testify.

> It was also the very circumstance of being inside the event that made unthinkable the very notion that a witness could exist, that is, someone who could step outside of the coercively totalitarian and dehumanising frame of reference in which the event was taking place, and provide an independent frame of reference through which the event could be observed.[289]

---

[289] Shoshana Felman, Dori Laub, *Testimony. Crisis of Witnessing in Literature, Psychoanalysis, and History*, Routledge, London and New York 1992, p. 81.

This unfathomability paralyses everyone involved, both executioner and victim, as well as those who lived during those times and must have had some idea of what was going on (typical in this respect is the distrust of the isolated "testimony" of those who managed to escape and offer reports of the extermination camps).[290] The victims who lost even the ability to turn to the other with the salutation "you" were unable to relate to themselves as to "you", i.e. they were *unable to bear witness as to themselves*. Their experience as victim became incommunicable even to themselves. But then this is *extermination*: the extermination of memory and history. Attempts to testify (albeit very belatedly) always transcend the boundary of the human capacity to understand. An "eyewitness" is someone who sees and yet does not see. In Lanzmann's film *Shoah* there is a scene that offers tragic proof of this. Richard Glazar describes the journey by train to the concentration camp:

> Then, very slowly, the train turned off of the main track, and rolled at a walking pace through a wood. While we looked out, we'd been able to open a window. The old man in our compartment saw a boy... Cows were grazing... And he asked the boy in signs, "Where are we?" And the kid made a funny gesture. This! Across the throat. A Pole? A Pole. Where was this? At the station? Not in words, but in signs, we asked "What's going on here?" And he made that gesture. Like this. We didn't really pay much attention to him. We couldn't figure out what he meant. (...) He says the Jews didn't believe it.[291]

They try to bear witness to something that escapes even them, the experience of which is rendered impossible, wiped out. They are

---

290 The Holocaust as philosophical theme first appears in the seventies. The texts that existed in the forties were isolated, albeit well known (Arendt, Jaspers, survivor testimonies). The "invisibility of Auschwitz" is well captured by, for instance, Enzo Traverso, *L'Histoire déchirée : Essai sur Auschwitz et les intellectuels*, Les Ed. du Cerf, Paris 1997.)
291 Lanzmann, *Shoah*, pp. 34–35.

separated from the "before" by the moat of extermination. But this means that they also have no "after". The fates of the survivors document this imprisonment in "rupture".

The testimony we are considering here is not the testimony of a *crisis* but the testimony of a *catastrophe*. Or rather, we are living in an age of testimony, because this catastrophe caused a *crisis of testimony*. But this is how the act of testimony becomes a privileged method of showing.

33

So what have we learned to date? That the Holocaust is an event that was supposed to remain without witnesses and be forgotten. The plan was to make the victims invisible, even if this meant denying the reality of dead bodies, which the Nazis called *Figuren* or *Schmattes* (rags). This invisibility is inadvertently confirmed even by revisionist historians: "I studied thousands of documents. I badgered specialists and historians with my questions. I tried in vain to find a single ex-convict who would be able to prove to me that they genuinely saw a gas chamber with their own eyes."[292]

A witness offers their testimony to this event, bearing witness in the present to a past that should never have become the present. This is a limit-situation. However, in the age of testimony, i.e. in the age of the crisis of testimony,[293] it is essential to understand the act of bearing witness as a completely specific means of showing, with its own special temporality. Is it in some way analogous to intentionality? Only to a certain extent. The witness is haunted by an event, the memory of which they cannot shake off, and offer their testimony regarding an "outside" that they wish to actualise. However, they bear witness to something that defies understanding and that must not be rationalised by identification: Auschwitz must not be explained or represented (Elie Wiesel), since any endeavour to understand this event is obscene (Claude Lanzmann). The witness comes up against the impossibility of any re-presentation of the event regarding which he is giving testimony. A chasm separates the witness with his testimony and those who are present to hear said testimony. The experience he recounts makes no sense. Testimony regarding the Holocaust is no *Sinngebung* (meaning), because that which it shows is the very absence of meaning. The witness refers

---

292 Robert Faurisson, *Le Monde,* 16. 1. 1979.
293 Cf. Felman – Laub, *Testimony: Crisis of Witnessing in Literature, Psychoanalysis, and History.*

to his experience in order to give expression to that which eludes it and in order to make of those before whom he bears witness witnesses to this elusion. The witness is the trace of that event. He is the sign that claims its own interpreter. It is for this reason that his testimony does not take the form of proof that would consist of an incontrovertible base of evident givenness.

The designation "after the Holocaust" is not a reference to calendar time, as Blanchot pointed out when he said that every story, whenever it is written, will henceforth always already be prior to Auschwitz since it refers to the collapse of linear temporality, the continuity of which guarantees the capacity of retention and protention. The event that fractures this time as though it were itself the source of a different temporality is present as past. In relation to itself it is always somehow deferred and only thus is it shown. This means that temporality is not a theoretical problem. It is not a condition of the possibility of the synthetic operations of the recognising (cognising) conscious, but is itself a structural requirement that is its own being endowed with speech and established "according to the time" inasmuch as its being in time lives through *récit*, narration. This is because, as Jean-Toussaint Desanti writes, only by virtue of the fact that we speak of yesterday do we live today as those we became yesterday, and in an always possible and updated discourse we thus summarise in time the disjointed moments of our lives that would otherwise disappear irrevocably. However, this is not as simple as it might appear at first glance:

In time we must constantly reckon with time, in such a way that time finally seems to speak to itself, organises itself in relation to itself as a discourse in which present, past and future refer mutually to each other, meld into one another, become reconciled, distance themselves from the other by mutual rejection, and yet interpenetrate each other in the development of an endlessly new story, the identity of whose narrator we do not know. Is it I who recounts my life or this life that is recounted in me? And am I something other than that which remains and preserves itself from this uninterrupted narration?[294]

A transforming philosophical discourse clearly understands time within a different context and grouped within a constellation with other questions. However, the possibility of a description of this other temporality is again implied or prefigured in Husserl's "analyses of the internal consciousness of time", in the paradox of continuity and discontinuity that phenomenology is incessantly confronted by and that it is unable to deal with. And here too phenomenology must somehow be nudged beyond its boundaries, so allowing us to uncover the traces of possible projects of a different thinking that will correspond to the new reality. Jacques Derrida will go on to claim, entirely legitimately, that Husserl's phenomenology is thinking on the very boundary of the deconstruction of the "metaphysics of presence", while Rudolf Bernet, who conducted a detailed examination into the interpretations of time in various phases of phenomenology, argues convincingly that Husserl's statements on time are often very non-metaphysical while not being independent of the metaphysical (the terms "metaphysical" and "non-metaphysical" can be read as distinguishing between tradition and transforming philosophical discourse), and thus his analyses of time operate on several different levels simultaneously.

Few of Husserl's analyses offer what Husserl expected from them, and his texts for the most part have a different effect to that intended by him. What Husserl wished to achieve is usually determined metaphysically, and often what he describes is directed against his own metaphysical understanding.[295]

294 Jean-Touissant Desanti, *Réflexions sur le temps. Conversations avec Dominique-Antoine Grisoni*, Bernard Grasset, Paris 1992, pp. 90–91.
295 Bernet, "Die ungegenwärtige Gegenwart", p. 42.

The unexpected beyond the horizon of the expected is the starting point of a transformation in the concept of time and heralds a much deeper transformation of the philosophical discourse.

However, the significance of the unexpected as the unidentifiable in the sense of unforeseeable is, like the significance of the traumatic past without presence, initially blurred, because interpretations of temporality that are situated before the threshold of the transformation of philosophical discourse, as well as those that operate on this threshold (as in the case of Husserl's phenomenology), lay emphasis on the continuity of time, on the flow of time. In *The Principles of Psychology*, William James coined the term *stream of consciousness*, and the technique of the same name this gave rise to in literature indicates that metaphors involving a flow or river are not a coincidence in philosophical texts either. With this in mind, the initial question that Husserl asks himself – how is it possible to perceive temporal objects such as melody in their entirety, i.e. within the whole of their temporal extension? – becomes comprehensible as soon as he realises that the temporality of consciousness is clearly the deepest problem phenomenology will have to confront. Since phenomenology places empirical or objective time in brackets, the origin of that which we call time must be found in consciousness and its constitutive acts, i.e. an investigation is necessary into the phenomenological content of the experience of time. The question is: where does our sense come from for that which for us has a sense of time (in Husserlian terminology something of the sort is meant by the word "constitution"). If the problem of temporality is formulated thus, one might surmise that the temporality of consciousness will be something like the final basis of all acts of the consciousness if it is not to be a disjointed sequence of its own immanent content. The internal temporality of consciousness is not only the condition of the possibility of the constitution of temporal objects, but equally of the preservation of the identity of that which appears through experience in different acts (perceiving, imagining, willing, etc.), and, equally, the condition of the possibility of memory and anticipation. However, the range of this deeper understanding of temporality will clearly be wider. It is the prerequisite for an understanding of the meaning of historicity, i.e. including the concept of teleology, and the essential framework of an investigation that aims to resolve the historical crisis afflicting the meaning of the return (across time) to the original establishment, and will aim to explain the very possibility of a crisis of meaning as (random or necessary) stories in time. However, if we place ourselves within an already transformed philosophical discourse, we can expect a different question: is it possible to describe the temporality of *testimony* on the basis of a phenomenological interpretation of time?

If phenomenology analyses intentional experiences and the noetic-noematic correlation in which the intended objectivities are manifest and understood "as" this and that, then time is clearly implicated in this investigation. The acts of consciousness must themselves have some temporal extension without which, for example, comparisons and "coverage" (co-incidence) of the diverse or the accomplishment of the intended, which are all synthetic acts, would be unthinkable. Identification requires time. This means that perception (temporal just like any other) of an object is itself a temporal object. Consciousness is temporal. However, we cannot say that it operates in time, because the origin of the temporality of consciousness must be located in its operations. Consciousness is thus, somehow, time. Its fundamental character is this internal consciousness of time. If this origin is to be uncovered and the constitution of time explained, it is appropriate to focus first on those experiences that make accessible the temporality of consciousness, i.e. on the experiences of temporal objects such as tone or melody.

The second step of our analysis must therefore be to reflect on the experience of the temporal object. This analysis will uncover the basic structural moments, namely the primary impression (*Urimpression*), retention and protention. These mark out the time horizon of (every) experience: the melody begins, continues and ends as the same melody. The first note is held as that resonating now and anticipation of the forthcoming note is linked to the held phase (phases). "Now" is this actuality, presence as a (certain field of) presentation. It is for this reason that Husserl does not designate this "now" only with the word presence (*Gegenwart*), but sometimes with the word presentation (*Gegenwärtigung*). The note is consciousness now. Inasmuch as certain of its phases are conscious as "now", the entirety of its duration is conscious as elapsed. The past continues to shine in the "now" as a *field* of presence as conscious of its having expired right now.

So how is it possible to perceive a melody in its entirety? Apparently thanks to retention and protention, which are specific in the sense of non-objectivising (non-thematising) intentions linking phase to phase and experience to experience in such a way that they form a connected nexus of a single flow, a continuity of flux into a temporal background (Husserl's well known comet's tail of retentions and the retentions of retentions). At every instant consciousness is a current into which new actualities constantly enter (from the "source point", which is the primary impression), which immediately become part of this compact flow, which does not begin and end, though it allows for a temporal unit (such as melody) to be perceived as beginning and ending.

In this way three levels of the constellation of time are gradually identified (along with the problem of their mutual interaction): 1) the level of transcendental theses (melody in objective time), 2) the level of immanent temporal objects and their appearance in the stream of time (the experience of the melody and reflections thereupon), and 3) the stream of consciousness that is the final base of the constitution of time and simultaneously constitutes itself. It is thus that I am able to explain, inter alia, that I perceive the melody in its entirety, since it is also clear that what the analysis of the internal consciousness of time finally discovered were the a priori conditions of all appearance, whether the experience has already thematised (intended and grasped) objects that are temporal or not. Husserl's texts devoted to temporality are spread over a long period of time. He worked intermittently on them from approximately 1905 to 1934.[296] The basic perspective does not change, though the terminology achieves a sharper focus and complexity. The analysis aims to go deeper. However, above all Husserl must deal with the problems or even paradoxes that emerge time and time again during this process. This relates mainly to the final level of the constitution of time, the level of the ur-phenomenon or primal phenomenon, regarding which in 1932 Husserl wrote:

We thus soon come up against a "pra-phenomenon", which has never been exposed, still less interpreted, and in which everything that can in any sense whatsoever be called a phenomenon has its source. It is the standing-flowing self-presence, the absolute ego present to itself in flowing in its standing-flowing life, which is still flowing through experience, intentionality and knowledge.[297]

---

296 Published gradually in the Husserliana edition: Edmund Husserl, *Zur Phänomenologie des inneren Zeitbewusstseins (1893–1917)*, ed. Rudolf Boehm, Husserliana X. Martinus Nijhoff, Haag 1966; Edmund Husserl, *Die 'Bernauer Manuskripte' über das Zeitbewußtsein (1917/18)*, Husserliana XXXIII, ed. Rudolf Bernet, Dieter Lohmar, Kluwer Academic Publishers, Dordrecht 2001; Edmund Husserl, *Späte Texte über Zeitkonstitution (1929–1934). Die C-Manuskripte.* Husserliana Materialienband 8, ed. Dieter Lohmar, Springer, New York 2006. Regarding the phenomenology of temporality cf. Klaus Held, *Lebendige Gegenwart. Die Frage nach der Seinsweise des transzendentalen Ich bei Edmund Husserl, entwickelt am Leitfaden der Zeitproblematik.* Phaenomenologica 23, Nijhoff, Haag 1966; Toine Kortooms, *Phenomenology of Time: Edmund Husserl's Analysis of Time-Consciousness.* Kluwer Academic Publishers, Dordrecht 2002; Ernst Wolfgang Orth (ed.), *Zeit und Zeitlichkeit bei Husserl und Heidegger*, Phänomenologische Forschungen 14, Verlag Karl Alber Freiburg, München 1983; D. Lohman, I. Yamaguchi (eds.), *On Time – New Contributions to the Husserlian Phenomenology of Time*, Phaenomenologica 197, Springer Science-Business Media, 2010; Alexander Schnell, *Temps et phénomène.* Georg Olms Verlag, Hildesheim, Zürich, New York, 2004. Jean-Toussaint Desanti, *Réflexions sur le temps. Conversations avec Dominique-Antoine Grisoni.* Bernard Grasset, Paris 1992.

297 Husserl, *Späte Texte über Zeitkonstitution*, p. 145. "So stoßen wir bald vor auf das nie herausgestellte, geschweige denn systematisch ausgelegte "Urphänomen", in dem alles, was sonst Phänomen heißen mag und in welchem Sinn immer, seine Quelle hat. Es ist die stehend-strömende

This brief example of Husserl's struggle with the possibilities of the language of phenomenological description supports the legitimacy of the observation he expressed in his early *Vorlesungen*: we lack a name for all of this. However, the formulation referred to is completely consequent. The final level must be something like a standing stream or *nunc stans*, a "place" in which experience (life) is embedded in such a way that it extends beyond this "now" into the flowing and arriving (retention is always already observed by protention). Consciousness is in the transcendence of itself. However, it is clear that on the level on which spatiality and temporality are first constituted it is impossible to use words like "place" or "presence" (*lebendige Gegenwart*), and so in his later works Husserl inclines to the neutral term "primordium", which in a less misleading way designates this constantly gushing source of (conscious) life. However, the expression *nunc stans* is revealing: by using it Husserl wishes to indicate that the outside is unthinkable in order to transcend consciousness via consciousness and that *nunc stans* potentially contains within itself everything thinkable (*alles Erdenkliche*). It is therefore something like the horizon of all horizons, which is why the same world appears constantly to us (and why the unknown is a modus of the known).

However, this level, though in principle distinct, cannot be completely separated from the constituted flow of immanent acts (temporal objects), because the absolute, i.e. constituting stream, namely consciousness, is "present" only in the experience of experiences, and experiences are *eo ipso* simply as experienced. The flow of consciousness is aware of itself, if it is aware of the constituted temporal unities. It is therefore essential that a specific property of life be this identity it possesses with the consciousness of time. This is also why the term *lebendige Gegenwart*, live or living presence, is replaced in the later texts by more complex terms, e.g. "stehend urtümliche

Selbstgegenwart bzw. das sich selbst strömend gegenwärtige absolute Ich in seinem stehend-strömenden Leben, einem Leben, das ständig strömendes Erleben, Intentionalität, Bewussthaben ist ".

Lebendigkeit" (lit: primally standing vitality) or "Urgegenwart" (ur-presence or primary presence).[298] However, an appropriate term is missing for a reason: that which is not a modality of time cannot be designated by names valid for that constituted in time.

The paradoxical idea of a flow that stands still is inevitable, because only it, along with the mutual implication of life and experience, the transitivity of life, guarantees that the postulate of the identity of thought and (appearing to it) being still applies and because only in this way is it possible to avert the threat of infinite regression, albeit at the cost of Husserl operating on the very edge of phenomenological demonstrability in this pre-reflexive layer of consciousness. All the more reason why conspicuous traces of the outside in the inside emerge from time to time in his texts.

This is above all the case with that structural moment of the field of presence or presentation (as we might translate the word *Gegenwärtigen*), which is the primary impression that is and is not the same as "now". Though something must differentiate past and present, this difference is part of the flow and can therefore only be expressed by means of abstraction as a continually shifting boundary (or "betweenness") in the movement of constant shifting, by means of which singularities entering consciousness are differentiated (this will be one of the possible keys to understanding Derrida's neologism *différance*), i.e. in a movement behind which reflection is always delayed without ever being able to hold the primary impression as such, unmodified by retention (and protention). The primary impression, or what Husserl calls the source point, is

> the running-off mode with which the immanent objects beings to exist. It is characterised as now (...) The "source-point" with which the "production" of the enduring object begins is a primal impression. This consciousness is in a state of constant change: the tone-now present "in person" con-

298 Edmund Husserl, *Phänomenologie der Intersubjektivität*, Husserliana XV, p. 668.

tinuously changes into something that has been; an always new tone-now continuously relieves the one that has passed over into modification. But when the consciousness of the tone-now, the primal impression, passes over into retention, this retention itself is a now in turn, something actually existing. While it is actually present itself (but not an actually present tone), it is retention *of* the tone that has been (...) Every actually present now of consciousness, however, is subject to the law of modification. It changes into retention of retention and does so continuously. Accordingly, a fixed continuum of retention arises in such a way that each later point is retention for every earlier point. And each retention is already a continuum. The tone begins and "it" steadily continues.[299]

If the primal impression is to designate the temporal forms of that which in consciousness emerges first of all as absolutely new and singular, then this very newness and singularity is problematised by the interpretation of the constitution of time flow. It is "present" for understanding only if held (additionally) by retention, i.e. if it appears as already modified by the entire structure of the temporal presentation, not in the mode of immediacy but as the already past. The primal impression may be present for its understanding in experience simply as a trace of (an escaping) singularity and newness, i.e. only as an *indexical* reference to the exterior. The now is here, but is not located in the movement of receding, and if it is held retentionally, it is only held as escaping. However, if this flow is the final base on which rests all showing to our consciousness (as well as consciousness showing to itself) and the establishment of meaning, then we have no choice but to say that the condition of this showing is the original escaping, because the last, which reflection on the flow of consciousness encounters, is this: what it still has within reach is already unarrestingly disappearing. Via primary retention the showing object is identifiable only when it is disappearing and

299 Edmund Husserl, *On the Phenomenology of the Consciousness of Internal Time (Collected Works* IV), trans. John B. Brough, Kluwer Academic Publishers, Dodrecht 1991, pp. 29–31.

thus eluding identification. This is why Klaus Held used the word *Entgleitenlassen* to describe retention as a passive operation of the consciousness: the synthetic presentation of that which is shown is possible only because consciousness permits its ongoing escaping from the present.

The primary impression in its constant transformation is always an escaping fulfilment, since it is inexorably replaced and overlapped with ever new current presentations. For this reason the tendency to fulfilment is never satisfied. The "ego" during perception is always also with something that is constantly arriving, because the constant flowing is forever pulling the rug of constant pra-impressional presence from under its feet, as it were.[300]

The last, founding level of showing, which is consciousness as the "temporalisation of time", is a special base, because its character is not firm. The final realm that Husserl's phenomenology reaches is *elapsus*, escape as the basis of all appearance and everything that can be thought. Showing is based on a retreat from the phenomenon as a special mode of resistance to recognition – as a sign of the outside, the past, that was never the present. The transcendental I (which is the same as transcendental consciousness) as constituting is at the mercy of the flow in which it is and which it is. It permits escape in order that it be able on all levels to carry out synthetic acts – coverage, identification, ideation.

Emmanuel Levinas has already drawn attention to these (unintended) consequences of the phenomenological analysis of the internal consciousness of time in texts from the sixties appended to later editions of his essay *Discovering Existence with Husserl and Heidegger*. Completely in character with his way of thinking, Levinas, like Husserl, deems the primary impression a key moment in the

300 Klaus Held, *Lebendige Gegenwart. Die Frage nach der Seinsweise des transzendentalen Ich bei Edmund Husserl, entwickelt am Leitfaden der Zeitproblematik*. Phaenomenologica 23, Nijhoff, Haag 1966, p. 44.

constitution of time, a "new beginning", a "continuous restarting ex novo" (this is also the meaning of his concept of "diachrony"). It is for this reason that in his early texts he examined the phenomenon of tiredness and exhaustion. A condition of a new beginning is the "death" of the previous moment. However, unlike Husserl, his concept of the original impression refers to discontinuity as the origin of the temporalisation of time (the moment is that by which something new always begins). This interpretation of time, precisely because it involves "impression", for Levinas begins on the level of sensation (though he does not differ here from Husserl), or *Empfindung*. However, he believes that the "newness" of each impression, its singularity, is precisely that which contradicts the idea of time as flow, because it is something that constantly precedes its own pre-predication (protention), precedes the very possibility of itself.[301] Like Derrida, Levinas sees the problem of Husserl's *Lectures* as being that intentionality is still understood as a model of an idealising identification: that which I intend surrenders itself to me through *Abschattungen* cast on the horizon of intended objectivity. In other words, I always intended something like an ideal pole, on which I constantly orientate via a multiplicity of aspects and which is gradually "constituted" as "ideality" in the experience.[302] Ideality transcends the flow of sensation, it is beyond time albeit constituted in and thanks to time. Husserl's descriptions of sensation are therefore problematic: if the original impression (singularity, newness, new beginning) is held by retention and understood in a certain way, then it is already "idealised" (I perceive redness as a quality intrinsic to the intended object and the noematic pole moves in the direction of coincidence with the neotic): the ideality of objectiveness pushes

301 Emmanuel Levinas, *Autrement qu'être ou au-delà de l'essence*. Martinus Nijhoff, Haag 1978, p. 41. Emmanuel Levinas, *Otherwise Than Being or Beyond the Essence*, trans. Alphonso Lingis, Kluwer Academic Publishers, Dordrecht 1991, p. 32.
302 Husserl's conception of retention and protention is clearly modelled on the idea of subtle gradation.

the "sensed" newness and singularity of the sensed (impression) into the background. However, there is something more important at play. I feel the impression, I am aware (consciousness is necessarily intentional) of this feeling. In other words, the intentional relationship implied in the sensation of impression necessarily, albeit minimally, separates the sensing from the sensed: here we are not talking of coincidence but of time.

> Time is not only the form that houses sensations and lures them into a becoming, it is the sensing of sensation, which is not a simple coincidence of sensing with the sensed, but an intentionality and consequently a minimal distance between the sensing and the sensed – precisely a temporal distance.[303]

To Husserl, for whom consciousness is necessarily present to itself, this is unacceptable. For Levinas, on the contrary, it is the very mystery of time and consciousness: consciousness lags behind itself.[304] "The mystery of intentionality lies in the divergence from (...) or in the modification of the temporal flux. Consciousness is senescence and remembrance of things."[305]

---

303 Emmanuel Levinas, *Discovering Existence with Husserl*, trans. Richard A. Cohen and Michael B. Smith, Northwestern University Press, Evanston 1998, p. 142.
304 Ibid., p. 144.
305 Ibid., p. 145. A later formulation of the origin of temporality is to be found in *Autrement qu'être*: "Even at this primordial level which is that of lived experience, in which the flow, reduced to pure immanence, should exclude even any suspicion of objectification, consciousness remains an intentionality, an 'intentionality of a specific kind' to be sure, but unthinkable without an apprehended correlate. This specific intentionality is time itself. There is consciousness insofar as the sensible impression differs from itself without differing; it differs without differing, is other within identity. The impression is illuminated by 'opening up', as though it plugged itself up; it undoes that coincidence of self with self in which the 'same' is smothered under itself, as under a candle extinguisher. It is not in phase with itself; *just* past, *about to* come. But to differ within identity, to maintain the moment that is being altered, is 'protaining' and 'retaining'". Levinas, *Otherwise than Being*, p. 32. From here, Husserl constitutes time that is not lost and that can always be returned: however, this is how it is possible to get from here to the primary impression that precedes every protention.

34

On the one hand, Husserl's concept of time is an attempt to resolve an eminently philosophical problem that cannot be avoided, especially when a "paradigm" changes (the impending philosophy of finality). On the other, Husserl cannot leave the problem of time to one side because he comes up against it again and again in his analyses, even though he nudges to one side the phenomenon of temporality at the start. He is not interested in the problem of the empirical or psychological genesis of idealities, but is nevertheless unable to rid himself of the problem of time, and whenever faced with the problem of history, attempts to resolve it through a "teleological" conception, i.e. the "ideal temporality" of the non-temporal establishment of history. However, as time passes it becomes clear that the phenomenological analysis of time is his fundamental problem inasmuch as the field of phenomenological investigation is *consciousness* as the field of *evidence* in reflection upon experience.

If phenomenology is thinking that aspires to be presuppositionless, then, somewhat paradoxically, it must be able to anticipate the possibility of the *full presence that guarantees this evidence* (i.e. the indivisible presence of the "now" without any trace of absence, uncontaminated by any exterior or any "otherness"). This is the condition that it has to demonstrate to be substantiated, i.e. to demonstrate consciousness as a realm that allows for the *unmediated* grasp of the experienced within reflection upon this experience. The contents and structures of the experience must be immediately given, in such a way that it is possible to apprehend and investigate them and thence to arrive at idealities and ideal laws.

This means that phenomenology must disclose consciousness *as presence in itself, of itself and for itself.* In other words, the prerequisite of phenomenology is the field of immanence (or the exterior without interior, or even better, the interior without exterior inside), the sphere of that which is *reelly* immanent in the experience of cognition,[306] i.e. an "*absolute and clear givenness*",[307] which is the genuine opinion of the thing itself at the moment that the relationship to something transcendent (the perception of the thing in the world) is the internal character of the phenomenon (perceived as the *noematic correlate* of acts of noesis: immanence in the intentional sense).

But along with this approach to the problem of time and its phenomenologically necessary preconditions (the paradigm of perception and intentional focus, intention as grasping), a paradox appears: reflection on the experience has the character of the perception of this experience, i.e. it is again an intentional act that now intends not a temporal object (melody), but its temporal determinacy, i.e. the constitution of the "temporalisation of time" itself as it appears in this experience. It detects/discovers the constituted stream, the flow of the stream. However, if this reflection as perception and intentional intentionality grasps, then it constitutes, while itself (as a certain specific perception) possessing a temporal extension:

> The actions of the intentional life, i.e. noesis, in which the transcendental noema are given, are themselves revealed under the gaze of reflection as givenness in "immanent time", i.e. they are inserted in the temporal flowing of the "current of consciousness" (...) noesis are also temporal objects...[308]

It therefore presupposes an even deeper level of temporality. In other words, analyses of the internal consciousness of time threaten an endless regress descending behind that "third" level as constantly receding. A possible solution might be found in the relationship of the second and third level as a completely specific relationship.

306 Edmund Husserl, *Die Idee der Phänomenologie* (Husserliana II), ed. Walter Biemel, Martinus Nijhoff, Haag, p. 35.
307 Ibid.
308 Held, *Lebendige Gegenwart,* p. 48 (Later on Husserl abandons the original content-apprehension schema in his analyses of time: see Alexander Schnell, *Temps et phénomène*, Georg Olms Verlag, Hildesheim, Zürich, New York 2004.

In Section 36 of the *Lectures on Internal Time Consciousness*, which summarises the outputs of his analyses, i.e. "time-constituting flow as absolute subjectivity", Husserl writes: "For all of this we have no names" and must resort to "images".[309] In doing so he is saying something fundamental about "concepts" and "conceptual thinking". He has stumbled upon something that eludes conceptual understanding and is problematising the very possibility of trans-historical concepts. He points the way forward that leads to Deleuze: philosophy is the *creation of concepts*. This is because Husserl's phenomenology is located on the edge of a major transformation of philosophical discourse in respect of a currently felt need to understand time and take finitude seriously as a dimension of thinking.

The deeper Husserl goes in his analyses of the internal consciousness of time, the more the *necessary assumption* becomes clear that these investigations are supposed to arrive at while at the same time establishing the legitimacy thereof, namely to overlay this initial gap between the assumption and the thinking without preconceptions that phenomenology claims to be. To put this slightly differently: with each further step of the investigation it becomes more and more clear why these analyses are essential and what they should aim at. They have to show how and whether that which must be given in order that phenomenology be possible is given: the basis of consciousness as *presence in itself for itself and of itself*.

The presence of consciousness in itself guarantees the *epoché* procedure and reduction to the sphere of immanence in which the outside becomes apparent inside as a phenomenon, i.e. a reduction to what and how consciousness is shown as *presence in consciousness and for consciousness* – consciousness precisely because it is *in itself*,

---

309 "It is absolute subjectivity and has the absolute properties of something to be designated metaphorically as 'flow'; of something that originates in a point of actuality, in a primal source-point, 'the now', and so on. In the actuality-experience we have the primal source-point and a continuity of reverberation. For all this, we lack names." (Husserl, *The Phenomenology of Internal Time Consciousness*, §36, p. 79.

it is *of itself* and is thus able to reflect upon its content and acts and to turn *in itself to itself* in movement, which does not abandon the field of immanence as the field of evidence. Consciousness is *immediately* present to itself, to its content and to its operations. However, consciousness is a stream, a flow, a flux (the condition of the possibility of syntheses, identifications and associations, the constitution of idealities, the completion of intentional opinion), and so it is essential that *presence* be retained in this flow that is also a *flowing* into the past. This important task of retaining that which is passing and has just passed (but not by means of re-presentation, which would introduce a certain discontinuity into the continuous stream of consciousness) is carried out by retentional and protentional (passively functioning) intentionality. This is why we cannot say that consciousness is in time (because it would then be necessary to find some other level of time prior to consciousness and the analysis would be threatened by infinite regress). Instead, it is necessary to show that the internal consciousness of time is in the end constituted and constitutive, i.e. that consciousness is time as perpetual "temporalising" or *Zeitigung*. However, this would mean that flowing, the stream, is somehow the same as *nunc stans*, standing time as "the moment from which consciousness radiates, reaching out to what is, what has been, and what will be",[310] and so every "now" has in a certain sense the dimension of the whole of time as lived presence (*lebendige Gegenwart*), a definition that is tightened up in Husserl's later texts as *stehend urtümliche Lebendigkeit*. This is something like *Urgegenwart*, which is not a modality of time and is not therefore the same as simply "the current immediate form of consciousness", as Husserl still called this "live presence" in the *Lectures*,[311] but is *im Strömen verharrende vieldimen-*

---

310 John B. Brough, "Notes on the Absolute Time-Constituting Flow of Consciousness", in: D. Lohmar, I. Yamaguchi (eds.), *On Time – New Contributions to the Husserlian Phenomenology of Time*, Phaenomenologica 197, Springer Science-Business Media, 2010, p. 44.
311 Husserl, *Vorlesungen*, Husserliana X, p. 83.

sionale Gegenwart,[312] which for the sake of differentiation Husserl also sometimes called *Primordium* and described it as "the primally original standing streaming (das urtümlich stehende Strömen).[313] This consciousness as the most original *lebendige Gegenwart* (as the *Primordium*) does not only allow for – as the continuum of intentional modifications of the primal "now" (to which the ur-impressional "now" corresponds in the specific experience) – the potential transcending of current consciousness via itself, and thus for recurrent recollection, but also – and this is important from the perspective of Husserl's *Crisis of the European Sciences* – the retrospective questioning of the original establishment and its restitution, as well as the concept of history as the fulfilment of the original *telos* and, finally, the element of evidence in which identification, *Wesensschau*, eidetic variation and a glimpse of idealities is possible. The fold in the reflexive relationship to itself is thus not a fold: the world as the horizon of all horizons has its final form of temporalising as the horizon of all temporal horizons, and in this way (transcendental) consciousness potentially includes everything that can be thought (*alles Erdenkliche*).[314]

312 Edmund Husserl, *Späte Texte über Zeitkonstitution (1929–1934)*, Husserliana, Materialien VIII, p. 129.

313 Edmund Husserl, *Zur phänomenologischen Reduktion*, Husserliana XXXIV, ed. Sebastian Luft, Springer 2002, p. 384. (1) Die Rückfrage von der Epoche aus führt auf das urtümlich stehende Strömen - in einem gewissen Sinne das nunc stans, stehende "Gegenwart", wobei das Wort "Gegenwart", als schon auf eine Zeitmodalität verweisend, eigentlich noch nicht passt. Eine erste Strukturanalyse ist also die der Form dieses Strömens als eines nur nach allgemeiner Form identifizierbaren. 2) Die erste Aussage ist: stehendes Strömen, stehendes Verströmen, stehendes Heranströmen. Im stehendem Strömen konstituiert sich der Strom; das Stehen besagt Ständigsein als "Prozess" – Prozess der Urzeitigung, Prozess der Zeitmodalitäten, der Wandlung, die ständig unterschieden hat Gegenwart, die in Vergangenheit sich wandelt (und Vergangenheit, die sich ihrerseits in Vorvergangenheit wandelt usw.), andererseits Zukunft, die sich wandelnd zu Gegenwart wird u. ff. Darin aber Konstitution von ständiger Zeit, ständigen Einheiten als zeitlichen Einheiten, die je in ihren Zeitmodalitäten strömend sich "darstellen", im zeitmodalen Strömen "stand"-halten, Stand haben, sich als Einheiten (Selbigkeiten) konstituieren."

314 Die Gegenwart ist allüberspannendes, sozusagen allwissendes Bewusstsein von sich selbst und all seinen intentionalen Bestanden - potentiell birgt ihre Struktur Allwissenheit der Welt in sich – als ideale Moglichkeit, wofem wir nur in Rechnung ziehen , dass der Dunkelheitshorizont,

It is for this reason that we can claim that everything unknown is a modus of the known.

However, would it not thus be possible to claim that the project of rationality, which effaces the incommensurability of the incommensurable and that works with *concepts* as the ur-form of objectivising thinking thanks to which man rids himself of fear by eliminating everything unknown from thinking, remains implicated in the very foundations of phenomenology, in its establishment of time, in its identification of time with consciousness that is in itself of itself and for itself, as the authors of the *Dialectic of Enlightenment* might say?

Nothing is allowed to remain outside, since the mere idea of the "outside" is the real source of fear.[315]

Husserl's concept of time wants to eliminate the event as the exterior with regard to the living present – and cannot do otherwise. For if the structural analogy still applied between the interpretation of the primary impression (*Urimpression*) forever retained by the order of retention, and the original establishment of the meaning or objective (*Urstiftung*) of a certain tradition that continually follows on from it, and if the idea was to show that this movement in itself and of itself (which is also the definition of teleological historicity) is irreducibly contaminated by some exterior – for example by the incalculable event that transcends existing horizons of understanding, or by a quality that is beyond our grasp – then this would mean that the very possibility of *Rückfrage*, the restitutive return to the

in dem Vergangenheit und Zukunft des Bewusstseinsstroms verschwimmen, und der (die) Vollkommenheit der Selbstwahrnehmung des Bewusstseins beschrankt, eine zufallige Schranke ist, die in infinitum erweitert gedacht werden kann, so dass als "Idee" erwachst ein allwissendes "gottliches" Bewusstsein, das sich selbst in vollkommener Klarheit umspannt. Auch das "endliche" Bewusstsein ist allwissend, auch seine Intentionalitat umspannt seine ganze Vergangenheit und Zukunft, aber nur partiell klar, im Ubrigen in einer Dunkelheit, die eine Potentialitat fur Klarheiten und Wiedererinnerungen ist" Husserl, *Bernauer Manuskripte*, pp. 45–46.
315 Adorno, Horkheimer, *Dialectics of Enlightenment*, p. 11.

original establishment of meaning (that would in that case always only be attainable "then", supplementarily (*nachträglich*), as always already modified in some way) would be at threat, and the *Urstiftung* would by analogy be something like the escaping quality of the ur-impression, a trace of meaning irrupting into the order of its apprehension/interpretations, without revealing itself in its presence in any of them. It would continue to differentiate itself and defer its full presence for consciousness. In other words (Derrida's in this case), tradition would be subject to the movement of *différance*. Or, as Derrida might also say: the meaning of Europe would be this "secretum" of its history, its re-founding in every moment of "crisis" (which is, however, every present).

Emmanuel Levinas will go on to say that Husserl's consciousness sleeps a dogmatic, because objectivising, sleep, but that it is a step away from its awakening precisely there where phenomenological reduction penetrates Life as such as it is present, albeit covered by its forced synchronisation with the "somnambulism of identifying reason" in the concept of live or living presence, i.e. in the basic objective of phenomenology to interpret *experience*, *Erleben*. If, therefore, phenomenology is not to break faith with this objective, the true meaning of phenomenological reduction must be rescued, i.e. this "permanent revolution", a revolution that will "reanimate or reactivate the life that is forgotten or weakened in [thematicising, objectivising] knowledge." This is the most intrinsic establishment of phenomenology, its "style". It turns the attention to that which shines from *behind consciousness*, which is the length and breadth of subjective life as layered by thinking that thematises, i.e. represents. In Levinas's reading of Husserl, reduction in the final analysis liberates thinking from the norms of adequation, from "obedience to the completed work of identification".[316] He then immediately poses

---

316 Emmanuel Levinas, "La philosophie et l'évei", in: *Entre nous*, p. 84. Levinas makes reference to Husserl's distinction between apodicticity and evidence in § 6 of *Cartesian Meditations*: apodicticity can obtain even when the evidence is not complete and adequate.

a question that hints at the non-mandatory link to Husserl that is peculiar to Levinas:

> Is it, under the label erleben (to live (something)) just a confused or obscure consciousness, merely something preparatory to the distinction between subject and object, a pre-thematization, a preknowledge? Must we not affirm our psychism otherwise? Does not the adjective living, from the beginning of Husserl's work on, underscore the importance of the word Erlebnis as expressing the way of the subject? The I's prereflective experience, designated by the term Erlebnis – the lived, is not just a moment of pre-objectification, like the *hulé* prior to the *Auffasen* (apprehending). The 'living present': we know the importance this term took on in Husserl's manuscripts on time. Its explosive and surprising character (similar to that of the present in the Bergsonian *durée*) is expressed in *The Phenomenology Internal Time-Consciousness* as the *primal impression*. Unforeseeable, it is in no way prepared in some germinating seed that would bear the past. The absolute traumatism that is inseparable from the spontaneity of its upsurge is of as much importance as the sensible quality that it offers to the adequation of knowledge. The living present of the *cogito-sum* occurs not only on the model of self-consciousness, absolute knowledge; it is the rupture of the equanimity of the 'even mind', the rupture of the Same of immanence; awakening and life.[317]

In other words, the *lebendige Gegenwart* is not the same as self-consciousness, but is an element of the emergence of the forever new (the ur-impression), perforating its presence in itself of itself and for itself, irrupting into immanence inasmuch as this invasion of the outside inside is an awakening to an alert life which is *sensibility*, which is living prior to *hylé* being transformed into the function of *Abschattung*. Our attention is therefore now turned to this point (and not only in the case of Levinas), to the pre-predicative sphere,

---

317 Emmanuel Levinas, "Philosophy and Awakening", in: *Entre Nous,* p. 85.

to the non-intentional operations of consciousness prior to the acts of thematisation, i.e. to its original openness to the outside, more to protention than to retention. This then returns, for instance, in Levinas's emphasis on suffering, i.e. a more passive experience that the passivity of receptivity, which through vulnerability refers to the presence of another as the other, and whence the only indisputable ethical principle of the 20th century that survived the "Holocaust as the paradigm of gratuitous human suffering, where evil appears in its diabolical horror."[318]

This shift of focus, which nevertheless remains a form of the continuation as well as of the non-continuation of phenomenology and which takes place conspicuously in connection with the "internal consciousness of time", continues in Derrida's exposure of the resistance within the framework of immanence or difference within auto-affection (or self-affection). Though it might at first glance seem that Derrida's thinking is closely linked to structuralist (or post-structuralist) semiology, a simple chronological list of his work shows that its starting point was in fact phenomenology.[319] His doctoral thesis *The Problem of Genesis in Husserl's Philosophy*[320] was written in 1953–54 and its choice of topic already makes reference to the problem of historicity, the history of meaning and by extension to temporality. Then there is his lecture *"Genesis and Structure in Phenomenology"* of 1995[321] and to a certain extent the preface to the translation of *The Origins of Geometry*,[322] one of the appendices to Husserl's *The Crisis of European Sciences*. Derrida deals explicitly

---

318 Emmanuel Levinas, "La souffrance inutile", in: ibid., p. 115. Emmanuel Levinas, "Useless Suffering", in: Ibid., p. 97.
319 For detailed information gleaned from archives, see Edward Baring, *Young Derrida and French Philosophy 1945–1968*. Cambridge UP, Cambridge 2011.
320 Jacques Derrida, *The Problem of Genesis in Husserl's Philosophy,* trans. Marian Hobson, The University of Chicago Press, Chicago & London, 2003.
321 Reprinted in Jacques Derrida, *L'écriture et la différence*, Ed. du Seuil, Paris 1967.
322 Jacques Derrida, *Introduction et traduction de "L'Origine de la géométrie", de Husserl*, P.U.F., Paris 1962.

with consciousness and its temporality in *Voice and Phenomenon*.[323] In general we can say that, at first indirectly, Derrida is constantly examining the very possibility of originally giving evidence as the *presence* of meaning in the original opinion of the thing itself, i.e. he asks whether this possibility is guaranteed by this concept of presence as elaborated by Husserl's phenomenological analyses of the last level of consciousness/time as *lebendige Gegenwart*. However, his "deconstruction" is not criticism, but rather a search for the traces of other possibilities of reading in the texts themselves. Inasmuch as Husserl is convinced, as he puts it in *Cartesian Meditations*, that the purely intuitive, concrete and apodictic way that phenomenology reports its findings "excludes all 'metaphysical adventure', all speculative excesses",[324] then Derrida seeks to verify whether this is the case. He asks whether the concept of presence in Husserl's texts is indeed non-metaphysical in relation to temporality and whether, on the basis of this concept, an eidetic science would be possible, capable of guaranteeing the ideality of its concepts and claims.

In other words he examines the sustainability of the principle of all principles.

It would be sustainable if it were not possible to prove the role of irreducible absence during the constitution of idealities or the impossibility of the contamination of the expression by indication. It would be sustainable if there existed something like a *phenomenological sign and phenomenological voice*: a physicality stripped of its physicality, i.e. of the *outside*.

Because Husserl must work with the "sign", he must simultaneously reduce the signification of the sign as outside, because the sign is traditionally the element of absence, non-originality. The sign is a sign of something because it takes the place of the thing in its absence. The sign cannot be the beginning or vice versa. In the

---

323 Jacques Derrida, *La voix et le phénomène*. P.U.F., Paris 1967.
324 Edmund Husserl, *Cartesian Meditations: An Introduction to Phenomenology*, trans. Dorion Cairns, Springer 1960, p. 139.

element of signs there is no beginning, we are always "in the middle". If phenomenology aims at a presentation of the thing itself, it must reduce re-presentation or convert it into a repetition of the identical. Whence Husserl's concept of "expression" as opposed to "indication" and whence the strategy that begins in the *Logical Investigations*: Husserl shifts the problematic of expression to the immanence of consciousness.

Derrida describes the specific approach to this reduction of the sign as follows: In order to distinguish expression from meaning (or signification), Husserl uses the German word "bedeuten" (nominative "Bedeutung"). When he says that the expression has *Bedeutung*, that *etwas bedeutet*, that it is *bedeutend*, he is saying that it is the expression of that which the speaker has immediately in mind, that which he intends to say, i.e. in Husserl's usage, which does not distinguish between *Sinn* and *Bedeutung* or meaning, "meaning", or to put it more precisely: the ideal meaning as the content of expression (see also *Ideas I*). However, this cannot apply in real communication, in which *Bedeutung* is always woven into the network of significations. The act of communication for Husserl is external to the act of "bedeuten"; it therefore only applies in speech without communication, in "monolithic discourse", in absolute silence (deprived of all materiality) of the voice of the solitary mental life, in which the relationship to the outside is suspended (though generally speaking this is the act establishing phenomenology).

In Husserl's semiology, expression is a sign bestowed with a signifying intention, i.e. *bedeutsames Zeichen*. "Bedeuten" is a key act: ideal objectivity (that which the speaker had in mind) is expressed without deserting, by virtue of its own exteriorisation, the interior, because everything takes place in the field of consciousness (the necessarily forever present in itself, of itself and for itself), which Husserl describes as *einsames Seelenleben,* the solitary life of the soul. It ensues from this that expression does not have to be genuinely articulated by speech, communicated (to someone else). Only consciousness itself is communicated (everything takes place, to draw on later terminology, within the noetic-noematic sphere of consciousness, within the framework of the international relatedness to the outside inside). A non-productive duplication is involved: the expressive intention emerges outside of itself only in the form of the phenomenological voice, while the content of the expression is ideality that does not exist in the world. If the expression as exteriorisation presupposes *sui generis* some kind of *Deutung*, then this is something like an "understanding listening":[325] everything is still under the control of "bedeuten", because all "involuntary associations" linked with factual communication are excluded. In other words:

> Sense wants to be signified; it is expressed only in a meaning (*vouloir-dire*) which is none other than a wanting-to-tell-itself proper to the presence of sense.[326]

Let us summarise for the sake of clarity. In his *Logical Investigations* Husserl attempts to lay the foundations of the scientism of science, formal logic. He must therefore demonstrate the possibility of a purely scientific speech, the unalloyed expression of ideal meaning or *Bedeutung*, i.e. the possibility of a purely expressive speech in which signifiers lead without equivocation to the signified. In this way, expression or *Ausdruck* would be "non-productive" (neither adding anything to nor subtracting anything from the ideal), simply "mirroring". It would be the double of ideal *Bedeutung*. It would retain the veracity of *Bedeutung*, which is not dependent on expression since *Bedeutung* belongs to a pre-expressive level. Its veracity is guaranteed by the illustrative "*presence*" of the object to which this *Bedeutung* is intentionally related. The veracity (objectivity) of testimony is thus transferred to the illustrative presence of the

---

325 Jacques Derrida, *Speech and Phenomena and other Essays on Husserl's Theory of Signs,* trans. David B. Allison, Newton Garver, Northwestern University Press, Evanston 1973, p. 34.
326 Ibid., p. 35.

object, i.e. the illustrativeness of the object for thinking that precedes speech (the aspect of that which Derrida terms "logocentrism"). And Derrida shows that the possibility of purely scientific speech is conditional upon what Husserl gradually eliminates from the game (the indicatory utilisation of signs, the impossibility of isolating the pure pre-expressive level of "labelling" and thus thinking).[327]

But what is the purpose of Derrida's observations regarding Husserl's concept of sign and signification? They point to a host of seemingly obvious eliminations. The *physical side* of speech is gradually excluded, along with everything that finds its origin in *bona fide communication* (the conveyance of something to someone else), because real communication is a dimension of (mere) meaning, i.e. also the atrophication of *Bedeutung* (of ideal meaning, which then returns in *The Crisis of European Sciences* as the cause of the "crisis" in meaning, namely the forgetting of the original looking in its real traditionalisation). Everything is orientated on the last field becoming *consciousness relating to itself in an internal monologue*, since, as seems clear, if I speak to myself, I simultaneously hear myself, and do not communicate anything to myself. Husserl's description of the sign pushes to one side its *signification* and with it its *materiality*. It eliminates the very moment of re-presentation, since (Husserl is convinced) consciousness does not need to re-represent its experiences to itself, because on the field of consciousness "every experience is *presently existing*". We relate to the acts of consciousness at the same moment that we experience them. Consciousness does not have to make anything known to itself from the power of the sign.[328] We are in the sphere of pure auto-affection, the outside has disappeared inside.

To put this in Derridean terms: Husserl wants to avoid all "metaphysical adventures" while at the same time repeating the founding gesture of the metaphysical tradition, which is the subordination of

327 See Bernet, "Differenz und Anwesenheit".
328 Derrida, *Speech and Phenomena*, p. 60.

the sign to logo, language to logic (to pure logical grammar). The one stands in opposition to the other, each contaminates the other, without its being possible to exclude either one or the other. Ideality should be able to retain its *Bedeutung* within the flow of time, even to appear as ideality within the stream of consciousness that is the internal temporality of life itself (through the operation of idealisation and synthesis in the coverage of the diverse). However, this appearance itself implies the exclusion of everything non-identical. But it is impossible to exclude the non-identical if we are to speak, for instance, of the primary impression. On the other hand, this is only "present" for consciousness subsequently (*nachträglich*), in retentional modification and after its materialism has, by virtue of being apprehended (something as something) become quality (of something as something). The presence of objectivity for consciousness is paid for by the absence of that which, in this manifestation as material, is its condition. It is as though we now read two texts without being able to decide which of them is the original. Ideality is unthinkable without its intersubjective communicability, thanks to which it only now becomes the ideal objectivity repeatable in its identity and only thus transcends empirical and individual consciousness (see Derrida's introduction to Husserl's *The Origin of Geometry*). This means genuine ideality is only in the element of language, in the order of meaning, i.e. exteriorisation, because its ideal being is nothing outside the world. "Sense, being temporal in nature, as Husserl recognised, is never simply present; it is always already engaged in the 'movement' of the trace, that is, in the order of 'signification'. It has always already issued forth from itself into the 'expressive stratum' of lived experience."[329]

To be more precise: this is not about pitting one text against another. It is about a double text and its internal movement in which its beginning, of which there should be only one, eternally returns,

---

[329] Ibid., pp. 85–86.

and this return is its trace. This is what Derrida characterises with his neologism *différance*, in which the temporality of the internal consciousness of time is transformed.

> For the ideality of the form (Form) of presence itself implies that it be infinitely re-peatable, that its re-turn, as a return of the same, is necessary ad infinitum and is inscribed in presence itself. It implies that the re-turn is the return of a present which will be retained in a finite movement or retention and that primordial truth, in the phenomenological sense of the term, is only to be found rooted in the finitude of this retention. It is furthermore implied that the relation with infinity can be instituted only in the opening of the form of presence upon ideality, as the possibility of a re-turn ad infinitum. (...) the presence of the present is thought of as arising from the bending-back of a return, from the movement of repetition, and not the reverse (...), bending-back is irreducible in presence or in self-presence (...), this trace or *différance* is always older than presence.[330]

It is no coincidence that Derrida first uses the neologism "différance" in his essay "Freud and the scene of writing"[331] in reaction to structuralist formalism, which pushes to one side the question of genesis, i.e. temporality (and the problem of history more generally). The term was also clearly inspired by Maurice Blanchot's "literary experience": the exterior of language is not outside the text, meaning does not precede the work. The basis of literature is that it has no basis until the text is interpreted, becomes significant, because the work escapes into the murmur of speech, its significance, which can never be stabilised with final validity, but is forever shifting. The "I" that speaks is flooded from within and without by an impersonal voice, writing in the sense of *écriture* differs from the written, etc. However, his reading of Freud led Derrida to a more

330 Derrida, *Speech and Phenomena*, pp. 67–68.
331 Jacques Derrida, "Freud and the Scene of Writing", in: *Writing and Difference*, trans. Alan Bass, Routledge & Kegan Paul, London 2001.

radical formulation of the temporality everywhere implied, of time before time through identification, escape from the presence, at that point where psychoanalysis, in connection with traumatic neurosis and repetition compulsion, comes up against "afterwardsness" or *Nachträglichkeit*. In his commentary on Freud, Derrida turns his attention to the central motif of Freud's later psychoanalysis, i.e. a concept of life in which, confronted by reality, life protects its survival by postponing the fulfilment of wishes demanded by the pleasure principle. However, is not that which establishes the relationship of pleasure to reality, primarily this shift, this postponement (*Aufschub*)? And is not death implied in the very principle of life, inasmuch as life cannot resist death otherwise than through an economy of death, differentiation (*différance*), repetition?[332] Derrida offers the most detailed answer to these questions thirteen years later in the second part of *La Carte Postale* entitled "Spéculer – sur Freud",[333] which can be read as one of the clearest demonstrations of the "concept" of deconstruction and *différance*. This again is another extraordinarily close reading of Freud, this time his essay *Beyond the Pleasure Principle*. Derrida poses what at first sight seems a simple question: did Freud ever arrive at something "outside" the pleasure principle; did he ever manage to step "outside" the realm of its control?

For it is noticeable that whenever Freud in his speculative metatheory dares to take a step in the direction of this principle and adds another moment or instance to his considerations – the reality principle, displacement, transference and countertransference, repetition compulsion leading to the discovery of the death drive, etc. – he opens up a new digression or postponement. And so the process of consideration is on the one hand diverted from its direction up until that point, and on the other repeatedly returns to older hypotheses that must now be corrected, and as a consequence repeats this repeti-

---

332 Derrida, *Writing and Difference*, p. 249.
333 Jacques Derrida, *The Postcard: From Socrates to Freud and Beyond*, trans. Alan Bass, The University of Chicago Press, Chicago, London 1987.

tion again and again. One is forced to conclude that there is nothing in this movement (highly reminiscent of the *fort/da* of little Ernst) that returns as identifiable and continually links to its beginning. What is even more remarkable is that, when looking back to the starting points of psychoanalytic theory, Freud repeatedly re-interprets its foundations (without giving them up), to such an extent that the path he is following cannot be distinguished from the deviations therefrom. He himself is finally aware that he is actually working with an equation "of two unknowns". Derrida's deconstruction – or to be more precise, the texts that deconstruct themselves in his reading – thus brings to the surface the strange "athetic" structure of Freud's discourse, its "athetic" functioning (Blanchot and Levinas would speak of thematisation without theme, a completely elliptical construction of an argument), which prevents us from finding any last instance in it, "that is to say, any instance whatsoever."[334]

That in turn is to say: any instance of beginning or origin. Derrida's reading of Freud is thus also the transformation of the early modern idea of tradition or traditionalisation as a continual linking up, an idea which persists in part in Gadamer's hermeneutics. An athetic or elliptical construction of the text ... the movement of reference now has nothing from which to deviate from, unless from its absenting focal point in the sense of principle or *arché*. The movement of deferral and transfer of *différance* dominates. Or perhaps *destinerrance*, another Joycean neologism, which designates the irrevocable possibility that a destination specified in advance may never be attained, that the original semantic intention is lost in indications and references in which only its traces will be retained without its ever being possible to restitute or re-present it. This is not a play on words but a consequent imagining of the openness to that which is arriving as that which cannot be anticipated and integrated without remainder into existing horizons of understanding. It involves

334 Derrida, *The Postcard*, p. 261.

revealing the event or "adventurous" temporality that was, albeit everywhere and completely, covered by the Husserlian consciousness of time and that means that in his analyses Husserl, too, must return at the very moment he wishes to transcend their boundaries. And this implies a thinking of history that differs from teleological history, in which the primal establishment (*Urstiftung*) of tradition is supposed to be the addressor of a certain aim (*telos*), and which is supposed to branch out and realise itself within history and lead it in "a meaningful, final harmony"[335] to the final destination or addressee.

> But to every primal establishment (*Urstiftung*) essentially belongs a final establishment (*Endstiftung*) assigned as a task to the historical process. This final establishment is accomplished when the task is brought to consummate clarity and thus to an apodictic method which, in every step of achievement, is a constant avenue to new steps having the character of absolute success, i.e., the character of apodictic steps. At this point philosophy, as an infinite task, would have arrived at its apodictic beginning, its horizon of apodictic forward movement.[336]

However, if the original establishment of meaning, like the original semantic intention (*Bedeutung*), does not produce contexts that it will have under its control and in which it will be "identified" (i.e. interpreted), and if the original task or reference is addressed to all of those who will receive, develop and fulfil it, i.e. to all the future couriers of this deed of foundation, we cannot avoid concluding that the recipient or heir will hand over "only the basics", i.e. "underlined, cut out, translated, commented, edited, taught, reset in a chosen perspective",[337] constantly replacing the escaping "origin",

335 Husserl, *The Crisis*, p. 73.
336 Husserl, *The Crisis*, p. 72.
337 Derrida, *The Postcard*, p. 373. Derrida's metaphor of postal relations and the postcard or letter (in French *lettre*, i.e. both letter and all "literature"), which is a continuation of what he had already analysed in connection with semiology and the sign, is intended to imply that the letter is a letter because it does not always have to reach the person it is addressed to. One thinks of Laclos' *Dangerous*

which in traditionalisation *in-sists* not as *instance* but as *restance-non-présente*,[338] as the constant trace of the missing origin that resists its actualisation. In this way, the "purposefulness" of transcendental historicity is transformed into a movement of return, in which, however, no-thing identical with itself is returned, but remains the movement of the returning of returns. This, too, is *différance*: the differentiation and deferral of the end of that movement, another thinking of tradition, another thinking of history, another thinking of *time*, of that whose traces Derrida discovers both in Husserl and in Freud's essay on the pleasure principle, when Freud rejects both philosophy and empirical speculation and prefers to speak of "speculation", realising that the very inevitability of the transition from observation to description, the very transfer of empirical givenness into specialist discourse, opens up a realm of problematic ambiguity, and that theory is always provisional and therefore necessarily *speculative*, because it is deprived of the possibility of naming the things itself in a special (to itself) way. Nothing remains but for Freud to progress by means of retrospective questioning (Husserl's *Rückfrage*, which is now lost), and each step outside ends inside in a movement that Derrida calls the movement of expropriation that problematises the value of "one's own". Is Freud convinced of the accuracy of his speculative hypotheses? "My answer would be that I am not convinced myself (...) I do not know how far I believe in them."[339]

Liaisons, in which letters drive the action precisely because they do not always reach their intended addressee, or arrive in the wrong sequence or late, and their interpretation is difficult because the sender is obliged in his next letter to rectify the misunderstandings caused by the previous letter, etc.
338 Cf. in: Derrida, *Marges de la philosophie* ("Signature, évenément, contexte"): "This structural possibility of being severed from its referent or signified (and therefore from communication and its context) seems to me to make of every mark, even if oral, a grapheme in general, that is, as we have seen, the nonpresent remaining of a differential mark cut off from its alleged "production" or origin. And I will extend this law even to all "experience" in general, if it is granted that there is no experience of pure presence, but only chains of differential marks. *Margins*, p. 318.
339 Sigmund Freud, *Beyond the Pleasure Principle,* trans. James Strachey, W.W. Norton, New York, London 1961, p. 53.

35

An interest in tradition and traditionalisation that, indirectly, is without doubt a response to Husserl's concept of history and its implied concept of time thus becomes a privileged site of the transformation of philosophical discourse. This takes the form of the deconstruction of assumptions regarding the continual temporality of the stream of consciousness, and, in the last instance, of horizontality as the last framework of synthesising identification. Unlike Husserl, Derrida views tradition using the "model" of inheritance and above all through the *non-evidentiality* of that which is traditionalised as testament (the legacy is a very paradoxical "beginning"), since if there exists some unity to inheritance, it

> can consist only in the injunction to *reaffirm by choosing* (...) one must filter, sift, criticise, one must sort out several different possibles that inhabit the same injunction. And inhabit it in a contradictory fashion around a secret. If the readability of a legacy were given, natural, transparent, univocal, if it did not call for and at the same time defy interpretation, we would never have anything to inherit from it. We would be affected by it as by a cause – natural or genetic. One always inherits from a secret – which says "read me, will you ever be able to do so?" The critical choice called for by any reaffirmation of the inheritance is also, like memory itself, the condition of finitude. The infinite does not inherit, it does not inherit (from) itself. The injunction itself (it always says "choose and decide from among what you inherit") can only be one by dividing itself, tearing itself apart, differing/deferring itself, by speaking at the same time several times – and in several voices.[340]

However, inasmuch as Derrida shows that in the phenomenon of the legacy the return to the origin is always a new beginning, the

340 Jacques Derrida, *Specters of Marx,* trans. Paggy Kamuf, Routledge, New York and London 1994, p. 18.

purpose of his considerations is not a polemic with Husserl's *Rück-frage* as the restitution of the original establishment of a certain tradition that deviated from its *telos*. His (deconstructive) reading of texts is not about revealing contradictions, gaps in arguments or unsubstantiated assumptions, but rescuing the possibility of *another* way of thinking, traces of which are as clear in these breaches as the manifest meanings themselves. Where Husserl attempts to bring an idea to a conclusion and give it systematic form, for instance even in the form of teleological history explicating in time that which is implied in its original establishment, Derrida shows that a genuine adherence to tradition (the legacy) consists in openness, that its time is not a continuity absorbing its own crises, but a continual discontinuity of *creative* reaffirmation, i.e. of productive continuation by the *new*. In other words, time must be thought from *différance*, from the movement of difference, which is open to the coming of that which is on the point of arrival. Or perhaps: thought is there where happening is taking place, it is not *ergon*, but *energeia*. Retrospective questioning of the origin is always its renewed updating, its establishment anew, which becomes apparent if we link traditionalisation with the legacy or the fulfilment of the testament. We must therefore do everything we can to receive the legacy (and phenomenology itself is a legacy), which is impossible other than by means of its reaffirmation, i.e. a decision as to what we deem to be alive in it. Confirmation of tradition is both its continuation and its interruption, since the heir is a finite being:

> If our heritage assigns contradictory tasks to us (to receive and yet to choose, to welcome what comes before us and yet to reinterpret it, etc.), this is because it is a testimony to our finitude. Only a finite being inherits, and his finitude *obliges* him. It obliges him to receive what is larger and older and more powerful and more durable than he. But the same finitude obliges one to choose, to prefer, to sacrifice, to exclude, to let go and leave behind. Precisely in order to respond to the call that preceded him, to

answer it and to answer for it – in one's name as in the name of the other. One is responsible before what comes before one but also before what is to come and therefore before oneself.[341]

The paradigm of inheritance is reaffirmation of the Husserlian concept of responsibility. This is a situated *response* in which the legacy is transformed into an event, the interpretation of which compels a withdrawal from the existing horizons of understanding. Inheritance is something like the givenness of the *gift*. However, though the word "situatedness" could be read as a reference to Heidegger, in this case too it is a completely Derridean acceptance of the testamentary legacy. This is best illustrated by Derrida's book *Spectres of Marx*. The framework of responses to the legacy is justice, in the name of which I ask the question of how to respond to the legacy of rights. However, justice establishes the principle of responsibility outside of all present living, I answer to the "phantoms" of those who are already dead or have not yet been born, and our present is inhabited by these very spectres, who demand that we respect them. In this way another temporality of tradition emerges. If we ask (thus situated between presently absent spectres, visitors to our present) where we want to head, then that which this question is driving at also always already precedes it. To put it slightly differently: the inheritance as a form of givenness is a *gift*, i.e. basically discontinuous time, time that is forever out of joint, outcast, dislocated, forever exiting continuity, the time of events. Our presence is constantly being visited by the *other*, which means that "There is first of all the doubtful contemporaneity of the present to itself".[342] As gift, the legacy is this task:

341 Jacques Derrida, Elisabeth Roudinesco: For What Tomorrow?, trans. Jeff Fort, Stanford University Press, Stanford 2004.
342 Derrida, *Specters*, p. 39.

It remains before us just as unquestionably as we are heirs of Marxism, even before wanting or refusing to be, and like all inheritors, we are in mourning (...) To be (...) means (...) to inherit. All the questions on the subject of being or of what is to be (or not to be) are questions of inheritance. There is no backward-looking fervour in this reminder, no traditionalist flavour. Reaction, reactionary, or reactive are but interpretations of the structure of inheritance. That we *are* heirs does not mean that we *have* or that we *receive* this or that, some inheritance that enriches us one day with this or that, but that the *being* of what we are is first of all inheritance, whether we like it or know it or not. And that, as Hőlderlin said so well, we can only *bear* witness to it.[343]

---

343 Ibid., p. 54.

36

Why must the transformation of philosophical discourse be tracked in the transformation of the concept of time and temporality? Because the condition of the possibility of a teleological understanding of history and the meaning guaranteed by history to be trans-historical, which is *lebendige Gegenwart* or living presence, i.e. the continuous unity of now and its subsequent retentions and protentions, is unsustainable face to face with real history – the crisis has inexorably morphed into catastrophe. The time is out of joint and open to the incalculable. Thinking after the Holocaust rewrites Husserl's *The Crisis of European Sciences*: the living present is co-present with the dead and, thus, with the still unborn. The origin (*Ursprung* and *Urstiftung*) is a legacy, traditionalisation takes place as the acceptance of the inheritance, the meaning of which will again be decided anew at the moment of its acceptance, because its reaffirmation is always a unique response in history. This is not anticipation, but expectation, a receptiveness to that which is forever to come and beyond the horizons of expectation not only *de facto*, but *de jure*. Temporality therefore implies a relationship via irreducible difference, a relationship to the event, the openness of the inside to the outside. As Derrida explains in uncommonly succinct fashion, this is because the event,

> must not be seen arriving. The event is that which arrives; the arrival of another as an event is only worthy of the name, i.e. it is an explosive, inaugural, singular event, if we do not see it coming. The event that we anticipate, that we see arriving and that we predict, is not an event, or rather it is an event whose character is neutralised, amortised, withheld by anticipation. The experience of an event is a passive experience, to which and, I would say, against which, arrives that which we do not see arriving and that is to begin with completely unpredictable, unforesee-

able; part of what makes an event an event is that it arrives in an utterly surprising way, *a l'improviste.*[344]

This event- (or "adventure"-) time is now inscribed in the identity of Europe. It is present, for instance, in Derrida's *Given Time*,[345] which inter alia examines Patočka's "European" interpretation of "care for the soul", and in the essay *L'autre cap* (translated as *The Other Heading*), which can be read as a direct response to Husserl's legacy since its central theme is that "what is still called Europe even if we no longer know very well what or who goes by this name".[346] Here, too, the transformation of discourse cannot be ignored: culture is necessarily special in that it is never identical to itself, it never has a single origin, and so any idea of "mono-genealogy" in its history is always mystification. The deviation from itself in an identity with itself resides in the *double bind* that a certain tradition must conform to: as "Europe" it anticipates something as objective (direction, the promise, etc.), though at the same time (as historical tradition) it anticipates that this objective is not given either in advance or once and for all. At this point we cannot fail to hear a discreet reference to how Husserl works with the concept of "idea in the Kantian sense". However, for Derrida this concept already belongs under the rubric of analogical logic, for which identity is that which, in its direction or aim, transcends the boundary of the empirical and is open to the infinite, and inasmuch as it accepts this logic, does so with a fundamental reservation:

> It is a logic (…) that I do not wish to criticize here. I would even be ready to subscribe to it, but with one hand only, for I keep another to write or look for

344 Jacques Derrida, *Penser à ne pas voir. Ecrits sur les arts du visible.* Textes réunis et établis par Ginette Michaud, Joana Masó et Javier Bassas. Collection Essais, Ed. de la Différence, Paris 2013, p. 55.
345 Jacques Derrida, *Donner le temps. 1. La fausse monaie.* Galilée, Paris 1991.
346 Jacques Derrida, *The Other Heading*, trans. Michael B. Naas, Pascale Anne Brault, Indiana University Press, 1992, p. 5.

something else, perhaps outside Europe. Not only in order to look — in the way of research, analysis, knowledge, and philosophy — for what is already found outside Europe, but not to close off in advance a border to future, to the to-come / à-venir/ of the *event*, to that which *comes* /*vient*/, which comes perhaps and perhaps comes from a completely other shore. [347]

Once again we have a relationship via irreducible difference inscribed in temporality. However, this prudent reservation on Derrida's part must be read against the backdrop of the phenomenological establishment of identity on the basis of the "coverage" of (simply) the analogous, i.e. against the backdrop of the world as the horizon of all horizons. Genuine openness (and another concept of time and history) is guaranteed only by the possibility that the horizon will be interrupted by something, though this does not imply an event that is by definition incompatible with the horizontal structure of showing and understanding.

Is this a polemic with Husserl? Absolutely not. Transformation, reaffirmation, response, acceptance of the inheritance, the gesture of responsibility toward tradition that is not irresponsible because it does not abide by a programme given in advance that it would simply fulfil, respect for the legacy. The origin is not givenness, but a gift.

347 Derrida, *The Other Heading*, p. 69.

37

Factually speaking, all of these provocative or seemingly esoteric themes in which the legacy of phenomenology is nevertheless constantly reaffirmed are already contained in Derrida's deconstructive reading of the structuralist semiology of the sixties, a reading that is a symmetrical counterpart to the problematisation of Husserl's differentiation between sign and indication, inasmuch as in both cases Derrida lays emphasis on the irrevocable interplay of presence and absence to which the neologism *différance* he had already devised refers, even though in connection with the sign the starting point is the Saussurian dictum that language is "a system of differential elements and not substance". Whence derives the primordiality or productivity of the trace and non-identity: in the system of language the value of the sign is defined by its difference from other signs, which means that the sign is marked by its presence in the form of absence, or by the *trace of the other*. In other words, the trace is a special "phenomenon". It must appear in the absence of that which left it (i.e. the trace), because otherwise it would not be a trace/sign, which in Peirce's terminology is called index, a pure, uncodified relationship (*secondness*). An example would be the language of semiology as Derrida works with it in his analysis of Austin's and Searle's theory of speech acts. Every sign must be capable of being cited, i.e. "it can break with every given context, and engender infinitely new contexts in an absolutely nonsaturable fashion", because it has no validity outside (independent) of context. Therefore, there exist "only contexts without any centre or absolute anchoring". Citationality is not a random property, since what "would a mark be that could not be cited? And whose origin could not be lost on the way?"[348]

---

348 Jacques Derrida, "Signature Event Context", in: Jacques Derrida, *Margins of Philosophy*, trans. Alan Bass, The Harvester Press, The University of Chicago 1982, pp. 320 and 321.

Inasmuch as Derrida on the one hand reveals the ellipticity or atheticity of various texts (see Freud's essay *Beyond the Pleasure Principle*),[349] while on the other hand himself writing such texts, his strategy is clearly already pointing to the deconstruction of the semiological concept of the sign. It is also hinting at a broader context: here, now, is the source of his mistrust of "centralisation" or the "original (primal) establishment" (*Urstiftung*). It is also worth noting that, in connection with his analysis of the concept of the sign (as the inheritance of modern philosophy, the metaphysical primacy of presence and the concept of temporality deriving therefrom), he cites Levinas's "past that has never been present".[350] And so we are not so far from the late books, which circle the phenomenon of the gift and the secret. This is why we already find neologism being used as a way of pointing to that which is absent without betraying that which resists appearance: the *restance non présente* already referred to, a way of denoting that which maintains in the phenomenon a resistance to becoming present and insists on its own disappearance.[351] To put it another way, the concept *restance* lays an emphasis on that which cannot be expressed within the framework of a theory of presence, a theory of identity, or within the framework of an interpretation of time that priorities the determination of permanence, succession and coexistence. In relation to texts, then, deconstruction shows that there always remains a certain trace of that which was subject to deconstruction and that a deconstructive reading "educes" without *actualising* (whence the link between the secret and the gift, the possibility of understanding deconstruction as a response to tradition, etc.). Each reading points to a certain remainder (*reste*), which resists its own dissolution and leaves a trace. This is why there cannot be any talk of re-presentation in the sense of a new presence, since the trace is never able to restore and resti-

---

349 See "Ellipsis", in: Derrida, *Writing and Difference*.
350 Derrida, "Différance", in: *Margins of Philosophy*, p. 21.
351 Derrida, "Signature événement contexte", ibid., p. 318.

tute that which is a trace, namely *restance non présente*. Resistance as a mode of showing.

It is no coincidence that at the start of *Of Grammatology* Derrida cites Peirce's description of an "infinite semiosis", which precedes not only the connection between sign and trace, but also that *restance* that does not allow the process of signification (thinking) to find closure and is the irreducibly absenting base (knowledge, meaning, the present of that which is shown). In addition, it is the trace of another project of modernity in modern thinking itself. The thinking of Peirce, as Derrida perhaps felt when he welcomed him as an ally in the deconstruction of structuralist semiology, cannot be reduced to his theory and classification of signs. It has its assumptions and consequences. Its assumptions are perhaps most cogently formulated in two published articles: "The Fixation of Belief" (1987) and "How to Make Our Ideas Clear" (1878). On the one hand, Peirce claims that it is necessary that the cause of our conviction (*belief*, but also knowledge) be something exterior, completely independent of us (an "external permanency"), and this means that reality shows itself to us exclusively by virtue of its resistance to cognition. And on the other hand, he says that knowledge has no beginning, since anyone who makes an effort to cognise is burdened by the mass of the already known, i.e. that regarding which there has (until now) been no doubt. For this reason cognition takes place in the form of the passage from one conviction (*belief* as *habit*) to another, and we are obliged to acquire this new habit by a sudden doubt regarding our existing knowledge. Life gradually leads us to new convictions and gives us the strength to question old beliefs. Derrida and Deleuze sometimes use the slightly strange phrase "transcendental empiricism", and it would be possible to apply this term to Peirce's philosophy, since to the question of how reality shows itself we would look to the close links between the theory of meaning, concept and thinking and the theory of the sign. Reality makes its presence felt there where it resists expectations or hypotheses and it is in this way that it is able to repeatedly disrupt our habits. However, we can encounter this resistance on the part of reality only when we act, i.e. we experiment. On the other hand, it is clear that this resistance is not a message regarding the properties of the resisting, but simply obliges us to think, to change our conduct, modify our image of the world, experiment in our thoughts and practice. As far as Peirce is concerned we relate to reality that gives itself to us in its denial, via irreducible difference. And this returns in his theory of endless semiosis and his understanding of the sign.

One of his definitions, the one cited by Derrida, reads in full as follows:

> Symbols grow. They come into being by development out of other signs, particularly from icons, or from mixed signs partaking of the nature of icons and symbols. We think only in signs. These mental signs are of mixed nature; the symbol-parts of them are called concepts. If a man makes a new symbol, it is by thoughts involving concepts. So it is only out of symbols that a new symbol can grow. Omne symbolum de symbolo. A symbol, once in being, spreads among the peoples. In use and in experience, its meaning grows. Such words as *force*, *law*, *wealth*, *marriage*, bear for us very different meanings from those they bore to our barbarous ancestors. The symbol may, with Emerson's sphinx, say to man, 'Of thine eye I am eyebeam.'[352]

Derrida cites this passage from Chapter III (Section 3 "The Character of Symbols") of Peirce's unpublished *Speculative Grammar* in order to demonstrate just what is implied in the concept of the symbol. Beneath the "game" of symbols there is no other level to which it would be possible to gain immediate access, for instance

---

[352] Charles Sanders Peirce, *Collected Papers of Ch.S. Peirce*, I-VI ed. Ch. Harsthorne and P. Weis. Harvard U.P., Cambridge Mass. 1931–35; VII-VIII ed. A.W. Burks, Harvard U.P., Cambridge Mass. 1958, here 2.302. Cited from Jacques Derrida: *De la Grammatologie*, Ed. de Minuit, Paris 1967, p. 70.

a phenomenological opinion of the thing itself, since the meaning of the symbol is not "motivated" naturally but by the system of language. However, if we examine Peirce's comprehensive theory of signs in more detail, we soon discover that we can find harbingers in it of what would only arrive a hundred years later, and not only in Derrida's texts. It is perhaps therefore easier to understand why later on the phenomenon of the gift, secrecy, non-identity and non-foundedness play such a role, i.e. a relationship via irreducible difference or the ineradicable traces of the outside inside and the method by which that which escapes the phenomenon and reveals itself only in this escape from the present shows itself. For instance, the "gift" is closely related to that which Derrida takes to be the movement of supplementarity and to the paradoxical temporality by which this movement appears. Time must be understood as that which gives (differentiation) and immediately takes, since it postpones until later – it is this that is *différance*. However, we are now close to endless semiosis: the interpreter "supplements" the symbol, but by revealing one aspect he postpones the revelation of others to later. This has been described very accurately by François-David Sebbah:

all operations of 'saying' are intercalated between us and the thing itself, deferring it; but it thus gives, since givenness occurs only in concealing. The text, which Husserl calls a spiritual object, is spirit in the sense of the phantomic, is fundamentally a phantomic object, a mixture of presence and non-presence, given in the very refusal of givenness. The text itself, an un-reimbursable debt constituted by the infinite delay of what it speaks about, as a result lacks generosity, transferring the debt to the receiver – and this is therefore what it gives: debt. In a sense, if we can speak of total presence while still recognising that it is not total presence; if we can speak of ghosts – that is, to let them speak, or to let them speak in us – this is in order to retain a little of what is lost to and in them if they are nothing but their escape, their flight, and thus to recognise them as such. Is not allowing to escape that which remains, fully itself in its escape, to be given it, as such? What remains is a *trace*.[353]

The link between semiotics and the phenomenological concept of showing and appearing is most apparent when Peirce specifies an infinite semiosis in relation to the fundamentally traditional character of the sign.

> A *Sign* or *Representant* is a First which stands in such a genuine triadic relation to the Second, called its *Object*, as to be capable of determining a Third, called its *Interpretant*, to assume the triadic relation to its Object in which it stands itself to the same Object.[354]

However, we must keep in mind the fact that for Peirce every thought is a sign inasmuch as the sign mediates between its object, which it is supposed to specify and whose cause it is supposed in some sense to be, and the meaning. The object and interpretant are two correlates of every sign: "the object is the antecedent, the interpretant the consequent of the sign." (MS. 318) This is obviously not a description of a static structure, for instance because of the need to show how new, hitherto unknown things might emerge, i.e. that it is a dynamic, open structure, and so we must clarify still further what is meant by the word sign.

> Since a sign is not identical with the thing signified, but differs from the latter in some respects, it must plainly have some characteristics which belong to it in itself, and have nothing to do with its representative function.

That is to say:

353 François-David Sebbah, *Testing the Limit: Henry, Levinas, and the Phenomenological Tradition*, Stanford UP, Stanford 2012, p. 101.
354 Peirce, *Collected papers*, 2.274.

Now a sign has, as such, three references: first, it is a sign to some thought which interprets it; second, it is a sign for some object to which in that thought it is equivalent, third, it is a sign, in some respect or quality, which brings it into connection with its object.[355]

If the sign is not identical with the thing signified, it is impossible to close the process, and in semiotics something is opened that Derrida (as far back as *Grammatology*) calls the movement of supplementarity: the supplement (Peirce would probably use the word interpretant) gives a certain text something in addition. However, we are equally entitled to say that it supplements that which is missing in the text inasmuch as the supplement is both inside and outside. This is a relatively accurate description of Husserl's aporia: when, for example, he takes written discourse as a supplement of speech but does not concede that he could add to the spoken word that which it lacks. If understood in this way, it is a threat to immediacy and causes crisis. In hindsight, however, from the perspective of the transformation of philosophical discourse, we can say that the irreducibility of the supplement, its productivity, had already been described by Peirce in connection with the endlessness of the semiotic process.

Here we need a more detailed description of this process:

I have already noted that a Sign has an Object and an Interpretant, the latter being that which the Sign produces in the Quasi-mind that is the Interpreter. But it remains to point out that there are usually two Objects and more than two interpretants. We have to distinguish the *Immediate* Object, which is the Object as the sign itself represents it, and whose Being is thus dependent upon the representation of it in the Sign from the *Dynamical* Object, which is the Reality which by some means contrives to determine the Sign to its Representation. In regard to the Interpretant we have equally

355 Ibid., 5.287 and 5.283.

to distinguish, in the first place, the Immediate Interpretant, which is the interpretant as it is revealed in the right understanding of the Sign itself, and is ordinarily called the *meaning* of the sign; while in the second place, we have to take note of the Dynamical Interpretant which is the actual effect which the Sign, as a Sign, really determines. Finally there is what I provisionally term the Final Interpretant, which refers to the manner in which the Sign tends to represent itself to be related to its Object. I confess that my own conception of this third interpretant is not yet quite free from mist. (…) Thus the division into Icons, Indices, and Symbols depends upon the different possible relations of a Sign to its Dynamical Object.[356]

Firstly, as opposed to Saussurean semiotics, here there is no mention of a code. The interpretant is an iconic relationship (or duality in Peirce's ontology: the "code" is a related interpretant for which the first interpretant is a new sign.)

Secondly, the relationship of the sign to its object is necessarily mediated by the relationship of the sign to the interpretant, without which there is no sign. The interpretant is itself a sign. Meaning resides exclusively in the relationship between signs that, however, do not belong to a system but are encountered during the process of understanding – "interpreting" in the strictest sense of the word, which is more and more robust the less it is restricted to simple repetition or synonymic substitution, since it is a new formulation from another point of view. Anything that arouses our interest in whatever way is therefore a Peircean sign. (It does not have to be interpreted: it suffices if I perceive it as interpretable. I feel that it would be necessary to exert some effort in order to get to know it, though the word effort in itself implies resistance on the side of the "giving" object. Resistance is implied wherever there is a sign.) Understanding is always risky, since it is not guaranteed but "real" by means of resistance, which obliges us to abandon existing knowledge and seek

356 Ibid., 4.536.

another way of understanding. The interpretant is above all a *response* to the event of an encounter (Deleuze: the encounter with the sign obliges us to think). The relationship of the sign to its object is mediated by the *relationship* between the sign and the interpretant. Meaning does not reside and is not implied *in* the sign, but *is found* (looked for) in the relationship between signs. And in the case of Peirce this is intended to illuminate more closely the differentiation between the immediate and the dynamical object.

We might simplify this difference using a trivial example. I am looking at an object that someone is holding in their hand and the word "book" crosses my mind (it is immaterial whether this is but a thought or spoken out loud). That which I see is a completely singular object. However, as soon as it occurs to me or say out loud the word "book", the object is classified within a certain group of similar things, by means of which I interpret the thing as a "book" and thus generalise by means of the meaning "book". I indicate it by means of a general meaning. "A sign, or *representamen*, is something which stands to somebody for something in some respect or capacity."[357] The object that "determined" that I denote it is now represented by a certain interpretant. It is an "immediate object", though the potentially endless series of other interpretants linked to this first finds its basis in what Peirce calls the "dynamical object". In other words, the dynamical object is something that is constantly revealed by virtue of escaping from its appearance (the immediate object).

In a letter to William James, Peirce writes:

> We must distinguish between the Immediate Object, – i.e. the Object as represented in the sign, – and the Real (no, because perhaps the Object is altogether fictive, I must choose a different term, therefore), say rather the Dynamical Object, which, from the nature of things, the Sign cannot express, which it can only *indicate* and leave the interpreter to find out by

357 Ibid., 2.228.

collateral experience. For instance, I point my finger to what I mean, but I can't make my companion know what I mean, if he can't see it, or if seeing it, it does not, to his mind, separate itself from the surrounding objects in the field of vision.[358]

This is why in an essay entitled *Four Incapacities* Peirce writes that every previous thought insinuates the thought that follows it, it is a sign of something for it. The following thought denotes that which was meant in the previous thought. It would be difficult to express Derrida's movement of supplementarity better. The interpretant is neither outside or inside, the dynamical object is both part of the endless semiosis and outside it, because the interpretant relates to it via irreducible difference, seals it and unseals it (as Derrida will go on to say in texts in which he explores the phenomenon of secrecy and the gift, the trace and the ellipsis), reveals it in its resistance to being revealed and in this way retains its uniqueness. The dynamical object could, therefore, be another name for *restance non présente*.

358 Ibid., 8.314.

38

Husserl works on the assumption that, if it is to be possible to treat Europe as a certain kind of "spiritual formation", then it must have its identity, the identity of tradition, history and meaning. For this reason it must acquire its identity from its (specific) *telos* as objective and task in light of which it is an identifiable whole, even though this whole is not givenness but directed movement. It is not defined in relation to the other, but by the elimination of the other. However, Derrida intervenes at this point: if Europe is to be part of real history (history *de facto*), this *telos* cannot be given *a priori* and forever; if it has such a telos, then it is only that which is manifest in history and its peripeteias or vicissitudes. If Europe is not to disappear in these peripeteias, its tradition must reside in the possibility of diverging from this tradition. A double bind. If Europe is to have its own identity, it must be equal to itself and to the other, unless tradition is to be same as the fulfilment of a programme. However, Husserl's concept of responsibility is both a sign of the fact that he was aware of this double bind and that he attempted to neutralise it.

The project of modernity, whose direct heir is Husserl, links Adorno, Levinas, Lyotard and Derrida with the figure of the Homeric Odysseus. In *Dialectic of Enlightenment*, Adorno and Horkheimer write that Odysseus is a hero who loses himself simply in order to find himself anew. He plunges into peril not in order to expose himself to the risk of becoming lost, but in order to prove to himself his ability never to lose sight of his objective. Odysseus is the story of a return, the overcoming of obstacles (the crisis) that prevent a return to the origin. Husserl's *The Crisis of European Sciences* reads the history of Europe in the same way: as an odyssey of the European spirit. The *Odyssey* is a story of the identity of the beginning and end in which an encounter with the outside represents a confrontation with a randomness that is indifferent to the beginning and end. This exterior, Levinas says, is always neutralised as soon as it is grasped rationally. In fact, Odysseus is still travelling around his island, and in the world through which he wanders he encounters himself everywhere. Levinas projects the economy of exchange into Odysseus's travels (whence to Derrida, who places the non-economy of the gift in opposition to the economy of exchange), and when he speaks of the relationship "face to face" he describes it as a relationship in which the "I", on the contrary, rids itself of being closed within itself, of that existence in which all adventures are simply an "odyssey", i.e. a return to the island.[359] It is this Odyssean nostalgia that afflicts traditional (Western) metaphysics. However, the movement towards the Other can never be a return to the same. I must give up the attempt to be a contemporary of the completion of my work. Lyotard adds that Odysseus lives in a world in which there is no such human being that would arrive "from elsewhere and from behind"[360], i.e. in a world that is not marked by the experience of exile. "To the myth of Ulysses return to Ithaca," he writes in one of the essays completing his interpretation of Husserl and Heidegger, "we would prefer to oppose the story of Abraham leaving his country forever for an as yet unknown land, and forbidding his servant to take back even his son to the point of departure."[361]

The break by which the transformation of philosophical discourse is marked could hardly be more striking.

"By faith Abraham, when he was called to go out into a place which he should after receive for an inheritance, obeyed; and he went out, not knowing whither he went." (Hebrews 11.8)

Now the Lord had said unto Abram, "Get thee out of thy country, and from thy kindred, and from thy father's house, unto a land that I will shew thee." (Genesis 12.1 King James Version)

359 Emmanuel Levinas, *Alterité et transcendence*, Fata Morgana, Paris 1995, p. 72.
360 Jean François Lyotard, "Return upon the Return", Humanities Press, Atlantic Highlands, NJ 1993, p. 192.
361 Emmanuel Levinas, "The Trace of the Other", *Tijdschrift voor Philosophie* (Sept. 1963), p. 610.

As Levinas writes in one of the texts commenting upon the Talmud, Abraham represents a "miracle of time", i.e. time as openness to that which is arriving and which it is forbidden to imagine according to the past and memory,since it transcends all of this,[362] time which is (already) liquidating human history, as Walter Benjamin would say. For this reason praise is due to those who wait without anticipating, i.e. without attempting to identify the future, and who thus differ from the prophets, because the latter are capable of foreseeing only events in historical time. Levinas's commentary is, moreover, very characteristically set within a concrete situation, within the present. The unimaginability of that which is on the point of arriving is announced by unimaginable horrors and inhumane trials – the Holocaust, Hitler's and Stalin's concentration camps, borne witness to in the novel by Vasily Grossman *Life and Fate*, which Levinas quotes extensively.

Abraham changes the situation, and much of that which during the 1930s and 40s is only hinted at finds expression once again. Thus, for example, Adorno's final aphorism from *Minima Moralia* is more understandable in light of this event-time. In its last sentence it suspends its base and is a performative demonstration of the thesis that the whole is untrue: "… the question concerning the reality or nonreality of redemption is, however, almost inconsequential." After the Holocaust there is nothing for it but to remind ourselves of the idea of redemption. And yet this idea has become highly problematic: the *double bind*. If it is still possible to think history, then it is not within the framework of a type of understanding that traces its roots back to modern, enlightened rationality. To look at things as they would be revealed from the perspective of redemption means forgetting them as we know them and proceeding from the inside (the *Bannkreis des Daseins*, the vicious circle of relations and existence within them) and finding the peace without. It means understanding

---

362 Emmanuel Levinas, *A l'heure des nations*, Ed. de Minuit, Paris 1988, p. 48.

history from the perspective of exile, i.e. as radical openness in relation to the "home" that is not given by the original foundation, but is a home where nobody is or ever has been. Derrida's *différance*, difference as articulating deferral, but at the same time an extremely significant intellectual operation: the reading of the "thesis" under erasure. Presence together with absence, a relationship via difference, ellipse, undecidability between outside and inside, because thinking must remain prepared for that which is on the point of arriving and be thus within itself turned to the outside (though not its own), the unidentifiable. If Levinas wants these most remote things to be the rule of all present days, it is impossible in this exchange not to hear a remote echo of Kracauer's patient waiting watchfully for the last things before the last, the non-anticipation of the "waiting", whose time is "hesitant openness". And it is impossible not to observe that the thinker of exodus is Maurice Blanchot, who, in an essay dedicated to Robert Antelme and his testimony regarding the concentration camps, understands exile as true movement, because it is the movement of the nomad who knows that "to go out (to step outside) is the exigency from which one cannot escape if one wants to maintain the possibility of a just relation."[363] Hence impatient anticipation, an identification of the future on the basis of the past, is, as Kafka knew,

an essential fault, because it misconstrues the very trueness of error which, like a law, requires that one never believe the goal is close or that one is coming nearer to it. One must never have done with the indefinite; one must never grasp – as if it were the immediate, the already present – the profundity of inexhaustible absence. (...) is impatience which makes the goal inaccessible by substituting for it the proximity of an intermediary figure. It is impatience that destroys the way toward the goal by preventing us from recognising in the intermediary the figure of the immediate.[364]

363 Blanchot, *The Infinite Conversation*, p. 125.
364 Blanchot, *The Space of Literature*, pp. 79 and 80.

39

The interpretation of temporality, which is based not on flow and continuity, but on the event, and therefore emphasises discontinuity and heterogeneity, can be understand both as the terrain on which it becomes a clearly intelligible transformation of philosophical discourse generating new "concepts" (in inverted commas because after Adorno even the status of the concept has become problematic, to say the least, and differently defined after Deleuze) and their specific constellation within such a transformed philosophy, and a field allowing for the actualisation of another project of modernity whose traces have been hidden until now in modern thinking. This proves in an almost self-referential way the now virtually general belief that presence is not present itself, either because (as Derrida shows) it is always being visited by ghosts and that responsibility for an inheritance is not the reproduction of the origin but its re-production, which in tradition establishes a new starting point, as it were, or because it is open to the outside, to that which is forever on the point of arriving. If we were then to combine Derrida's ghosts or spectres from *Spectres of Marx* with his neologistic locution *restance non présente* (see above), i.e. with a past that was never present and that is, to simplify matters, a trace of escape or a trace of the unrealised, then this would be an "instance" that turns to us in every "now" and requires us to bear witness to it in our response. Here there can be no talk of the continuity of Husserl's "living present" as the flow of retentions constantly linked via the present moment to protention, even though Husserl's phenomenon of crisis could be considered as one of the junctions of this transformation. Time is open to the "other" in both directions, i.e. to the incalculable past that can at any time irrupt into the present "now". However, this is another example of actualisation, since we can encounter this concept of time as far back as Walter Benjamin, above all in his emphasis on the operation of "remembrance" (*Eingedenken*), partly inspired by

Proust's *mémoire involontaire* and inspiring in its turn Adorno, who, for instance, in *Minima moralia*, writes: "No other hope is left to the past than that, exposed defencelessly to disaster, it shall emerge from it as something different."[365] Adorno also speaks of the necessity of remembering the suffering that is sedimented in concepts.[366]

To formulate this radically: time is for Benjamin something that only has meaning via history because primarily it is not a dimension of that which was but that which is not yet and perhaps never will be. Perhaps a key to understanding this idea is what he says in Section II from *On the Concept of History* regarding happiness, namely that our image of happiness is indissolubly bound up with the image of redemption. Adorno's aphorism "Zu Ende" from *Minima Moralia* suggests how this Messianism was understood by his contemporaries (and how it would later be understood by Derrida). This then ties in to what immediately follows:

> The past carries a secret index with it (*führt mit sich einen zeitlichen Index*), by which it is referred to redemption... If so, then there is a secret protocol between the generations of the past and that of our own. For we have been expected upon this earth.[367]

Happiness points to redemption (and thus to another time), because on the one hand it is something that, though possible in the past, was wasted by us, and on the other it is precisely in this knowledge of its wastage that hope is maintained that it will be attained in some "other time" as a still genuine possibility. Time is almost by definition the time of missed opportunities that are not part of that series of events as presented by traditional history.[368]

365 Adorno, *Minima moralia*, p. 167.
366 Adorno, *Zur Metakritik der Erkenntnistheorie*, GS 5, p. 47.
367 Benjamin, *Selected Writings* 4, p. 390.
368 Cf. Werner Hamacher, "'Now': Walter Benjamin on Historical Time." In: Heidrun Friese (ed.), *The Moment. Time and Rupture in Modern Thought*, Liverpool University Press, Liverpool 2001, pp. 161–196.

If we were to transfer Benjamin's idea of happiness into thinking after the Holocaust, the result would in all likelihood be that which Derrida understands as justice, which, as he himself says, is undeconstructible.[369] Or as he also says: deconstruction is justice. Throughout his many riffs on this theme, the following argumentation always returns: the law prescribes, and this means that a decision in accordance with the law (not only in the positivist sense of the word) reduces the moment of personal responsibility for the decision, the moment of personal guarantee. Derrida invokes Montaigne and Pascal, both of whom claim that anyone who obeys the law simply because it is the law is not obeying it as they should. If a decision is to be just in the sense of justice, then in the act by which it takes place it must both be subject to the rule (it cannot be arbitrary or random) and at the same time must be outside of the rule, since the situation in which a decision must be taken is always unique, every case is *sui generis* (no two are identical, they do not "coincide" with each other) and requires a unique interpretation which, for this reason – without it being purely arbitrary – cannot be guaranteed by any of the existing (past and present) rules. And yet as a decision that seeks to be true to the idea of justice, it cannot be without any relation to the law. "(O)ne cannot speak *directly* about justice, thematize or objectivize justice, say 'this is just' and even less 'I am just'."[370] Therefore justice can never be thought of as something realised: not in the past, present or historical future. In this sense a just decision would be an answer to a unique situation. When Derrida says that no first principle is the first, he also has in mind this *critical* situation and at the same time overturns the idea of the "principle of all principles" on which Husserl's phenomenology is based. These are not simple aporia, but elliptical formulations:

369 Jacques Derrida, "Force of Law. The Metaphysical Foundation of Authority", in: Drucila Cornell et al. (eds.), *Deconstruction and the Possibility of Justice,* Routledge, London 1992, p. 15.
370 Ibid., p. 10.

I cannot thematise justice by uttering the sentence "this is just", because in doing so I deny its idea.

Similarly, in the case of Benjamin happiness is knowable only through its absence; we know of happiness because we perceive it as a possibility that has passed us by. And this knowledge then casts another light on history: every possibility that was missed in the past remains an opportunity for the future precisely because it has not encountered its fulfilment. The past has a future, and it has this future inasmuch as that which was missed seeks its realisation from a different "now" to that in which it was missed. This is undoubtedly the point to draw attention to the introductory sentence of Adorno's *Negative Dialectic*: "Philosophy, which once seemed obsolete, lives on because the moment to realise it was missed."[371]

The true dimension of history is the past's address to our "now": "we were expected".

It is to the expectation of the unnamed and lost in the history of progress, which Benjamin identifies with catastrophe in Section IX of *Theses on the Philosophy of History*, that the concept of remembrance (*Eingedenken*) corresponds, a remembrance in which the past first understands itself in the correct way, i.e. with regard to justice. It is via remembrance that the dimension of history is opened in which there is space for every singularity and in which the past is saved because its unique meaning returns to it, as opposed to historicism, which "contents itself with establishing a causal connection between various moments in history. But no fact that is a cause is for that very reason historical. It became historical posthumously, as it were, through events that may be separated from it by thousands of years." (XVIII A). The true meaning of the unique event or fate is not given by its identification in respect of some whole or "grand narrative", as Lyotard would go on to call it. In other words, the measure of history is justice, which must do justice to that which is

---

371 Adorno, *Negative Dialectics*, p. 3.

for historicism qua the non-identifiable outside the history of progress qua historical norms, and because it is inadmissible that we justify the present in the name of those who were eliminated from history. That which is irredeemable in history (as it is understood by historicism) can therefore only be saved in another dimension of time. The historian of historicism empathises with the victor (VII). Translated into the language of Derridean deconstruction, it is only under the erasure of the history of the victors that the history of their victims becomes intelligible.

For Benjamin, that which fractures the continuity of the history of progress (which is in its own way teleological history) is the "dialectical image":

> It's not that what is past casts its light on what is present, or what is present its light on the past; rather, image is that wherein what has been comes together in a flash with the now to form a constellation. In other words, image is dialectics at a standstill. For while the relation of the present to the past is a purely temporal, continuous one, the relation of what-has-been to the now is dialectical: is not progression but image, suddenly emergent. – Only dialectical images are genuine images (that is, not archaic); and the place where one encounters them is language. The read image, by which is meant the image in the Now of recognisability, bears to the highest degree the stamp of the critical, dangerous moment which is at the basis of all reading. Awakening.
>
> (...)
>
> Every present is determined by those images which are synchronic with it: each "now" is the "now" of a particular recognizability.[372]

Remembrance is an act capable of bringing to light that which should be preserved from past events or destinies. In the act of remembrance, the present is unexpectedly (an "awakening") connected

372 Walter Benjamin, *The Arcades Project*, trans. Howard Eiland and Kevin McLaughlin, The Belknap Press, Cambridge 1999, pp. 462–463.

to the past (the past that awaits it) and is capable of illuminating the singularity of the singular, which only possesses its own purpose if there is within it a clear claim to a vindication other than that which the time of historicism offers it. This "tiger's leap" from the past to the here and now creates a completely specific constellation and averts the threat of an irretrievable image of the past that threatens to disappear "in any present that does not recognize itself as intended in that image" (V.). The constellation is something like a complex symbol (image, graph or mosaic) of an indexical nature. It indicates without discouraging the indicated. In the "Epistemo-Critical Prologue" to *The Origin of German Tragic Drama*, Benjamin has similar things to say about truth. "(...) truth is not a process of exposure which destroys the secret, but a revelation which does justice to it",[373] and thus far his *Theses* link up to his concept of the "idea", which appears only when various fragments of the past find themselves in the correct arrangement. A simpler form of this idea would be Adorno's *Vexierbild* or picture puzzle. However, if thinking in constellations replaces thinking in concepts, this does not entail an abandonment of the concept, but its re-construction. Along with Gilles Deleuze we might say that the concept is a certain organisation of components and gives them their coexistence. As such, a completely specific organisation of moments refers to a problem for which it is the response.[374]

Benjamin's conception of history clearly foreshadows themes that will characterise the philosophical discourse transformed by the event of the Holocaust, whether this be in Derrida's texts (secrecy, the heterogeneity of time, justice), Lyotard's *differend* (the problem of the suffering of the individual), or in the work of other writers. His "Messianism" refers to a relationship through irrevocable dif-

---

373 Walter Benjamin, *The Origin of German Tragic Drama*, trans. John Osborne, Verso, London, New York 1998, p. 31.
374 Gilles Deleuze and Félix Guattari, *What Is Philosophy?*, trans. Hugh Tomlinson and Graham Burchell, Columbia University Press, New York 1994, ch. 1 "What is a concept?", esp. p. 16.

ference, and his concept of the constellation or dialectical image already implies a turn to showing that which escapes in the act of escaping: "The dialectical image is an image that flashes up. The image of what has been – in this case, the image of Baudelaire – must be caught in this way, flashing up in the now of its recognizability. The redemption enacted in this way, and solely in this way, is won only against the perception of what is being irredeemably lost."[375] And if we recall Derrida's reading of Freud, we cannot overlook the section from the "Epistemo-Critical Prologue" where Benjamin characterises his preferred form of writing. What is characteristic of the treatise is the fact that "A writer must stop and restart with every new sentence."[376]

It is for this reason that the return to Benjamin's *Theses* (and *Arcades*) is at the same time an entry into thinking of the latter half of the twentieth century, or a sign of which this thinking is the interpretant. Take one example from Derrida's *Spectres of Marx* as proof:

If I am getting ready to speak at length about ghosts, inheritance, and generations, generations of ghosts, which is to say about certain others who are not present, nor presently living, either to us, in us, or outside use, it is in the name of justice. Of justice where it is not yet, not yet there, where it is no longer, let us understand where it is no longer present, and where it will never be, no more than the law, reducible to laws or rights. It is necessary to speak of the ghost, indeed to the ghost and with it, from the moment that no ethics, no politics, whether revolutionary or not, seems possible and thinkable and just that does not recognise in its principle the respect for those others who are no longer or for those others who are not yet there, presently living, whether they are already dead or not yet born. No justice – let us not say no law and once again we are not speaking here of laws – seems possible or thinkable without the principle of some responsi-

375 Benjamin, *Selected Writings 4*, pp. 183–184.
376 Benjamin, *The Origin*, p. 29.

bility, beyond all living present, within that which disjoins the living present, before the ghosts, of those who are not yet born or who are already dead, be they victims of wars, political or other kinds of violence, nationalist, racist, colonialist, sexist, or other kinds of exterminations, victims of the oppressions of capitalist imperialism or any of the forms of totalitarianism.[377]

Above all, however, the *Theses on the Philosophy of History* are concerned with the phenomena of crisis and catastrophe.[378] Benjamin probably began working on the *Theses* in 1938 and intended them to form the theoretical framework of a book he was preparing on Baudelaire. However, progress on the work was shattered by the Ribbentrop-Molotov Pact signed on 23 September 1939 between Hitler and Stalin. In a letter to Gershom Scholem, Soma Morgenstern writes that reports of this event caused Benjamin an "incurable wound". Benjamin's response to this crisis is clear in the *Theses* themselves, for instance when he writes of the "moment when the politicians in whom the opponents of Fascism had placed their hopes are prostrate and confirm their defeat by betraying their own cause." (X) His *Theses* now found themselves in a new situation and the concept of remembrance acquired a new dimension ("a memory ... flashes up at a moment of danger"), and the text a new independence. Benjamin continued working until the final weeks prior to his suicide on the Spanish border on 26 September 1940. If remembrance is an act that "leads the past to bring the present into a critical state",[379] then it is now clear that a crisis is essential if the time of historicism, the time

---

377 Derrida, *Spectres de Marx*, p. xix.
378 The *Theses* exist in seven different versions, including a French translation, of which none can be regarded as definitive. They were first printed in a mimeographed booklet entitled *Walter Benjamin zum Gedächtnis* (In Memory of Walter Benjamin) by the Institute in its American exile in 1942. The title fluctuates around "On the Concept of History" ("Über den Begriff der Geschichte", "Geschichtsphilosophische Reflexionen" and "Geschitsphilosophische Thesen"). A detailed analysis of the genesis, variants and notes is to be found in the 19th volume of *Kritische Gesamtausgabe: Walter Benjamin, Über den Begriff der Geschichte*, ed. Gérard Raulet, Suhrkamp, Frankfurt a.M. 2010.
379 Benjamin, *Selected Writings* 4, p. 184.

of the victors, is to be fractured. However, all of this was only illuminated by the catastrophe that Benjamin presciently intuited from its first symptoms. "The concept of progress must be grounded in the idea of the catastrophe," he wrote in his study of Baudelaire's *Central Park*. The exterior is not outside but inside.

40

Ghosts reveal time to be anachronistic. They are with us as both behind us and before us, and as that which fixes its gaze upon us: we are expected. When Derrida says that "it is necessary to do everything to appropriate a past even though we know that it remains fundamentally inappropriable",[380] this is the credo of Jacques Derrida as heir to a long philosophical tradition. However, this credo is also a philosophical response to a recent past that expected this response. If it is the case that the concept of responsibility makes no sense outside of the experience of inheritance,[381] then it is also the case that our relationship to the past and our response to the past are always situated in real history. And that to which a response must be given in the second half of the twentieth century, in "the calm that settles after all hope has died", as Hannah Arendt puts it in the preface to *Elements and Origins of Totalitarianism*,[382] is this manifestation of bare life, i.e. to the ghosts, which at present take the form of the "Musulman" ("deathly pale, exhausted zombies that trudged weakly only a few centimetres from a fatal dose of phenol"[383]) and the "drowned".

Bare life, *la nuda vita*, is Giorgio Agamben's answer to the question implied by the title of Primo Levi's *If This is a Man*. It is a response that concretises the claim made by Michel Foucault that forms the foundation of his concept of "biopower": "modern man is an animal whose politics places his existence as a living being in question".[384] It is a provocative answer, since according to Agamben

380 Jacques Derrida, *De quoi demain... Dialogue*, Libraire Arthème Fayard et Galilée, Paris 2001, p 12.
381 Cf. ibid., p. 13.
382 Hannah Arendt, *The Origins of Totalitarianism*, Harcourt Brace, San Diego, New York, London 1973, p. vii.
383 Rudolf Vrba, *44070 – The Conspiracy of the Twentieth Century*, Star & Cross, Washington 1989; *I Escaped from Auschwitz*, Robson Books, London 1964.
384 Michel Foucault, *The Will to Knowledge. The History of Sexuality* 1, trans. Robert Hurley, Pantheon Books, New York, p. 143.

the biopolitical paradigm of the modern era is the extermination camp as a place in which the most terrible *conditio inhumana* the world has ever seen became reality. When he says, however, that the subterranean river of biopolitics only gushed to the surface in the twentieth century, but otherwise ran its course in a hidden but continuous fashion, he is closer to Hannah Arendt, who in the preface to the first edition of *Elements and Origins of Totalitarianism* speaks of the concealed tendency of the history of the West, which spilled over its manifest tradition in the twentieth century. The interpretation of the concept of "bare life" must therefore return to the ancient distinction between *bios* and *zoé*, where *bios* is a concrete form or way of life (belonging to the public sphere, to the *polis*), whereas *zoé* is the simple fact of life (in the private sphere, the *oikos*). This distinction is the key to opening the limit-concept of Roman law, i.e. the ambivalence of the word sacred in the concept of the *homo sacer*, as an individual was referred to, who was exiled from the community after committing a serious crime. From the moment of ritual ostracism, i.e. the announcement he was "*sacer*", such a figure could be killed by anyone but not be sacrificed in a religious ritual. He could not be sacrificed for the community from which he was expelled because he no longer belonged to it. He was excluded from community law, and the sole justice applied to him was that which expelled him irrevocably from the community. From the perspective of the community, his life is not *bios* – if the rights associated with human existence are revoked, all that remains is the human being and his purely biological, i.e. bare life, *la nuda vita*.

Homo sacer is a strange, ambiguous form of exclusion. A person is abandoned by the law. And yet it cannot be said that he is outside or that he is inside, since in his capacity as ostracised he is subject by virtue of this exclusion to the justice that ostracised him. This situation, in which the outside cannot be distinguished from the inside, then allows for a link to be made with the modern concept of sovereignty (e.g. as in the case of Carl Schmitt), and above all with Benjamin's state of emergency that becomes the rule. The state of emergency or "Verordnung zum Schutz von Volk und Staat", which was enacted by the Nazis in 1933 (in the same year as Martin Heidegger gave his first address as Rector of the University of Freiburg), was never recalled during Nazi rule. If the sovereign is he who is entitled to declare *Ausnahmezustand*, by which the legal order is suspended, this creates a strange sphere of jurisprudence that is capable of suspending itself – it is the threshold between inside and outside where the one does not exclude the other. However, it is here (according to Agamben) that the law manifests its pure form: it is applied by virtue of not being applied, it is power that refrains from exerting itself,[385] it is valid without this meaning anything. It is in this space, and only in this space, that bare life appears, life abandoned by law, left to itself. Agamben thus reconstructs the hidden genealogy of biopower that Foucault situates in the modern era as the successor to sovereign power and discipline:

> one of the basic phenomena of the nineteenth century was what might be called power's hold over life. What I mean is the acquisition of power over man insofar as man is a living being that the biological came under State control, that there was at least a certain tendency that leads to what might be termed State control of the biological. [386]
> Now I think we see something new emerging in the second half of the eighteenth century: a new technology of power, but this time it is not disciplinary. This technology of power does not exclude the former, does not exclude disciplinary technology, but it does dovetail into it, integrate it, modify it to some extent, and above all, use it by sort of infiltrating it, embedding itself in existing disciplinary techniques. This new technique does not simply do away with the disciplinary technique, because it exists at a different level,

385 Giorgio Agamben, *Homo Sacer: Sovereign Power and Bare Life*, trans. Daniel Heller-Roazen, Stanford UP, Stanford 1998, p. 23.
386 Michel Foucault, *Society Must Be Defended. Lectures at the Collège de France 1975–76*, trans. David Macey, Picador, New York, pp. 237–238.

on a different scale, and because it has a different bearing area, and makes use of very different instruments. Unlike discipline, which is addressed to bodies, the new nondisciplinary power is applied not to man-as-body but to the living man, to man-as-living-being; ultimately, if you like, to man-as-species. To be more specific, I would say that discipline tries to rule a multiplicity of men to the extent that their multiplicity can and must be dissolved into individual bodies that can be kept under surveillance, trained, used, and, if need be, punished. And that the new technology that is being established is addressed to a multiplicity of men, not to the extent that they are nothing more than their individual bodies, but affected by overall processes characteristic of birth, death, production, illness, and so on. So after a first seizure of power over the body in an individualising mode, we have a second seizure of power that is not individualising but, if you like, massifying, that is directed not at man-as-body but at man-as-species. After the anatomo-politics of the human body established in the course of the eighteenth century, we have, at the end of that century, the emergence of something that is no longer an anatomo-politics of the human body, but what I would call a "biopolitics" of the human race.[387]

Along with biopower appears something new, a "person", recognised neither by law nor discipline (neither the individual under the terms of a contract, nor the individual as individual body), but a person-population that appears as a *political* problem, as a *biological* problem, as a problem of *power*. "Biopolitics (...) tries to control the series of random events that can occur in a living mass."[388] And it is in this turn to life that the fundamental transformation of power resides: "And now we have the emergence of a power that I would call the power of regularization, and it, in contrast, consists in making live and letting die."[389]

---

387 Ibid. pp. 242–243.
388 Ibid. p. 246.
389 Ibid. p. 247.

In an effort to demonstrate that, as a stable realisation of an exception, the concentration camp is a hidden matrix of the political arena in which we live, Agamben goes further back in time.

> The Foucauldian thesis will then have to be corrected or, at least, completed, in the sense that what characterizes modern politics is not so much the inclusion of zoē in the polis – which is, in itself, absolutely ancient – nor simply the fact that life as such becomes a principal object of the projections and calculations of State power. Instead the decisive fact is that, together with the process by which the exception everywhere becomes the rule, the realm of bare life – which is originally situated at the margins of the political order – gradually begins to coincide with the political realm, and exclusion and inclusion, outside and inside, bios and zoē, right and fact, enter into a zone of irreducible indistinction. At once excluding bare life from and capturing it within the political order, the state of exception actually constituted, in its very separateness, the hidden foundation on which the entire political system rested.[390]

It now becomes clear at least in part why the third part of *Homo Sacer* is entitled "The Camp as Biopolitical Paradigm of the Modern".[391] The concentration camp is a real fact, a historical fact. As such it is present, for instance, in Adorno's claim that to write poetry after Auschwitz is barbaric. Philosophy must reflect this fact and reassess the meaning of the Enlightenment project of the modern era. This line of thinking abandons the traditional philosophy of history, but emphasises (Adorno again) that concepts of reason must constantly be corrected by their own subjects, and that it is essential that the idea be "affected" by real history. Similarly, after the war the con-

---

390 Giorgio Agamben, *Homo Sacer*, p. 12.
391 The book *Homo sacer: Il potere sovrano e la nuda vita*, Torino: Einaudi, 1995, is the first volume of a long series that includes *State of Exception; Stasis: Civil War as a Political Paradigm; The Kingdom and the Glory; Homo sacer II, 2; The Sacrament of Language; Homo sacer II, 3; Opus Dei; Homo sacer II, 5; Remants of Auschwitz; Homo sacer III; The Highest Poverty; The Use of Bodies; Homo sacer IV, 2*, etc.

centration camp becomes a "sign" around which the idea circles, concerned with cannot be named, what cannot be thought, what cannot even be understood, because understanding the Holocaust would mean the destruction of ethics. However, Agamben does not use the "concentration camp" as an empirical fact, nor as a sign, but as a *paradigm*. And so in order to understand his proposition fully we must remind ourselves of what he has in mind when he speaks of a paradigm. In a certain regard this term is one of the fundamental concepts of Agamben's thinking, inter alia because it implies an ambiguitiy vis-à-vis the inside and outside that is manifest at such time as a state of affairs pertains during which the exception becomes the rule. Moreover, though it is not obvious on first glance, as soon as exception and rule take their place in the centre of philosophical attention, the classical (metaphysical) assumption of the identity of thinking and being is excluded from the game. Given that the "camp" is a historical fact or event in real history, it is impossible when attempting to understand it to reduce the *quaestio facti* to a *quaestio iuris* (a reduction that Husserl's idea of teleology and the ensuing understanding of crisis is marked by).

The idea of the paradigm and the paradigmatic method of investigation brings us to Michel Foucault. What is perhaps his best known analysis from *Discipline and Punish* sets out to demonstrate how Bentham's prison reforms (the panopticon as a completely concrete architectural figure or *dispositif*) exemplify the new organisation of power at a certain point in time. The panopticon is a kind of diagram of power, an ideal form of political technology,[392] which at any one moment in time is updated so as to meet the needs of many different institutions (school, factory, regulatory and administrative measures, scientific findings, etc.) as a hidden network that con-

392 Cf. Michel Foucault, *Discipline and Punish*, trans. Alan Sheridan, Vintage Books, New York 1995, pp. 276 et seq.

nects them. This network or *dispositif* then mediates the relationship between power and knowledge[393].

The *dispositif* in the position of exemplar or paradigm is thus both part of that of which it is an example and, in exemplary form, excluded from this subset. It is both the rule and the exception to the rule, both inside and outside. The peculiarity of the paradigmatic method as a means of knowledge is that it does not proceed from the particular to the universal, but from the universal to the particular. It remains on the level of the unique and thus problematises the antinomy of the particular or universal (which is, on the contrary, the basis of induction and deduction). The exemplum is a singularly representing instance and does not relate to the exemplified by virtue of "belonging to...", i.e. not by virtue of what is common to the element of the exemplified subset in which everything is "covered". The example is a unique case that is isolated from the context of which it is a part only until such time as it allows us to understand the whole by virtue of its singularity.[394] In other words, the paradigm (the exemplum) does not allow for the identification of "that *as* that", but recognises without converting singularity into the members of a certain class.

> On the one hand, every example is treated in effect as a real particular case; but on the other, it remains understood that it cannot serve in its particularity. Neither particular nor universal, the example is a singular object that presents itself as such, that shows its singularity. Hence the pregnancy of the Greek term, for example: *paradeigma*, that which is shown alongside (like the German *Bei-spiel*, that which plays alongside). Hence the proper place of the example is always beside itself in the empty space in which its undefinable and unforgettable life unfolds.[395]

393 Cf. Giorgio Agamben, *What is an Apparatus*, Stanford UP, Stanford 2009.
394 Giorgio Agamben, *The Signature of All Things: On Method*, trans. Luca D'Isanto with Kevin Attell, Zone Books 2009, pp. 16 et seq.
395 Giorgio Agamben, *The Coming Community*, trans. Michael Hardt, University of Minnesota Press, Minneapolis, London 1993, p. 17.

The testimony of all those who survived the Holocaust can be read in this way, as an example in the Agambenian sense. And it is in this way, from the particular to the particular, without generalisation, without integration into an overarching narrative, that Claude Lanzmann proceeds in his film *Shoah*.

41

The testimony of the survivors – *If This Is a Man* (Primo Levi), *The Human Race* (Robert Antelme) – indicates in its titles the extreme limits whose extension is the concentration and extermination camps in which the modern form of "bare life" appears: *häftling* or *zek* (convict).

> The conviction that life has a purpose is rooted in every fibre of man, it is a property of the human substance. Free men give many names to this purpose, and many think and talk about its nature. But for us the question is simpler.
> Today, in this place, our only purpose is to reach the spring. At the moment we care about nothing else.[396]

People do not die in the camp, but corpses are manufactured here. Life is not life here, nor does death die here. Foucault's biopolitics, as Agamben says, here coincides with *thanatopolitics*[397], which is the result of what had until then been more a latent process, a description of which could be understood as a parallel or concretisation of Adorno and Horkheimer's dialectic of enlightenment.

In his lectures entitled *Security, Territory, Population*, Foucault sets out the initial phase of this process, namely the transition from sovereign power to an emerging biopolitics. During the era of sovereign power the criminal, thief or murderer is punished exclusively on the basis of their crime, whereas in the era of disciplinary power they are punished only after a thorough analysis of their character and after ascertaining both individual and collective conditions under which they perpetrated their crime. It is important these facts be ascertained in order that it be possible to predict whether they can

---

396 Primo Levi, *If This Is a Man*, trans. Stuart Woolf, Orion Press, New York 1959, p. 79.
397 Giorgio Agamben, *Remnants of Auschwitz. The Witness and the Archive*, Zone Books, New York 1999, p. 83.

be remedied or not. This is why the criminal is subjected to psychological examination, surveillance and rehabilitation. New "tactics" of power appear: prison, psychiatric institution, suspended sentences, etc. A more detailed examination then ascertains the number of murders or thieves in the population as a whole, decides whether crime figures are rising or falling, in what demographic groups specific types of crime feature, and how it would be possible to regulate and control all of these variables in the optimal way. Discipline and biopower overlap: both represent a power over life (*bios*) that can be exerted on both individuals and groups: school workshops, prisons and psychiatric institutions relate to bodies inasmuch as they deviate from the norms, though there also exist population norms: fertility rates, death rates, public health and migration (average values and deviations therefrom). Though all of this takes place through the good offices of both institutions and the state, the state is already implicated in many institutions (e.g. schools and hospitals). We can therefore say that discipline relates to the micro-level of power relations, while biopower operates on the macro-level. Biopower in the form of "care" then creates a situation in which death becomes a scandal and suicide is understood as a subversive act of resistance, since death is beyond the reach of biopower. Power does not impact on death, it impacts on mortality rates.

In the right of sovereignty, death was the moment of the most obvious and most spectacular manifestation of the absolute power of the sovereign; death now becomes, in contrast, the moment when the individual escapes all power, falls back on himself and retreats, so to speak, into his own privacy. Power no longer recognises death. Power literally ignores death.[398]

---

398 Foucault, *Society Must Be Defended*, p. 248.

Biopower is therefore what we might call the administration of life, because it needs estimates, statistics, the specification of various demographic factors, population censuses, which, however, are not simply censuses, but the point of intersection of the population and the individual body. The Auschwitz crematorium for which the prisoners were simply statistical units or *Stücke* was able to burn up to ten thousand dead bodies a day.[399] In the Soviet gulags, the number of victims was given in *recommended figures* specifying how many "boxes of soap" (which is how the prisoners were referred to) were to be delivered to the gulag slaughter house.[400]

If sovereignty is characterised by the right to "take life or let live", then modern biopolitics embodies the principle of "make live, let die". However, according to Giorgio Agamben, in totalitarian regimes both principles intersected in the paradox formulated by Foucault himself when he posed the question of how biopower can let die if its objective is to let live, and yet be manifest in the form of murder. In order to explain this we need to follow the process of gradual separation and exclusion during the biologisation of the originally body politic, the moment the "people" is doubled by the "population". This opens up a space for racial theory, the differentiation of Aryan and non-Aryan, i.e. the singling out of an outside in the hitherto homogenous realm of life. From here it is but a short step to "homo sacer". This general schema using which we must clarify Foucault's analyses then only needs a concrete *Massnahmen*, a measure of the Nazi state. Extermination, annihilation, *Vernichtung*, begins at the moment that non-Aryans are excluded from economic and political life as *Fremdkörper* or a foreign element, whose physical separation begins with exclusion into a ghetto and continues with deportations beyond the borders of the Third Reich. This is how, up until 1939 at the latest, the Germans managed to

---

399 Filip Müller, *Eyewitness Auschwitz. Three Years in the Gas Chambers*, ed. and trans. Susanne Flatauer and Helmut Freitag, Ivad R. Dee, Chicago 1979, pp. 59 et seq.
400 Alexander Solzhenitsyn, *The Gulag Archipelago*.

make of German Jews socially dead persons,[401] a term that Goldhagen adopts from the book by Orland Patterson *Slavery and Social Death* (1962): "Members of a society conceive of the socially dead as being bereft of some essential human attributes and undeserving of essential social, civil, and legal protections." [402]

The legal system gives up on them *de facto* and *de iure*; proof of this is, for example, the letter written (*Richterbrief*, which had the status of a directive) by Otto Georg Thierack, Reich Minister of Justice from 1942 and president of the *Academy for German Law* on 13 September 1942:

> In order to liberate the German nation from Poles, Russians, Jews and Gypsies and in order to release eastern territories joined to the empire as settlement areas for the Germany people, I intend to submit criminal proceedings against Poles, Jews, Russians and Gypsies to the imperial chief of the SS. I am taking these measures on the basis that justice can only to a small extent contribute to the extermination of members of these nationalities.[403]

Along with the occupation of Europe, and above all after the invasion of Western Poland by Germany and of Eastern Poland by the Soviet Union, stateless zones began systematically to emerge as extraterritoriality, non-places of concentration and extermination camps, which in a sense were nowhere. The mechanism of this process is outlined by Timothy Snyder. It begins with the establishment of different racial institutions (to counter the racial threat) and continues with the destruction of states in an aggressive war that allows

401 Daniel Johan Goldhagen, *Hitler's Willing Executioners. Ordinary Germans and the Holocaust*, Alfred Knopf, New York 1996, pp. 90 et seq.

402 Cf. Goldhagen, *Hitler's Willing Executioners*, p. 168.

403 Ota Kraus, Erich Kulka, *Noc a mlha*, Naše Vojsko-SPB, Praha 1958, p. 16. After a meeting with Himmler on 18 September 1942, Thierack observed: "Korrektur bei nichtgenügenden Justizurteilen durch polizeiliche Sonderbehandlung. Es wurde auf Vorschlag des Reichsleiters Bormann zwischen Reichsführer-SS und mir folgende Vereinbarung getrofffen ... 2. Auslieferung asozialer Elemente aus dem Strafvollzug an den Reichsführer-SS zur Vernichtung durch Arbeit." (cited from John M. Steiner, *Power Politics and Social Change in National Socialist Germany*, de Gruyter 1975, p. 325.)

these institutions to operate outside Germany and in a legal vacuum in which property and civil rights guaranteeing legal protection are suspended. A case study in this respect would be Estonia. After being occupied by the Red Army, Soviet laws were retroactively applied "under the logic that the Estonian state not only did not exist, but had never existed."[404] As soon as Germany invaded this non-existent state at the start of July 1941, anyone who was murdered there did not legally exist. The concentration camp – a Bartholomew's Eve that lasted twelve years – is a replica of statelessness; the survival of unidentifiable deportees would be a legal paradox.

It was for this reason, however, that the "true backbone of the camp" (Primo Levi) was the person called in camp jargon the *musulman*; the tottering body, a living corpse, bare life, which is possible only in this extension of the extreme limits of the human where life and death become indistinguishable. "The living dead (...) whose eyes were empty, whose flesh had fled, whose blood was near to water",[405] the "irereversibly exhausted, worn-out prisoner close to death",[406] the prisoner "who was giving up and was given up by his comrades, no longer had room in his consciousness for the contrast of good or bad... He was a staggering corpse, a bundle of physical functions in its last convulsions."[407] "The drowned" of the title of Primo Levi's final book.

> I must repeat – we, the survivors, are not the true witnesses. This is a uncomfortable notion, of which I have become conscious little by little, reading the memoirs of others and reading mine at a distance of years. We survivors are not only exiguous but also an anomalous minority; we are those who by their prevarications or abilities or good luck did not touch the bottom.

---

404 Timothy Snyder, *Black Earth. Holocaust as History and Warning.* Tim Duggan Books, New York 2015.
405 Vrba, *44070 – The Conspiracy of the Twentieth Century*; idem, *I Escaped from Auschwitz*, ch. 6 passim.
406 Primo Levi, *The Drowned and the Saved,* trans. Raymond Rosenthal, Abacus, London 2013, p. 107.
407 Jean Améry, *At the Mind's Limits*, trans. Sidney Rosenfeld and Stella P. Rosenfeld, Indiana University Press, Bloomington 1980, p. 9.

Those who did so, those who saw the Gorgon, have not returned to tell about it or have returned mute, but they are the 'Muslims', the submerged, the complete witnesses, the ones whose deposition would have a general significance. They are the rule, we are the exception. Under another sky, and returned from a similar and diverse slavery Solzhenitsyn noted (it) ... We speak in their stead, by proxy.[408]

In a place where the state of emergency is a quotidian rule, there emerges what Primo Levi called the "grey zone", or (as translated by Agamben) the "zone of indistinction". If it is essential to understand this state as marginal or borderline, and if the border commonly refers to a line whose function is to separate (life and death, the outside and the inside), then its spatial extension in the form of zones does not allow for such differentiation. Neither life nor death, but both life and death, neither inside nor outside, but inside and outside. "We were all living beings in the process of crossing the frontier into death", writes Shlomo Venezia.[409]

Thus the musulman, this Derridean ghost, becomes what Agamben uses as a paradigm: the living dead (one hesitates to call their death death, as Primo Levi says), an example of the non-differentiability of the human and not of the human as already simply human. However, always *on this side* of humanity, because to deny him as a person (as that which still belongs to the human species[410]) would mean adopting the perspective of the SS, repeating its gesture.[411] The bare life to which the human being is reduced is thus the norm. It does not confirm to any existing norms, because even categories

408 Levi, *The Drowned and the Saved*, pp. 89–90.
409 Shlomo Venezia, *Inside the Gas Chambers. Eight Months in the Sonderkommando of Auschwitz*, Polity Press, Cambridge 2009, p. 100.
410 "(H)eroes we know about, from history or from literature (…) we do not believe that they were ever brought to the point of expressing as their last and only claim an ultimate sense of belonging to the human race." Robert Antelme, *The Human Race*, trans. Jeffrey Haight and Annie Mahler, Marlboro Press 1992, p. 5.
411 Agamben, *Remnants of Auschwitz*, p. 63.

of dignity and self-respect lost all meaning in this zone. However, it is unavoidable that we remain with the musulman and say that it is he that is "the guard on the threshold of a new ethics, an ethics of a form and life that begins where dignity ends".[412] It is a person, without our being able to label him as such within the categories of traditional anthropology and ethics. He is something irreducible, unthematisable, because he is outside discursivity. He is something like Derrida's *restance non présente*, a pre-echo of which is to be found in the title of Agamben's book *Quel que resta di Auschwitz*. Primo Levi was already aware of this when he wrote:

> Have we – we who have returned – been able to understand and make others understand our experience? What we commonly mean by "understand" coincides with "simplify": without profound simplification the world around us would be an infinite, undefined tangle that would defy our ability to orient ourselves and decide upon our actions. In short, we are compelled to reduce the knowable to a schema (...) language and conceptual thought."[413]

However, it is not enough to transform the philosophical discourse by introducing other (less discursive) categories. Another form of "showing" is necessary, a showing of that which escapes being shown, wherein resides its escape. We must understand the resistance to the phenomenon as a method of appearance and part company from a cognition consisting of identification. Experience banished from philosophy must be articulated, and in philosophical language.[414] For instance, through the separation of ethics from ontology, as in Levinas and Lyotard. However, all of this is on the basis of testimony and bearing witness, into which Husserl's responsibility for showing has been transformed.

---

412 Ibid., p. 69.
413 Levi, *The Drowned*, p. 31.
414 Cf. Simon Critchley, *The Ethics of Deconstruction. Derrida and Levinas.* Edinburgh UP, Edinburgh 21999, p. 44.

42

That which governs the phenomenological discourse is the principle of all principles, to wit, the need to accept that which shows itself as it shows itself and within the limits set by this showing. We must bracket out everything we already know or only assume we know. The thing must *show itself*. This is the original ideal of descriptive phenomenology that, however, will always be retained as the base layer of the phenomenological approach. Objectivity thus showing itself *bears witness to itself*, it *bears witness to its own presence*. This is why in Husserl's essays the verb "zeugen" (testify) or the noun "Zeugnis" (testimony) in the strict sense of the word almost never appear, and if so, then exclusively in the reflexive form "sich bezeugen". *Testimony* in the strict sense of the word is something that is necessarily subject to reduction. It has an indexical character, it is indication, *Anzeige*, and not an expression in the sense of *bedeutsames Zeichen*. However, the presence of that which is borne witness to is not manifest in itself, but through testimony, even the testimony of someone else, be this eyewitness testimony, an interview, photography, or some other type of document. In respect of showing or self-showing (*Zeigen, Erscheinen*) and the looking that corresponds to it (*Schauen* or watching, *Anschauen* or looking at), testimony, i.e. *Zeugen, Zeugnis*, is secondary. It actualises and represents, without presenting the thing itself.

Testimony as a form of showing is further complicated by the fact that it is (somehow) inseparable from the experience of the specific testifying subject. Testimony always implies the formula "I was there", which clearly shows that the reality of the testified is inseparable from the presence of the witness *there and then*. Through the grammatical category of the personal pronoun "I" (*shifter*), the witness draws attention to himself as the mouthpiece of verbal testimony and thus declares himself a witness. The preterite has a similarly deictic character in relation to the actual presence of the witness "then" and "there" in relation to a specifically defined "here". The character of pointing something out is then underlined by the fact that the witness somehow (perhaps even implicitly) must or should be able to say "believe me", even though that in which we are to place our faith is not objectively verifiable. In short, that which is witnessed is phenomenologically undemonstrable, partly because of the irreplaceability of the witness who embodies the uniqueness of the testimony, and partly because the past does not in and of itself make itself present, *bezeugt sich nicht* (does not bear witness to itself), but is actualised only through the witness. Testimony is not proof.

This is the *formal* structure of testimony. However, another dimension must be taken into account. If testimony is submitted to a court under oath, this means that the witness who appeals to those who are listening to him is responsible for his testimony, and so a challenge is implicit in his speech: trust me. The testimony is not only constative but performative. This becomes abundantly clear when the witness is giving testimony regarding an event that was supposed to have remained without witnesses (in the "crisis of witnessing"[415]), since the extermination camp not only liquidated the witnesses, but sought to remove so much as any trace of their liquidation.

Here, "you have to believe me" means "believe me because I tell you to, because I ask it of you," or, equally well, "I promise you to speak the truth and to be faithful to my promises, and I commit myself to being faithful." In this "it is necessary to believe me", the "it is necessary", which is not theoretical but performative-pragmatic, is as determining as the "believe". Ultimately, it is perhaps the only rigorous introduction to the thought of what "to believe" might mean. When I subscribe to the conclusion of a syllogism or to the delivery of a proof, it is no longer an act of belief, even if the one who conducts the demonstration asks me to "believe" in the truth of the

415 Cf. Shoshana Felman, Dori Laub, *Testimony: Crisis of Witnessing in Literature, Psychoanalysis, and History*, Routledge, London and New York 1992, pp. 76–77.

demonstration. A mathematician or a physicist, a historian, as such, does not seriously ask me to believe him or her. He does not appeal in the last analysis to my belief, at the moment when he presents his conclusions.[416]

Whence the fundamental question: what is being borne witness to as "Auschwitz", the "Holocaust", "Shoah"?

I have already mentioned the elusiveness, the incomprehensibility of that to which the survivors bear witness. However, here too we can differentiate. Adorno claims that any explanation would mean denying the exceptional nature of the event of the Holocaust. It is a traumatic event, i.e. its "apprehension", its appropriation, its very acknowledgement is constantly being denied. It returns as a nightmare, though this is also a sign of its unassimilability. Maurice Blanchot reaches a radical conclusion: Auschwitz is that which is still before us. This points to an important aspect of testimony within the context of philosophical discourse, namely that we cannot push aside that which we do not understand even if the witness is speaking of something that escapes even his understanding (the witness himself embodies the testimony in such a situation). Or, as Derrida would have it: we cannot avoid the ghosts, who are waiting to see whether we respond to them.

All of is confirmed by the facts. The public was not willing or able to accept reports of the death camps submitted by those who managed to escape them (e.g. Rudolf Vrba). Thanks to the Polish resistance, the Allies had been informed of the Final Solution as far back as 1941, and a similarly reserved stance to the survivors pertained even in the years immediately following the war. Reports were received with scepticism and disbelief during the war, even in Jewish communities:

---

416 Jacques Derrida, "Poetics and Politics of Witnessing", in: Jacques Derrida, *Sovereignities in Question: The Poetics of Paul Celan*, ed. by Thomas Dutoit and Outi Pasanen, Fordham University Press, New York 2005, pp. 76–77.

(T)hose who were lucid enough to warn the Jewish communities about the forthcoming destruction either through information or through foresight, were dismissed as 'prophets of doom' and labelled traitors or madmen.[417]

The unassimilability of the event is also addressed by Robert Antelme:

> Two years ago, during the first days after our return, I think we were all prey to a genuine delirium. We wanted at last to speak, to be heard. We were told that by itself our physical appearance was eloquent enough; but we had only just returned, with us we brought back our memory of our experience, an experience that was still very much alive, and we felt a frantic desire to describe it such as it had been. As of those first days, however, we saw that it was impossible to bridge the gap we discovered opening up between the words at our disposal and that experience which, in the case of most of us, was still going forward within our bodies. How were we to resign ourselves to not trying to explain how we had got to the state we were in? For we were yet in that state. And even so it was impossible. No sooner would we begin to tell our story than we would be choking over it. And then, even to us, what we had to tell would start to seem *unimaginable.*[418]

Others could be cited in this regard: Améry, Levi, Richard Glazar and many many others. Susan Sontag generalises when she says that one's first encounter with the photographic inventory of ultimate horror is a paradigm of what "revelation" means for the twentieth century: negative epiphany. That which is given as testimony by survivors is somehow radically *untransferrable*, an experience eluding expression. Testimony regarding the Holocaust can never be *bedeutsames Zeichen*, because a horizon within which it could be incorporated cannot exist. Salmen Lewenthal, a member of the Auschwitz Sonderkommando, who buried his notes in the grounds of

417 Felman – Laub, *Testimony*, p. 83.
418 Antelme, *The Human Race*, p. 3.

the crematorium (where they were discovered only in 1962), speaks of "events unimaginable for human beings".[419]

The Nazi extermination centres produced not only dead bodies as though on a conveyor belt, but were also the site of a war on memory. They thwarted the very possibility of grieving inasmuch as "to remember the death of other humans *in spite of their annihilation* remains the last possible human act of ethical resistance against their desolation",[420]and inasmuch as they systematically destroyed intergenerational continuity, i.e. the basis of lived or natural time, that wave that carries the individuals of each successive generation[421], and even the possibility of being with the other that persists in mourning.

To have a friend, to look at him, to follow him with your eyes, to admire him in friendship, is to know in a more intense way, already injured, always insistent, and more and more unforgettable, that one of the two of you will inevitably see the other die. One of us, each says to himself, the day will come when one of the two of us will see himself no longer seeing the other and so will carry the other within him a while longer, his eyes following without seeing, the world suspended by some unique tear, each time unique, through which everything from then on, through which the world itself – and this day will come – will come to be reflected quivering, reflecting disappearance itself: the world, the whole world, the world itself, for death takes from us not only some particular life within the world, some moment that belongs to us, but, each time, without limit, someone through whom the world, and first of all our own world, will have opened up in a both finite and infinite – mortally infinite – way. That is the blurred and transparent testimony borne by this tear, this small, infinitely small, tear, which the

419 *Inmitten des grauenvollen Verbrechens. Handschriften von Mitgliedern des Sonderkommandos*, ed. Jadwiga Bezwinska et al., Verlag des Staatlichen Auschwitz-Birkenau-Museums, 1996, p. 34.
420 James Hatley, *Suffering Witness: The Quandary of Responsibility after the Irreparable*. State University of New York Press, Albany 2000, p. 41.
421 Ibid., p. 60.

mourning of friends passes through and endures even before death, and always singularly so, always irreplaceably.[422]

If the Holocaust is an event beyond all standards and referential frameworks to which our understanding relates, it is this way because it is an event that did not "create" witnesses. Firstly, its incomprehensibility made it impossible for the survivors to find it within themselves to bear witness to it (a characteristic of the traumatic event), which is a condition of the possibility of their being able to bear witness before others. Secondly, the very institution of the death camp liquidates witnesses physically and without trace: only the dead victims would be genuine witnesses. Hence the title of the book oft-cited by Primo Levi: *The Drowned and the Saved*. The true witnesses are the "drowned", while the survivors bear witness to the missing testimony of missing witnesses. The event itself is *effaced.*

To the question of *what* is actually being borne witness to as the "Shoa", "Holocaust" or "Auschwitz" we must therefore add another: *Who* is bearing witness? On the one hand, it is he who survived and who can speak. However, this is an atypical *häftling* or inmate, an anomalous minority, in the words of Primo Levi (*I sopravvissuti sono una minoranza anomala*). On the other, it is he who touched the bottom and looked into the face of the Gorgon (*visto la Gorgone*) – he should be the one to speak, but cannot. The survivors represent him and speak on his behalf. He is dead until such moment as the living lend him their voice, until he testifies to what is being said through him; the witness's speech transcends the witness (Levinas). Although the voice of silent victims is heard in the words of those who survived, there is nobody here who could say of themselves that they are a genuine witness. Silence is both at the very bottom and yet enters the speech of the survivors, which means that it is impossible to distinguish between the silent and the speaking in this

422 Jacques Derrida, "The Taste of Tears", in: *The Work of Mourning*, ed. by Pascale-Anne Braul, Michael Naas, Chicago University Press, Chicago, London 2001, p. 107.

testimony. This is an indistinguishability that in its highly radical way demonstrates the presence of the outside inside, the relationship via irreducible difference.

However, in the testimony of survivors not only man and speech find themselves in a problematic and risky relationship, but the very definition of man as *zóon logon echón*, or a living being who has language, especially if the experience of the death camps is sometimes designated "unspeakable", even though there are witnesses who talk about it. Levi's paradox can only be resolved by a change of discourse, i.e. by a critical revision of our traditional understanding of speech. This forms the subject of Agamben's *Remnants of Auschwitz*.[423] The chapter "The Archive and Testimony" touches tangentially on Benjamin's reflections on the atrophy of experience and directly on Émile Benveniste, who in his *Problèmes de linguistique générale*[424] concludes that the "I" is primarily constituted as an instance of speech, i.e. a human being becomes a subject when he or she enters the order of speech. Subjectivity is the speaker's ability to position himself as the subject of speech, and it cannot, therefore, be defined either by some original perception or experience in itself, because this is but a secondary effect dependent on the linguistic establishment of the "I", or by some psychological substance. "'Ego' is he who says 'ego'".[425] The singular first person pronoun does not relate either to the concept (in Saussure's terminology), or to the individual, but designates its speaker in the act of individual speech at the moment of its utterance. The reality to which it refers is the reality of this speech. Benveniste adds that if we are consistent in our considerations, then "there is no other objective testimony to the identity of the subject except that which he himself thus gives

423 Agamben, *Remnants of Auschwitz.*
424 Emile Benveniste, *Problèmes de linguistique générale I.* Gallimard, Paris 1966.
425 Emile Benveniste, "De la subjectivité dans le langage", in: *Problèmes de linguistique générale* I, p. 260.

about himself."[426] That which is designated the subject is the materialised shadow that his speech casts upon the speaker, and this is why various traditional ideas of "transcendental subjectivity", including Husserl's, are chimerical. This is a rough approximation of the first stage in Agamben's argument.

In the second stage, in which he refers back to earlier publications,[427] he turns his attention to this discrepancy between the human being and language. The human being is that place in which we must localise that which we call experience, as well as the connection between experience and testimony. That which opens up access to this dimension is *experimentum linguae*: the speaker experiences the overthrow of the classical idea of man as a being gifted with speech upon realising that language comes to him from without and that he must first embrace it. But then it would be possible to speak of silent inarticulate experience and of experience before it is expropriated by language. However, it is clear that only a person who already speaks, i.e. a subject, could thus describe his state prior to entering the regime of speech. In other words, only and precisely the ability to speak refers to the "base", which Agamben names *infanzia*, i.e. to the experience of speech as pure potentiality.

This non-speaking does not refer to some chronological prevenience or originality; *infanzia* coexists in the human being with speech. However, this has consequences within broader contexts. For instance, the "origin" (including Husserl's *Urstiftung* or original institution and including the early modern concept of the base) is not that which constantly recedes into the past, but that "which has not yet ceased to occur".[428] Experience from the perspective

426 Ibid., p. 263.
427 Giorgio Agamben, *Infanzia e storia: Distruzione dell'esperienza e origine della storia* (1978) and *La potenza del pensiero: Saggi e conferenza* (expanded edition 2005).
428 Giorgio Agamben, *Infancy and History. On the Destruction of Experience*, trans. Liz Heron, Verso 2007, Verso, London, New York, 2007, p. 57.

of *infanzia* is the difference between the human and the linguistic, which is a claim that can be illuminated by contrast: if "experience" did not exist, speech would be the same as using language according to rules. However, because man is not identical with language, speech is like the ex-position of experience, a place in which experience finds expression but is never identical to it – it is the site of a relationship via irreducible difference.

Here, as in Agamben and elsewhere, an understanding of difference as a threshold or limit that does not belong to one or the other side (a separator links, a link separates) and is a zone of indistinguishability (see, for instance, the relationship of the human and in-human in man) plays a fundamental role. This concept, in which the *infanzia* preceding speech is the potentiality of speech, i.e. both in-speech and speech, frees the transition from one to the other of incomprehensibility, for instance the transition (a problem inherited from Saussurean structural linguistics) from *langue* to *parole*, from language to system to speech as communicating meaning, the transition that, according to Benveniste and Agamben, is essential if the subject is to constitute itself (from this perspective *infanzia* is the de-subjectivised possibility of subjectification).

To express matters using Benveniste's terminology: it allows us to understand the transition from the semiotic to the semantic. If a mode of designation belongs to the semiotic that is particular to language, i.e. the sign designates, if it is recognised, identified as a sign with a certain value, then the semiotic is actually a designation that only comes into being in speech, in the act of testifying: significance is not recognised but understood. Between both is discontinuity – and Agamben's concept of non-speech is supposed to explain how it is possible that in fact this hiatus is constantly being bridged.

It is the fact of man's infancy (in other words, in order to speak, he needs to be constituted as a subject within language by removing himself from infancy) which breaks the closed world of the sign and transforms pure language into human discourse, the semiotic into the semantic.[429]

For this very reason, however, it is not possible to posit the semiotic and the semantic as two completely different realities. Instead, bearing in mind *infanzia* as potentiality, they should be regarded as transcendental limits. The semiotic would then be something like a pre-linguistic vocalisation (an idea very close to the hum and murmur of speech; elsewhere in his speculations Agamben refers to glossolalia), which becomes the essential substratum of the semantic the moment that man acquires speech and abandons his muteness.

Because Agamben's paradigmatic method is a method by analogy, this argument is aimed at both "ineffability" and at testimony as discourse imparting speech to the person who is not capable of speech as well as to the concept of the subject. For if the "I" is a subject only at the cost of accepting his de-subjectivisation, his inseparable link with the a-subjective *infanzia*, then analogously we might understand the survivor as the subject of testimony that is de-subjectivised by virtue of having him speak in his testimony the experience of the bottom unattainable by him. Man is able to become a witness precisely because he has speech as a being capable of not having speech:

> because there is an inseparable division and non-coincidence between the inhuman and the human, the living being and the speaking being, the *Muselmann* and the survivor. Precisely insofar as it inheres in language as such, precisely insofar as it bears witness to the taking place of a potentiality of speaking through an impotentiality alone, its authority depends not on a factual truth, a conformity between something said and a fact or between memory and what happened, but rather on the immemorial relation between the unsayable and the sayable, between the outside and the inside of language. *The authority of the witness consists in his capacity to speak*

---

429 Agamben, *Infancy*, p. 64.

solely in the name of an incapacity to speak – that is, in his or her being a subject. Testimony thus guarantees not the factual truth of the statement safeguarded in the archive, but rather its unarchivability, its exteriority with respect to the archive – that is, the necessity by which, as the existence of language, it escapes both memory and forgetting. It is because there is testimony only where there is an impossibility of speaking, because there is a witness only where there has been desubjectification, that the *Muselmann* is the complete witness and that the survivor and the *Muselmann* cannot be split apart.[430]

This theme is expanded on in *Remnants of Auschwitz*, especially as regards the categories of potentiality and contingency. We can leave these aside, though not without pointing to their motivation, which is not a reinterpretation of traditional concepts, but an examination of the necessity for a radical transformation of the philosophical discourse as a response to the event of the Holocaust. Auschwitz means the collapse of the traditional ontological operators, namely categories, because it is the event "in which the impossible is forced into the real. Auschwitz is the existence of the impossible (...) The *Muselmann* produced by Auschwitz is the catastrophe of the subject, the subject's effacement as the placer of contingency and its maintenance as existence of the impossible."[431] In *Potentialities* Agamben states quite explicitly that the task of the next philosophy will be "to redefine the entire domain of categories and modality."[432]

Two brief comments in conclusion.

Firstly: Agamben summarises a complex argument by saying that testimony places the inside and outside of language, the sayable and unsayable (*indicibile*), in a relationship. We might simplify matters thus: that which was thus or, to put it another way, was designated

430 Agamben, *Remnants of Auschwitz*, pp. 157–8.
431 Ibid., p. 148.
432 Giorgio Agamben, *Potentialities. Collected Essays in Philosophy*, ed. and trans. with an introduction by Daniel Heller-Roazen Stanford, Stanford University Press, Stanford 1999, pp. 76–5.

by language as this or that; if we wanted to eliminate "as", we would come up against unsayability or ineffability. Or to put things another way (whence Agamben's analyses of the concepts of potentiality, actualisation, contingency[433]): the existence of language itself is unsayable. Perhaps this is how we should understand the following paragraph from the "Prologue" to *Infanzia e storia*:

> The *ineffabile*, the unsaid, are in fact categories which belong exclusively to human language; far from indicating a limit of language, they express its invincible power of presupposition, the unsayable being precisely what language must presuppose in order to signify.[434]

Among other things, however, Agamben also wants to say that unsayability is a category that tradition has long surrounded with an aura of the sacred. If we wanted to rid ourselves of it in this form, this would mean having to remain silent about Auschwitz, so sacrificing its victims a second time.

> This why those who assert the unsayability of Auschwitz today should be more cautious in their statements. If they mean to say that Auschwitz was unique event in the face of which the witness must in some way submit his every word to the test of an impossibility of speaking, they are right. But if, joining uniqueness to unsayability, they transform Auschwitz into a reality absolutely separated from language, if they break the tie between an impossibility and a possibility of speaking that, in the *Muselmann*, constitutes testimony, then they unconsciously repeat the Nazis' gesture.[435]

Secondly: the Prologue to *Infanzia e storia* cited above begins with a Blanchotesque consideration of the work. Agamben says that every written work must be understood as an introduction to that which

---

433 Conducted most thoroughly in the chapter "Bartleby, or On Contingency", in: *Potentialities*.
434 Agamben, *Infancy and History*, p. 4.
435 Agamben, *Remnantsof Auschwitz*, p. 157.

has never been written and which is destined to remain unwritten forever. All works that follow it will again be simply an introduction to others. The absent work defines each already written work as a *prolegomenon* or *paralipomenon* of the non-existent work. This too is a description of an elliptical or a-thetic text and it too we may read as an analogy of irrevocable difference or discrepancy between language and experience, the outside (*infanzia*) and inside (language), or unsayability as the prerequisite of denotation, i.e. of a relationship via difference. However, were we to seek a wider analogy, we could interpret this ellipticity as unambiguous confirmation of the non-identity of thinking and being, and thus as a break with the classical philosophical discourse. This analogy would bring us back to Adorno's response to the event of the Holocaust in *Negative Dialectics* (published in 1966) and in his university lectures from 1963 entitled *Metaphysics: Concept and Problems,* in which he presents several of the ideas that appear in the final section of *Negative Dialectics.* As opposed to "metaphysics" (the contents of the spirit's thinking is the spirit itself), Adorno demands we return to concepts their embeddedness in time (in what Adorno calls *Relevanz des Innerzeitlichen*[436]), i.e. in real history. After Auschwitz this step is essential, since it is clear that that which was played out in time impacts fundamentally on thinking whose concepts and categories cannot be situated outside historical, event- or adventurist-time.

---

[436] Theodor W. Adorno, *Metaphysik. Begriff und Probleme*, ed. Rolf Tiedemann, Suhrkamp, Frankfurt a.M. 2006, p. 159.

43

The Auschwitz Musulman is he who finds himself in the centre of the concentric circles of a camp in a non-place, the last boundary of which is *Selektion*. Though every prisoner recognises himself in his disfigured face, if he does not want to be liquidated, he must constantly hide him within himself. Even the first American soldiers to arrive at the Nazi concentration camps in Germany found looking at the prisoners' faces intolerable. George W. King, who was present during the liberation of the prisoners in Mauthausen, recorded his feelings as follows: "there was no way of distinguishing them. Shaved heads and sunken faces... it is impossible to see people in them. Under these circumstances one avoids looking at them. It is too painful."[437] Not even the prisoners spoke with the Musulman, as though not speaking and not seeing was the only reasonable conduct towards those beyond help.

The existence of the Musulman was corroborated by Primo Levi in *If This is a Man*.

> But with the mussulmans, the men in decay, it is not even worth speaking, because they have no distinguished acquaintances in camp, they do not gain any extra rations, they do not work in profitable Kommandos and they know no secret method of organising. And in any case, one knows that they are only here on a visit, that in a few weeks nothing will remain of them but a handful of ashes in some near-by field and a crossed-out number on a register (...) they suffer and drag themselves along in an opaque inteimate solitude, and in solitude they die or disappear, without leaving a trace in anyone's memory. (...) All the mussulmans who finished in the gas chambers have the same story, or more exactly, have no story; they followed the slope down to the bottom, like streams that run down to the sea... Their life

---

[437] Cited from Cornelia Brink, "Bilder vom Feind. Das Scheitern der 'visuellen Entnazifierung' 1945." In: Sven Kramer (ed.), *Die Shoah im Bild*. Edition text+kritik, Richard Boorberg Verlag, München 2003, p. 52.

is short, but their number is endless; they, the *Muselmänner*, the drowned, form the backbone of the camp, an anonymous mass, continually renewed and always identical, of non-men (...) One hesitates to call them living: one hesitates to call their death death, in the face of which they have no fear, as they are too tired to understand. (...) They crowd my memory with their faceless presences, and if I could enclose all the evil of our time in one image, I would choose this image which is familiar to me: an emaciated man, with head dropped and shoulders curved, on whose face and in whose eyes not a trace of a thought is to be seen.[438]

Giorgio Agamben, whose book *Remnants of Auschwitz* is a running commentary on Primo Levi's work cited above, examines the way that this absence in the sense of the unrepresentability of the Musulman is borne witness to and can be regarded as a paradigm of testimony. He captures the echo of the empty centre of the death camp where Levi remembers a small, paralysed three-year old boy (a child of Auschwitz, a child of death), who didn't know how to speak and whom the prisoners called Hurbinek because of the unintelligible sounds he made. However, suddenly Hurbinek began to repeat a word that nobody could understand and that Levi transcribes as "mass-klo, matisklo"[439]. Nobody knew what he was saying, even though the prisoners in Auschwitz came from all over Europe and spoke many different languages.

Hurbinek died in March 1945 and Levi writes: "Nothing remains of him: he bears witness through these words of mine." However, this would mean that that regarding which testimony is given no longer has to be language. The sound "matisklo" emerges from that "lacuna" in testimony. It is non-speech to which speech replies and in which speech is born. If Levi, even as a survivor, is unable to bear full witness ("by my words" his voice, which mumbles something

438 Levi, *If This is a Man*, pp. 101–103.
439 Primo Levi, *La tregua*, Einaudi, Torino 1989, p. 14 ("Non sapeva, una parola difficile, non ungherese: qualcosa come 'mass-klo', 'matisklo'.")

unintelligible), then Agamben infers the following: if language is to testify, it must free up the space of non-speech so that the impossibility of testifying appears.

> But not even the survivor can bear witness completely, can speak his own lacuna. This means that testimony is the disjunction between two impossibilities of bearing witness; it means that language, in order to bear witness, must give way to a non-language in order to show the impossibility of bearing witness. The language of testimony is a language that no longer signifies and that, in not signifying, advances into what is without language, to the point of taking on a different insignificance − that of the complete witness, that of he who by definition cannot bear witness. To bear witness, it is therefore not enough to bring language to its own non-sense, to the pure undecidability of letters (*m-a-s-s-k-l-o, m-a-t-i-s-k-l-o*). It is necessary that this senseless sound be, in turn, the voice of something or someone that, for entirely other reasons, cannot bear witness. It is thus necessary that the impossibility of bearing witness, the "lacuna" that constitutes human language, collapses, giving way to a different impossibility of bearing witness − that which does not have language.[440]

The voice of someone who themself cannot speak: the movement of traditionalisation, the acceptance of the legacy, like the act of testimony or responding and responsibility, can be (and often is) expressed metaphorically. For instance, James Hatley in his book *Suffering Witness* (dedicated to Hurbinek) says, in Derridean style: we live time in such a way that we reply to those who existed before us, and in this way become bearers of their voice. And responding, we turn to the voices of those who will arrive after us, "voices who arise out of one's own flesh (be it bodily or figuratively) only to articulate a time utterly beyond one's own death."[441]

---

440 Agamben, *Remnants of Auschwitz*, p. 39.
441 Hatley, *Suffering Witness*, p. 62.

However, this mode of expression both is and is not a metaphor, because the voice itself is and is not inside language. It is midway between two limits (molar and molecular, as Gilles Deleuze might put it), with which, however, it can never merge: language uttered out loud can escape to its wording and become sound, but precisely in this way it may at the opposite end be sublimated into pure concept, become lost in the ideal significance of the spoken. It does not completely belong either to the semiotic or the semantic. As the inseparable purport of language, the voice is the unattainable exterior of its unattainable interior. This is perhaps what Foucault had in mind when he was examining the ontology of literary language and wrote the following in the essay *Language to Infinity*:

> Writing, in our day, has moved infinitely closer to its source, to this disquieting sound which announces from the depths of language – once we attend to it – the source against which we seek refuge and toward which we address ourselves. Like Franz Kafka's beast, language now listens from the bottom of its burrow to this inevitable and growing noise. To defend itself it must follow its movements, become its loyal enemy, and allow nothing to stand between them except the contradictory thinness of a transparent and unbreakable partition. We must ceaselessly speak, for as long and as loudly as this indefinite and deafening noise – longer and more loudly so that in mixing our voices with it we might succeed – if not in silencing and mastering it – in modulating its futility in the endless murmuring we call literature.[442]

This is what speech is for Agamben: the voice as the trace of a trace of the bottom of the camp. In its ambivalence (the spoken must merge with the element of semiotics in order to become audible) it is the "medium" of the relationship via irreducible difference. The voice is that which can never be the theme of language; in the spo-

442 Michel Foucault, Le langage à l'infini , Tel Quel, n° 15, automne 1963, pp. 44–53; in: Foucault, *Dits et écrits* I, p. 255.

ken it remains like an ossified echo. It disappears as soon as the word is uttered. *Le dire* is always already lost in *le dit*, as Levinas will go on to say. Language as the manifestation of this difference, this incommensurability or asymmetry (since, to use another example from Agamben, there does not exist a human voice that would be a sign of a man in such a way as the chirping of a cricket is the voice of a cricket), is the condition of the possibility of testimony.

> I shall not write about what all of these unhappy wretches told me... However, what I can say is that, if I had not seen everything with my own eyes, I would never have believed that something like this was possible. I was especially shaken by the report of a Polish Jew who spoke Yiddish. The very intonation of his voice embodied the horrific tragedy of our nation.[443]

> But what is this voice?
> – Not something to hear, perhaps the last written cry, what is inscribed in the future outside books, outside language.
> – But what is this voice?[444]

The work that was never written, referred to by Giorgio Agamben in the prologue to *Infanzia e storia* as elliptical, because the absent centre of all of his written books could, as he himself suspects, carry the title *The Human Voice* or *Ethics, an Essay on the Voice*. After reading his book *Remnants of Auschwitz* this becomes more understandable: the voice allows speech to testify. However, we must not ignore the broader context. Language is not the same as speech. Speech needs a voice that is on this or the other side of "subjectivity" in order to become audible. These are not theoretical niceties, but an explication of human historical experience, the experience of non-coincidence, a fundamental experience, because it becomes a new measure of philosophical discourse traditionally linked to the

---

443 Susanne Fall, *Terezín, ráj mezi lágry*, trans. Věra Koubová, Revolver Revue, Praha 2015, p. 76.
444 Maurice Blanchot, *The Infinite Conversation*, p. 331.

categories of the subject and consciousness or self-consciousness, whose identity with itself (coincidence) is the basis of thinking as knowledge. However, testimony, which clearly belongs to a different order than that of pure knowledge or cognition, shows that the subject is something split or decentred, because it is located in the gap between the living being and language, between the life function and life history (which is why the destruction of life history does not entail the liquidation of the subject's humanity). This is experience that is brought to light by the testimony of survivors, both by virtue of what they testify and how they testify; the experience of incommensurableness, of the relationship via irreducible difference, is that which "makes us think", i.e. forces us to think differently. Blanchot formulated it in its most extreme manifestation in his reflections accompanying the testimony of Robert Antelme: we are beginning to understand that man is the indestructible that can be destroyed.[445] He experiences this at exactly the moment he approaches the limits of suffering where he is nothing but that "other" that as pure "subject" he is not. It is therefore not unreasonable to say that man is capable of surviving man, because the latter is also a man whose humanity has been devastated (a reply to the implied question in the title of Primo Levi's *If This Is a Man*), and even he belongs to the human species (confirmation of the title of Robert Antelme's *The Human Race*). That which we designate "I" is the assisting witness to this de-subjectivisation: the man experiencing shame.

The third chapter of *Remnants of Auschwitz* entitled *Shame, or On the Subject*, makes explicit reference to Levinas's essay *On Escape (De l'évasion)* from the mid-1930s,[446] in which the author first sketched out the trajectory of his future work beyond the boundaries of ontology and the philosophy of knowledge in the position of *prima philosophia*. It is here, by means of a subtle analysis of the phenomenon of shame, that he deconstructs the postulate of identity

---

445 Ibid., pp. 191–192.
446 Emmanuel Levinas, *De l'évasion*, Montpellier, Fata Morgana, 1962 (1935).

with itself in self-consciousness that, according to him, simply conceals a deeper conflict in the subject. Because shame is not primarily a moral phenomenon, but rather stems from our inability to identify with what is in us and is alien to us (it approximates to the distinction between the life function and life history, or Binswanger's difference between the dreaming and waking state), which, however, emerges in the borderline situation of the destruction of humanity. It is something that we would want to conceal but cannot, either from the other or from ourselves. We cannot escape ourselves, we are bound to ourself, we are permanently present to this difference (the non-coincidence in us, the irreducible crisis inside), in our completeness. It is in this sense we should understand the statement that the "I" is present to itself (*présence du moi à soi-même*), i.e. that the "I" is witness to its own de-subjectivisation at precisely the moment it becomes a subject (in Agamben's subsequent formulation). Shame, as Levinas says, reveals being, which reveals itself and seeks an apology.[447] Shame is a sign of this non-identity as it reveals itself, the impossibility of concealing the outside inside, the fact that the subject is affected by its own receptivity.

Voice, speech, shame, traumatic experience and the witness thereof, the semiotics of indexical signs (trace, ellipsis, secrecy), the relationship via irreducible difference, the non-identity of thought and being or consciousness and being, experience and language ... all of this is closely connected if philosophy responds to the event of the Holocaust by means of a root-and-branch transformation of its discourse. However, this transformation must be monitored not only wherever concepts change their meaning, wherever new concepts appear and old ones fade into the background, wherever accents and the like shift, but wherever it is possible to observe something like an internal resonance between various different places of this discourse (whether we give them their authors' names or label them by

447 Ibid., p. 114.

specific problems or questions) that lends the transformed discourse its coherence. As Adorno wrote in *Minima Moralia*: "the soundness of a conception can be judged by whether it causes one quotation to summon another."[448] This applies not only to specific texts or works of a particular author, but also to the discourse of philosophy as a whole. For this reason it would be difficult to find some minimal common denominator. It is more a case of strategic proximity, though this is not always clear at first sight. If, for example, in Derrida's neologism *différance* we hear not only "difference" but also "deferral" in the sense of postponement, then the meaning of this invented concept is respect for resistance: if thinking does not attempt to identify something "as" something mediated via the already constituted horizon of expectation, this is not about becoming resigned to the failure of cognition, but rather an attempt to rescue that which always remains, since that which escapes, i.e. which resists exposure of this type, must be shown in this resistance, in the act of escape. In this way a mutual correspondence will be found between testimony and Derrida's untranslatable "concept" *restance non présente*, the echo of which is present in Agamben's *Remnants of Auschwitz*.

If we overlook the theological messianic connotations that the concept of the remainder or remains is surrounded by in the case of this author, the original interpreter of the texts of Walter Benjamin, in the phrase *il resto* we find firstly the present absence of the nonidentical (of the outside inside), and secondly (above all, one might add), another concept of temporality concealed within, a different dimension of time beyond chronology and teleology. In this sense *il resto* further develops the impulse provided by Benjamin's reflections on the *Jetzt-Zeit*, the here-and-now.

Il resto, remnant, restance – under no circumstances is this part of the whole[449]; the remainder or remains must be understood as an

---

448 Adorno, *Minima Moralia*, p. 87

449 See, for instance, Leland de la Durantaye, *Giorgio Agamben: A Critical Introduction*. Stanford UP, Stanford 2009, p. 298 et. seq.

excess. It indicates a divergence from the whole and as such refers to the impossibility of the identification of whole and remainder, their mutual cover (*Deckung*) as a means of cognising the unique (of an event), i.e. it refers to the remainder of non-identity in every act of identification. In this sense, and to a extent that does not exclude either shifts or polemical dialogue between them, both Derrida's and Agamben's thinking links up to Adorno's negative dialectics. However, at the same time Agamben's *il resto* and Derrida's *restance* refer to another temporality. In Agamben's case a comparison offers itself with the "operational time" of the linguist Gustave Guillaume:[450] the time that human thinking requires in order to construct for itself a certain image of time must be set aside from linear time. The idea thus created then refers back to chronological time. However, operational time is heterogeneous in respect of this time (all the more so in that, in order to create an image of time, we must be able to "contract" it in our thinking.[451] This comparison illuminates Agamben's conception of messianic time especially: "the time that time takes to come to an end" [452] (*il tempo che il tempo ci mette per finire*), the time that remains between time and its end.

However, perhaps all of this is prefigured, albeit in simpler form, both in Kracauer's approach to waiting (*Warten*) as hesitant openness that does not look for when and whether time will end, because it is necessary that life focus on the last thing before the last in the "antechamber" (*Vorraum*) of the end, and in Adorno's requirement of a relationship with the unconditional, the condition of which, however, is that it does not pose a question regarding the possibility (or impossibility) of its attainment – or redemption.

Again, Derrida's *différance* is not as remote as it might seem.

450 Gustave Guillaume, *Foundations for a Science of Language*. John Benjamin's, Amsterdamn 1984, p. 123.
451 Cf. Giorgio Agamben, *The Time That Remains*, trans. Patricia Dailey, Stanford University Press, Stanford 2005, p. 65 et seq.
452 Ibid., p. 67.

44

An integral aspect of the transformation of philosophical discourse is a transformation in the hierarchy of philosophical genres. The essay, fragment, dialogue, philosophical miniature or sketch initiated by apparently marginal or random observations once more comes into its own. Texts that say something by speaking of something else, texts whose content is presented by the very method of its presentation. This state of affairs was described by Adorno in *Aesthetic Theory*: art needs philosophy, since philosophy says what art cannot say, although it is art alone which is able to say it: by not saying it.[453]

And so the example of "internal architecture" from Benjamin's *One-Way Street* is actually not even an example:

> The tractatus is an Arabic form. Its exterior is undifferentiated and unobtrusive, like the façades of Arabian buildings, whose articulation begins only in the courtyard. So, too, the articulated structure of the tractatus is invisible from the outside, revealing itself only from within. If it is formed by chapters, they have not verbal headings but numbers. The surface of its deliberations is not enlivened with pictures, but covered with unbroken, proliferating arabesques. In the ornamental density of this presentation, the distinction between thematic and excursive expositions is abolished.[454]

[453] Theodor W. Adorno, *Ästhetische Theorie*, GS 7, p. 13.
[454] Walter Benjamin, "One-Way Street", in *Selected Writings* 1, p. 402.

45

The question reads as follows: how do we show that which resists being shown, that which remains as *il resto, remnant,* as *restance non-présente*? How do we not lose that to which testimony refers? And in any case, what is testimony? These questions bring to life thinking that is not driven by method but declares itself as strategy. The very word strategy is already an explanation of sorts of this turn. Strategy, an approach that is not secured in advance, whose calculations are neither certain nor evident. In Adornian terms, the approach is justified by its outcome. Strategy implies a gamble, whence the importance of the essay ("attempt" or "trial") as a philosophical genre and Michel Montaigne as its predecessor, for instance in Derrida's *Force of Law*. Adorno provides a more detailed explanation in *The Essay as Form*, in which the word "method" becomes a paleonym.

> With regard to scientific procedure and its philosophic grounding as method, the essay, in accordance with its idea, draws the fullest consequences from the critique of the system. Even the empiricist doctrines that grant priority to open, unanticipated experience over firm, conceptual ordering remain systematic to the extent that they investigate what they hold to be the more or less constant preconditions of knowledge and develop them in as continuous a context as possible. Since the time of Bacon, who was himself an essayist, empiricism – no less than rationalism – has been "method". Doubt about the unconditional priority of method was raised, in the actual process of thought, almost exclusively by the essay. It does justice to the consciousness of non-identity, without needing to say so, radically unradical in refraining from any reduction to a principle. (...) It proceeds, so to speak, methodically unmethodically. (...) It is not so much that the essay ignores indisputable certainty, as that it abrogates the ideal. The essay becomes true in its progress, which drives it beyond itself, and not in a hoarding obsession with fundamentals. Its concepts receive their light from a *terminus*

ad quem hidden to the essay itself, and not from an obvious *terminus a quo*. In this the very method of the essay expresses the utopian intention.[455]

Strategy is a relationship to the incalculable, i.e. a relationship via irreducible difference, a relationship to that which is on the point of arrival. If we attempt to calculate this, it is precisely because we confront the unpredictable, we do not know:

> If a strategy were guaranteed in and of itself, if its calculation were sure, there would be no strategy at all. Strategy always implies a wager — that is, a certain way of giving ourselves over to not-knowing, to the incalculable. We calculate because there is something incalculable. We calculate where we do not know, where we can make no determination.[456]

The substitution of the method by strategy, which on the one hand is anticipated by Benjamin and his constellations and dialectical image, and on the other by Hans-Georg Gadamer in his book *Truth and Method* (1960), can almost be followed step by step during the latter half of the twentieth century. In addition, in the background of Derrida's *différance* is Saussure's *Course in General Linguistics*, in which the operation of language is compared to a game of chess: every move changes the entire system and so its scope cannot be precisely forecast. The response to this comparison is Derrida's early essay *Structure, Sign and Play in the Discourse of the Human Sciences* (1966),[457] in which the internal movement of the decentred structure is called the "play of structure",[458] clearly in polemic with the classical concept in which transformations of the structure are limited or regulated by its "centre" (or the principle or origin, as it

455 Theodor W. Adorno, *Noten zur Literatur*, Suhrkamp, Frankfurt a.M. 1981, pp. 16, 21.
456 Jacques Derrida and Maurizio Ferraris, *A Taste for the Secret*, trans. Giacomo Donis, Polity Press, Cambridge 2002, p. 13.
457 Jacques Derrida, *Writing and Difference*, trans. Alan Bass, University of Chicago Press, Chicago 1978, pp. 351–370.
458 Ibid., p. 352.

would be possible to say in other contexts). The game, as Benjamin knew (since he often had gambling in mind) requires more "presence of mind" than method, because only (the) presence of mind – open to that which is on the point of arrival – is capable of quickly clarifying the situation.

> He who asks fortune-tellers unwittingly forfeits an inner intimation of coming events that is a thousand times more exact than anything they may say. He is impelled by inertia, rather than by curiosity, and nothing is more unlike the submissive apathy with which he hears his fate revealed than the alert dexterity with which the man of courage lays hand on the future. For presence of mind is an extract of the future, and precise awareness of the present moment is more decisive than foreknowledge of the most distant events.[459]

In other words, the paradigm of the game leads to the substitution of method by strategy. For Derrida this is one of the ways of introducing the movement of differánce:

> There are thus two interpretations of interpretation, of structure, of sign, of freeplay. The one seeks to decipher, dreams of deciphering, a truth or an origin which is free from freeplay and from the order of the sign, and lives an exile the necessity of interpretation. The other, which is no longer turned toward the origin, affirms freeplay and tries to pass beyond man and humanism, the name man being the name of that being who, throughout the history of metaphysics or of ontotheology – in other words, through the history of all of his history – has dreamed of full presence, the reassuring foundation, the origin and the end of the game.[460]

---

459 Benjamin,"One-Way Street", pp. 402–403. Cf.: "Presence of mind as a political category comes magnificently to life in these words of Turgot: 'Before we have learned to deal with things in a given position, they have already changed several times. Thus, we always perceive events too late, and politics always needs to foresee, so to speak, the present.'" Walter Benjamin, *The Arcades Project*, trans. Howard Eiland and Kevin McLaughlin, The Belknap Press, Cambridge, Mass. and London 1999, pp. 477–478.
460 Derrida, "La structure, signe et jeu...", p. 427.

Strategic thinking is called for, because the game is neither teleological movement nor the development of that which is wrapped in origin (Husserl's history is still both to a certain extent): neither is it movement without internal meaning. The turn toward strategy is a turn to an approach of hesitant openness that allows for the unpredictable and so is always in a relationship with that which is on the point of arrival and is capable of understanding appropriately both the event and its time. Within this context the inspiration of messianic time is unsurprising, though this traditional idea is deconstructed in various different ways by all the authors mentioned (beginning with Benjamin, moving onto Kracauer and Adorno and ending with Levinas, Derrida, Agamben et al.)

Precisely because strategy calculates with the incalculable, it is able to relate to the event, i.e. to that which occurs earlier than is possible, and for this reason this relationship is a relationship via irreducible difference. Though asymmetrical, it is a relationship. However, thinking is only in this relationship to the event when it corresponds to it.

The Holocaust, this "event unimaginable for human beings" (S. Lewenthal), in its capacity as event is a challenge to thinking, since it problematises it. It is unimaginable, it defies understanding, it is that which subverts the rationality of even attempting to understand. For this reason, however, the response to the fact of the Holocaust is the transformation of philosophical discourse. This response does not attempt to assimilate, identify or explain the event of the Holocaust, but seeks to present its testimony regarding the Holocaust. This is not easy: in modern (traditional, classical or modern) philosophy, testimony is a minority genre. Testimony does not submit direct proof. Its evidence is controvertible, which puts it on the lowest level of epistemological relevance. All the more so because it is singular and without guarantee (as Paul Celan says:"Niemand zeugt für den Zeugen", "No one bears witness for the witness"), and that which it testifies to it only actualises through the mediation of indication. It is not therefore on the side of the necessary but the probable, it belongs to rhetoric not to philosophy. If philosophy is to bear witness regarding the Holocaust, its response must consist of a transformation of the philosophical discourse (or as Deleuze would say, the "image of thought"), by means of which testimony becomes one of the central concepts or methods of showing. However, this presupposes, on a completely general level, that philosophy will turn its attention to the resistance that events place in the way of our (identifying, assimilating) understanding, and cease to regard this resistance as that which is to be broken. Respect for the event-character of the event assumes respect for the other, the unique, the inappropriable. Respect for the escape of that which resists its own showing. The philosophical response does not explain the event but embodies it as testimony.

This understanding of the event is formulated radically by Derrida. The event is that which we do not see coming because it is outside all horizons that anticipate and allow for cognition. It is outside the world inasmuch as the world is understood in the Husserlian way as the horizon of all horizons. If it is that which the framework of its understanding has within itself, then we can say that upon the arrival of the event our world is cited within another context. The known is strange, the event is not inscribed within the continuous flow of time, but refers to a time that is somehow adventurist, reveals the event-meaning of time.

The event relates to everything because it relates to meaning. The event's intervention is radical inasmuch as it unsettles the horizon of all horizons by virtue of the consciousness of meaning that is irreducible to the horizon (that which makes sense is a deviation, a change of direction). It was this that Husserl had before his eyes, without being conscious of it, when he created the phenomenological base of evident cognition in the act of identification as the conformity of like with like that pushes the incompatible to the side, as well as when he came across the problem of "hyletic data" when analysing perception and the internal consciousness of time. He left to one side the fact that the carrier of meaning could in fact be the incompatible, i.e. the event.[461] For this reason the world must be defined differently, namely as that which can be reconfigured by an event in response to an event.[462] The world does not determine possibilities. Instead, this function is performed by events, namely *crises* of the world.

Whence another way of thinking about time. The event as external in relation to the current hermeneutic horizon of all horizons transcends presence. More precisely, the event is always present only as the past in the light of its future, and it can only ever be turned into a theme after the event, as it were. However, this does not only involve what is known as a traumatic relationship with the past, i.e. Freud's *Nachträglichkeit* or "afterwardsness", since at this juncture Benjamin's concept of time as expressed in the *Theses on the Philosophy of History* once again enters the equation: the past can only be seen in an instant of danger. This could be rephrased as follows: in a world after the Holocaust hitherto concealed traces come to light, traces of an unrealised project of *another* modernity that we call postmodernism.

---

461 See Claude Romano, *L'événement et le temps*, P. U. F., Paris 1999, pp. 146–147.
462 Ibid., p. 55.

46

Our world is cited as though within another context. The exterior is indistinguishable from the interior, the known is suddenly strange, the appearance of the world, i.e. that which it shows me when I look for what is possible, has changed. The elsewhere is here. The event is the irruption of reality into the world. The sensation novel personalises this non-identifiability – the mysterious villain could be anyone, the relationship between cause and effect is interpreted as a hypnotic influence.[463] Its defining feature qua genre is the improbability that lurks in the shadows of the quotidian. This was why the surrealists were so fascinated by Fantômas, who electrified the nerves of his readership.

If Literature is confronted with the event, if it attempts to find a response to it, it tries in its own special way – determined by the meaning of the word "fiction" – to create a context that could be the referential framework of the event. It seeks meaning in crisis. However, above all it is able to register accurately this uncertainty in advance. Kafka's strange worshipper suffers seasickness on dry land due to the fact that he has forgotten the real names of things and now in his haste casts random names over them. He observes that from time to time tall buildings collapse for no apparent reason.[464] Elsewhere a giant mole is caught sight of[465] and the elderly bachelor Blumfeld is followed in his room by two bouncing balls that follow him wherever he goes.[466] And this is not to speak of Odradek. Eduard Raban, separated from the outside world, which he observes,

---

463 A motif that survives, beginning with *The Cabinet of Dr. Caligari* via the novel *Grey Face* by Sax Rohmer (1924), the Czech translation of which, published in 1933, features a swastika on its cover, and Fritz Lang's film *Dr. Mabuse, der Spieler* (1922) to *The Manchurian Candidate* by Richard Condon (1959). Starting in 1939, Hermann Broch worked on *Theory of Mass Hysteria*.
464 Franz Kafka, "Conversation with a Worshiper" (Early Stories).
465 Franz Kafka, "A Country Doctor".
466 Franz Kafka, "Blumfeld, an Elderly Bachelor".

departs. His journey has a destination, but he sets off in no clear direction without its being possible to say that he is lost.[467]

In trivial novels the relationship to Literature is silently suspended. But not, however, to real history. The sheer variety of such novels is unthinkable without history. The detective story envisages the institutionalisation of the police force (The Metropolitan Police Act, 1828). The Western reflects the uncertain, shifting frontier that, though indefinable, thus forms the identity of America.[468] The gangster movie appears simultaneously with the enforcement of prohibition (1919) and depicted the city as an asphalt jungle.[469] Spy novels and conspiracy thrillers are a transposition of paranoia onto the political map of the world, and enjoy a renaissance during the Cold War before this was replaced by the threat of terrorism. If the conventionalised schema of literature assumes a movement from the outbreak of a crisis that destabilises the existing balance (murder, conflict on still lawless borderlands, the rational business enterprise of gangsters who have become public enemy no. 1, a traitor operating within the system, etc.) to the return of the original stability, we cannot overlook the fact that the resolution of the crisis postpones the problem to which it has unwittingly pointed, even though it appears to have ironed out the crisis (in this respect it is possibly close to myth as described by Levi-Strauss). When the perpetrator is revealed the scales fall from our eyes and the mystery is stripped from a person who is capable of murder. The restoration of order by means of the arrival of the law enables us to forget the difference between law and justice, and the liquidation of organised

---

467 Franz Kafka, "Wedding Preparations in the Country".

468 See Frederick Jackson Turner, *The Significance of the Frontier in American History* of 1893. The book begins by citing an official document from 1890: "Up to and including 1880 the country had a frontier of settlement, but at present the unsettled area has been so broken into by isolated bodies of settlement that there can hardly be said to be a frontier line." Penguin Books – Great Ideas, p. 1.

469 W. R. Burnet, *The Asphalt Jungle*, Knopf, New York, 1949 and *The Asphalt Jungle* directed by John Huston (MGM, 1950).

crime glosses over the fact that a desire for success ends inevitably in failure.

> At bottom, the gangster is doomed because he is under the obligation to succeed, not because the means he employs are unlawful. In the deeper layers of the modern consciousness, *all* means are unlawful, every attempt to succeed is an act of aggression, leaving one alone and guilty and defenceless among enemies: one is *punished* for success. This is our intolerable dilemma: that failure is a kind of death and success is evil and dangerous, is – ultimately – impossible. The effect of the gangster film is to embody this dilemma in the person of the gangster and resolve it by his death. The dilemma is resolved because it is *his* death, not ours. We are safe; for the moment, we can acquiesce in our failure, we can choose to fail.[470]

In short, lowbrow literature is covertly and unconsciously elliptical, unlike serious or highbrow literature.

If we wanted to corroborate and illustrate this difference, a single example would suffice. The event brackets the world, the context appears to be lost, and Europe as cultural formation can seem as though it has suddenly found itself in Africa. This is literally how things are in one of the African novels by Edgar Wallace *Sandi, the Kingmaker*, 1922. In this book, one Mr. Sanders resorts to machine gun to civilise ruthlessly the natives, whose status as such is evinced by their names: M'sufu, K'salugu M'popo, Kofalaba, etc. and the fact that they have a single word for the concepts "law" and "power", while the idea of justice is conveyed with a word that means "revenge".

> From each of the twelve districts of Rimi-Rimi you shall send me the best makers of huts and weavers of straw and thatchers of roof, and you shall

470 Robert Warshow, "Gangster as Tragic Hero", in: Robert Warshow, *The Immediate Experience. Movies, Comics, Theatre and Other Aspects of Popular Culture*, enlarged edition, Harvard UP, Harvard 2001, p. 103.

each contribute the straw and the wood I desire, for I am going to build a great Palace house in this space and here I and the king I make shall site down and give laws so that all may live comfortably."

"Lord," said one of the deputation in dismay, "We heard you were not staying with us and our hearts were glad."

"I am staying with you," said Sanders, without a smile, "and if your hearts are not glad, your backs will be sore."[471]

However, this is how Europe is represented in *Heart of Darkness* by Joseph Conrad (published serially in 1899). The continent is present in the figure of Kurtz, a product of Europe and the embodiment of its underbelly[472]. However, it is here, in a strange inversion, that Europe, supposedly the basis of universal meaning, becomes the other and strange. The way that Conrad presents the "event" is antithetical to Wallace: the outside was a world absorbed by reality. Furthermore, he is aware of the ellipticity of speech, which is unavoidable where reference must be made to "the heart of darkness":

The yarns of seamen have a direct simplicity, the whole meaning of which lies within the shell of a cracked nut. But Marlow was not typical (if his propensity to spin yarns be excepted), and to him the meaning of an episode was not inside like a kernel but outside, enveloping the tale which brought it out only as a glow brings out a haze, in the likeness of one of these misty halos that sometimes are made visible by the spectral illumination of moonshine.[473]

Kurtz's report for the International Society for the Suppression of Savage Customs is

471 Edgar Wallace, *Sandi, the King-maker*, Project Gutenberg Australia, 2009, unpaginated.
472 "All Europe contributed to the making of Kurtz; and by and by I learned that, most appropriately, the International Society for the Suppression of Savage Customs had entrusted him with the making of a report,for its future guidance." Joseph Conrad, *Heart of Darkness*, ed. with Introduction and Notes by Owen Knowles, Penguin Classics 2007, p. 61.
473 Ibid., p. 10.

very simple, and at the end of that moving appeal to every altruistic senti-
ment it blazed at you, luminous and terrifying, like a flash of lightning in
a serene sky: "Exterminate all the brutes."[474]

474 Ibid., p. 62.

47

Only one thing remained reachable, close and secure amid all losses: language. Yes, language: In spite of everything, it remained secure against loss. But it had to go through its own lack of answers, through terrifying silence, through the thousand darknesses of murderous speech. It went through. It gave me no words for what was happening, but went through it. Went through and could resurface, "enriched" by it all.[475]

The poems of Paul Celan are not only testimony but bear witness to testimony itself. This is true (not only) of *Niemand zeugt für den Zeugen*, i.e. the observation that there is nobody who could testify to the truth of what the witness says. Testimony is not a document. It is in fact incompatible with the imperative of security and demonstrability, since, as Derrida says, that which it is talking about "is linked to a singularity and to the experience of an idiomatic mark (...) It is elliptical."[476] And yet it has its own particular way of showing, and that is through indication.

We can "read" this poem, we can desire to read, cite, and re-cite it, while giving upon interpreting it, or at least on going over the limit beyond which interpretation encounters, at the same time, its possibility and its impossibility. What we have here is a compulsion to cite and re-cite, to repeat what we understand without completely understanding it, feeling at work in the economy of the ellipsis a power more powerful than that of meaning and perhaps even than that of truth, of the mask which would manifest itself *as* mask. The reciting compulsion, the "by heart" desire, stems from this limit to intelligibility or transparency of meaning.[477]

475 Paul Celan, Speech on the Occasion of Receiving the Literature Prize of the Free Hanseatic City of Bremen, in Paul Celan, *Collected Prose*, trans. Rosemarie Waldrop, Psychology Press, 2003, p. 34.
476 Jacques Derrida, *Poétique et politique du témoignage*, L'Herne, Paris 2005, p. 15.
477 Ibid., p. 16.

The poems of Paul Celan bear witness to testimony by virtue of their idiomaticity. This does not reside simply in German and its possibilities, nor simply in the fact that the language of "willing executioners" is obliged to become the bearer of the voice of their victims, but in what is another name for strategy: in their poetics.

> A poem can "bear witness" to a poetics. It can promise it, it can be a response to it, as to a testamentary promise. Indeed it must, it cannot not, do so. But not with the idea of applying a previously existing art of writing, or of referring to one as to a charter written somewhere else, or of obeying its laws like a transcendent authority, but rather by itself promising, in the act of its event, the foundation of a poetics. It would be a matter, then, of the poem "constituting its own poetics," as Krieger puts it, a poetics that must also, *through* its generality, become, invent, institute, offer for reading, in an exemplary way, signing it, at the same time sealing and unsealing it, the possibility of *this* poem.[478]

Since bearing witness is not synonymous with providing proof, it must appeal to faith. A unique experience is involved and thus no proxy may stand in for the witness. "Deep down, the witness knew then, as he does now, that his testimony would not be received. After all it deals with an event that sprang from the darket zone of man. Only those who experienced Auschwitz know what it was. Others will never know."[479] But is it not then necessary to take another step and to ask the question whether everything I tell the other is not bearing witness? If I tell you what I am thinking, I want you to believe me. And do I not always seek recourse in my speech to some strategy, some poetics? If testimony is irreducible to concepts, because it refers to a specific time and place, the I must work on the concept in order that it become expression (Adorno). Poetics is

---

478 Ibid., p. 8.
479 Elie Wiesel, *Night*, trans. Marion Wiesel, Hill and Wang, New York 2006, Preface to the new translation by Elie Wiesel, unpaginated.

an essential context that allows for an understanding of meaning. However, testimony does not accept meaning from elsewhere, but carries it within itself. It is a poetics specific to this and only this method of speech, this poem, this discourse. It is the inherent framework of every "inspection" (if we may take the liberty of using Husserl's term) of that to which speech refers, and simultaneously delays its complete presence. Ellipsis cannot be avoided, it may only be denied. The constative is contaminated by the performative: testimony belongs to the "dimension of performative interpretation, that is, of an interpretation that transforms the very thing it interprets"[480]. In this way "inspection" becomes a matter of responsibility – to ghosts.

This can be expressed in a way that pays its respects both to Levinas's motivations and Derrida's philosophy: the witness is the hostage of ghosts by which he is persecuted and to which he provides shelter thanks to his testimony:

> The witness is not reducible to the relationship that leads from an index to the indicated. That would make it a disclosure and a thematization. It is the bottomless passivity of responsibility, and thus, sincerity. It is the meaning of language, before language scatters into words, into themes equal to the words and dissimulating in the said the openness of the saying...[481]

The witness testifies to something that escapes him as soon as he submits his testimony. Hence trauma became the key to understanding the phenomenon of testimony and whence the poetics of elliptical discourse. In the poems of Paul Celan the ellipsis designates that which is crucial. The witness is guardian, heir, keeper of the legacy of that which was and disappeared.[482]

Phenomenology begins with the methodical exclusion of everything we know from elsewhere, all assumptions and, above all, the

480 Derrida, *Spectres*, p. 89. Jacques Derrida, *Specters of Marx*, p. 51.
481 Emmanuel Levinas, *Autrement qu'etre*, Martinus Nijhoff, Haag 1978, p. 192.
482 Cf. Derrida, *Poétique et politique du témoignage*, p. 28.

"general thesis of the world". It begins with *epoché* and reduction, with a procedure that Husserl calls *Einklammerung* or bracketing. However, that which is bracketed does not disappear completely. It is present, in brackets, but its operation is cancelled, suspended. Heidegger continues with this retaining elimination when he refers to the original or inaugural understanding of being, which was forgotten in the history of ontology (a kind of *Urstiftung* and *Rückfrage*, original foundation and retrospective questioning), with a strange graphic gesture: *Seyn* or "Beyng". This usage (again with its meaning slightly shifted) is taken over by Derrida, who generalises it as a method of designating undecidability or cross-contamination (*"Le dehors est le dedans"*[483]) as the presence of absence or as a sign of paleonymy (an old word used in a different way) or trace. Showing *sous rature*, under erasure. However, this graphic intervention then evokes the elliptical or a-thetic text (see Freud's *Beyond the Pleasure Principle*), the phenomenon of the gift or secrecy that is betrayed without being divulged. Or the presence of the voice in speech and the presence of the event borne witness to in testimony. A showing of that which escapes the phenomenon, *restance non-présente*.

It is necessary to retain the word (accept the legacy), in order that it be possible to show that which remains, *il resto*; to bequeath the outside to meaning and thus to be inside in relation to the outside. A method of return to the start, to the original establishment that becomes clear now, within a new context created by the response to the event.

When Derrida writes the essay "Ellipsis" in the margin of a book of poems by Edmond Jabès,[484] he summarises all of this and thus reaffirms at a distance Husserl's *Rückfrage*:

483 Derrida, *De la grammatologie*, p. 65 et seq.
484 Derrida, *Writing and Difference*, p. 295 et seq.

And Yukel said:

The circle is acknowledged. Break the curve. The route doubles the route.
The book consecrates the book.

The return to the book here announces the form of the eternal return. The return of the same does not alter itself – but does so absolutely – except by amounting to the same. Pure repetition, were it to change neither thing nor sign, carries with it an unlimited power of perversion and subversion. This repetition is writing because what disappears in it is the self-identity of the origin, the self-presence of so-called living speech. That is the centre.[485]

Erasure is paradigm, a necessary ellipticity and thinking that is only there where it happens, because it is looking for a way of thinking differently and thus exposes itself to its own erasure, by means of which it actualises itself again and again in order to be true to that which is on the point of arrival. Or to express the same idea more simply: the irruption of reality into the world.

It might seem as though this speech on showing that which does not show itself but which is not entirely absent is simply another in a sequence of sophisticated speculations begot by postmodernism. However, it has a distinguished predecessor in modernism. For instance, take the well known poem by Charles Baudelaire "A une passante":

The deafening road around me roared.
Tall, slim, in deep mourning, making majestic grief,
A woman passed, lifting and swinging
With a pompous gesture the ornamental hem of her garment.

Swift and noble, with statuesque limb.
As for me, I drank, twitching like an old roué,
From her eye, livid sky where the hurricane is born,
The softness that fascinates and the pleasure that kills.

---

485 Ibid., p. 296.

A gleam... then night: O fleeting beauty,
Your glance has given me sudden rebirth,
Shall I see you again only in eternity?

Somewhere else, very far from here! Too late! Perhaps never!
For I do not know where you flee, nor you where I am going,
O you whom I would have loved, O you who knew it![486]

This is a clinically accurate description of an encounter with something that shows itself without unveiling itself. It is this resistance to that which escapes in its disappearance that is a sui generis phenomenon. The unattainability of that which left a trace of itself in this encounter resides in the fact that that which could have happened never happened and never will happen, even though in the ephemeral moment of the encounter (*éclat*) it nevertheless somehow (under erasure) shows itself. The limits of this "noema" from the order of secrecy, *secretum*, is expressed quite clearly: it will be fully present in eternity.

In his essay *On Some Motifs in Baudelaire* Walter Benjamin associates this poem with the idea of the flâneur, who wanders the city aimlessly, watching the passersby:

In a widow's veil, mysteriously and mutely borne along by the crowd, an unknown woman comes into the poet's field of vision. What this sonnet communicates is simply this: Far from experiencing the crowd as an opposed, antagonistic element, this very crowd brings to the city dweller the figure that fascinates. The delight of the urban poet is love – not at first sight, but at last sight. It is an eternal farewell which coincides in the poem with the moment of enchantment. (*Es ist ein Abschied für ewig, der im Gedicht mit dem Augenblick der Berückung zusammenfällt*).[487]

---

486 Trans. Geoffrey Wagner.
487 Walter Benjamin, "On Some Motifs in Baudelaire", in: *Illuminations: Essays and Reflections*, trans. Harry Zohn, Schocken Books, New York 1968, p. 168.

If we strip away from Baudelaire's definition of the modern era the Christian connotations of "ephemerality" and cleave purely to this image of a brief encounter, we are in the midst of what is termed postmodern philosophy, a transformed discourse in which emphasis is placed on the asymmetrical relationship with the other (Levinas), the relationship with unrealised justice (Derrida), i.e. a relationship respecting difference, the movement of difference as the meaning of temporality. There is nothing that would be compatible with the certainty and evidence according to the rules of a cognitive, identifying discourse, a relationship heterogeneous in respect of the logic of consciousness, intentionality and representation. This is associated with the fact that in a privileged way appearance is not showing in the sense of Husserlian phenomenology, but withdrawal (*Entzug*) in the sense that Dieter Mersch uses this word, where withdrawal or escape (*Entziehen*) he characterises (with the aid of "bracketing") as an event: "(It) shows (itself) – (it) offers (itself) as a 'gift' of original otherness". Mersch goes on to remind us that "perception (…) is not cognition, differentiation, designation or representation, but above all answering."[488]

Thinking after the Holocaust discovers traces of another project of modernism in modernism itself. It discovers the very phenomenon of the trace, the trace as phenomenon. However, the trace is no longer a fleeting encounter with a promise of happiness, but the ash of the concentration camps: *dein aschenes Haar Sulamith,* "your ashen hair Sulamith."

---

488 Dieter Mersch, *Ereignis und Aura. Untersuchungen zu einer Ästhetik des Performativen.* Suhrkamp, Frankfurt a. M. 2002, pp. 50 and 46.

48

The Holocaust is an unimaginable and unrepresentable event. Yes, if the philosophical discourse, part of which is a phenomenology consisting of intuition, is not transformed in such a way that, in addition to intuition, it respects another method of showing, i.e. glimpsing.

In the summer of 1944, the Polish resistance smuggled a camera into Auschwitz intended for members of the *Sonderkommando*, i.e. those prisoners whose job was to service the crematorium, look after the operations of the gas chambers, and liquidate any trace of the Holocaust. They knew that as witnesses they stood no chance of surviving. When new members took the place of old, their first job was to bury the bodies of their shot predecessors. Those who knew what was taking place in the camp tried to preserve their testimony, and since escape was out of the question, they buried their journals, reports and other documents they had gathered in the ground. Shortly after the liberation of the camp the manuscripts of three of them (Haïm Herman, Zelman Gradowski and Leib Langfus) were discovered, and later of another two (Salmen Lewental in 1961 and 1962 and Marcel Nadsari in October 1980.)[489] As soon as they obtained a camera, they availed themselves of the fact that the roof of one of the crematoria was being repaired and managed to take four photos of it. They shot the liquidation of corpses and the path of prisoners to the gas chamber from the alley between the buildings. As Didi-Huberman says, these photos are more rare than all possible artworks, because they were taken in a world that was attempting to make them impossible.[490] However, in this case we must correct the claim of unimaginability, all the more so since calling this event

---

[489] An edition of these "Auschwitz Scrolls" was published in *Revue d'histoire de la Shoah. Le monde juif* in a special issue "Des voix sous les cendres. Manuscrits des *Sonderkommando* d'Auschwitz", (no. 171, 2001) care of P. Mesnard and C. Saletti.

[490] Georges Didi-Huberman, *Images in Spite of All*, trans. Shane B. Lillis, The University of Chicago Press, Chicago 2012, p. 20.

unrespresentable and inexplicable risks shifting it into the realm of mystical adoration. In addition, even a non-problematising understanding of the image needs correcting too.

> Photography, from this angle, shows a particular ability – illustrated by certain well-or lesser-known examples – to curb the fiercest will to obliterate. (...) A single look at this *remnant of images*, or erratic corpus of *images in spite of all*, is enough to sense that Auschwitz can no longer be spoken of in those absolute terms – generally well intentioned, apparently philosophical, but actually lazy – "unsayable" and "unimaginable". The four photographs taken in August 1944 by the members of the *Sonderkommando* address the unimaginable with which the Shoah is so often credited today – and this is the second period of the unimaginable: tragically, the Shoah refutes it. Auschwitz has been called *unthinkable*. But Hannah Arendt has shown that it is precisely where thought falters that we ought to persist in our thought or, rather, give it a new turn. So, if we say that Auschwitz exceeds any existing juridical thought, any notion of fault or of justice, then political science and law must be rethought entirely. And if we believe that Auschwitz exceeds all existing political thought, even anthropology, then we must rethink the very foundations of the human sciences as such.[491]

The book *Images in Spite of All* by Georges Didi-Huberman, which is devoted to these four photographs, inevitably broadens out into a consideration of the relationship between image and imagination, image and text, image and archive. The starting point is the proposition that there is no one image, no image is complete, or as Godard might say: though there are two images here, there is already a third. The images change. If they encounter other images or texts, each can be the commencement of many such series in which they intensify. This encounter is the work of the imagination. If we want to know, we must imagine. Knowledge consists of assembly,

491 Ibid., p. 23 and 25.

i.e. an operation evoking resonance and difference. A dimension of time other than chronology corresponds to assembly, a different dimension in which the contemporaneity of the non-contemporary predominates, i.e. Walter Benjamin's *Jetzt-Zeit*, in which every moment may become filled if it encounters something past that expects it. The singularity of the unique is preserved in this time because the aim of the assembly is not the overlapping coverage of elements, eliminating the difference between the similar, but a constellation of conflicts. That which remains flashes in the resulting interstices, gaps or differences. This *in spite of an impossibility* that is unpronounceable, unimaginable, unrepresentable. The relationship to the non-identical via irreducible difference. Showing despite its impossibility.

> The very existence and the possibility of such testimony – its *enunciation in spite of all* – refute the grand idea, the closed notion, of an *unsayable* Auschwitz. It is to the very core of speech that testimony invites us, compelling us to work there. It is harsh work, since what it concerns is a description of death at work, with the inarticulate cries and the silences that are implied.[492]

As tragic experience the unrepresentable requires its antithesis, i.e. an act in which we represent it *in spite of all*. This is why the Nazis wanted their crime to be unrepresentable. This is why the members of the *Sonderkommando* decided to take these four photographs of extermination. And this is why, though the words of the witnesses paralyse our ability to image what they depict, *in spite of all* we must attempt to understand better what their testimony is saying.

In his essay *Glimpses/Aperçues* Didi-Huberman then suggests how to understand this method of appearing in interstices: the thing

---

492 Ibid., p. 25.

that appears before it disappears leaves something like the trace of a question, memory or desire. To glimpse means to look in passing. He reminds us of Baudelaire's sonnet *To a Passerby* and concludes with a quote from a book by Anne-Lise Stern, who survived Auschwitz and incorporated this experience into her psychoanalytical practice:

> The other memory: also on the way back from work, an uncovered truck crosses our path, filled with more or less naked men, already reduced to nothing. The eyes of one of those men met mine. We were still fresh, our convoy had not quite all been shaved. He still had a fine look in his eyes. The look of a man who knew that he was looking at a woman for the last time in his life. We stayed looking into each other's eye for as long as possible, holding each other's gaze. Then the truck disappeared into the birch wood, in the direction of crematorium.[493]

---

[493] Anne-Lise Stern, *Le Savoir-déporté. Camps, histoire, psychanalyse*, Seuil, Paris 2004, p. 38, quoted in: Georges Didi-Huberman, "Glimpses. Between Appearance and Disappearance", *Zeitschrift für Medien- und Kulturforschung*, 7/1/2016, Felix Meiner Verlag, Hamburg 2016, p. 124.

49

Auschwitz did not take place so that elegant philosophical treatises might be written about it.

Bibliography

A

Adorno, Theodor W., Horkheimer, Max, *Dialectic of Enlightenment*, trans. E.F.N. Jephcott, Stanford UP, Stanford 2002.

Adorno, Theodor W., *Einführung in die Dialektik* (1958), in: *Nachgelassene Schriften*, IV, *Vorlesungen*, 2, ed. Ch. Ziermann, Suhrkamp, Frankfurt am Main 2010.

Adorno, Theodor W., *Gesammelte Schriften*, I–XX, ed. Rolf Tiedemann, Suhrkamp, Frankfurt am Main 1970.

Adorno, Theodor W., *Metaphysik. Begriff und Probleme* (1965), in: *Nachgelassene Schriften*, IV, *Vorlesungen*, 14, ed. Rolf Tiedemann, Suhrkamp, Frankfurt am Main 2006.

Adorno, Theodor W., *Minima Moralia. Reflections from Damaged Life*, trans. E.F.N. Jephcott, Verso, London, New York 2005.

Adorno, Theodor W., *Probleme der Moralphilosophie* (1963), in: *Nachgelassene Schriften*, IV, *Vorlesungen*, 10, ed. Thomas Schröder, Suhrkamp, Frankfurt am Main 1996.

Adorno, Theodor W., *Ontologie und Dialektik* (1960/61), in: *Nachgelassene Schriften*, IV, *Vorlesungen*, 7, ed. Rolf Tiedemann, Suhrkamp, Frankfurt am Main 2008.

Adorno, Theodor W., *Vorlesung über Negative Dialektik. Fragmente zur Vorlesung 1965/66*, in: *Nachgelassene Schriften*, IV, *Vorlesungen*, 16, ed. Rolf Tiedemann, Suhrkamp, Frankfurt am Main 2003.

Agamben, Giorgio, *The Comming Community*, University of Minnesota Press, Minneapolis 1993.

Agamben, Giorgio, *Homo Sacer: Sovereign Power and Bare Life*, trans. Daniel Heller-Roazen, Stanford UP, Stanford 1998.

Agamben, Giorgio, *Quel che resta di Auschwitz. L'archivio e il testimone. Homo sacer*, III, Bollati Boringhieri, Torino 1998.

Agamben, Giorgio, *Potentialities. Collected Essays in Philosophy*, ed. Daniel Heller-Roazen, Stanford University Press, Stanford 1999.

Agamben, Giorgio, *Il tempo che resta. Un commento alla «Lettera ai romani»*, Bollati Boringhieri, Torino 2000.

Agamben, Giorgio, *State of Exception. Homo sacer*, II, University of Chicago Press, Chicago, London, 2005.

Agamben, Giorgio, *Language and Death: The Place of Negativity*, University of Minnesota Press, Minneapolis, Oxford 2006.

Agamben, Giorgio, *Infancy and History. On the Destruction of Experience*, Verso, London, New York 2007.

Agamben, Giorgio, *Signatura rerum. Sur la méthode*, Vrin, Paris 2008.

Améry, Jean, *At the Mind's Limits*, trans. Sidney Rosenfeld and Stella P. Rosenfeld, Indiana University Press, Bloomington 1980.

Aliez, Eric (ed.), *Gilles Deleuze. Une vie philosophique*, Institut Synthélabo, Paris 1998.

Aliez, Eric et al. (ed.), *Gilles Deleuze. Immanence et vie*, Qudrige, P.U.F., Paris 1998.

Al-Saji, Alia, "The Memory of Another Past: Bergson, Deleuze and a New Theory of Time", *Continental Philosophy Review* 37, 2005, pp. 203–39.

Arendt, Hannah, "The Achievement of Hermann Broch", *Kenyon Review* 11 (3), 1949, pp. 476–83.

Attridge, Derek, "Derrida and the Questioning of Literature", in: Jacques Derrida, *Acts of Literature*, ed. Derek Attridge, Routledge, New York, London 1992.

Attridge, Derek, *The Singularity of Literature*, Routledge, New York, London 2004.

Baring, Edward, *Young Derrida and French Philosophy 1945-1968*, Cambridge UP, Cambridge 2011.

Barnouw, Dagmar, "Vielschichtige Oberflächen", in: Frank Grunert, Dorothee Kimmlich (ed.), *Denken durch die Dinge. Siegfried Kracauer im Kontext*, Wilhelm Fink Verlag, München 2009.

Bates, David, "Crisis Between the Wars: Derrida and the Origin of Undecidability", *Representations* 90 (1), 2005, pp. 1–27.

Beauvoir, Simone de, *Pour une morale de l'ambiguïté*, Gallimard, Paris 1947.

Bell, David F., "Technologies of Speed, Technologies of Crime", *Yale French Studies* 108 (Crime Fictions), 2005, pp. 8–19.

Belpoliti, Marco (ed.), *Hovory s Primo Levim 1963-1987*, trans. Drahoslava Janderová, Paseka, Praha, Litomyšl, 2003.

Benjamin, Walter, *Das Passagen-Werk*, I–II, ed. Rolf Tiedemann, Suhrkamp, Frankfurt 1982 (*GS* V/1–2).

Benjamin, Walter, *Einbahnstrasse. Werke und Nachlass. Kritische Gesamtausgabe*, VIII, ed. Detlev Schötker in coop. with Stefen Haug, Suhrkamp, Frankfurt am Main 2009.

Benjamin, Walter, *Gesammelte Schriften* (GS), ed. Rolf Tiedemann, Hermann Schweppenhäuser, I–VII, Suhrkamp, Frankfurt am Main 1972–1989.

Benjamin, Walter, *Über den Begriff der Geschichte. Werke und Nachlass. Kritische Gesamtausgabe*, XIX, ed. Gérard Raulet, Suhrkamp, Frankfurt am Main 2010.

Bennington, Geoffrey, "Is It Time?", in: Heidrun Friese (ed.), *The Moment. Time and Rupture in Modern Thought*, Liverpool University Press, Liverpool 2001.

Bennington, Geoffrey, *Lyotard: Writing the Event*, Manchester UP, Columbia UP, New York 1988.

Benveniste, Emile, *Problèmes de linguistique générale* I, Gallimard, Paris 1966.

Bernet, Rudolf, "Die ungegenwärtige Gegenwart. Anwesenheit und Abwesenheit in Husserls Analyse des Zeitbewusstseins", in: Ernst Wolfgang Orth (ed.), *Zeit und Zeitlichkeit bei Husserl und Heidegger* (Phänomenologische Forschungen 14), Verlag Karl Alber, Freiburg, München 1983, pp. 16–57.

Bernet, Rudolf, "Differenz und Anwesenheit. Derridas und Husserls Phänomenologie der Sprache, der Zeit, der Geschichte, der wissenschaftlichen Rationalität", in: Ernst Wolfgang Orth (ed.), *Studien zur neueren französischen Phänomenologie*, Verlag Karl Alber, Freiburg, München 1986.

Bernet, Rudolf, "Derrida and His Master's Voice", in: W. R. McKenna, J. C. Evans (ed.), *Derrida and Phenomenology*, Kluwer Academic Publishers 1995, pp. 1–21.

Bernet, Rudolf, "Husserl's New Phenomenology of Time Consciousness in the Bernau Manuscripts", in: D. Lohman, I. Yamaguchi (ed.), *On Time - New Contributions to the Husserlian Phenomenology of Time* (Phaenomenologica 197), Springer Science-Business Media 2010.

Bernet, Rudolf, Kern, Iso, Marbach, Eduard, *Edmund Husserl: Darstellung seines Denkens*, Felix Meiner Verlag, Hamburg 1996.

Biceaga, Victor, *The Concept of Passivity in Husserl's Phenomenology* (Contributions to Phenomenology 60), Springer, Dordrecht, Heidelberg, London, New York 2010.

Bidney, David, "The Concept of Cultural Crisis", *American Anthropologist, New Series* 48 (4), 1946, pp. 534–52.

Blanchot, Maurice, *La Part du feu*, Gallimard, Paris 1949.

Blanchot, Maurice, *Celui qui ne m'accompagnait pas*, Gallimard, Paris 1953.

Blanchot, Maurice, *Le livre à venir*, Gallimard, Paris 1959.

Blanchot, Maurice, *L'Attente L'Oubli*, Gallimard, Paris 1962.

Blanchot, Maurice, *L'Entretien infini*, Gallimard, Paris 1969.

Blanchot, Maurice, *L'Ecriture du désastre*, Gallimard, Paris 1980.

Blanchot, Maurice, *The Space of Literature*, trans. Ann Smock, University of Nebraska Press, Lincoln, London 1982.

Blom, Philipp, *Die zerrissenen Jahre. 1918-1938*, Carl Hanser Verlag, München 2014.

Boltanski, Luc, *Énigmes et complots. Une enquête à propos d'enquêtes*, Gallimard, Paris 2012.

Borowski, Tadeusz, *Wybor Opowiadan*, PIW, Warszawa 1959.

Brandlmeier, Thomas, *Fantômas. Beiträge zur Panik des 20. Jahrhunderts*, Verbrecher Verlag, Berlin 2007.

Bratu Hansen, Miriam, *Cinema and Experience. Siegfried Kracauer, Walter Benjamin and Theodor W. Adorno*. University of California Press, Berkeley, Los Angeles, London 2012.

Brough, John B., "Notes on the absolute Time-Constituting Flow of Consciousness", in: D. Lohman – I. Yamaguchi (ed.), *On Time – New Contributions to the Husserlian Phenomenology of Time* (Phaenomenologica 197), Springer Science-Business Media 2010, pp. 21–49.

Callarco, Mathew, DeCaroli, Steven (ed.), *Giorgio Agamben. Sovereignity and Life*, Stanford University Press, Stanford 2007.

Cattaruzza, Marina, *Storia della Shoah. La crisi dell'Europa, lo sterminio degli Ebrei e la memoria del XX secolo*, I–IV, UTET, Torino 2005–2006 (contrib. by Marina Cattaruzza, Marcello Flores, Simon Levis Sullam and Enzo Traverso).

Celan, Paul, *Meridian. Endfassung - Entwürfe - Materialien* (Werke. Tübinger Ausgabe), ed. Bernhard Böschenstein, Heino Schmull, Suhrkamp, Frankfurt am Main 1999.

Clarke, I. F., "Future-War Fiction: The First Main Phase, 1871–1900", *Science Fiction Studies* 24 (3), 1997, pp. 387–412.

Clarke, I. F., "Forecast of Warfare in Fiction 1803–1914", *Comparative Studies in Society and History* 10 (1), 1967, pp. 1–25.

Clemens, Justin, Heron, Nicolas, Murray, Alex (ed.), *The Work of Giorgio Agamben. Law, Literature, Life*, Edinburgh University Press, Edinburgh 2008.

Conrad, Mark T. (ed.), *The Philosophy of Film Noir*, University Press of Kentucky 2006.

Cornell, Drucilla, "Post-structuralism, the Ethical Relation and the Law", *Cardozo Law Review* 9, 1988, pp. 587–628.

Cornell, Drucilla, *The Philosophy of the Limit*, Routledge, New York, London 1992.

Crépon, Marc, Worms, Frédéric (ed.), *Derrida, la tradition de la philosophie*, Editions Galilée, Paris 2008.

Critchley, Simon, "Il y a - Holding Levinas's Hand to Blanchot's Fire", in: C. B. Gill (ed.), *Maurice Blanchot: The Demand of Writing*, Routledge, London 1996, pp. 108–22.

Critchley, Simon, Bernasconi, Robert (ed.), *The Cambridge Companion to Levinas*, Cambridge UP, Cambridge 2004.

Critchley, Simon, *The Ethics of Deconstruction. Derrida and Levinas*, 2. ed., Edinburgh UP, Edinburgh 1999.

Critchley, Simon, "Who Speaks in the Work of Samuel Beckett?", *Yale French Studies* 93, The Place of Maurice Blanchot, 1998, pp. 114–30.

Delbo, Charlotte, *Auschwitz et après I. Aucun de nous ne reviendra*, Ed. de Minuit, Paris 1970.

Delbo, Charlotte, *Auschwitz et après. Une connaissance inutile*, Ed. de Minuit, Paris 1970.

Delbo, Charlotte, *Auschwitz et après. Mesure de nos jours*, Ed. de Minuit, Paris 1971.

DeRoo, Neal, *Futurity in Phenomenology. Promise and Method in Husserl, Levinas and Derrida*, Fordham University Press, New York 2013.

Derrida, Jacques, "Introduction", in: E. Husserl, *L'Origine de la géométrie*, PUF, Paris 1962.

Derrida, Jacques, *L'écriture et la différence*, Ed. du Seuil, Paris 1967.

Derrida, Jacques, *De la grammatologie*, Ed. de Minuit, Paris 1967.

Derrida, Jacques, *La voix et le phénomène*, P.U.F., Paris 1967.

Derrida, Jacques, *Marges - de la philosophie*, Ed. de Minuit, Paris 1972.

Derrida, Jacques, *La Carte postale. De Socrate à Freud et au-delà*, Flammarion, Paris 1980.

Derrida, Jacques, *Parages*, Galilée, Paris 1986.

Derrida, Jacques, *Psyché. Inventions de l'autre*, Galilée, Paris 1987.

Derrida, Jacques, *Le problème de la genèse dans la philosophie de Husserl*, P.U.F., Paris 1990.

Derrida, Jacques, *L'autre cap suivi de La Démocratie ajournée*, Ed. de Minuit, Paris 1991.

Derrida, Jacques, *Donner le temps*, I, *La fausse monaie*. Galilée, Paris 1991.

Derrida, Jacques, *Acts of Literature*, ed. Derek Attridge, Routledge, New York, London 1992.

Derrida, Jacques, *Passions*, Galilée, Paris 1993.

Derrida, Jacques, *Spectres de Marx*, Galilée, Paris 1993.

Derrida, Jacques, *Le toucher – Jean Luc Nancy*, Galilée, Paris 1998.

Derrida, Jacques, *De quoi demain... Dialogue*, Libraire Arthème Fayard et Galilée, Paris 2001.

Derrida, Jacques, *Násilí a metafyzika*, trans. Jiří Pechar et al., FILOSOFIA, Praha 2002.

Derrida, Jacques, *Copy, Archive, Signature. A Conversation on Photography*, ed. Gerhard Richter, Stanford UP, Stanford 2010.

Derrida, Jacques, Ferraris, Maurizio, *A Taste for the Secret*, trans. Giacomo Donis, Polity Press, Cambridge 2002.

Desanti, Jean-Touissant, *Réflexions sur le temps. Conversations avec Dominique-Antoine Grisoni*, Bernard Grasset, Paris 1992.

Dickos, Andrew, *Street With No Name. A History of the Classic American Film Noir*, 2. ed. (2002), University Press of Kentucky 2013.

Didi-Huberman, Georges, *Devant l'image. Question posée aux fins d'une histoire de l'art*, Ed. de Minuit, Paris 1990.

Didi-Huberman, Georges, *Images malgré tout*, Ed. de Minuit, Paris 2003.

Dimendberg, Edward, *Film Noir and the Spaces of Modernity*, Harvard UP, Cambridge (MA) 2004.

Diner, Dan, *Beyond the Conceivable. Studies on Germany, Nazism, and the Holocaust*, University of California Press, Berkeley, Los Angeles, London 2000.

De La Durantaye, Leland, *Giorgio Agamben. A Critical Introduction*, Stanford University Press, Stanford 2009.

Düttmann, Alexander Garcia, *The Gift of Language. Memory and Promise in Adorno, Benjamin, Heidegger and Rosenzweig*, trans. A. Lyons, The Athlone Press, London 2000.

Düttmann, Alexander Garcia, *So ist es. Ein philosophischer Kommentar zu Adornos "Minima Moralia"*, Suhrkamp, Frankfurt am Main 2004.

Eisenzweig, Uri, "Violence Untold: The Birth of a Modern Fascination", *Yale French Studies* 108 (Crime Fictions), 2005, pp. 20–35.

Fall, Susanne, "Terezín, ráj mezi lágry", trans. Věra Koubová, *Revolver Revue* 2015.

"Fantômas", *Europe, Revue littéraire mensuelle*, Juin–Julliet 1979.

Felman, Shoshana, Laub, Dori, *Testimony. Crisis of Witnessing in Literature, Psychoanalysis, and History*, Routledge, London, New York 1992.

Ferraris, Maurizio, "The Aporia of the Instant in Derrida's Reading of Husserl", in: *The Moment. Time and Rupture in Modern Thought*, ed. Heidrun Friese, Liverpool University Press, Liverpool 2001.

Fornabai, Nanette L., "Criminal Factors: Fantômas, Anthropometrics, and the Numerical Fictions of Modern Criminal Identity", *Yale French Studies* 108 (Crime Fictions), 2005, pp. 60–73.

Foucault, Michel, *Les anormaux. Cours au Collège de France (1974-1975)*, Gallimard, Seuil, Paris 1999.

Foucault, Michel, *La Société punitive. Cours au Collège de France (1972-1973)*, Gallimard, Seuil, Paris 2013.

Foucault, Michel, *Vůle k vědění. Dějiny sexuality*, I, trans. Čestmír Pelikán, Herrmann a synové, Praha 1999.

Foucault, Michel, *Dits et écrits*, I, Gallimard, Paris 2001.

Foucault, Michel, *Zrození biopolitiky. Kurz na Collège de France (1978-1979)*, trans. Petr Horák, Centrum pro studium demokracie a kultury, Brno 2009.

Foucault, Michel, *Society Must Be Defended. Lectures at the Collège de France (1975-1976)*, trans. David Macey, Picador, New York.

Freud, Sigmund, *Beyond the Pleasure Principle*, W.W. Norton and Company (Standard Edition), New York, London 1990.

Friedländer, Saul, *The Years of Extermination: Nazi Germany and the Jews*, HarperCollins 2007.

Friedler, Eric, Siebert, Barbara, Kilian, Andreas, *Svědkové z továrny na smrt. Historie a svědectví židovského sonderkommanda v Osvětimi*, trans. Vladimír Čadský, Rypka Publishers 2007.

Gadamer, Hans-Georg, *Pravda a metoda*, I, *Nárys filosofické hermeneutiky*, trans. David Mik, Triáda, Praha 2010.

Gasché, Rodolphe, "European Memories: Jan Patočka and Jacques Derrida on Responsibility", *Critical Inquiry* 33 (2), 2007, pp. 291–311.

Gibbs, Robert, *Correlations in Rosenzweig und Levinas*, Princeton University Press, Princeton 1992.

Girard, René, *Des choses cachées depuis la fondation du monde*, Grasset, Paris 1978.

Girard, René, *Lež romantismu a pravda románu*, Dauphin, Praha 1998.

Goldhagen, Daniel Johan, *Hitler's Willing Executioners. Ordinary Germans and the Holocaust*, Alfred Knopf, New York 1996.

Glazar, Richard, *Treblinka, slovo jak z dětské říkanky*, G plus G, Praha 2012.

Gunning, Tom, "Lynx-Eyed Detectives and Shadow Bandits: Visuality and Eclipse in French Detective Stories and Films Before WW I", *Yale French Studies* 108 (Crime Fictions), 2005, pp. 74–88.

Haase, Ulrich, Large, William, *Maurice Blanchot*, Routledge, London, New York 2001.

Haller, Mark H., "Urban Crime and Criminal Justice: The Chicago Cae", *Journal of American History* 57 (3), 1970, pp. 619–635.

Hanson, Jeffrey, "Returning (to) the Gift of Death: Violence and History in Derrida and Levinas", *International Journal for Philosophy of Religion* 67 (1), 2010, pp. 1–15.

Hatley, James, *Suffering Witness. The Quandary of Responsibility after the Irreparable*, State University of New York Press, Albany 2000.

Heidegger, Martin, *Die Grundprobleme der Phänomenologie* (Gesamtausgabe 2/24), Vittorio Klostermann, Frankfurt am Main 1975.

Hejdánek, Ladislav, *Nepředmětnost v myšlení a ve skutečnosti*, OIKOYMENH, Praha 1997.

Hilberg, Raul, *The Destruction of the European Jews*, I–III, Holmes & Meier, New York, London 1985.

Hillis Miller, J., "Derrida's Destinerrance", *MLN* 121 (4), French Issue, 2006, pp. 893–910.

Hobbes, Thomas, *Leviathan*, trans. Karel Berka, Jiří Chotaš, Zdeněk Masopust, Marina Barabas, OIKOYMENH, Praha 2009.

Hodge, Joanna, *Derrida On Time*, Routledge, New York, London 2007.

Hollenstein, Elmar, *Phänomenologie der Assoziation. Zu Struktur und Funktion eines Grundprinzips der passiven Genesis bei E. Husserl* (Phaenomenologica 44), Martinus Nijhoff, Den Haag 1972.

Holton, Robert J., "The Idea of Crisis in Modern Society", *British Journal of Sociology* 38 (4), 1987, pp. 502–20.

Hume, Robert D., "Gothic versus Romantic: A Revaluation of the Gothic Novel", *PMLA* 84 (2), 1969, pp. 282–290.

Husserl, Edmund, *Analysen zur pasiven Synthesis. Aus Vorlesungen und Forschungsmanuskripten 1918-1926*, ed. Margot Fleischer, Martinus Nijhoff, Haag 1965.

Husserl, Edmund, *Zur Phänomenologie des inneren Zeitbewusstseins* (1893–1917), ed. Rudolf Boehm (Hua 20), Martinus Nijhoff, Haag 1966.

Husserl, Edmund, *The Crisis of European Sciences and Transcendental Phenomenology: An Introduction to Phenomenological philosophy*, trans. David Carr, Northwestern University Press, Evanston 1970 (Hua 6, 1954).

Husserl, Edmund, *Erfahrung und Urteil* (1939), Felix Meiner Verlag, Hamburg 1985.

Husserl, Edmund, *Aufsätze und Vorträge* (Hua 27), Kluwer Academic Publishers, Dordrecht, Boston, London 1989.

Husserl, Edmund, *Die 'Bernauer Manuskripte' über das Zeitbewußtsein* (1917/18; Hua 33), ed. Rudolf Bernet, Dieter Lohmar, Kluwer Academic Publishers, Dordrecht 2001.

Husserl, Edmund, *Natur und Geist: Vorlesungen Sommersemester 1927* (Hua 32), ed. Michael Weiler, Kluwer Academic Publishers, Dordrecht 2001.

Husserl, Edmund, *Idea fenomenologie. Pět přednášek*, trans. Miroslav Petříček, OIKOYMENH, Praha 2001 (*Die Idee der Phänomenologie*, Hua 2, 1950).

Husserl, Edmund, *Einführung in die Phänomenologie der Erkenntnis* (1909), ed. Elisabeth Schuhmann (Hua 7), Springer Verlag 2005.

Husserl, Edmund, *Späte Texte über Zeitkonstitution (1929-1934). Die C-Manuskripte*, ed. Dieter Lohmar (Hua Materialienband 8), Springer, New York 2006.

Irwin, John T., *Unless the Threat of Death Is Behind Them. Hard-boiled Fiction and Film noir*, John Hopkins UP, Baltimore 2006.

Iyer, Lars, "Literary Communism. Blanchot's Conversations with Bataille and Levinas", *Symposium, Journal of the Canadian Society for Hermeneutics and Postmodern Thought* 6 (1), 2002, pp. 45–62.

Jarvis, Simon, *Adorno. A Critical Introduction*, Routledge, New York 1998.

Kalifa, Dominique, "Criminal Investigations at the Fin-de-siècle", *Yale French Studies* 108 (Crime Fictions), 2005, pp. 36–47.

Katz, Claire, Trout, Lara, *Emmanuel Levinas. Critical Assessments of Leading Philosophers*, I, Routledge, London, New York 2005.

Klemperer, Victor, *LTI. Notizbuch eines Philologen*, Reclam, Leipzig 1975.

Klemperer, Victor, *Ich will Zeugnis ablegen bis zum letzten. Tagebücher 1933-1945*, I–VIII, Aufbau, Berlin 1999.

Knight, Stephen, *Crime Fiction 1800-2000. Detection, Death, Diversity*, Palgrave, Macmillan 2004.

Kracauer, Siegfried, *Die Angestellten*, Suhrkamp, Frankfurt am Main 1971.

Kracauer, Siegfried, *Der Detektiv-Roman. Ein philosophischer Traktat*, Suhrkamp, Frankfurt am Main 1979.

Kracauer, Siegfried, *Geschichte - Vor den letzten Dingen*, in: *Siegfried Kracauer Werke*, IV, ed. Ingrid Belke, Suhrkamp, Frankfurt am Main 2009.

Krämer, Sybille, *Medium, Bote, Übertragung. Kleine Metaphysik der Medialität*, Suhrkamp, Frankfurt am Main 2008.

Kraus, Ota, Kulka, Erich, *Noc a mlha*, Naše Vojsko-SPB, Praha 1958.

Lèbre, Jérôme, *La justice sans condition*, Michalon Editeur, Paris 2013.

Levi, Primo, *If This Is a Man*, trans. Stuart Woolf, Orion Press, New York 1959.

Levi, Primo, *If Not Now, When?* Penguin Books 2000.

Levi, Primo, *The Drowned and the Saved*, trans. Raymond Rosenthal, Abacus, London 2013.

Levi, Primo, *Prvky života*, trans. Hana Benešová, Odeon, Praha 1981.

Levinas, Emmanuel, *De l'évasion*, Montpellier, Fata Morgana, Paris 1962 (1935).

Levinas, Emmanuel, "On the Trail of the Other", *Philosophy Today*, 10. 1. 1966.

Levinas, Emmanuel, *Autrement qu'être ou au-delà de l'essence*, Martinus Nijhoff, Haag 1978.

Levinas, Emmanuel, *Existence and Existents*, trans. Alphonso Lingis, Martinus Nijhoff, Haag 1978.

Levinas, Emmanuel, *Collected Philosophical Papers*, trans. Alphonso Lingis, Martinus Nijhoff, Haag 1987.

Levinas, Emmanuel, *A l'heure des nations*, Ed. de Minuit, Paris 1988.

Levinas, Emmanuel, *Entre nous. Essai sur le penser-à-l'autre*, Figures, Grasset, Paris 1991.

Emmanuel Levinas, *Otherwise Than Being or Beyond the Essence*, trans. Alphonso Lingis, Kluwer Academic Publishers, Dordrecht 1991.

Levinas, Emmanuel, *Alterité et transcendence*, Fata Morgana, Paris 1995.

Levinas, Emmanuel, *Difficult Freedom*, trans. Seán Hand, Johns Hopkins University Press, Baltimore 1997.

Levinas, Emmanuel, *Totalita a nekonečno*, trans. Miroslav Petříček and Jan Sokol, OIKOYMENH, Praha 1997.

(Levinas, Emmanuel, *Totalité et Infini. Essai sur l'exteriorité*. Martinus Nijhoff, Haag 1961).

Levinas, Emmanuel, *Discovering Existence with Husserl*, trans. Richard A. Cohen and Michael B. Smith, Northwestern UP, Evanston, Illinois 2000.

Levinas, Emmanuel, *Etika a nekonečno*, trans. Věra Dvořáková, Miloš Rejchrt, OIKOYMENH, Praha 2009.

Levinas, Emmanuel, *En découvrant l'existence avec Husserl et Heidegger*, 4. ed., Vrin, Paris 2010.

Lescourret, Marie-Anne, *Emmanuel Levinas*, Flammarion, Paris 1994.

Lyotard, Jean-François, *Au Juste*, Christian Bourgois, Paris 1979.

Lyotard, Jean-François, *La Condition postmoderne*, Ed. de Minuit, Paris 1979.

Lyotard, Jean-François, *Le Différend*, Ed. de Minuit, Paris 1983.

Lyotard, Jean-François, *Tombeau de l'intellectuel*, Galilée, Paris 1984.

Lyotard, Jean-François, *Le Postmoderne expliqué aux enfants*, Galilée, Paris 1986.

Lyotard, Jean-François, *L'Inhumain. Causeries sur le temps*, Galilée, Paris 1988.

Lyotard, Jean-François, *La Faculté de juger* (contrib. by J. Derrida, V. Descombes et al.), Ed. de Minuit, Paris 1989.

Lyotard, Jean-François, *Témoigner du différend*, ed. Franis Guibal, Jacob Rogozinski, Osiris, Paris 1989.

Lyotard, Jean-François, *Putování*, trans. Miroslav Petříček, Herrmann a synové, Praha 2001 (*Pérégrination: Loi, forme, événement*, Galilée, Paris 1990).

Lyotard, Jean-François, *Návrat a jiné eseje*, trans. Ladislav Šerý, Miroslav Petříček, Herrmann a synové, Praha 2002.

Lyotard, Jean-François, *Logique de Levinas*, ed. Paul Audi, Verdier, Paris 2015.

Marion, J.-L. (ed.), *Emmanuel Levinas. Positivité et transcendance (suivi Lévinas et la phénoménologie)*, P.U.F. Epiméthée, Paris 2000.

Mappen, Marc, *Prohibition Gangsters. The Rise and Fall of a Bad Generation*, Rutgers University Press, New Brunswick, New Jersey, London 2013.

McLaughlin, Daniel, "The Sacred and the Unspeakable", *Theory and Event* 13 (1), 2010.

McLaughlin, Kevin, Rosen, Philip (ed.), "Benjamin Now", *Boundary* 30 (1), 2003.

Marcel, Gabriel, *K filosofii naděje*, trans. Věra Dvořáková and Miroslav Žilina, Vyšehrad, Praha 1971.

Marder, Michael, *Groundless Existence. The Political Ontology of Carl Schmitt*, Continuum, New York 2010.

McCormick, John P., "Derrida on Law: Or, Poststructuralism Gets Serious", *Political Theory* 29 (3), 2001, pp. 395–423.

Merleau-Ponty, Maurice, *Fenomenologie vnímání*, trans. Jakub Čapek, OIKOYMENH, Praha 2013.

Michaud, Ginette, *Tenir au secret (Derrida, Blanchot)*, Galilée, Paris 2006.

Monkkonen, Eric H., "The Organized Response to Crime in Nineteenth- and Twentieenth-Century America", *Journal of Interdisciplinary History* 14 (1), 1983, pp. 113–28.

Morrison, James C., "Husserl's 'Crisis': Reflections on the Relationship of Philosophy and History", *Philosophy and Phenomenological Research* 37 (3), 1977, pp. 312–30.

Moss, Jeremy (ed.), *The Later Foucault. Politics and Philosophy*, Sage Publications, London 1998.

Müller, Filip, *Eyewitness Auschwitz. Three Years in the Gas Chambers*, ed. and trans. Susanne Flatauer, Ivad R. Dee, Chicago 1979.

Müller, Ulrich, *Theodor W. Adornos "Negative Dialektik"*, Wissenschaftliche Buchgesellschaft, Darmstadt 2006.

Nancy, Jean-Luc, *L'Oubli de la philosophie*, Galilée, Paris 1986.

Nancy, Jean-Luc, *Une pensée finie*, Galilée, Paris 1990.

Nancy, Jean-Luc, *Le Sens du monde*, Galilée, Paris 1993.

Naremore, James, *More than Night. Film Noir in its Contexts*, University of California Press, Berkeley, Los Angeles, London 2008.

Nicol, Bran, McNulty, Eugene, Pulham, Patricia, *Crime Culture. Figuring Criminality in Fiction and Film* (Continuum Literary Studies), Continuum, London, New York 2011.

Ombrosi, Orieta, *Le crépuscule de la raison. Benjamin, Adorno, Horkheimer et Levinas à l'épreuve de la Catastrophe*, Hermann Editeurs, Paris 2007.

Pan, David, "Against Biopolitics: Walter Benjamin, Carl Schmitt, and Giorgio Agamben on Political Sovereignity and Symbolic Order, *German Quarterly* 82 (1), 2009, pp. 42–62.

Paetzold, Heinz, Schneider, Helmut, *Schellings Denken der Freiheit*, Kassel University Press, Kassel 2010.

Panek, LeRoy L., *The Special Branch. The British Spy Novel, 1890-1980*, Bowling Green University Popular Press, Ohio 1981.

Patterson, David et al., *Encyclopedia of Holocaust Literature*, Oryx Press, Westport, London 2002.

Perivolaropoulou, Nia – Despoix, Philippe (ed.), *Culture de masse et modernité. Siegfried Kracauer sociologue, critique, écrivain*, Maison des Sciences de l'Homme, Paris 2001.

Priestman, Martin (ed.), *The Cambridge Companion to Crime Fiction*, Cambridge University Press, Cambridge 2003.

Rajchman, John, "Crisis", *Representations* 28, 1989, pp. 90–98.

Rajchman, John, "Foucault's Art of Seeing", *October* 44, 1988, pp. 88–117.

Rees, Laurence, *The Holocaust. A New History*, Viking (Penguin), 2017.

Richter, Gerhard, *Thought-Images. Frankfurt School Writers' Reflections from Damaged Life*, Stanford University Press, Stanford 2007.

Richter, Gerhard, *Afterness. Figures of Following in Modern Thought and Aesthetics*, Columbia University Press, New York 2011.

Rothberg, Michael, *Traumatic Realism. The Demands of Holocaust Representation*, University of Minnesota Press, Minneapolis, London 2000.

Rousset, David, *L'univers concentrationnaire*, Ed. de Minuit, Paris 1965.

Salzani, Carlo, "The City as Crime Scene: Walter Benjamin and the Traces of the Detective", *New German Critique* 100, 2007, pp. 165–87.

Sartre, Jean-Paul, *Bytí a nicota*, trans. O. Kuba, OIKOYMENH, Praha 2009 (1943).

Sartre, Jean-Paul, *Situations*, I, Gallimard, Paris 1947.

Scaggs, John, *Crime Fiction*, Routledge, London, New York 2005.

Schelling, Friedrich Wilhelm Joseph, *Schriften 1804-1812*, Union Verlag, Berlin 1982.

Schmitt, Carl, *Der Nomos de Erde im Völkerrecht des Jus Publicum Europaeum*, 2. ed., Dunckler & Humblot, Berlin 1974 (1950).

Schmitt, Carl, *Theorie des Partisanen*, 2. ed., Dunckler & Humblot, Berlin 2006 (1963).

Schmitt, Carl, *Pojem politična*, trans. Otokar Vochoč, OIKOYMENH, Brno, Praha 2007.

Schmitt, Carl, *Politická theologie. Čtyři kapitoly k učení o suverenitě*, trans. Jan Kranát and Otakar Vochoč, OIKOYMENH, Praha 2012.

Schnell, Alexander, *Temps et phénomène*, Olms Verlag, Hildesheim, Zürich, New York 2004.

Seshagiri, Urmira, "Modernity's (Yellow) Perils: Dr. Fu-Manchu and English Race Paranoia", *Cultural Critique* 62, 2006, pp. 162–194.

Seltzer, Mark, "Serial Killers (II): The Pathological Public Sphere", *Critical Inquiry* 22 (1), 1995, pp. 122–149.

Shelton, Marie-Denise, "Le Monde noir dans la littérature dadaïste et surréaliste", *French Review* 57 (3), 1984, pp. 320–328.

Silverstein, Marc, "After the Fall: The World of Graham Greene's Thrillers", *Novel: A Forum on Fiction* 22 (1), 1988, pp. 24–44.

Simmel, Georg, *Individualismus der modernen Zeit und andere soziologische Abhandlungen*, Suhrkamp, Frankfurt am Main 2008.

Simmel, Georg, *O podstate kultury*, trans. Ladislav Šimon, Kalligram, Bratislava 2003.

Simmel, Georg, *Soziologie. Untersuchungen über die Formen der Vergesellschaftung. Gesamtausgabe*, II, Suhrkamp, Frankfurt am Main 2013.

Snyder, Rober Lance, *The Art of Indirection in British Espionage Fiction. A Critical Study of Six Novelists*, McFarlan Publishers, Jefferson, London 2011.

Snyder, Timothy, *Black Earth. Holocaust as History and Warning.* Tim Duggan Books, New York 2015.

Solzhenitsyn, Aleksander, *Souostroví Gulag*, I–II, trans. Kruh překladatelů, OK Centrum, Praha 1990.

Srajek, Martin C., *In the Margins of Deconstruction. Jewish Conceptions of Ethics in Emmanuel Levinas and Jacques Derrida*, Springer Science & Bussiness Media, Dordrecht 1998.

Stafford, David A. T., "Spies and Gentlemen: The Birth of the British Spy Novel. 1893–1914", *Victorian Studies* 24 (4), 1981, pp. 489–509.

Sutherland, Edwin H., *The Professional Thief, by Professional Thief*, annotated and interpreted by Edwin H. Sutherland, The University of Chicago Sociological Series, Chicago 1937.

Tarde, Gabriel, *Les Lois de l'imitation*, 2. ed., Ed. Kimé, Paris 1993 (1895).

Tillich, Paul, "Schelling und die Anfänge des existenzialistischen Protestes", *Zeitschrift für philosophische Forschung* 2 (9), 1955, pp. 197–208.

Tritten, Tyler, *Beyond Presence. The Late F. W. J. Schelling's Criticism of Metaphysics* (Quellen und Studien zur Philosophie 111), De Gruyter, Boston, Berlin 2012.

Thompson, George J., *"Rhino", Hammett's Moral Vision*, Vince Emery Production, San Francisco 2007.Venezia, Shlomo, *Inside the Gas Chambers. Eight Months in the Sonderkommando of Auschwitz*, Polity Press, Cambridge 2009.

Venezia, Shlomo, *Inside the Gas Chambers. Eight Months in the Sonderkommando of Auschwitz*, Polity Press, Cambridge 2009.

Veyne, Paul, *Jak se píšou dějiny*, trans. Čestmír Pelikán, Pavel Mervart, Červený Kostelec 2010.

Vrba, Rudolf, *I Escaped from Auschwitz*, Robson Books, London 1964.

Vrba, Rudolf, *44070 - The Conspiracy of the Twentieth Century*, Star & Cross, Washington 1989.

Walker, John, "City Jungles and Expressionist Reification from Brecht to Hammet", *Twentieth Century Literature* 44 (1), 1998, pp. 119–33

Walz, Robin, *Pop Surrealism. Insolent Popular Culture in Early Twentieth-Century Paris*, University of California Press, Berkeley, Los Angeles, London 2000.

Watkin, William, *The Literary Agamben. Adventures in Logopoiesis*, Continuum, London, New York 2010.

Weber, Max, "Science as a Vocation", Duncker & Humblot, München 1919, p. 5.

Wiesel, Elie, *Night*, trans. Marion Wiesel, Hill and Wang, New York 2006.

Wilke, Sabine, "Adorno and Derrida as Readers of Husserl: Some Reflections on the Historical Context of Modernism and Postmodernism", *Boundary* 16 (2/3), 1989, pp. 77–90.

Willits, Curt G., "The Blanchot/Beckett Correspondence: Situating the Writer/Writing at the Limen of Naught", *Colloquy. Text. Theory. Critique* 10, 2005, pp. 257–268.

Worthington, Heather, *The Rise of the Detective in Early Nineteenth-Century Popular Fiction*, Palgrave Macmillan, London 2005.

Wyschogrod, Edith, *Spirit in Ashes. Hegel, Heidegger and Man-Made Mass Death*, Yale University Press, New Haven, London 1985.

B

Ambler, Eric, *Background to Danger* (orig. *Uncommon Danger*, 1937).

Ambler, Eric, *The Dark Frontier*, Fontana Books 1967 (1936).

Ambler, Eric, *The Journey into Fear*, Vintage Crime 2002 (1940).

Buchan, John, *39 Steps* (1915).

Burnett, W. R., *The Asphalt Jungle*, Rosetta Books (electronic edition), New York 2011 (1929).

Horler, Sidney, *The Secret Service Man* (1929).

John, Juliet (ed.), *Cult Criminals: The Newgate Novels, 1830-1847*, I–VI, Routledge, London 1998.

Childers, Erskine, *Riddle of the Sands* (1903).

Conrad, Joseph, *The Secret Agent* (1907).

Greene, Graham, *The Ministry of Fear* (1943).

Le Carré, John, *Smileyho lidé*, trans. Ivan Němeček, Svoboda, Praha 1994.

Le Queux, William, *The Great War in England in 1897* (1894).

Le Queux, William, *Invasion of 1910* (1906).

McNeile, H. C. *The Black Gang* (1922).

McNeile, H. C., *Bull-Dog Drummond* (1920).

McNeile, H. C., *The Female of the Species* (1926).

McNeile, H. C., *The Third Round* (1924).

Oppenheim, Edward Phillips, *The Traitors* (1902).

Penzler, Otto (ed.), *The Black Lizard Big Book of Black Mask*, Vintage, Reprint Edition 2010.

Rohmer, Sax, *The Mystery of Dr. Fu-Manchu* (1913).

Rohmer, Sax, *The Yellow Claw* (1915).

Rohmer, Sax, *The Daughter of Fu-Manchu* (1931).

Rohmer, Sax, *The Island of Fu-Manchu* (1941).

Rohmer, Sax, *The Shadow of Fu-Manchu* (1948).

Wallace, Edgar, *The Four Just Men* (1905).

Wallace, Edgar, *The Council of Justice* (1908).
Wallace, Edgar, *The Just Men of Cordova* (1918).
Wallace, Edgar, *The Law of the Just Men* (1921).
Wallace, Edgar, *Sandi, the Kingmaker* (1922).
Wallace, Edgar, *The Mind of Mr. J. G. Reeder* (1925).
Wallace, Edgar, *The Three Just Men* (1924).
Wallace, Edgar, *Again the Three Just Men* (1928).
Wallace, Edgar, *When the Gangs Came to London* (1932).
Wells, Herbert George, *The War in the Air* (1908).
Wells, Herbert George, *The War of the Worlds* (1898).
Wells, Herbert George, *The World Set Free* (1914).

C
Souvestre, Pierre, Allain, Marcel, *Fantômas* (1911).
Souvestre, Pierre, Allain, Marcel, *Juve contra Fantômas* (1911).
Souvestre, Pierre, Allain, Marcel, *Le mort qui tue* (1911).
Souvestre, Pierre, Allain, Marcel, *L'Agent secret* (1911).
Souvestre, Pierre, Allain, Marcel, *Un Roi Prisonnier de Fantômas* (1911).
Souvestre, Pierre, Allain, Marcel, *Le Policier Apache* (1911).
Souvestre, Pierre, Allain, Marcel, *Le Pendu des Londres* (1911).
Souvestre, Pierre, Allain, Marcel, *La fille des Fantômas* (1911).
Souvestre, Pierre, Allain, Marcel, *Le Fiacre de nuit* (1911).
Souvestre, Pierre, Allain, Marcel, *La Main coupée* (1911).
Souvestre, Pierre, Allain, Marcel, *L'Arrestation de Fantômas* (1912).
Souvestre, Pierre, Allain, Marcel, *La livrée du Crime* (1912).
Souvestre, Pierre, Allain, Marcel, *La mort de Juve* (1912).
Souvestre, Pierre, Allain, Marcel, *L'Evadée de Saint-Lazare* (1912).
Souvestre, Pierre, Allain, Marcel, *La disparition de Fandor* (1912).
Souvestre, Pierre, Allain, Marcel, *Le marriage de Fantômas* (1912).
Souvestre, Pierre, Allain, Marcel, *L'Assassin de Lady Beltham* 1912).
Souvestre, Pierre, Allain, Marcel, *La Guêpe Rouge* (1912).
Souvestre, Pierre, Allain, Marcel, *Les Souliers du Mort* (1912).
Souvestre, Pierre, Allain, Marcel, *Le Train perdu* (1912).
Souvestre, Pierre, Allain, Marcel, *Les Amours d'un Prince* (1912).
Souvestre, Pierre, Allain, Marcel, *Le Bouquet tragique* (1912).
Souvestre, Pierre, Allain, Marcel, *Le Jockey masque* (1913).
Souvestre, Pierre, Allain, Marcel, *Le Cercueil Vide* (1913).
Souvestre, Pierre, Allain, Marcel, *Le Faiseur de Reines* (1913).

Souvestre, Pierre, Allain, Marcel, *Le Cadavre Géant* (1913).
Souvestre, Pierre, Allain, Marcel, *Le Voleur d'Or* (1913).
Souvestre, Pierre, Allain, Marcel, *La Série Rouge* (1913).
Souvestre, Pierre, Allain, Marcel, *L'Hôtel du Crime* (1913).
Souvestre, Pierre, Allain, Marcel, *La Cravatte de Chanvre* (1913).
Souvestre, Pierre, Allain, Marcel, *La Fin de Fantômas* (1913).

The Václav Havel Series aims to honor and extend the intellectual legacy of the dissident, playwright, philosopher, and president whose name it proudly bears. Prepared with Ivan M. Havel, and other personalities and institutions closely associated with Václav Havel, such as the Václav Havel Library and Forum 2000, the series focuses on modern thought and the contemporary world – encompassing history, politics, art, architecture, and ethics. While the works often concern the Central European experience, the series – like Havel himself – focuses on issues that affect humanity across the globe.

Published titles
Jiří Přibáň, *The Defence of Constitutionalism: The Czech Question in Post-national Europe*
Matěj Spurný, *Making the Most of Tomorrow: A Laboratory of Socialist Modernity in Czechoslovakia*
Jacques Rossi, *Fragmented Lives: Chronicles of the Gulag*
Jiří Přibáň & Karel Hvížďala, *In Quest of History: On Czech Statehood and Identity*
Miroslav Petříček, *Philosophy en noir: Rethinking Philosophy after the Holocaust*

Forthcoming
Petr Roubal, *Spartakiads: The Politics of Physical Culture in Communist Czechoslovakia*
Martin C. Putna, *Rus - Ukraine - Russia: Scenes from the Cultural History of Russian Religiosity*
Olivier Mongin, *The Urban Condition: The City in a Globalizing World*
Jan Sokol, *Power, Money, Law*
Josef Šafařík, *Letters to Melin: A Discourse on Science and Progress*
Ivan M. Havel et al., *Letters from Olga*